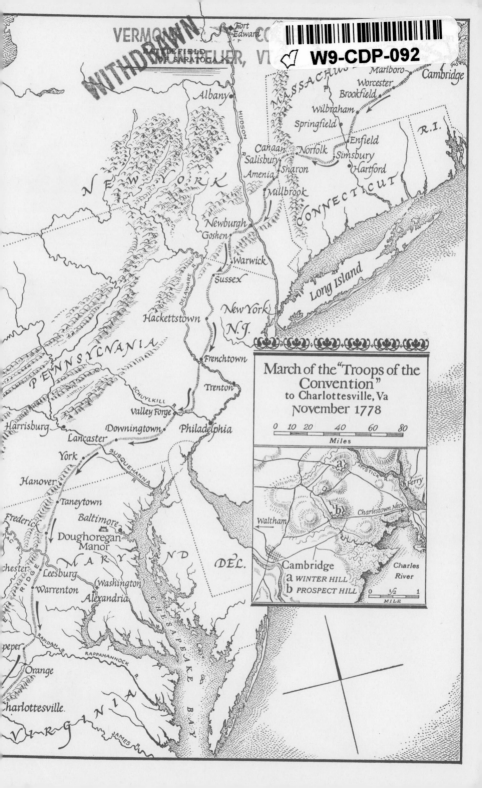

W9-CDP-092

VERMONT

BATTLEFIELD
OF SARATOGA

MONTPELIER, VT.

Fort Edward

Albany

HUDSON R.

NEW YORK

Newburgh
Goshen

Warwick

Sussex

Hackettstown

DELAWARE R.

Frenchtown

Trenton

New York

N.J.

Long Island

MASSACHUSETTS

Cambridge

Marlboro
Worcester
Brookfield
Wilbraham
Springfield
Norfolk Enfield
Canaan Simsbury
Salisbury Sharon Hartford
Amenia
Millbrook

CONNECTICUT

R.I.

PENNSYLVANIA

SCHUYLKILL R.

Valley Forge

Harrisburg
Lancaster
York
SUSQUEHANNA R.
Hanover
Taneytown
Frederick Baltimore
Doughoregan
Manor
BLUE RIDGE
chester
Leesburg
Warrenton
(Washington)
Alexandria

MARYLAND

DEL.

CHESAPEAKE BAY

Downingtown
Philadelphia

peper
RAPIDAN R.
Orange

RAPPAHANNOCK R.

harlottesville

VIRGINIA

JAMES R.

March of the "Troops of the Convention" to Charlottesville, Va

November 1778

0   10   20   40   60   80
Miles

MYSTIC R.

a

b

Charlestown Neck

Ferry

Waltham

Cambridge

a WINTER HILL
b PROSPECT HILL

Charles
River

0   ½   1
MILE

BOOKS BY
Louise Hall Tharp

CHAMPLAIN: NORTHWEST VOYAGER

COMPANY OF ADVENTURERS
The Story of the Hudson's Bay Company

THE PEABODY SISTERS OF SALEM

UNTIL VICTORY
Horace Mann and Mary Peabody

THREE SAINTS AND A SINNER
Julia Ward Howe
Louise, Annie and Sam Ward

TORY HOLE

ADVENTUROUS ALLIANCE
The Story of the Agassiz Family of Boston

LOUIS AGASSIZ: ADVENTUROUS SCIENTIST

THE BARONESS AND THE GENERAL

The Baroness and
the General

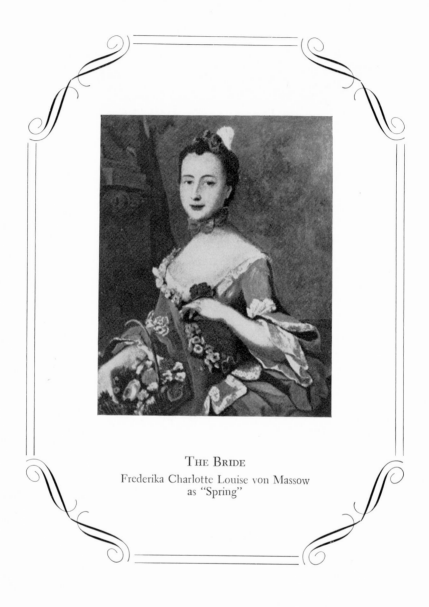

THE BRIDE
Frederika Charlotte Louise von Massow
as "Spring"

The Baroness and the General

LOUISE HALL THARP

With Illustrations

LITTLE, BROWN AND COMPANY · BOSTON · TORONTO

LIBRARY OF CONGRESS CATALOG CARD NO. 62-17955

FIRST EDITION

Published simultaneously in Canada
by Little, Brown & Company (Canada) Limited

PRINTED IN THE UNITED STATES OF AMERICA

To my husband
Carey Edwin Tharp

Contents

Main Characters

Frederika Charlotte Luisa von Massow, Baroness von Riedesel

Baron Friedrich Adolphus von Riedesel of Lauterbach, Duchy of Brunswick, General in charge of troops rented to King George III of England by Duke Ferdinand of Brunswick

Riedesel children: Augusta, Frederika, Amerika ("Miss America"), Canada, Charlotte, Georg Karl

Charles I and Charles II, Dukes of Brunswick, overlords of Ferdinand

Ferdinand, Duke of Brunswick, hero of Minden and field marshal of the Brunswick regiments

George III, of the House of Brunswick, King of England

Charlotte Sophia of Mecklenburg-Strelitz, Queen of England

George Sackville, Lord Germain, British Secretary of State for the Colonies, director of American campaign

Sir John Burgoyne (Gentleman Johnny), General of the British Army, von Riedesel's commander

Captain Edward Foy, commissary

Hannah Van Horne Foy, his wife

Mr. and Mrs. Russell of London

Sir Guy Carleton, Governor of Canada

Lady Mary (Maria) Carleton, his wife, and Lady Anne, her sister

Lady Harriet Acland and Major Acland

Mr. and Mrs. Mich Murray of Quebec

Major General William Phillips of the British Army, second in command to Burgoyne

Lieutenant Colonel Baum of the Brunswick dragoons

Captain Willoe, aide to General Riedesel

Rockel, chasseur, jaeger for the von Massow family, and bodyguard and coachman for the Baroness von Riedesel on her American journey

General Philip Schuyler of the Continental Army

General Benjamin Lincoln of the Continental Army

General Horatio Gates of the Continental Army

General Seth Warner of the Green Mountain Boys
General John Stark of the militia of New Hampshire
General William Heath of the Continental Army, stationed at Cambridge,
Mass.
Philip Mazzei, Esquire, of Charlottesville, Virginia
Thomas Jefferson, Esquire, of Charlottesville, Virginia
Charles Carroll of Carrollton, Maryland, and Mrs. Carroll
General Sir Henry Clinton, supreme commander of the British Army in
America after 1778
Sir Frederick Haldimand, Governor of Quebec
Also: Women; Savages; sea captains; and a knave of a cook

NARRATORS

English	German	American
Thomas Anburey, volunteer with the 89th Regiment, Foot	Lieutenant Du Roi of the Brunswick Prince Frederick Regiment	Captain Benjamin Warren
Lieutenant James Murray Hadden of the Royal Artillery	Captain Georg Pausch, chief of Hanau Artillery, Burgoyne campaign	Henry Brockholst Livingston, aide to Schuyler
Lieutenant William Digby of the 53d Shropshire Regiment, Foot	Heinrich Urban Cleve, adjutant of the Brunswick troops	Richard Varick, aide to Schuyler and Arnold
Loyalist Colonel (Tory) Thomas Jones	Ernst Johann Schuler von Senden	Ebenezer Mattoon (later general)
	Baron and Baroness von Riedesel	Ebenzer Fletcher of New Ipswich, N.H., fifer under General St. Clair
		James Thacher, M.D.
		Mrs. Hannah Winthrop

Illustrations

The Bride, *frontispiece*

Between Pages 240 and 241

General Baron von Riedesel; The Baroness von Riedesel

The Five Riedesel Daughters

George III and Family

General John Burgoyne by Sir Joshua Reynolds

General Sir Guy Carleton; General Sir Frederick Haldimand;
Major General William Phillips; The Bridegroom

General Philip Schuyler; General Horatio Gates;
General William Heath

Castle at Lauterbach; St. James's Palace Mall

Quebec

Fraser's Funeral at the "Great Redoubt" at Saratoga

Barracks of the Prisoners of Saratoga

Plan of Boston

Burgoyne's Positions at the Battles of Saratoga

End Papers

Route of Burgoyne-Riedesel
March of the Surrendered Army to Cambridge, Massachusetts
March of the "Troops of the Convention" to
Charlottesville, Virginia

The Baroness and the General

The Baroness

IT WAS the year 1762, and at the Court of Charles I, Duke of Brunswick, a military wedding was being planned to climax a gay winter season. Professional soldiering was the chief occupation in this small German duchy, and soldiers its most profitable export — along with cavalry horses. But the wars in which the troops of His Most Serene Highness were hired to engage were usually fought only during the summer months. Winter was the time to quarter the troops in barracks, while the officers rested upon their laurels, boasted about past and future campaigns, and otherwise amused themselves. Everyone at Court was happy about the prospect of wedding festivities, especially Tischbein, the German artist who had been commissioned by the Duke to paint the wedding party.[1]

Tischbein began with the bride, who sat in the artist's great armchair looking pleased. Frederika Charlotte Luisa von Massow was seventeen and, since symbolism was all the rage, the artist painted her as "Spring." Her dark hair had been pinned up in a brisk little pompadour, crowned with blue flowers and a stiff white feather that stood up like a brush. Around her neck she wore a blue ribbon tied in a demure bow just under her chin, although her blue satin dress was cut extremely low. Pink flowers in a

3

basket and a flower garland carried out the springtime theme but the bride's youth and gaiety made such stage properties super-fluous. Her dark blue eyes were full of laughter and her smile was one of pure delight. "Fritschen," as her family called her, looked ready to jump down from the painter's dais and dance away laughing, in her grown-up-lady's gown.

The time was not far off when Fritschen would be known as "the Baroness." She would ride into a wilderness fort in a strange sort of carriage, and British troops under Gentleman Johnny Burgoyne would stare and ask her name. German mercenaries would tell them that here was their German General's wife, and to English ears it would sound as if they said her name was "Red 'azel" ("Red Hazel" with the H dropped off, cockney-fashion). Indignantly, the troops of the Duke of Brunswick would explain that this was the Baroness von Riedesel — "Ree-day-zel," they would repeat loudly, as to a stupid foreigner; and perhaps one of those altercations all too common between English and German soldiers would break out.[2] But to rank and file of the English the Baroness remained "Red 'azel" — soon to be a term of admiration and affection. Not that liberties would be taken, for the Baroness was an aristocrat — called "Mrs. General" to her face, or "Lady Fritz." With her in the high-wheeled carriage would be her three little girls, known as "the little ladies."

The Baroness von Riedesel would one day write a firsthand account of her six years' adventures in America during the Revolution. Later as a book it would need a frontispiece, and an engraver would reproduce the Tischbein portrait to the best of his ability. The sentimental re-drawing would only faintly resemble the gay young girl who sat to Tischbein, or the forthright, fine-looking woman painted in later life. "Madam Riedesel" was never senti-mental, although she was sometimes naïve and believed tall tales about North America. She was cheerful and optimistic, making many a grim situation bearable for her serious and rather solemn husband. She spoke of herself as "frolicsome."

It would be reasonable to suppose that in eighteenth-century Germany the marriage of a wellborn young lady would be arranged for her; and at least officially, Frederika's marriage was a model of proper procedure. Duke Ferdinand of Brunswick, with the approval of his brother Charles I, the reigning Duke (and with the consent of the would-be bridegroom's father), approached Commissary General von Massow on behalf of Baron Friedrich Adolphus von Riedesel, who wanted to marry the commissary general's second daughter. Riedesel was Duke Ferdinand's favorite aide-de-camp, and this request had the force of a command which von Massow was delighted to obey. Of course there was no record of the future bride's being consulted. But Fritschen's marriage was a love match just the same.

Friedrich Adolphus was twenty-one and already a captain of cavalry when he first met the entrancing Frederika. He was a hard-working, conscientious young man among a group of gay young blades who frequented the von Massow house, which was never far from the seat of war. Minden, an ancient town on the banks of the Weser, was the von Massow home when Fritschen met her cavalry captain. Built upon a hill with city walls and winding streets, it was only four and a half miles from the field of the battle where English and German military reputations were lost and won in 1759, during the Seven Years' War. George Sackville, the future Lord George Germain, was the coward of Minden — too drunk to advance his troops, as his court-martial appears to show. Major General William Phillips, a captain at Minden, was one of the heroes, if breaking four canes over the backs of his artillery horses be proof of courage. He received a "gratuity" of one thousand pounds. Captain Edward Foy was another on the scene. He "commanded 4 twelve-pounders, 3 six-pounders and 2 howitzers," collecting "a special commendation from Duke Ferdinand" (known as the hero of Minden) and a "gratuity of 30 crowns." Years later Frederika von Massow as Baroness would remember having met Foy before, so perhaps his field was also the von Massow drawing room. And Riedesel, an ensign when the action began, was made captain on being sent to announce the victory to the Landgrave of Hesse. The French and Austrians being driven out, the von Massows took a house in Minden, where Fritschen met many officers, heroes and otherwise, some of whom she would meet again during the American Revolution.

Riedesel saw all he could of Fritschen and he was always a welcome guest at her father's house. She must have been about thirteen when she decided that just one, out of the many young officers she knew, pleased her thoroughly. "Frederika is much prejudiced against me and treats me like a coach-horse," one of Riedesel's friends complained to him. "She has confessed to Madame H — that she loves you most tenderly. I congratulate you from the bottom of my heart and hope that an early peace will aid you in attaining the possession of so many charms."

Although Frederika had fallen in love at an early age there was no early peace. In 1761, her captain of cavalry had time to become even more of a hero in her eyes. Sent to command some hussars defending a bridge on the Weser, Riedesel was so successful that the Duc de Broglie, commanding for the French, ordered an aide to go and see why the bridge was not taken. The aide saw a young officer in brilliant uniform, mounted on a fine horse, directing the defense. Jumping from his own horse, Broglie's aide took over one of the small cannon, aimed and fired it himself. When the smoke cleared, the defending rider and his horse were down. The attackers cheered. Then they saw a man in mud-spattered, smoke-blackened uniform struggle out from under the dead horse, get himself another horse and mount again, a tempting target at the head of the defenders of the bridge. Whether target practice continued or whether chivalry prevailed is not clear, but in any case a messenger under a flag of truce arrived at the German camp that evening leading a horse "richly caparisoned" as a gift for the "brave officer." Only then did Captain Riedesel discover that the marksman on the other side of the bridge had been his own brother, enlisted under the French. It was very much the custom for an officer to take service under any command that paid well and offered a chance for advancement. Young officers were like modern professional athletes, pleased by the compliment of being traded to a winning team.

It was understandable, none the less, that Baron Johann Wilhelm von Riedesel wanted only one son in military service. He had decided on the law for Friedrich. The boy was tutored by a clergyman in Frischborn, near the ancestral castle at Lauterbach, and then packed off to Marburg to study at the university. Apparently the only thing in mediaeval Marburg that appealed to young Riedesel was the castle, with its parade ground where a Hessian infantry battalion drilled daily. He soon struck up a friendship with the officers, but there was no use in his thinking about an army career when his father had chosen otherwise. A Hessian major offered to write to the Baron, however, and in due course announced that he had received permission for Friedrich to enter the battalion as "vice ensign." The boy wrote home joyfully to thank his father, only to learn that no letter had ever been received from the major and no permission granted. "Since you, as a nobleman, have taken the oath, you must get along the best you can without help from me," Fredrich's father decreed — and this was disaster indeed. Without an allowance from home, the boy, "aged about fourteen," could hardly pay for the relatively small amount of gold braid on a vice ensign's coat. Young Riedesel determined to work hard and rise in rank. He did; and eventually his father forgave him.[3]

Born June 3, 1738, Friedrich von Riedesel was about eighteen when he first went to England — with a German regiment in the service of George II. He spoke French with a strong German accent — as evidenced by his phonetic spelling. His written French emerged with German sentence structure; but French was the language of diplomacy, and he wrote it to the best of his ability in most of his letters. English was an entirely new language to him. Thirty years later and after considerable further experience, Riedesel was forced to confess: "I am obliged to write in French as I cannot compose two lines in English. I can, however, read English and thoroughly understand it."

At the outbreak of the Seven Years' War, Riedesel with his Hessian regiment was ordered back to Germany. It was the ambition of most young officers to join the staff or "family" of a prominent general, so Riedesel felt fortunate now on being appointed to the staff of Duke Ferdinand, while still serving officially as captain under the Landgrave of Hesse.

Duke Ferdinand's star was rising, and, after Minden, Riedesel withdrew from Hessian service, where he felt he was not getting ahead, to enter the service of the Duke of Brunswick. Unquestionably, Riedesel had both charm and tact. Soon the reigning Duke, Charles I of Brunswick, was signing letters to him "Affectionately." Riedesel also became the friend of Prince Charles William — later Charles II of Brunswick — who married a sister of George III of England. But it was Duke Ferdinand, his own general and the victor at Minden, whom Riedesel really loved; and it was Duke Ferdinand who gave Riedesel the military wedding at the little town of Neuhaus, near his headquarters at Wolfenbüttel.

Of course Tischbein was painting Friedrich now as a bridegroom. Round of face, with earnest eyes and plump pink cheeks, there stood Friedrich Adolphus von Riedesel on the artist's dais. Tischbein was going to need a lot of crimson and gold paint. Riedesel's hair was powdered white, gold braid covered him from shoulder to ample waistline which was wrapped in a scarlet sash. Red also were his pantaloons, although what could be seen of his coat was blue, and sky-blue was the cape slung over his shoulder. Ornamenting the cape was still more gold braid with a border of white fur.

The groom's uniform probably outshone the bride's dress when

December 2 came at last. But Frederika's vivid blue eyes and her look of happiness upon her wedding day would be a match for anything a military tailor could devise.

Carriages full of petty nobility from Brunswick, seven miles away, filled the streets of Neuhaus and Wolfenbüttel. Townspeople and country people gathered to see the sight, and it is reasonable to suppose that the populace were not forgotten when good things to eat and drink were passed around. After all, of what use is a general, or a lieutenant colonel for that matter, without recruits? Many men had to be forced into the armies of some German hereditary princes, but Brunswickers had a reputation for willing service. They felt genuine affection for their leaders, which was reciprocated.

There was dancing in the streets and dancing in the houses of the landed gentry. No Brunswick regiment ever set out on a campaign without musicians; and when they were in garrison, as now, there was music everywhere. As the good beer flowed from casks set up in street and courtyard, there was singing: new songs composed in honor of the bride and groom; old songs sung from time immemorial.

Then suddenly the festivities were over. Frederika could be called the Baroness von Riedesel, but her husband must remain in service in Wolfenbüttel while she went home to her parents. After every summer's campaign, however, young Riedesel could usually depend upon returning to Wolfenbüttel, and eventually he bought a home there. But meanwhile Fritschen discovered that being a married daughter living with her parents was not much fun. On the grounds that she needed experience, she was given a great deal of work to do, with servants to help her of course, in her father's large and complicated household. She ordered provisions, kept accounts, managed servants. But her mother was fond of authority, delegating only responsibility and meting out praise in small measure. There were other daughters in the family who now had first priority when it came to entertaining guests.

They must marry at their social level if possible, for if they stepped above it this would cost their father extra money for a dowry. Frederika had already done just this. But that the other girls should marry beneath their station was also unthinkable, and eligible young army officers continued to be cordially received. Frederika loved her husband, but she had always been the popular one at home and now she must remember to sit with the dowagers after dinner and let her sisters play the harpsichord or sing the Italian arias which all the girls had learned to do so well.

Three years went by. Fritschen had at least a temporary home of her own in Berlin by the time her first child was born — January 6, 1766. To her great joy, it was a son. Giving him all the names an eldest son could possibly need to gain favor throughout life, the boy's parents began with the ruling house of Brunswick and ended with family friends. The child was called Christian Charles Louis Ferdinand Henry William Herman Valentine. He lived to the enchanting age of thirteen months and died February 2, 1767. The happy-hearted young Baroness learned the meaning of grief in her twenty-second year.

Frederika waited a long four years for her second child, a girl this time, whom they named Philippina. She was born on March 29, 1770, and died on that same fatal date of February 2, in the year 1771. Frederika had been brought up as a strict Lutheran and believed that the death of her children was the will of God, foreordained before the world began. But resignation does not put an end to sorrow.

At the time of her first little girl's death, Frederika was expecting another child. Augusta, they named her. She was born August 3, 1771, and this time it was the will of God that she would live to maturity. The next child, born May 12, 1774, also a girl, was named for her mother; she too survived infancy to face still further hazards in a strange land. Each girl in due course became a Countess.

If the Baroness's passionate desire for a son was not quite in keeping with her fatalistic belief, this was perfectly understandable. Most of her husband's property was entailed and could not be inherited by a woman. The castle at Lauterbach, other real estate and buildings, much income, all family silver and jewels, must go to a brother or a nephew of her husband's unless von Riedesel had a male heir. With succeeding pregnancies, Frederika prayed earnestly for a boy, felt certain her prayers would be answered — and then loved the baby girl with all her heart.

In the year 1776, the Riedesels were at last living in a home of their own in Wolfenbüttel. They loved the place, even though they took for granted its many half-timbered houses, winding streets, and the ducal castle rising grim and authoritative in the *Schlossplatz*. Stone walls, with ramparts and gates of oak and iron protected the town, while the River Oker, like a moat, flowed outside the walls. As long as cannon remained a clumsy invention, as long as primitive gunpowder proved an inefficient means of destruction, Wolfenbüttel would be a fortress — a safe place to look upon as home.

A state of peace is the most desirable of situations in this world. But to a man like Riedesel, now almost thirty-eight years old and a colonel of carabineers, peace presented nothing but problems. No one permanently in charge of the garrison at Wolfenbüttel could hope to rise in rank. Family estates, however large, could never produce enough income to satisfy the needs of all the sons in the family — and of course there was no gainful occupation, such as gunsmithing or innkeeping, that a member of the aristocracy could consider. But no one ever looked askance at the sharing-out of booty among officers, according to rank, at the end of a successful campaign: what Riedesel needed was a good, active, not too long or dangerous war where he could be on the winning side.

How fortunate, then, that George III should be having a little trouble with a few rebellious subjects in his provinces of North

America! Prosperous Hanover, Brunswick's neighbor to the north-ward, belonged to the King of England personally, and so he sent five battalions of his Hanoverians to Gibraltar and to Minorca, calling home the British garrisons at those posts. In the early autumn of 1775 he negotiated with Russia for twenty thousand men, but the deal fell through. Colonel William Faw-citt, British commissioner, agreed to sound out a few German princes about the price of troops for hire. Some of these absolute rulers wanted money to pay for extravagant living in imitation of the French court; others were actually interested in building back an inheritance after the destruction of the Seven Years' War; but whatever the reasons, they all wanted money, and Brunswick was the first to come to terms with George III.

On January 9, 1776, Charles, Duke of Brunswick (brother and overlord of Duke Ferdinand), promised His Britannic Majesty a corps of 3936 infantrymen and 336 *unmounted* dragoons. The men were to be equipped by the Duke, except that he was not to supply horses. This was curious, because Brunswick was famous for the raising of fine horses; but perhaps the Duke had hoped to sell rather than to rent them, since the King of England seemed ready to open his purse.

There were clauses in the agreement that would benefit rank and file. George III was to pay and feed the German troops ex-actly as his own men were paid and provisioned. They were to have equal hospital care and, if unable to continue to serve be-cause of wounds, they were to be sent by Great Britain to some port in Europe, on the Elbe or the Weser.

"Levy money" was to be paid, at the rate of seven pounds, four shillings and four and a half pence for each recruit; and as men dropped out, either killed or wounded, the Duke promised to train new recruits for the same price, equip and send them in to British service. But if a whole regiment, a battalion or a com-pany should be lost at sea on the voyage to America, or wiped out in battle or by an uncommon epidemic of sickness, His Britannic Majesty must bear all expense of new recruits and make good in cash, the loss of the Duke's men. For every man killed, the King of England would owe the Duke of Brunswick thirty thalers (or about $22.50). For the maimed, the Duke would receive about half that sum, but he must replace at his own expense those who died of sickness or who deserted.

From the day the treaty was signed, the King of England agreed to pay an annual subsidy of 11,517 pounds, 17 shillings, 1½ pence. Double that amount would be due each year for the next two years after the Duke's men had come home again.[4] This sounds like a stiff bargain, but the Landgrave of Hesse-Cassel got more than twice as much per man. Hesse-Hanau, also, stood out for more money. These two principalities between them sent 8145 men, as against Brunswick's final total of 5723. It is not surprising, then, that in America all of King George's German troops were called "Hessians," no matter where they came from. Riedesel's Brunswickers resented this.

As far as the Baron Riedesel was concerned, one clause of the treaty interested him more than the others. Duke Charles was to nominate the officers to serve under a British high command, and it was written into the agreement that these officers should be of "high caliber." Who then would be sent? The Riedesels did not have long to wait for the answer. On January 10, 1776, the day after the treaty with Great Britain was signed, Colonel Riedesel was appointed commander of the first contingent from Brunswick.

Madam the Baroness now announced that she was going to America with her husband, and that she would take the children. This is not as surprising as it might seem. After all, Commissary von Massow had followed the Brunswick army taking his wife and family with him and establishing them near the field of action, as at Minden. Frederika was used to war, at least at a reasonably safe distance.

This following of the troops was not just a German custom. In

England, Lady Maria Carleton was preparing to join her husband in Canada, and Lady Harriet Acland[5] was going to America with Major Acland, as were the wives of sundry other officers. Then there were the generals that Madam Riedesel would call "rebels" — Washington, Greene, Gates, for example; they too would have their wives with them from time to time, and young "Master St. Clair" would be with his father at Ticonderoga, sent home when the action began.

Perhaps it was Colonel Riedesel who reminded his wife that since she was expecting their fifth child in March, a son ought to be born in his fatherland. Probably Frederika burst into tears. She admitted that she wept upon occasion but always recovered rapidly. Very well, she would wait until her son was born, and then bring the two girls and the baby to America as soon as she was able to travel. Colonel Riedesel consented to this plan, admiring his wife for her courage, yet not quite believing that she would actually attempt such a journey.

On the sixteenth of February the Brunswick troops were ready to march. They paraded in the courtyard of the ducal palace, and in the streets of Brunswick and Wolfenbüttel, with regimental flags flying, for all the world to watch and applaud. At their head rode Colonel Riedesel in his most brilliant uniform, mounted on his finest horse. There were 2282 men in this first contingent.

Walking behind the baggage wagons, as the troops left Brunswick, were seventy-seven women "camp followers." They were not harlots but wives of soldiers, because the chaplains were strict and a woman was either sent packing or married to the man she followed if her status was unclear. They carried pots and pans, bedding and supplies — and babies. They led children ("not counted") by the hand, and they were entitled to one half a man's ration, the children to a quarter. Of course only the fittest survived, but these were amazingly tough and strong. They were *women*, not ladies, as Madam Riedesel would in due course make clear.[6]

Out marched the Duke of Brunswick's troops—and then back they marched again. The boats which were to carry them down the river to the sea had not arrived. A week went by before they finally marched away.

2

Mrs. General

THE Baroness Riedesel received the first letters from her husband headed "Liefert, February 22, 1776." "Dearest Wife," he began: "Never have I suffered more than when I left you this morning. My heart was broken. If I could have gone back, who knows what I would have done! But, my darling, God has placed me in my present calling and I must follow it."

Riedesel asked anxiously about the health of his wife, whose "approaching confinement" caused him great anxiety. And she must "guard most preciously the two little girls," for he loved them fondly. But he had saved some good news for the end of his letter. On leaving the city of Brunswick he had been given sealed orders which he had now opened and read. "I have this evening been raised to the rank of major general. Therefore, my own Mrs. General, take good care of your health so that you can follow me as soon as possible after a happy delivery."

It was pleasant to be a Baroness. Frederika frankly enjoyed the rights and privileges to which her birth and marriage entitled her. She believed in the divine right of Kings and Queens, Dukes and Duchesses, on down the line. Military rank was another matter. Her husband had earned his promotion himself, and she could not help feeling especially pleased to be called "Mrs. General."

Riedesel was marching northward across country toward the Elbe with four regiments of infantry, a battalion of grenadiers and a battalion of jaegers (riflemen).[1] They covered thirty miles a day and at night various towns and villages had the doubtful pleasure of receiving about forty-three hundred uninvited guests. Riedesel was anxious to acquit himself well in this new command — and he remembered that deserters would not be paid for. Much was to be written about the passage of troops across the various small German principalities at this time. Johann Gottfried Seume, a theological student at Leipzig, would tell of false arrest, of being recruited by force and shipped to North America after imprisonment for attempted escape. But this was done by the Landgrave of Cassel, "the great broker of men" as he put it, and Seume did not reach America until the war was almost over.[2] General Riedesel was able to report to Duke Ferdinand on February 24, 1776: "Our march has progressed better than I expected. We have not had a single desertion . . ."

Twelve days later, the Brunswick troops were at Stade, quartered on the town and in the surrounding villages, and Colonel Fawcitt, King George's commissioner, began his inspection. He was pleased with the dragoons, Riedesel said. But Fawcitt complained that the men in the battalion of grenadiers were not tall enough and that some of them were too old. General Riedesel was able to talk the King's representative out of these objections. The reviewing of regiments continued with questions raised and answered until March 12, when "ships arrived to the number of seven." Colonel Fawcitt said that he had never seen an embarkation of troops that was so quiet and orderly: "Not a single man was drunk!"

Six more ships arrived at Stade to accommodate the Brunswick troops, and five days went by, full of intense activity. Horses belonging to the officers were lifted in slings and set down on the deck of the last riverboat — a procedure most of them took exception to. But "the same order prevailed." There had been no angry complaints from villagers on the march, nor in the area of Stade.

"Everyone was joyful and in good spirits," Riedesel wrote. And once more he could report "no desertions." Fawcitt had insisted upon counting the Brunswick troops twice, which was not according to contract. Riedesel was annoyed but allowed it, "because my conscience is clear," he said.

The official account sent to Duke Ferdinand sounded calm and almost casual, just as the newly-made General meant it to be. Only to his own Mrs. General did he confide that he had been unable to sleep, night after night. He was a good executive officer, attentive to every detail, but he was a perfectionist — and he suffered agonies lest the least thing go wrong.

"I hope you will soon be in marching trim," he wrote to his wife, realizing how much he needed her cheerful, optimistic presence.

Mrs. General could hardly wait for the son she so confidently expected. But the baby took its own good time, and when it came it was a girl. It was hard for her to write the letter announcing this disappointment. There was still no future heir to the castle at Lauterbach. But the baby's mother felt that there could hardly be a sweeter little girl than her Caroline. If only her husband would not feel too badly! Duke Ferdinand sent the letter to General Riedesel by special courier, for the troops were just about to sail for England. And back by courier came the answer. "Come to Portsmouth as soon as your health and that of our newly born little daughter Caroline will permit. . . . Be not impatient. Embrace our dear, dear children for me. The ship awaits me. Love me always. Take care of your precious health and be assured I am wholly yours."

The ship *Pallas* did not leave Stade at once, however, because of contrary winds. And when the vessel finally got under way there were many miles of river sailing ahead of the *Pallas* before she could reach the North Sea. General Riedesel described his routine aboard ship to amuse and reassure his wife. "I rise about seven in the morning after having said my prayers in bed. We dress ourselves quickly and breakfast after the English fashion upon tea and bread and butter. Then I go on deck and smoke my pipe. After that I write, read, drink my coffee, walk up and down the deck with both Englishmen and, with one or two more pipes, pass the time until two o'clock, when we have dinner." One of the two Englishmen mentioned was Captain Edmonston, appointed as English-speaking adjutant to Riedesel and soon to become his devoted friend. The other was Captain Edward Foy, a British artillery officer, now appointed commissary to the German troops in Canada. "You will remember Captain Foy from Minden," General Riedesel reminded the Baroness. Madam Riedesel was to hear more of him — and eventually she would wish that she had never met his wife, the former Hannah Van Horne of New York.

Dinner was the high point of the day on board ship. "We have nine people at table, have three courses and eat for nearly an hour," Riedesel wrote. When the cloth was cleared away they spent "half or three quarters of an hour drinking healths." First came that of the King — His Majesty George III of England; "second, the Duke; third, yours and the children's; fourth Captain Foy's wife; fifth a good sea voyage; and sixth a successful campaign in America. At four o'clock dinner is over. We consume four bottles of wine a day along with half a bottle of arrack [a liqueur from the East Indies] for punch. Afterwards I drink coffee with the Englishmen."

At the time of writing the fleet was still becalmed in the Elbe, so Riedesel spoke of visiting other vessels "after coffee." In the evening he played a rubber of whist and "at half past eight cold meat is brought on — also wine for anyone that wants it, and beer, and at ten o'clock all of us go to bed."

This was how things went, day after day, the General assured his wife. Now that the responsibility of marching the troops over-

land was ended, he was sleeping well and enjoying life. All that
was lacking was Mrs. General to keep him company, and he was
confident she would soon set out. Couriers galloping across
country still carried letters to Brunswick and returned with
packets for the General from the reigning Duke Charles, from
Duke Ferdinand and from the Baroness. But on the twenty-
second of March, "Here we are upon the open sea," the General
wrote. "The pilots are leaving and I will give them my last letter
from the outermost border of Germany. Fear nothing. We are all
very well and I hope we shall make the entire passage to Spithead
safely and, once accustomed to open ocean, reach America in
perfect health."

General Riedesel proved to be a remarkably good sailor, but
his account of the North Sea crossing, written to amuse his wife,
was pathetic as well as funny. For a man accustomed to a great
deal of personal service, he was a good sport — and it would seem
that he was also a good cook. His account was headed Dover,
March 26, 1776.

"Sunday morning we had had a heavy fog, then the sea grew
rough. Two guns were fired from our ship to indicate our course.
The fog lifted, the wind and waves rose although there was
actually no storm. Now everyone was seasick. The cook could not
cook. Müller could not dress me. Valentine could find nothing.
To sum up, great lamentations and great blundering on all sides.
I was starved but had nothing to eat. Finally, Captain Foy and I
cooked a pea soup in the ship's galley and ate cold roast beef,
which made up our whole dinner. The sailors ate nothing at all.

"Monday, the weather was somewhat milder; some people felt
better, but the majority were still sick. Captain Foy and I made
bouillon, cooked a cod with anchovy sauce, a ragout of beef and
roast veal with potatoes.

"On Tuesday we had beautiful weather and more people recovered. The soldiers cooked for themselves but the cook could
still do nothing. So Foy and I did the cooking again. We had rice

soup, yellow turnips with beef, codfish with anchovy sauce and a ragout of lamb."

It is to be hoped that the officers entitled to sit at Riedesel's table were sufficiently grateful to the commissary and the General for being such accomplished chefs. They sighted land on Tuesday, and on Wednesday they were "opposite Dover" with Captain Foy going ashore, carrying letters.

This would seem to be General Riedesel's first sea voyage and he was more than ever anxious about his wife, soon to be traveling alone. "Remember, dearest Angel, everyone may be sick upon the water," he told her. "You might have very little help from your servants so you must choose the shortest route to England. I think the best one will be by way of Calais."

On reaching Dover, Riedesel had expected to get news of the progress of the war between England and her rebellious colonies. He mentioned that the *Pallas* had been the ship to bring General Gage back to England after a rather unfortunate affair in Boston. People were saying that the Battle of Bunker Hill had been "more bloody than Minden" — but doubtless the rebels had learned their lesson. Quebec had been under siege. Captain Foy told Riedesel that "if Quebec is still ours and there is no American army this side of Montreal" he was going to have his wife join him, and General Carleton would do the same.

In view of his experience on the North Sea, General Riedesel decided that the Baroness "must positively not leave England before Lady Maria Carleton and Mrs. Foy. Then you can go with them and travel more safely," he said. This was about the worst advice he could have given, and he underestimated his "own Mrs. General." But she would do her best to obey his orders.

The German transports left the vicinity of Dover on March 26 and arrived off Spithead three days later. Riedesel had himself rowed ashore to call on British Commodore Sir Charles Douglas (later Admiral) whose headquarters were in Portsmouth. For the Atlantic crossing, transportation aboard a man-of-war had been promised to General Riedesel. After the usual civilities had been exchanged, he asked Commodore Douglas the name of the frigate assigned to him. But "other generals bound for America" had reached Portsmouth first and just now all space was taken. General John Burgoyne had the best cabin — aboard the *Blonde*, a frigate of thirty-six guns, whose name must have pleased "Gentleman Johnny," noted for his taste in pretty women.

Also sailing on the *Blonde* was Major General William Phillips, eventually to be appointed second in command to Burgoyne. A captain when Riedesel had known him at Minden, Phillips had an exalted opinion of his own importance, although he was major general in America only. Later, and because of Madam Riedesel's charm and tact, he would become a very good friend. But right now it was evident that there was no room aboard the *Blonde* for another high-ranking officer.

So back to the *Pallas* went the commander of the Brunswick troops. Douglas was aware that a touchy situation could develop, as indicated by the exertions he made in Riedesel's behalf. Thirty carpenters were sent aboard the *Pallas* to tear out partitions and build a large private cabin for the General and better quarters for his aides. Meanwhile, Riedesel was given quarters on shore with a guard of honor before his door. He dined on shore with Sir Charles on the night after his arrival in Portsmouth and two days later the commodore gave a dinner for him on board the flagship — when Riedesel was piped aboard.

Douglas gave a dinner for Burgoyne also, aboard the flagship, to which Riedesel was invited. He entertained all the frigate captains and they reciprocated with breakfasts and dinners. For seven days there was a continual round of festivities; then on April 4, 1776, at eleven o'clock in the morning, the fleet sailed. They had a prosperous voyage of only forty-four days before land was sighted.

For the Baroness, there was no such smooth sailing, but she organized her own affairs with efficiency. First of all came the matter of her mother. Madam von Massow was determined that no daughter of hers was going to the dreadful wilds of North America, even after the expected grandchild was born. Madam von Massow was coming to Wolfenbüttel herself to take charge of everything. "It is the duty of a wife to leave all and follow her husband," Frederika wrote, knowing there was no answer to this argument. The threat of an impending visit was a little harder to handle. "In spite of the happiness of seeing you at my house . . ." Frederika was definitely not inviting her mother to come, because "the parting afterwards" would be "too hard to bear." Mrs. General proved to be a good strategist — but nearly a month went by before she could write, "How rejoiced I am that you begin to be more reconciled to my journey."

Friends at Wolfenbüttel and at the Court in Brunswick proved almost as much of a problem. They told the Baroness Riedesel that North American Indians were all cannibals and that she and the children would be eaten alive. It was also a well-known fact, they assured her, that the English in North America ate horsemeat and likewise cats. The Baroness believed these tales, as she afterwards admitted. But she said the stories frightened her less than the thought of going into a country where she could not speak the language. She knew she had a faculty for making friends but how do you persuade a cannibal not to eat you when he can't understand a word you say? And how do you say "No thank you, no roast cat," in English? Madam Riedesel spoke only French and German.

As soon as Mrs. General received her husband's orders to go by way of Calais and Dover, she began to plan her route. She was a little disappointed not to see the Elbe because her husband had described "beautiful villages" on the banks of the river and castles on nearby hills. But maps were brought out and the Post Road through Brussels chosen. Post-horses would be used, but the Baroness would travel in her own carriage.

Mrs. General had a carriage built to her specifications. It was high off the ground, with big wheels because there would be deeply rutted roads, and it had steps to let down so that she could climb in. Since there was sure to be bad weather, the carriage was covered with oilcloth with gay designs painted on it. There was a high seat in front for the coachman and another at the back for the footman, with a musket strapped firmly under each seat. Luggage was also carried outside. Within, there was room for Madam Riedesel, her two women servants — and the children. Augusta had reached the advanced age of four years and nine months, while Frederika was two. Their mother carried and nursed the baby Caroline, who was ten weeks old.[3]

"Rockel" was the coachman's name. He had served under General Riedesel as a chasseur, or light infantryman, but had been retired for some years. The word *chasseur* ("huntsman") came from the days when huntsmen or jaegers were the most trusted servants on a lord's domain. They supplied venison for the table, showed no mercy to poachers, and would protect their master and his family with their lives if necessary. Rockel was at this time a huntsman for Madam Riedesel's father, but he "dropped everything to go with her," the Baroness said. He was utterly devoted to his lady and her children, and for the next eight years he served as a sort of noncommissioned officer with footmen and postilions under him in Mrs. General's little army.

"Get all the letters of introduction you can, especially to people in England," General Riedesel had advised his wife. So she collected all sorts of documents, and her friends were anxious to help her — since it was clear that their horrible tales of America were not going to keep her at home.

Then there was the matter of clothes. A French general might lose a battle at Minden, but French dressmakers ruled the fashion world at the court of the Duke of Brunswick. The Baroness ordered a new-style material called "chintz" (from the Hindu word for "spotted" or patterned India cotton) and she had pretty, full-skirted dresses, decidedly low at the neck, made for herself and her girls. This was the style favored by the young queen, Marie Antoinette, the dressmaker said. The children's hats were round and flat, their petticoats were many. Madam the Baroness was extremely style-conscious, and she never worried about how ruffles would be washed and ironed in the North American wilderness among the cannibals.

The date of departure had been set for the thirteenth of May, and on the fourteenth at five in the morning Mrs. General's carriage rumbled over the cobblestones of Wolfenbüttel and out the city gate. She would never meet a general who came so close to setting out on time.

Capacious pockets inside the carriage were stuffed with provisions, but at noon they stopped to change the post-horses and Madam the Baroness ordered some beer soup.[4] This was a hearty snack much appreciated in Germany, and at this inn it was probably good, because Mrs. General made no complaint. But when the innkeeper charged her ten grochen, or about thirty cents, she complained bitterly. The man told her she would have to pay six times as much farther down the road, and the Baroness replied with spirit that he was being uncivil. If she didn't like it she should have stayed at home, he said; and suddenly, army child though she had been, the Baroness realized that she had lived a sheltered life. She had always been surrounded by officers under her father's command or aides of her husband's or servants to do her bidding. Now she was on her own. She would have to overlook rudeness, and she did so.[5]

At the next post, where the horses were changed, the Baroness heard news that made a little incivility seem a mere trifle. There were highway robbers on the road ahead. "One hundred and thirty had been executed during the last fortnight, most of them by hanging." This would seem like mass execution, but Madam Riedesel was told that three times as many more "were still at large." "This news threw me into a great fright," she admitted.

She had money which her husband had left for her, and she planned "to live very frugally" to make it last. She also had a little store of personal jewels. They were not really important compared to the pearls and diamonds unscrupulous ladies were constantly collecting from grateful princes, but they were pretty trinkets of sentimental value. Mrs. General was prepared to sell them if necessary, but she would keep them for her daughters if she could and she was certainly not going to have them or her money stolen. She ordered Rockel to whip up the horses — and have his musket ready.

The horses supplied at the last post were worn out and incapable of that "post-haste" travel the Baroness had a right to expect. Twilight came just as the road entered a forest. In Mrs. General's own words, "Suddenly, some object hanging in the air struck me through the open window of my carriage. I seized it and felt something hard and rough. It was the body of a hanged man." She had "seized" the leg, which had a woolen stocking on it.

On they drove, and within a few minutes came to a sinister-looking house standing alone in the forest. The postilions the posthouse had supplied were so frightened that they refused to go a step farther and a man "of a suspicious appearance" came out who said he would put up the Baroness and her party for the night. He led Madam Riedesel with the children and her maid-servants "into a remote room with only one bed." The room was deathly cold and the man agreed to have a fire built in the fire-place, but he had no food to offer except tea and black bread.

Before long the "faithful Rockel" came to Madam's door with "a very anxious face, and said, 'Things are not right in this place; there is a room full of guns.'" He thought they had picked the headquarters of a robber band in which to spend the night but that the robbers themselves were out marauding. "'I shall sit at the door of your room all night with my gun in my hand,'" Rockel promised. He would "sell his life dear." The other manservant he had posted in the carriage with the other gun.

Mrs. General put her little children to bed, praised the older servingwoman for keeping calm and scolded the younger one for shedding tears. If the children cried, their mother never mentioned it. They had been told to remember that their father was a general and that therefore they must be brave. Their mother sat on a stool and leaned her head against the bed, and to her surprise she finally slept. At four in the morning came a knock on the door. It was Rockel, to say that the horses were harnessed, the postilions ready to start.

"I put my head out of the window," said the Baroness, "and saw in the wood where we were a great number of nightingales, who, by their sweet singing, made me forget all my fears."

3

They Point the Finger

MRS. General described the rest of her European journey as "very prosperous." She passed through Brussels, Tournai and St. Omer, in what is now Belgium. In 1776, Brussels belonged to Austria, Tournai to the Netherlands and St. Omer to France. Passports and visas were not a part of the Baroness Riedesel's problems, but her letters of introduction proved important, for at every city gate guards wanted to know who she was and where she was going with those three little children in that canvas-covered carriage.

There was time for sight-seeing, but Mrs. General paid little or no attention to city walls and battlements or cathedrals, no matter how many centuries old. She had never seen a city entirely without walls and, as a loyal Lutheran, she could not approve of eleventh-century basilicas or medieval Gothic vaulting. She did, however, "visit a mountain" all of 485 feet high. From the summit, she could see "thirty-two towns exclusive of hamlets."

On the first day of June, in 1776, the British convoy and the transports of German troops reached Quebec. On that same day, Mrs. General was in Calais, preparing for her first sea voyage — across the English Channel. The weather was stormy. She put up at a well-recommended inn "and immediately sent for a ship's captain." Friends had advised her to hire "a packet boat," and a captain presented himself whom she liked and whose terms were favorable.

But the innkeeper was not a man to be trusted and Mrs. General took too much of his advice. First of all, he told her to leave her carriage "in his care." If she took it aboard the boat she would have to pay a high duty on it in Dover. This was an argument which won over the thrifty Baroness, much as she hated to part with the coach, which had been home to her and the children for a month and a half. Probably she thought she would be coming back through Calais before long. But there was the matter of packing up all the belongings that had been so neatly stowed inside. Boxes had to be acquired, and cord, and Madam Riedesel and her maids worked feverishly. When all was packed and stowed aboard the packet freight charges came to an alarming sum.

The innkeeper had a second suggestion. "He advised me to take with us a trusty man for our protection, without whom I would run great risk. He therefore pretended to take great pains to find me such a one and at length brought me an extremely well-dressed man, whom he introduced to me as a nobleman and a very good friend of his." The English nobleman said he would with great pleasure accompany the Baroness Riedesel to London. He had elegant manners and somehow he made it seem quite natural that the Baroness should pay his expenses, since he was temporarily out of funds. Frederika was now "escorted" by a confidence man!

Now winds were contrary. Boxes had been packed in great haste and taken to the ship, but for two days there was nothing to do but stay at the inn and wait for the wind to change. It was nerve-racking, because the Baroness was afraid of the water and so were the children. "In order to increase their courage" their mother told them that they would see their father as soon as the voyage was over. She neglected to say *which* voyage, and so there was trouble later, as she knew there would be.

At last both wind and tide were right. The Baroness rode down to the quay with the servants following on foot. Caroline, now three months old, was in her mother's arms, but when they got to the water the two little girls scrambled out of the carriage, a sailor picked them up, "and when I looked around me for the children . . . to my great surprise they were already on board the boat, playing with the crew!" Frederika had been "pretending to be courageous to dispel their fears," but now she was terrified. "I had the little one also lifted on board, and now, my heart having a magnet, I found it not so hard as I had imagined," she said. "A plank was thrown across from the shore to the ship over which I walked with firm steps."

"The ship was handsome and clean, which at once relieved me of all fear," the Baroness commented. Cleanliness came next to godliness with her always, stormy seas and treacherous reefs a far lesser evil than dirt. "I had a love of a cabin in which there were eight beds. All the furniture was mahogany and brass, polished like a mirror." Mrs. General had been told that she and the children must lie down at once. "But there was no air in the cabin," so they came on deck "and ate and drank with excellent appetite." This time, Frederika followed her own instincts instead of taking advice and she did exactly the right thing. She and the children proved to be good sailors, and "although the wind was pretty strong" they had the time of their lives.

Members of the crew played with the children. "Husband, your arm," said little Frederika, to one of the sailors, and he solemnly escorted her up and down the deck. One "large, brown-complexioned fellow" picked up the baby Caroline and "it was droll to see him carrying her about and taking care of her while she laughed up at him."

The gay voyage was over all too soon. The captain said he had rarely had so favorable a crossing — it took only five hours. But next came retribution for the children's mother. The children "were now determined to have their father, which troubled me greatly," she confessed. "I beguiled them by saying that we must embark once more — but they teased me continually."

At Dover there was a crowd of men sent to solicit customers for various inns. Mrs. General chose a French inn, which proved "magnificent" with "everything about it remarkably clean." Then came the customs man to search the baggage "which is very troublesome, but I had letters addressed to him," she said. "As soon as he heard that I was following my husband to America he was very gallant and said that it would be cruel to worry the wife of a general who had gone to America in the King's service."

The Baroness said not a word about her "titled" English escort while they were on board the packet ship, and it is to be hoped that he was seasick for his sins. The baggage which the customs had just cleared contained all sorts of goods belonging to the Calais innkeeper and to this confidence man. Madam Riedesel had just unwittingly become the accomplice of smugglers.

This adventurer now took seats for himself and Madam Riedesel's party in the stagecoach for London and then handed her a bill for luggage carried on the coachtop, much of it his own, and "charged for by the pound." The Baroness made her children sit on narrow seats, their backs to the horses, so that the English gentleman would have a comfortable seat for himself in the coach. At stopovers for meals, he ate with her at table, "giving himself the airs of a man of consequence." But she noticed that the servants at the inns along the road acted rather as if they were old cronies of his. At times it almost seemed as if they shared a private joke with the English "milord."

In London, the Baroness went to an inn which friends back in Brunswick had recommended. She had been told that it was delightful, so she was surprised when the landlord showed her "a very wretched apartment on the fourth floor," up under the roof, but she assumed that the inn was full and that she would have better rooms later. She told the landlord to look after her gentleman escort, although now that the traveling was over she did not wish him to share her meals. Then she sent messengers with letters to friends living in London.

Next day the calls of ceremony began. "General Schieffen, three ladies to whom the Duchess of Brunswick had written, and many others, arrived. They were surprised to find me in such miserable quarters," the Baroness said, and before long the innkeeper came to her. Who was the man she had brought with her from Calais? he wanted to know.

"A nobleman," the Baroness explained, and told how the landlord at Calais had arranged that this English gentleman "would be so courteous as to escort" her on her "journey."

"This is another of his tricks!" exclaimed the London innkeeper. The so-called English gentleman was a former valet who had been dismissed — doubtless for good reason. He now lived by his wits, imitating the manners of former masters with considerable success. His reputation as a swindler was pretty well known in London, however, so that the landlord, seeing a lady ride up with him, had assumed that she was no better than she should be. When this lady announced that she was the Baroness von Riedesel, the landlord never believed a word of it. But when callers of quality arrived, he began to have second thoughts.

The London innkeeper was now very much distressed. He gave the Baroness "splendid rooms" for which he charged no more than for the "wretched" ones and "entreated her forgiveness." She asked him to get rid of the crook for her, but the confidence man, not in the least abashed, demanded "five or six guineas for his escort."

The Baroness next discovered that the Calais innkeeper had persuaded her to leave her carriage behind so that he could rent it out himself. She wrote directly to Lord North, Prime Minister of England. Lord North ordered the carriage brought over duty free and driven to London without cost to the Baroness. But it all took time, and Frederika, who had supposed she would be in

London only two days, waited eight days for her carriage to come. It worried her to be in an expensive hostelry in Suffolk Street close to St. James's, Palace, so she sent for her bill. Sure enough, it was high. Of course the innkeeper urged her to stay on, assuring her that he knew her husband would pay. But she was determined not to waste money. As soon as her carriage arrived, she would go to the seaport town of Bristol and take ship from there to Canada. It was what her husband advised, the Baroness said.

Meanwhile there was no harm in a little sight-seeing, and St. James's Park was "a lovely place for walking." In Brunswick, Germany, it was the custom to stroll about without hat or coat in summer — and it was now early June. But her English friends warned the Baroness that such informality would not do in London. She must "wear a cloak and hat." Obediently, she did so, and set out, early one afternoon, with Madam von Hinüber, wife of the Hanoverian Minister. Augusta, now almost five years old, went along, "dressed in a little hooped skirt and a pretty round hat."

They had not walked far before the Baroness saw that "people pointed at us with the finger." It was a strange sensation. Soon "almost everyone was doing it" and Frederika felt her face grow hot. She asked Madam von Hinüber what the matter was and the lady from Hanover explained one did not carry a fan while wearing a hat. Hastily, the Baroness closed and tried to conceal her fan in the folds of her skirt, but people continued to point and she heard them say, "French woman. Pretty girl." (These words she wrote down in English in the journal in which she recorded, in German, the events of her journey.) There was evidently still something wrong, and Madam von Hinüber thought the little girl's hoopskirt might be too fancy and her mother's dress "too formal." Madam von Hinüber realized that it was the French fashion to wear low-cut dresses at almost any hour of the day, but "the French were not very popular in London," she said — putting it mildly.

Next day, when the Baroness and her children went walking in St. James's Park, "we were all of us dressed throughout in the English fashion," she said. "Now we thought we would not be specially noticed." It was all the more embarrassing to hear the same words, " 'French woman. Pretty girl.' " Her friends had found an English manservant for her and she asked him what people were staring at this time. He said it was because she "had put ribbons on" her children. She "tore them off" and put them in her pocket, Augusta and Frederika apparently making no protest. But their mother was almost ready to cry. It seemed also "that the children's hats were differently shaped" from the hats the English children wore. "I learned from this," she said, "the necessity of conforming to the fashions of the country if one would live pleasantly, for a mob is soon collected and if you engage in an argument, you may be insulted." This last the Baroness wrote long afterward, perhaps for the information of her fellow countrywomen who might travel abroad. For the present, she tried hard to "conform," only to remain conspicuous one way or another.

Friends in London urged the Baroness to stay in the city because it was headquarters for news and she would be sure to know when the next convoy would sail for America. But Mrs. Foy, wife of Captain Foy the commissary, was in Bristol, and General Riedesel had designated her as his wife's traveling companion. The Baroness accordingly wrote to Mrs. Foy, asking her to engage lodgings in Bristol. Captain Foy's family were Bristol merchants and his uncle, now an alderman, was formerly the mayor.[1]

Mrs. Foy herself, the former Hannah Van Horne, was the daughter of John Van Horne, merchant, of New York and Kill's Hall — a manor on the Raritan River in New Jersey. Most of the Van Hornes were Tories, but there were "five well bred and beautiful Van Horne daughters who were the much admired toasts of both armies." Some of these "bright-eyed girls who

welcomed friend and foe alike" were Hannah's sisters, and some
her cousins; for her uncle, Philip Van Horne lived nearby at
"Phil's Hill," also known as "Convivial Hall." Hannah had captured the heart of Captain Foy when he came to New York as
secretary to the Earl of Dunmore, British Governor of New York
Province. The bewitching Hannah married Captain Foy on July
26, 1772.[2]

Captain Foy sailed for England around 1775 with his wife and
a sister-in-law, and left them in Bristol with his uncle. He obtained
the job of commissary to the troops in America. He had been
exploiting the colonists under Lord Dunmore, and for a man of
his talents, the new post was sure to turn out well both for himself and his relatives. To be sure, a few accidents happened. General Riedesel, on opening packing-cases supposed to contain British
boots for Brunswick troops, found them full of ladies' slippers.
But Riedesel forgave the man who had proved such a good cook's
helper aboard the *Pallas*.

Mrs. General, as her strange-looking German carriage rumbled
into the outskirts of Bristol, dispatched a messenger to Mrs. Foy's
uncle-in-law, "the Mayor of the City."[3] According to the records
he was mayor no longer, but she thought he was, and she took
it for granted that he would direct her personally to the lodgings
provided for her. In due course her carriage pulled up at the inn
on the city square. A crowd gathered. "They stared at the strange
appearance of my coach and at the two muskets fastened on
top," the Baroness said. "They raised the oilcloth cover of my
carriage to see how it was painted." This was too much for the
faithful Rockel, who had sworn to protect his Baroness with his
life. He spoke only a few words of English but he shouted at
the crowd telling them to get away and he "called them names."
They returned the compliment.

"Upon this," wrote the Baroness, "Rockel lost all control of
himself and knocked one of them down with a blow under the

ear." The crowd swarmed in upon him. There was no telling
what might have happened except that "the Mayor of Bristol
arrived on the scene in the nick of time."

Order was restored, but Mrs. Foy had to be sent for before the
"mayor" could find out who the very pretty but somewhat im-
perious German lady was and what she wanted. Mrs. Foy "could
converse a little in French." She got into Madam Riedesel's carriage and they drove to "fine and spacious apartments." But the
Baroness Frederika stayed here only a short time, because the
landlady refused to allow her to have the children's clothes
washed and because the apartments were extremely expensive.
She went house-hunting for herself and found rooms from which
she "had a most delightful view." They "overlooked the whole
College Green, a promenade filled with trees in the midst of clean
grass and paths where men, women and children were in the
habit of walking." It was a place where her own children "ran and
played" on the grass among the flower beds and borders.

Bristol was a fine old city with half-timbered houses reminiscent
of Wolfenbüttel — with Gothic churches, a cathedral and much
wealth derived in part from trade with America. But there was
another unhappy ordeal in store for the Baroness. She was wearing one of the new dresses made for her back in Germany, a
"calico trimmed with green taffeta." Mrs. Foy had come for her
and they went out walking, when "more than a hundred sailors
gathered around us and pointed at me with their fingers, at the
same time crying out, 'French whore!'" Just barely managing to
keep from bursting into tears, the Baroness ran into a shop and
"pretended to examine the merchandise and, shortly after, the
crowd dispersed." When she got home, she cried bitterly — and
gave away the dress.

The children asked constantly for the ship that was to take
them to their father, but no fleet bound for America was setting
out. The servants "lost heart" in this strange land where no one

spoke their language. Mrs. General did her best to appear cheerful so as to encourage her little army, but in her journal she confessed that "she wept for hours in secret in her lonely room." And then she "took courage." The thing to do was to learn English. In six weeks she could read the English newspapers and she could order whatever she wanted to eat and ask for merchandise in the shops.

Plenty of ships, though not in convoy, sailed out of Bristol. Again and again the Baroness went to Mrs. Foy to see if there wasn't one they could engage passage on. But Mrs. Foy said she was waiting for letters from her husband.

Hannah Foy lived in "a pretty and well-furnished house where she did a great deal of entertaining." At first, the Baroness assumed that the parties, much frequented by ships' officers, were for the sister, Miss Van Horne. But gradually it became clear that Mrs. Foy had no great desire to join her husband. "At last the long-expected letter" from Captain Foy came to hand, and "upon this, my impatience showed itself and also the irresolution of Madam Foy," the Baroness wrote. "Finally I persuaded her to consent to our departure."

Frederika had already written to Lord Germain and he had "answered her very politely." But Mrs. General had asked for orders and she did not get them. "It was indeed true that winter was drawing near and that I must . . . wish to embark, especially since my husband had written for me. But since he had, at the same time, imposed the condition that I must travel with Madam Foy . . ." Germain "did not know what advice to give." Lord George was confidently directing a war against far-distant colonials, but he left it to Mrs. General Riedesel to persuade Mrs. Foy to go to America, promising "passage on a packet ship" if this could be accomplished.

The Baroness finally got Mrs. Foy's reluctant consent. She again wrote to Lord Germain, who replied that he "owned a packet ship" about to sail from Portsmouth. The Baroness could have free passage and all provisions and Mrs. Foy "could share with me if I so desired," Frederika said. Lord George ordered a cow put on board so the Riedesel children could have milk.

"In proportion as the moment for our departure approached, the more irresolute Madame Foy became," but they all set out for Portsmouth. "Here Madam Foy and her sister found many officers who were old acquaintances. They passed a very gay evening." First Madam Riedesel put her children to bed and then she went to join the company. She found the officers telling Mrs. Foy and her sister that "it was a thousand pities that such pretty ladies should expose themselves to such a risk" as taking passage to America so late in the year. They said other things to the pretty ladies which Frederika, "not being a sufficient mistress of the English language" could not understand very well. But she gathered that if Mrs. Foy and Miss Van Horne should spend the coming winter in England, they would not be lonely. Madam Riedesel went back to her own room.

Sometime in the night, Mrs. Foy came to the Baroness and announced that she was not going to sail. "I urgently besought her not to decide so hastily," Frederika said, and Mrs. Foy "returned to her company. At eight next morning, Mrs. Foy and her sister appeared and informed me that we must start back. I wept, but all in vain, for she well knew that my husband had laid it upon me not to undertake the voyage without her." The baggage had already been sent along the road to Bristol by Mrs. Foy's orders. The carriage was at the door.

But on the road to Bristol, Mrs. General saw a wagon going toward Portsmouth under armed escort. She had an English maid by this time, who had agreed to go to America, and she asked this girl why the cart was guarded. It was a money chest going aboard the packet with gold and silver to pay the troops in Canada, the girl said.

"If they risk so much money, it can't be too late to attempt the voyage," Mrs. General exclaimed.

"Go ahead, then," said Hannah Foy, laughing.

"But you sent our baggage back to Bristol without telling me."

And to this, Mrs. Foy replied "in a bantering tone" that, since Mrs. General was so brave, why shouldn't she go aboard ship with the clothes she was wearing and just her hand luggage?

Madam Riedesel had been altogether too patient with Hannah Foy. Now she lost her temper, and back to Bristol she went. She sent Rockel to catch up with the baggage cart and bring back the general's wine she had bought for him, the fresh limes they needed to prevent scurvy on the voyage, the bedding, and the warm clothes. "Fortunately the cartman understood a little German," she said, for the ship "was expected every moment."

Three weeks went by and no packet ship owned by Lord George Germain arrived in Portsmouth. This was heartbreaking, because with every day lost winter came closer and the St. Lawrence River might be closed to navigation. Madam Riedesel made friends in Portsmouth, however, and the family of Commodore Douglas was particularly nice to her.

"I often dined at the Douglas mansion," Frederika wrote. But she still suffered from embarrassment because of being in a foreign land. At table, for instance, "each person in turn honored me by offering me a glass of wine. I had heard of this custom and that it was considered an insult to refuse. But I was nursing my little daughter Caroline and therefore dared not take any wine at all. The first day I lacked courage to refuse," she confessed, "but I feared it would injure my child, so the next day I asked if it would be all right if I drank water." Everybody smiled and reassured the Baroness. Only "people in low life" would dream of being insulted, they told her.

At first the Baroness was also worried because she "could not bring" herself "to eat vegetables boiled after the English fashion, merely in water." But she observed that they "sometimes poured an excellent sauce of butter over them" and after that she liked

English boiled cabbage with melted butter almost as well as
sauerkraut.

Portsmouth, England, was a beautiful city, the Baroness said.
She and the children took daily walks upon the walls and ramparts to watch the ships sailing in and out of the harbor. With
every incoming sail they wondered, "Is this the packet?" At night
they heard a gun which was fired in salute to each arrival and
early in the morning they eagerly asked, "Did Lord George Germain's ship come in?" The answer was always no.

Now Madam Riedesel's money began to run low, no matter
how frugal she tried to be. At this point, however, a Captain
Young and his wife arrived from Tobago. Captain Young had
been Adjutant to Duke Ferdinand during the Seven Years' War
and knew General Riedesel well. He was on his way to London
and it was known that Lord Germain's packet was tied up in the
Thames. Captain Young suggested that Madam Riedesel go to
London where she could share the expenses of a modest lodging
with him and his wife. She could get in touch with the Riedesel's
English banker and board the packet when it left London.

This seemed good advice. Mrs. General marshaled her little
army and set out. When she arrived in London, the packet ship
had sailed and she had missed it.

4

Meanwhile, the General...

GENERAL Riedesel arrived off the city of Quebec on the first day of June, 1776, at six o'clock in the evening. There was still plenty of daylight and he could see the broad St. Lawrence stretching onward into endless forest. On a great cliff overlooking the city his practiced eye caught a glimpse of iron howitzers on a wall built of wood. There were wooden houses beyond the wall and down on a narrow shelf on land close to the river there was another wooden town.

The General "lost no time" but jumped into a strange-looking two-wheeled vehicle and told the driver to take him to the Governor's palace. The driver of the calash, who sat on a "narrow board in front with his feet on the shafts," shouted and cracked his whip and the little horse sprang up a steep and winding road. Riedesel hung on to the sides of his boxlike seat for dear life, then leaned forward with a jerk as the horse slowed to a crawl. They passed through a narrow, fortified gate and, with more cracking of the whip and shouting, they drew up at a barracklike building. After a brief but violent colloquy, in German French on Riedesel's part and Canadian French on the part of the driver, the General strode into the building "to pay his respects to Sir Guy Carleton, Governor of the Province of Canada."[1]

Carleton was tall, thin, austere. "Put a black wig on him and a long black gown and he would be the image of the Abbé of Jérusalem," tutor to the Hereditary Prince Charles William of Brunswick, General Riedesel thought. "He has the same way of walking — the same tone of voice." After polite formalities had been exchanged, Sir Guy invited the General to come to dinner next day.

The American rebels still held Montreal, Sir Guy Carleton told Riedesel, but they had nothing that could be called an army. With the reinforcements brought by Burgoyne, they would soon be defeated. Only five months previously, Sir Guy himself, disguised as a Canadian voyageur, had barely escaped from the rebels by slipping down the St. Lawrence from Montreal in a canoe. But now the tables were turning. He had just taken Three Rivers from the Americans, and had left a British garrison at that important little city and trading post halfway between Quebec and Montreal.

June 3, 1776, was General Riedesel's birthday. He was thirty-eight years old and his military advancement had been rapid, which should have given him satisfaction. But he spent the day aboard the *Pallas* writing letters, packing to disembark, and feeling morose. Orders had already come from Carleton to leave the "Regiment Prince Frederick" and the dragoons under Lieutenant Colonel Baum to garrison Quebec and Levis, across the St. Lawrence. A general is anything but pleased to have troops taken from his command; Riedesel confided in a letter to his wife that he did not think Carleton was fair.

The next day was the birthday of George III. The city of Quebec was "illuminated" in the evening by means of lighted candles set in every window. It was well known that a good many French people living in Quebec had hoped that the Americans would win.[2] Yet it seemed that in all of Quebec's fifteen hundred houses, everyone was joyously burning candles in honor of the

King of England. The reason for this was soon apparent, however. Soldiers were going about heaving rocks through any unlighted windows.

Quebec was "for the most part on a high mountain," General Riedesel said. The "whole west side is fortified, but the fortifications are in a bad state of repair although they worked hard last winter and are still feverishly at work to rebuild them." Mortars had been hauled out of old frigates and mounted on the walls and there were eighty-one iron cannon. Riedesel concluded that the American rebels "must be a miserable lot of soldiers," because, if those wood and mud fortifications had been in Germany, "four to eight cannon would make such a hole in them in a few hours that half a battalion could march through it."

General Riedesel went to visit "the memorable mountain" which the English General Wolfe climbed when he took the city from Montcalm in 1759. Then he went to see the place where the American General Montgomery had been killed on December 3, 1775. And General Carleton "passed in review some 600 American prisoners of war" taken after Montgomery's failure to capture Quebec. The German Baron Riedesel was shocked to learn that "among the so-called colonels and other officers captured from the rebel army, many were tailors, shoemakers and base mechanics."

Riedesel was given "command of a corps," and this, he said, "surprised everyone." He was especially fond of "Regiment Riedesel," named in his honor, and this was given to him along with Breymann's Grenadier battalion, a British battalion of 150 Canadians and 300 Indians.

After his conferences with Carleton, Riedesel felt that the plan of campaign for the summer of 1776 was a simple one. All they had to do was, first, drive the American rebels out of Canada; then, after pursuing them into the British colonies to the southward

Carleton, with Riedesel's help of course, would quickly subdue them and the American rebellion would be over.

The first lesson General Riedesel needed to learn concerned the vast distances in North America and the primitive condition of all so-called "roads." He was proud of the Brunswick-bred horses he had brought with him on the ship *Martha*. They would have carried a man in armor, and they were trained not to bolt from the flash and roar of cannon but lead a charge against an enemy as steadily as they led a parade. His horses, General Carleton now told Riedesel, would at present be of no use to him — because the army must "cross little rivers where there are no bridges." They were to march to the northern end of Lake Champlain, and "thither I shall go on foot, like the rest of the army." Such a thing could not happen to a general in Europe. "I hope I shall set a good example to my men," Riedesel said.

Without waiting to unload baggage, Carleton planned to send the fleet which had just arrived from Great Britain up the St. Lawrence to recover Montreal, still held by Americans. But the wind came whirling down the river in the wrong direction. News traveled faster than the fleet.

"The small-pox has broke out in such a manner that [the American Army] is almost ruined," wrote Benedict Arnold, who was in command after the death of Montgomery. He began his retreat.[3]

"The chiefs of the wild nations" met in Quebec at noon on the seventh of June, and on that same day "orders suddenly came that the wind was right and the fleet was to weigh anchor at four in the afternoon." General Riedesel went back to the *Pallas* and the fleet left Quebec for Three Rivers, making three leagues, or between nine and ten miles that day and anchoring off Cap Rouge for the night. Riedesel, although still regretting the horse he had left behind, was not yet required to set an example to his troops by slogging along on foot. Getting under way again at eight next morning, the fleet made over thirty miles by two in the afternoon. Riedesel admired the "beautiful landscape" on both banks of the St. Lawrence where "woodland and cultivated fields were interspersed with many neat settlements." They anchored off Cap L'Oiseau to take on river pilots.

Anchored all around them in the river were the frigates *Triton* and *Blonde* and "many transports with British infantry." When no pilots appeared, Riedesel had himself rowed over to the *Triton* to see what was the matter. There were many more ships than pilots, he was told. Nothing could be done while they waited for French Canadian river men to see them past the Richelieu Rapids.

At ten o'clock on the morning of June 9 the fleet set out again with a favorable wind. Every ship flew a blue flag in honor of the captain of the *Blonde*, who was commodore. The Laurentian Mountains rose on the north shore and at the foot of a cliff they saw the wreck of "a rebel ship." They cast anchor at ten at night, having sailed over forty miles. News reached them that "an engagement at Three Rivers" was still in progress. But a small force of Americans had already been defeated. General Riedesel had missed it and he was very much annoyed.

On the morning of the tenth of June, Riedesel reached Three Rivers, where he interviewed some of the American prisoners. To his astonishment, "most of them were Germans from the Province of Pennsylvania." He had believed, on setting out, that this rebellion which he had come to help suppress consisted of a rabble of peasants who had seized whatever crude weapons came to hand, being "deluded by unprincipled leaders." He still thought so, and was the more puzzled because "judging by their uniforms the Germans were soldiers."[4]

General Burgoyne, already in Three Rivers, treated the captured American officers with extreme politeness, ordering food for

them and "serving them himself." Burgoyne never missed an opportunity to be dramatic, and in this account of his excessive
civility there is more than a hint of the sardonic.

The thing to do now was to follow up their advantage as
quickly as possible, but contrary winds kept Carleton and his
fleet anchored in front of Three Rivers for two days. On the
morning of June 12, a breeze served to move the ships as far as
Lake St. Peter, where they were becalmed. Fog swept in over this
twenty-five-mile section of the St. Lawrence, where the river is
nine miles wide. Orders were to load all guns, decks were to be
manned by soldiers under arms, and ships must hail each other
every fifteen minutes. Boats from the frigates patrolled "around
the ships constantly to keep everybody alert," while "savages
and also Canadians patrolled the shores." The *Blonde* and the
Triton returned to Quebec, the river being too shallow for them.
General Carleton went aboard the "ship-of-war *Martin*, fourteen
guns" and on June 14 they "cautiously continued their voyage,
the *Martin* leading the way in a light breeze." Canoes filled with
"savages" and Canadians went close to shore, and from time to
time news was brought from patrols on land: The Americans were
making a stand. . . . They were fortifying Sorel. . . .

Carleton ordered all troops to be ready to disembark. Small
frigates could approach close to the little town of Sorel with its
square, its church, its few wooden houses. Artillery could make
short work of whatever log and mud ramparts the Americans had
thrown up. But now word came that the Americans had retreated up the Richelieu River to Chambly — one of the few well-
built stone fortresses on the overland route to the Hudson. General Riedesel was still aboard the *Pallas*, the ship which had
carried him across the Atlantic. It was small enough to sail on
Lake St. Peter!

Orders to disembark and draw four days' rations were given

at three in the afternoon. Although the ships were opposite Sorel, bateaux were needed to get the men ashore. Rain began to come down, steadily, pitilessly — such rain as Brunswickers assumed could fall only in short showers. The sodden German troops were told that no baggage wagons would be supplied and they must carry their blankets, "which grew heavier every moment by the rain." It took three hours to disembark, and then they marched along a rough road in the gathering darkness. The Americans had made no stand at Sorel — they had gone, but Carleton was after them.

"We marched about fourteen miles in six days," General Riedesel reported to the Duke of Brunswick. He referred to German miles; the distance covered was about sixty-five miles English measurement. "During the whole of this journey, I and the other officers were obliged to go on foot. This is the seventh day that I have worn the same shirt and stockings." What a novel experience for the Baron General Friedrich Adolphus von Riedesel!

Carleton was bitterly disappointed to find that the Americans had also evacuated Chambly before he got there. Only the stone shell of the fort remained. Inside, soldiers' quarters, galleries, staircases — all were a heap of still smoking embers. According to the Americans' own account, their rear guard left just as the British advance guard was seen coming down the road.

All the previous day and night, the Americans had been frantically loading their sick and wounded into bateaux. They could spare only two able-bodied men to each boat and these men could barely make headway against the swift Richelieu as it swept down the long miles from Lake Champlain. They paused at St. Johns, then camped briefly twelve miles farther south at Isle aux Noix, men dying along the way from wounds, from dysentery — and from smallpox. At last Sullivan with men from Sorel reached Crown Point on Lake Champlain, as did Arnold with his men from Montreal. Here were gathered about 5200 Americans, nearly 2000 of them too ill to move. Their only food was raw pork, hard bread and unbaked flour.

General Riedesel's estimate of the American army, at this point, was hasty but understandable. "Their soldiers are not what they were thought to be in Germany," he wrote his overlord. "They are a miserable race of men with poor officers. They have no money, only paper . . ." and Riedesel thought the "confederation of provinces" to the southward could not last long. If Howe "lands safely, captures New York and gains a footing, we can cross the lake with a few brigades, one after the other." Then the American Revolution would be over, "this winter" of 1776–1777.

General Riedesel was posted at "La Prairie" or Laprairie, a town midway between Chambly and Montreal on the south bank of the St. Lawrence and commanding the portage at the Lachine Rapids. This was an important post, having a road leading to Chambly and waterways in several directions. "We are at this place masters of the whole Province of Canada," he wrote to Duke Ferdinand on July 25. "If we had ships and sloops of war in which to cross Lake Champlain, we would soon be in the rear of the colonies. But all our vessels are yet to be built and this delay will cost us three weeks."

Riedesel spent most of his time traveling from town to town, getting an idea of the lay of the land, urging on the work crews who were repairing forts at Sorel, Chambly, St. Johns and Isle aux Noix. The terrain of England's North American provinces did not please the German General. "Aside from a few cultivated regions on the rivers, all the hills are covered with woods," he complained. You could not choose a good spot to have a battle. All you could do was to build forts and "go with the Indians through primeval forests." Riedesel had come to the conclusion that "in the whole of America, there is no spot where six battalions could be placed in a good position."

Things were not going well with the Prince Frederick Regi-

ment, under Riedesel but left back in Quebec. They had scurvy
and were on the point of mutiny. Instead of ordering floggings,
Riedesel went to Quebec to listen to complaints. He found that
the commissary had been feeding the men salt beef, and he went
straight to Carleton who ordered that fresh meat and vegetables
be supplied at once. Riedesel's first thought must have been that
his old friend Captain Foy, as commissary, had been cheating the
troops. But he found that Foy, after being offered the post of
barrack master without rise in rank, had refused it and was now
secretary to Carleton. This was certainly a position to which his
experience entitled him, and Foy already knew that it could be
made financially worthwhile. He had made a fortune as Secretary to Lord Dunmore in New York Province and in Virginia.

On returning to his post at Laprairie, Riedesel found his troops
were accused of pillaging. But they were not a conquering army in
enemy territory, as Reidesel was well aware, and he made strict
rules. He established a market day at Sorel when the French
Canadian peasants (he called all farmers "peasants") were to
bring in produce for which his deputy commissaries were to pay
cash. Of course the inhabitants were required to bring in fresh
meat, fish and vegetables, whether they wanted to or not. And of
course they hid food and sold it at black market prices whenever they got a chance. But the new system worked well on the
whole.

More than three hundred men came down with dysentery.
General Riedesel seems to have had a pretty good idea that this
disease was caused by filth, and his orders concerning sanitation
were strict. Latrines must be dug and soldiers must use them. It
was understood that any army camp smelled to high heaven, but
latrines must be filled and new ones dug at stated intervals, before
the stench became overpowering.

Aside from the statement that the seventy-seven women were
with the Brunswick troops, these poor souls rarely appeared in

general orders, in journals or in orderly books. Captain Georg Pausch, in charge of the Hanau artillery, and a journal writer of note, observed of accommodations on shipboard: "The married men and women occupy beds . . . six in number, very narrow and arranged in two tiers, one above the other and separated . . . to prevent misbehavior as much as possible." A child was born aboard a ship in the St. Lawrence and named "Lorenz." The German women's costumes caused comment, as Madam Riedesel was to discover.

But one of the functions of women camp followers was to forage, and as soon as the Brunswickers encamped a few orders concerning women began to appear in the orderly books of the various officers. Women were to stop trading with the Indians. Above all, they were to stop giving rum to the Indians as a medium of exchange. Rum was served out to soldiers, those on fatigue duty getting more than others and those in hospital receiving special rations. Sutlers and traders hung around the camp with rum for sale, and it was a dull woman who could not set herself up in business and acquire fresh deermeat from the Indians to supplement her half-ration, or moccasins for herself and her children and extra blankets as nights grew cold — all with rum for money. Indians "walked freely through our camp, came into our tents without ceremony wanting rum or brandy" was the report, and control was next to impossible.[5] Riedesel insisted that his German women camp followers were above rum selling, but investigation proved otherwise.

Boatbuilding went slowly, it seemed to Riedesel, who wanted to get on with the campaign and perhaps spend a pleasant winter in New York. At Sorel, at St. Johns, "carpenters from all the ships were ordered" to report along with "artificers" from the different regiments.[6] Most of the Canadians in the area were "building roads through the woods, bringing up cannon, provisions and all kinds of stores. . . ." The Canadians who had greeted General Sullivan at Sorel with enthusiasm either fled with the retreating army or now "worked in irons on the roads."

There was a portage of about seven miles between Chambly and St. Johns. Boats and bateaux were pulled along the road beside the rapids here "by a great number of horses" — all requisitioned from the "Inhabitants." But two sloops of war "were attempted to be brought up" — in vain. Their guns were taken out of them, loaded on creaking wains and hauled laboriously. The sloops were dismasted and hauled overland piecemeal. At St. Johns, they were building the *Carleton,* a twelve-gun schooner, the *Inflexible,* a twenty-eight-gun frigate and "a floating battery of great strength carrying mortars, shells and twenty-four-pounders." The weather was extremely hot, for it was mid-July.

"We have already conquered the whole of Canada and shall, as soon as our boats are ready, force our way into New England," General Riedesel wrote to his wife with understandable optimism. He expected to see her soon, for surely she was on the ocean by now. The war would be over in a few more weeks. Then "I will try to manage to take you comfortably home in my ship," he promised.

5

The First Thrust

I N JULY General Riedesel went to Montreal to see the city. It was "somewhat handsomer than Quebec," he thought, but "its wall is nothing more than an apology for a wall with loopholes for cannon and firearms. What is called the citadel is only a log house in poor condition." Riedesel attended another "meeting of wild men."

Chiefs from all the tribes of the Iroquois nation had been invited to gather at a church built by the Jesuits but no longer in use because the Jesuits had withdrawn from Montreal. Holy images and symbols had been taken down and in the choir, once mumurous with Latin prayers and responses, rugs were spread and stools lined up on either side. In the center was an armchair and behind, in place of the high altar, there was a table. Down the main aisle were rows of stools, three hundred in all.

Governor Carleton marched into the church, followed by his high command — Generals Burgoyne, Phillips, Riedesel. Behind the officers came Carleton's secretaries — Captain Foy, and Captain Christopher Carleton,[1] nephew and brother-in-law of the Governor — who seated themselves at the table, prepared to take notes. Governor Carleton sat in the armchair. He seems to have been the only person with a reasonably comfortable seat, but what impressed Riedesel was that Carleton kept his hat on during the whole proceedings. The nave of the church was filled with

52

Indian chiefs, who lighted their ceremonial pipes and sat on their stools, pipe in mouth.[2]

Each tribe spoke, through its chief and its French interpreter who acted as orator. Carleton had his own interpreter, just to check, and his nephew was also competent in the Iroquois language. The Indians said they knew that revolt had arisen against the King of England. They praised the valor of General Carleton in chasing the rebels out of Montreal and explained that those tribes living near Laprairie who had remained neutral had been misled. An old man, not present, had told them lies. They were now ready to hire themselves out for a year to General Carleton.

Next came the "gifts." Powder and ball, over and above that needed to kill the English settlers to the southward, was agreed upon. The Indians had grown dependent upon the white man's weapons for the hunt, to procure food as well as furs. Kettles, blankets, all sorts of civilized luxuries had become necessities and Carleton was adept at promising enough but not too much. He never paid everything at one time but doled out "gifts" on the installment plan, after receiving services.

When the first day's conference was over, the chiefs filed past Governor Carleton and shook hands. "They had brought with them a few scalps of rebels whom they had killed and with which they honored Generals Carleton, Burgoyne and Phillips," General Riedesel wrote. Apparently, he didn't get one.

Next came the "feasting." Rum was given out to seal the bargain, and another conference was called for the following day, but by then the chiefs were too drunk to stand up and the meeting was postponed. As soon as negotiations were over, Governor Carleton had himself paddled down the St. Lawrence in his Indian war canoe, leaving Burgoyne in charge of British and Brunswick forces poised on the southern border of Canada. General Riedesel went back to Laprairie, and he was embarrassed to have to report to his Duke as to what happened next.

"With an army in Germany it would scarcely be possible for

an enemy to steal into a cantonment," he said. "But here, with the way the armies are posted, it is easier." And with grudging admiration, Riedesel added: "The only wonder is how the rebels could make this long march of forty leagues through deserts and dense woods and carry, at the same time, rations for fifteen days on their backs." Brigadier General Patrick Gordon, in command of the British First Brigade, had been shot at by an American rebel while riding along the road from St. Johns to Laprairie. Gordon had put spurs to his horse and escaped with two musket balls in his shoulder. He reached St. Johns, but fainted from loss of blood on arrival, recovered consciousness long enough to tell what had happened, and then died of his wounds. "I have gone over that road myself more than thirty times," Riedesel exclaimed. He would no longer ride alone.

This small affair was a jolt to the "Masters of Canada." Burgoyne, in his general orders, let himself go in his best bombastic style: "The Rebel Runaways not having dared to show their Faces as Soldiers, have now taken the part of the vilest Assassins and are lurking in small Parties to murder, if any single or unarmed Officer or Soldier may be passing the Roads, near the Woodside." Carleton offered a reward of fifty guineas to any inhabitant who would capture or betray the American scouts — or, in Burgoyne's words, "these infamous Skulkers."

General Riedesel wrote that "the person who commanded the party which attacked General Gordon" was known to be "Whitcomb of Connecticut calling himself Lieutenant." And in Burgoyne's general orders was a description: "He is between 30 and 40 years of age, to appearance near 6 feet high, rather thin than otherwise, light brown hair tied behind, rough face, not sure whether occasioned by small-pox or not. He wears a kind of under Jacket without Sleeves, slash Pockets, leather Breeches, grey woolen or yarn Stockings and Shoes. Hat flapped, a gold Cord tied round it. He had a Firelock, Blanket, Pouch and Powder Horn."

The American Lieutenant Benjamin Whitcomb wrote his own laconic report of what happened: "Twenty-third, early in the morning, I returned to my former place of abode, stood there the whole day, saw twenty-three carts laden with barrels and tents going to St. Johns. Twenty-fourth, staid at the same place till about twelve o'clock, then fired on an officer, and moved immediately into Chambly road . . . finding myself discovered was obliged to conceal myself in the brush till dark. The 25th instant, on which I made my escape by the guards, I saw upwards of 40 carts preparing to go to St. Johns and I judge there were lying at that place and on the road about one full regiment of regulars." Far from being at the head of an expedition, Lieutenant Whitcomb had come alone from Fort Ticonderoga to get information about British preparations and if possible to bring back a prisoner. He had tried to capture Brigadier Gordon — had fired to stop him — and was unaware that Gordon was wounded.

On August 13, Whitcomb was back again with two men, "disguised as countrymen." He stationed himself on the road as before, observed "seventy-two Indians, armed, returning from St. Johns for Montreal." Then along came two men, "found to be the enemy. I immediately stepped out and told them they were my prisoners. . . . They were sure I was no soldier. I told them, soldier or not, they must go with me to Ticonderoga. . . . They offered me money to let them go. I told them I would not, for all the money King George was worth." Whitcomb and his two fellow scouts carried off Quartermaster Alexander Saunders and an ensign. Saunders had a loaded fusee and a brace of pistols and had boasted that he would like to meet Whitcomb and claim the reward. After what was to the Englishmen "a terrifying journey" through the forest to Ticonderoga, they were "forwarded" to Congress under guard, and Lieutenant Whitcomb's rank was raised to major.[3]

Riedesel never ceased to protest because some of his Brunswickers were kept at Quebec when old men and soldiers just out of hospital could have garrisoned the city just as well. Finally, the dragoons were released to him. Germans worked at tasks far beneath their dignity as soldiers when they built blockhouses and barracks and repaired the walls at St. Johns. Riedesel's men had to learn to row a boat — and most of them had never done such a thing before. But he praised them and said they learned quickly. Lacking Burgoyne's dash and fire that made his men cheer at the sight of him, Riedesel was nonetheless loved by the Brunswickers, who trusted him to look after them the best he could.

It was the ninth of October 1776 when the fleet (built or reassembled) was finally set afloat on Lake Champlain. On the tenth Captain Carleton, in Indian dress and in full war paint, set out along the lake shore with four hundred Indians in canoes. The next day the Brunswick brigade was ordered to embark seventy-six men from each company — the remainder to stay in camp. Riedesel was ordered to Isle aux Noix. "Am I forever to bring up the rear!" he exclaimed.

Isle aux Noix, eight and seven tenths miles north of the present Canadian border, was a small, marshy island long occupied and lightly fortified as an Indian trading post. It was extremely unhealthy. Orders for digging latrines were all well and good, but water seeped into any hole, filled it and overflowed. In case of rain, soldiers' quarters were always flooded. The American army had retreated, but the mosquitoes had not — their forces were nightly reinforced, their weapons always ready. General Riedesel hated this post and with good reason, but it was the depot for provisions for the fleet now about to cross Lake Champlain.

Carleton advanced into the lake with the *Inflexible*, carrying eighteen twelve-pounders. She had been completed just eight days previously. Next came the *Lady Mary* (or *Maria*), named in honor of Carleton's wife, a schooner with fourteen six-pounders. The schooner *Carleton* carried twelve six-pounders — and the "radeau," or raft, was a floating battery armed with six twenty-four-pounders, six twelve-pounders and two howitzers. Much was expected of the radeau when it came to breaching the walls of Fort Ticonderoga. Then there were ten gunboats each carrying three cannon which had just arrived from England, and there were two twelve-gun vessels captured from the Americans. Various parties had reconnoitered the northern part of the lake and had seen no sign of Americans and it was concluded that the newly-built British fleet could sail without opposition.

The fleet headed along the west coast of Champlain in the direction of Grand Isle. They passed the northern channel between a long, heavily wooded island and the western mainland without seeing a sail — but they were seen. During the summer months, the Americans had also been building a fleet. General Benedict Arnold had been allowed to take it out into the lake, but Horatio Gates (briefly in command) had warned him not to sail too far from Ticonderoga. Arnold, however, was anchored between Valcour Island and the mainland, more than fifty miles north of the fort. Arnold was tremendously outnumbered and outgunned, but his position — in a channel only three quarters of a mile wide—would prevent the whole British fleet from attacking him at once. He ordered the schooner *Royal Savage* to show herself at the southern entrance to the channel and he sent four armed galleys, to work with the *Royal Savage* like dogs with a hunter.

When the British caught sight of "a frigate slipping behind an island" the *Carleton* was sent in pursuit but could not catch her. The water shoaled off, and the *Carleton* had to give up the chase, but the *Inflexible* hit the *Royal Savage* three times, which so confused the crew (Arnold said) that they grounded her. She was by no means out of commission, however, and her crew continued to fire her guns until she had to be abandoned.

Lieutenant Georg Pausch, in his journal, told of the Battle of Valcour Island as it looked to him from the deck of what was probably one of the ten English gunboats.[4] Pausch knew by five o'clock in the morning of October 11 that there was an engagement going on, but his gunboat sailed slowly. It was half past ten before he heard the sound of artillery.

The first thing Pausch saw was "a frigate of the enemy stuck fast on a stone cliff and abandoned." But "soon after, we saw two other frigates sending forth a lively fire. Besides this they [the Americans] had several armed gondolas which, one after the other, emerged from a small bay of the island firing rapidly and effectively. Every once in a while they would vanish in order to get breath, and suddenly reappear.

"Our attack, with about 27 bateaux armed with 24 12- and 6-pound cannon and a few howitzers, became very animated. But now our frigates approached. One of them, the *Maria,* having His Excellency von Carleton on board, advanced and opened a lively cannonade. This one was replaced by the frigate *Carleton* and, as she in turn retreated, the *Inflexible* took her place, only to retreat as the others had done. One of the enemy's frigates . . . began to career over on one side but in spite of this continued her fire. The cannon of the rebels were well served; for I saw afterwards that our ships were pretty well mended and patched with boards and stoppers.

"Close to one o'clock in the afternoon, this naval battle began to get very serious. Lt. Dufais came very near perishing with all his men for a cannon-ball going through his powder magazine, it blew up. . . . Dufais's bateau came back burning and I hurried to it to save, if possible, the lieutenant and his men. All who could, jumped on board my bateau, which, being thus overloaded, came near sinking. . . ."

Pausch had "nine cannoneers and nine sailors" added to his own force of "10 cannoneers, 1 drummer, 1 sergeant, 1 boy and 10 sailors; in all 48 persons." He noted that the radeau had proved so unmanageable that it never arrived on the scene till dusk and never got a shot at Arnold's fleet.

Carleton was certain now that he had but to wait for morning to polish off the Americans. As Pausch told it, "This night a chain was formed of all the bateaux; and everyone had to be wide awake and on the alert. The captain's frigate, which had run aground, was set on fire by the orders of His Excellency and her ammunition blowing up caused a fine fire lasting all night."

Next morning Arnold was gone! It was a masterly retreat, executed in black darkness and in complete silence. Carefully shielded lanterns were hung at the stern of each ship to show the way. There must have been a gap in the "chain of bateaux," or a weak link, and the fire from the frigate must have burned to embers. "Landlubbers," Arnold had called his crew, but they rowed without a splash or creak of oars.

"Carleton was in a rage," General Riedesel said. He was so excited that he set out in pursuit forgetting to give any orders to his land forces. The Americans were only twelve miles away, however, having limped as far as Schuyler's Island where they were trying to repair their fleet. Carleton might have pulverized them and marooned their crews except for "the violence of the wind and a great swell" which made his ships rock as though in midocean. He came about and returned to Valcour Island, where he anchored. Towards evening the weather moderated and he set out again, "the boats using their oars to make headway against the wind."[5]

Having completed repairs, Arnold and his Americans started for Crown Point, where there was a fort, a small garrison and a harbor in which to make a stand. But the "wind proved fair" — for the British — and they overtook the Americans about noon. The Americans were outranged by the British guns, and now there was no channel where they could force a close engagement, but only the great open lake all around them. After using up their ammunition and seeing their iron balls fall uselessly into the water while British well-aimed shot came aboard, the "three stern-most vessels struck their colors."

Arnold ran his ship *Congress* aground and blew her up. Afterwards, the British General Phillips told Riedesel that he heard the groans and cries of wounded men abandoned by Arnold in the flaming hull. Five vessels were burned, the crews escaping to Ticonderoga. Once more Carleton was angry because his Indians, swarming ashore from their canoes, were supposed to have been harvesting scalps, letting no one get away.

It was a sad story or a triumphant one, all depending on the point of view. But, once more, General Riedesel had missed an engagement. He had been at Isle aux Noix, industriously gathering provisions and drilling his men, just as he had been doing for the last three months. He gave "a great dinner of thirty-six covers [for General Carleton] and the principal officers of the army," he wrote his wife, and assured her that he "had made friends with everyone" and thought he "stood well with all officers and men." But he was too good at detail to be spared from routine tasks. Finally, he asked for and received an invitation aboard ship.

"On Board the *Washington,* a prize taken from the Rebels," Riedesel put at the top of a letter dated October 26, 1776. "I am here as a volunteer for six days. We have sailed close to Fort Carillon [the French name for Ticonderoga]." He had observed the arm of Lake Champlain leading toward Skenesborough. At "Buttonmole Bay," where Arnold's ships were burned,[6] Riedesel watched the British raising guns. They salvaged thirty within a few days. But Carleton was again angry. The Americans had dismantled the fort at Crown Point in order to get guns to arm their fleet, and they had done nothing at all to repair the place! He had expected to find it in good shape, so that he could use it himself.

At Crown Point there was nothing and no one. Once there had been a French fort all of cut stone with medieval keep, battlements, moat and portcullis. The Americans had found it in a ruinous condition, but containing a treasure nonetheless. One Lieutenant Job Cook, writing in phonetic style to his Commander

in Chief, Philip Schuyler, in January, 1776, tells of what went on:
"Sir as i have Received your Honours orders to imploy the Men
under my charge in Digging in the old fort for Led But the Men
that i have inlisted Eair all most neaked and the weather very
Cold; . . . if it is your Honours plesuer that I should Eopen that
tresuer, I will set as many men to work as have clothes Surfis-
sant . . ."[7]

It was indeed His Honor's "plesuer," and Job Cook soon found
six hundred pounds of lead. This was a scarce commodity among
the colonists, who had been melting down everything from George
the Third's statue to pewter plates in order to make bullets. Ten
days later, Job Cook reported the discovery of six hundred and
fifty pounds more of lead, a cache perhaps dating from the days
of the French and Indian wars. Job's mission at the fort was now
about over. He made another report:

A RETURN OF FIREARMS IN STORE

Servisable—NONE

Unservisable—ELEVEN

General Riedesel had received an outline of British strategy
before he left Portsmouth, England, and this had been enlarged
upon since his arrival in Canada. For the benefit of the Duke of
Brunswick, he set it all down: "Howe, after leaving 200 men at
Boston, will rendezvous on Long Island and make that the base
of future operations. His army will go up the Hudson, mostly by
water, and thus operate against Crown Point. . . ."[8]

It was not in the cards that Howe should leave "200 men at
Boston." He had evacuated Boston March 17, 1776, assisted to
this decision by guns taken from the British and brought overland
from Ticonderoga. Riedesel heard about it only after Howe
arrived in Halifax, a detour not on his original schedule. Hessian
soldiers, sent direct to Halifax, then taken to Long Island, had
much to do with Howe's brilliant victory and the British

occupation of New York. Howe should, now, have been at Crown Point, according to those plans which looked so well on paper. It was unfortunate, perhaps, that, in evacuating Boston, Howe had taken the beautiful Mrs. Loring with him to Halifax and then had brought her to New York. She did not care for wilderness forts; she liked cities.

Carleton decided that it was too late in the season to continue the campaign. The Americans could easily be finished off in the spring. But there were wheels within wheels, and General Riedesel set to work to explain matters to the Duke of Brunswick, writing in French and marking his letter "to be put into cypher":

"There comes upon us a new political season. General Howe has been appointed Chief in New England. If Carleton, an officer with seniority, should cross the Lake to join the other army, he would have to put himself under the orders of Lord Howe, a thing which the former would not like to do, if I know him." In an undated but earlier letter, probably written in August, Riedesel had already suggested that there were difficulties between Howe and Carleton. Carleton was "haughty and taciturn by nature," while Howe was "proud, and intoxicated with being so much in the good graces of the King and the Ministry, so that he wants to carry off all the honors himself." Riedesel hoped that this incompatibility between the two generals "would not have a bad effect upon the common cause."

There was a bit of interesting advice which General Riedesel gave the Duke of Brunswick, with many polite apologies for presuming to do so. He thought the Duke should try to see that the British did not get in arrears in their payments for the Brunswick soldiers. If possible the Duke "should get payment in advance," because British accounts were in a hopeless muddle. And the "commissary is still in the greatest confusion."[9]

Riedesel's letters to his wife were of the sort to reassure her, for he knew that she loved him dearly. "If this war is carried on like this next year," he wrote after describing how he missed taking part in the Battle of Valcour Island, "I shall be more sure of my life here in the midst of it than upon the parade grounds of Wolfenbüttel and Brunswick." The men were now going into winter quarters, and he had been assigned to Three Rivers. It was going to be "very quiet, and I should be able to live entirely for you," he said.

In another letter — "The nights are beginning to be a little cold," Riedesel wrote; "we already speak and think of winter. What a comfort it would be for me, if I could quietly enjoy the society of you and the children. Truly that would be worth more to me than all else. But where may you now be? Perhaps on the broad sea, perhaps in great peril. Night after night my mind is filled with anxiety for your safety. I hope that God will soon end my anguish and grant me the joy of seeing you in my arms." The General's most recent letters from his wife had been dated April and May 1776, although she wrote him regularly.

6

Winter in London

WHEN the Baroness von Riedesel arrived in London in
September 1776, to discover that her ship had sailed without her, she needed all her courage to conceal her grief from her
children and the servants. Everyone told her that it was already
too late in the season to attempt a voyage to Quebec but this
was only a mildly comforting thought. Eventually the news came
that Lord George Germain's packet had arrived safely and that
the captain had made General Riedesel pay for that cow put
aboard to supply the children with milk. For the thrifty Baroness,
this was almost the last straw. But another ship, which sailed at
the same time, had been crushed in the ice.

Life in London was pleasant at first. Captain and Mrs. Young
from Tobago urged Mrs. General Riedesel to live with them and
she agreed on condition that she share expenses. They lived in
great style, however, and the Baroness began to feel anxious
about her share of the cost. The Youngs insisted that she owed
them nothing — they just wanted her as their guest. "I thought
they must be immensely wealthy," Frederika said. But of course
she could not accept largesse from anyone. She had some small
diamonds in the little bag of family ornaments she had brought
with her and so she had her portrait painted in miniature, then

64

framed in gold, surrounded by the diamonds and mounted in a bracelet for Mrs. Young. It must have been a charming ornament.

"I was tolerably happy," Mrs. General said. But the friendship with the Youngs did not prosper. "Madam Young . . . bought gowns and headdresses by the dozen, kept the house full of milliners and mantua-makers," and when she had a whole new wardrobe assembled she announced that she and the Baroness were going out in society. They would visit "public resorts" and go to all sorts of private parties. Captain Young, who was much older than his wife, had little use for gadding, but it would be all right—Madam von Riedesel could be the chaperone for the giddy Mrs. Young.

"I excused myself," the Baroness wrote. She could not leave the baby, whom she was still nursing, nor would she entrust the older children to servants in a strange land. "I was too sad and uneasy on account of my absent husband," she added — and there was also "the great expense."

Mrs. Young took all this very badly. She was "almost rude" — and rarely did anyone dare to go that far with Madam Riedesel. "To make matters worse," her husband applauded Mrs. General's stand and held her up as an example his wife ought to follow. Although Frederika understood perfectly that Captain Young was not helping matters, she was unprepared when Mrs. Young came to her and asked her if she had found any other lodgings yet! She quickly assured the lady that she was ready to go any time. "Mrs. Young said she knew of a place and would go" with her to see it.

They set out in the Youngs' carriage and after many twistings and turnings they came to "a truly mean house" in a narrow alley of doubtful appearance. She must have "respectable lodgings" because she had "letters of introduction to several ladies of quality and planned to receive them in a manner befitting their station," the Baroness said. Mrs. Young "answered spitefully" that she had supposed this miserable roominghouse would be just the thing for someone who was "such a good housewife" and "loved to be so retired."

As they were driving back, Frederika "noticed an advertisement on a corner house in a very good neighborhood." The Baroness told the coachman to pull up and she went into the house to inquire. It was "a small dwelling although clean and respectable." But alas — the price! Four pounds a week would be out of the question, and Mrs. General employed strategy. "I always have my door closed and locked by ten o'clock at night," she remarked. The little girls, docile and polite, had come with her and the landlady, who was childless, loved them at sight and so did her husband. A bargain was struck for three pounds a week, "furniture, kitchen utensils and clothes-washing facilities included."

"I was not only comfortably lodged but my landlord and landlady, whose name was Russell, became my warmest friends," the Baroness said. She told them frankly that all she had in the world, at the moment, was ten guineas, and that money from Germany was not due for six weeks. Besides being owners of property for rent, the Russells were in the provision business and they promised to market for the German family at wholesale. "You can pay at your own convenience," they said.

"They both taught my children English," the Baroness wrote. Mr. Russell became so fond of little Caroline that he offered to adopt her and promised to leave her "his entire fortune." Both the Russells were always buying little presents for the children and searching food markets for special items which might please them and their mother.

The Baroness Frederika had perfect faith in Providence, and she "thanked God for the Russells and all the more so" when she heard what happened to the Youngs after she left them. Mrs. Young continued to live extravagantly until she was threatened with arrest for debt. "Milliners, tailors and mantua-makers seized some of her belongings," and Captain Young finally fled the country to avoid a debtor's prison. His wife was "supported by friends."

Among the belongings that Mrs. Young would have been willing to part with was the bracelet with a miniature set in diamonds. Perhaps now, in some museum or private collection, the Baroness Frederika von Riedesel, painted in London at the age of thirty-one, smiles from her setting. She would have had herself painted smiling, for the loneliness she suffered she kept to herself. She was unusually pretty, and the painter, whose name she did not mention, would have done justice to lovely white shoulders and sparkling blue eyes. Perhaps the portrait bears a label, "Unknown young woman, Georgian period," or some such sad indication that Frederika's portrait has become a mere "collector's item."

The year 1776 was almost over when Frederika's friends persuaded her to be presented at court. She had a "court dress" made and Lady Germain was her sponsor. At this time, no one was in higher favor with the King than Lord Germain. His disgrace at Minden was forgotten, his court-martial verdict of guilty having been ordered reversed by George III while still Prince George. The former George Sackville had even changed his name on inheriting "a vast fortune" from Lady Betty, wife of Sir John Germain. He neglected nothing for his own advancement and had married Lady Diana, an heiress.[1]

"I found the castle very ugly and furnished in an old-fashioned style," wrote Madam Riedesel. She was talking about St. James's Palace, built by Henry the Eighth and said to have been designed by Holbein. The initials *H. A.* carved above the fireplace in the Presence Chamber meant nothing to the German Baroness, but she would have shuddered if she had realized that they stood for Henry VIII and the ill-fated Anne Boleyn. Squared-off Tudor windows with leaded diamond-shaped panes served to keep out rather than let in the light, while the portraits of a long line of kings and the carved oak and tapestries all depressed Frederika. She liked white walls ornamented in plaster relief with gilded shells and scrolls. Delicate gilded furniture with bright brocaded cushions pleased her — although this taste of Fritschen's was to undergo a change.

"All the ladies and gentlemen were standing in their allotted places" in the audience room. Then the King entered, "preceded by three cavaliers." George III was at this time thirty-eight years old, somewhat red-faced with full cheeks and heavy-lidded eyes. He was by no means as fat as cartoonists liked to pretend, and sometimes fasted to avoid obesity, but at other times he did full justice to the enormous meals it was the custom to set before royalty. He had suffered one period of insanity and would end his days totally blind and deaf, an old man with a long white beard, suffering from hallucinations. In 1776 he was as sane as he ever would be. Although the first of the Georges to be born in England, George III looked German, which must have pleased the Baroness. She whispered to Lady Germain: Was it true that the King always kissed all the ladies?

"Oh, no," said Lady Diana. " 'Only Englishwomen and Marchionesses."

The Queen entered the Presence Chamber right behind the King. A chamberlain preceded her and a lady-in-waiting carried her train. Queen Charlotte had been a Princess of Mecklenburg-Strelitz. Seventeen at the time of her marriage, she was now thirty-three. She had never been pretty; her mouth was heavy, with an undershot lower lip, but she had fine, dark eyes and, at the time of her marriage, a slim figure. She was now the mother of eleven children, and the Baroness von Riedesel was being presented to her at one of the rare intervals when Her Majesty was not pregnant. Eventually, she was the mother of fifteen.

At the door of the Presence Chamber, the King turned to the right and the Queen to the left. They circled the room and spoke

a word or several words to each person "stationed" around the
walls, while anxious eyes followed them to see who might be
honored by more attention than another. When the King and
Queen met at the end of the room they "made each other a
profound bow" and proceeded with their solemn, slow circuit.

The Baroness must have been on the right side, for scarcely
had she whispered her anxious inquiry when George III of England came up and kissed her. "I turned red as fire," Frederika
declared.

The King asked her if she had any letters from her husband
and she recovered sufficiently to tell him that the last letters had
arrived November 22. His Majesty graciously remarked that he
had asked about General Riedesel specifically and that "everybody
is satisfied with him." The King hoped the cold in Canada would
not injure the General's health.

"Oh, no, Your Majesty, he was born in a cold climate," replied
the Baroness. This was a comparatively long conversation, and
there must have been envious glances. But the Queen, who "soon
came up," had even more to say. How long had the Baroness
been in London? Frederika said it was now two months. The
Queen had thought it was longer. "I have been seven months in
England," the Baroness explained and the Queen asked her if
she didn't fear an ocean voyage. The Queen hated the sea, herself, she said, perhaps remembering an ocean voyage to marry
a man she had never met and who loved someone else, as she
would soon enough be told.

"I do not like the sea," confessed the Baroness, "but as it is the
only way I can see my husband again, I shall joyfully set sail."

"I admire your courage, especially with three children," Her
Majesty said in parting, and Mrs. General was pleased — because
she had not told the Queen about the children: someone at court
must have given Queen Charlotte information which really interested her.

"During the reception I saw all the royal children except one who was ill," Frederika said. "They were ten in number and all beautiful as pictures."

This cordial reception at court pleased the Baroness, and she was still more pleased to be asked to return informally. She "visited the Queen several times afterward," and when spring came at last and plans were completed for Frederika's voyage to America she went to bid Queen Charlotte good-by. Once more, the Queen spoke of the terrors of an ocean voyage. "They wrote me that you take this journey unknown to your husband," the Queen remarked. Frederika was indignant. "Your Majesty is a German Princess and therefore you know that I could not possibly have come here without my husband's consent," she cried. "For one thing, no one would have given me the money necessary for the journey." That a married woman would never have money of her own, even though she might be an heiress, was something Queen Charlotte understood perfectly well.

"What is the name of your ship?" the Queen asked. "I shall often inquire about you."

"She kept her word," Frederika said. "She often asked about me, and frequently sent her remembrances." The Queen of England might easily have envied the Baroness Riedesel. The Queen would never long for the sight of her husband, and she would never joyfully brave the perils of the sea to go to him.[2]

General Burgoyne was now in London, having left the quartering of the troops in Canada in Riedesel's competent hands. He carried letters to the Baroness, and "had promised my husband that we should travel together," when he returned to Canada in the spring. She was both innocent and naïve to put it that way, as time would show.

Burgoyne's star was in the ascendant in London. He was seen riding in St. James's Park with the King! Together he and Lord George Germain pored over maps of the English colonies in North America — those delightfully simplified affairs that made it

seem but an easy step from Quebec to Albany and from Albany
to New York. Great waterways — the St. Lawrence, the Richelieu,
Lake Champlain, the Hudson — seemed provided by a special
Providence for the convenient transportation of a British army
with ships, guns and mercenaries. A short and glorious campaign,
a triumphant meeting between Burgoyne and Sir William Howe
at Albany — and the rebellion would collapse.

But what to do about Mrs. General Riedesel, her three little
girls and several servants? Burgoyne would be aboard a man-of-
war, naturally. Nothing less would suit his dignity. In response
to Frederika's question, Lord George Germain told her that he
didn't think a man-of-war would be very comfortable. He said,
however, that Mr. Watson, a very wealthy London banker and,
like Dick Whittington, "thrice Lord Mayor of London," would
let Mrs. General Riedesel "have his ship." He happened to be the
Riedesel's family banker in London, and Mrs. General knew him
well already, so she went to see him again. She described him as
"a worthy man who had one foot bitten off by a shark in the
West Indies." Madam the Baroness made sure that she was
getting passage at a low cost, could have accommodations to suit
her and could pay on arrival in Quebec. (If she drowned let him
just try to collect!)

Lord Germain gave Mr. Watson a letter of marque for his
merchant ship and two officers with sixty men to protect her. In
other words, the vessel became a privateer and Lord Germain
assured Madam Riedesel that this made everything much safer
for her. The owner promptly bought up the most valuable cargo
he could lay hands on, for here was a venture almost sure to make
money. He was so pleased to have his merchantman armed that
he took the Baroness on a tour of the ship, which was "large and
spacious," and he "immediately arranged everything just as I
wished," she said. Mr. Watson summoned Captain Arbuthnot
and crew and told them that "whoever should offend me might
expect the same punishment as though he had offended the

owner." Anyone she complained of would be fired. This was very
flattering, but it did not please the captain overmuch.

In a glow of pleasure over her good fortune, Madam Riedesel
wrote to Mrs. Foy and invited her to share the voyage. "I knew
it would please my husband," she said. "She accepted and all
past misunderstandings were forgiven and forgotten. We met at
Portsmouth and on the 15th of April we went on board of our
ship."

Mrs. General had a long list of articles her husband had asked
her to buy and bring to him. First in importance of course were
the wines. He required the best Madeira and bought it by the
pipe, which was a cask containing about 126 gallons. Banker
Watson was very helpful in seeing about this. Then there were
the limes to eat so that she and the children should not have
scurvy. Mr. Watson provisioned his ship unusually well and this
was great good fortune, because the Baroness had heard horrible
tales of "officers" actually running short of food and having to
eat soldiers' or sailors' rations. "Unpacking, setting the cabin to
rights," trying to make sure that everything she or the children
might want on the voyage could be found easily, Frederika was
"very busy the entire evening before the ship set sail."

The man-of-war *Blonde* was in charge of the convoy, but Burgoyne was not on board. He had sailed earlier, on the *Apollo*. This
second convoy left Portsmouth April 16 with thirty sail. They
headed for St. Helena to rendezvous with the man-of-war *Porpoise*
for additional protection, because — although no one had told the
Baroness — the Americans were all too successful at sea, their
privateersmen playing havoc with British shipping. At first everyone was seasick and it surprised Mrs. General to discover that she
felt worse while the ship was tossing at anchor, waiting for a
favorable wind, than when actually under sail.

By the nineteenth of April, 1777, "we passed Plymouth under
a fine breeze," Mrs. General said. "Everyone was well again and

we danced on deck." In her capacity as owner's representative, she had discovered and commandeered from among the soldiers or the crew "a capital fifer and three drummers." But the breeze blew into a gale, winds were "contrary," and seas ran high for the next four days.

"I believe there is nothing better for seasickness than to be right busy," said the Baroness. Her servants were "nearly the sickest of all," and, as she could not bear to see her children "without care," she staggered out of her berth, "washed and dressed them, afterwards, myself," and went out on deck. The fresh air was of course the best antidote, the ship's cook seems to have been a good sailor, and "every day we had four and often five and six dishes that were right well prepared."

So many people had talked to the Baroness about the terrors of an Atlantic voyage that she felt almost guilty when she found herself enjoying it. "I know not whether it was the hope of so soon seeing my husband that gave me good spirits but I had not the least repentance of having undertaken the journey," she said. Her servants were frightened and she would have sent them back if she could, but when she asked the children if they wanted to go back they said, " 'Oh, no. We will cheerfully be sick if we can only reach our father."

There was a church service on deck on the twenty-seventh of April and it touched Frederika's heart to see "the entire ship's crew kneel down" and to "hear the fervency with which they prayed." By evening she knew why they had prayed so hard. The wind shifted and the "ship staggered so dreadfully" that she "often fell down." The following Sunday the seas ran so high that there was no church service and the crew were kept constantly at work handling the sails.

Somehow the convoy managed to stay together, and when there was calm weather "all were delighted and paid visits to the different ships." One hundred and thirty-four German reinforcements were aboard the *Henry*, which sailed alongside and dipped her colors to the Baroness Riedesel. Men lined her rail and shouted "Long live the General's wife! Long live the General!" At which Mrs. General was so delighted that she held up the children for the men to see and cried "Long live all of you!" The men shouted, "Hurrah, hurrah!"

Now the German chaplain led the men in a glorious Lutheran hymn. "My whole heart stirred within me," said the Baroness.

The man-of-war *Porpoise* came alongside almost every day to inquire for the health of Mrs. General. The captain had been a lieutenant on the *Pallas* when General Riedesel sailed on her the previous year. The General had promised to speak a good word for him — and here he was, with the command.

Wind freshened or turned slack, wind was contrary or rose to gale strength as day after day went by. When fog blew in "it was necessary in the night to blow trumpets." It rained, and by the middle of May it was cold most of the time. The captain of the *Blonde*, a new one evidently, "had never been in this region before" and discovered that "he had run too far northerly by some five hundred sea miles." They would have to "wait for a north wind" to take them to the banks of Newfoundland.

The ship *Silver Eel* lost her mainmast and "in the night of May 23 the man-of-war *Porpoise* separated" from them. At St. Helena, where the convoy had waited for the *Porpoise*, there must have been some transfer of cargo because the Baroness worried over the missing ship: "My entire baggage and my husband's wine and regimentals were on board that ship," she said. But both the *Silver Eel* and the *Porpoise* caught up with the convoy on May 30.

They "arrived without mishap" off the Grand Banks and the ship's cook caught a big cod. Everyone was hungry for fresh food by this time, and the cook made a great ceremony of preparing to present his codfish to the Baroness Riedesel. Tempers had worn thin, however, and the captain of the vessel actually so far forgot himself as to snatch the fish out of the cook's hands and throw it into the sea. It seems he had wanted that cod to give to Mrs. Foy.

"I gave the good man a guinea for his kind intention," said Frederika. Everyone not on duty was fishing from the deck by now, but no more cod were caught.

Apparently the *Porpoise* had been sailing so close that the captain's childish performance had been observed. "I had my triumph," said Frederika, "when, soon after, the captain of the *Porpoise* sent me four codfish bound on a board, to which someone had fastened a string for safety in case our captain should throw them overboard. I treated the whole ship's crew to them, as if nothing had happened." Coals of fire were her favorite weapon on many occasions, and this time the captain "seemed ashamed of his rudeness." Before long, codfish, though still esteemed a delicacy, were in good supply. On May 29 the *Blonde* caught "one hundred fish, a large proportion of them cod."

The Baroness was already sorry that she had invited Hannah Foy to share the voyage. Madam Foy's conduct with the ship's captain amazed and shocked the virtuous Mrs. General, who, nevertheless, seemed to think that Hannah's reasons for it made sense. Because of "her old intimacy with the captain of our ship, Mrs. Foy dared not refuse him those liberties to which he had formerly been accustomed," Frederika said.

That Hannah Foy had again become the captain's mistress was bad enough. But Hannah's maid was "a most beautiful creature" who came along "solely for the sake of leaving a country where she was already too well known and in order to find among the sailors such licentious friends as she was best pleased with."

The voyage had not long been in progress when it was discovered that someone was stealing the captain's wine. "My poor jaeger, Rockel, was accused of it," Madam Riedesel said, and she "felt deeply for this honest man." But "the true culprit was discovered one night when the ship gave a sudden lurch" which knocked down Nancy, Mrs. Foy's maid, who was carrying off two bottles. The bottles crashed; the girl gave "a loud scream which brought every one to her on the run."

There was an outer cabin, just beyond Madam Riedesel's cabin door, "where the maid and her lover were conducting themselves wantonly" one night. The helmsman and "other under officers" broke up the party and then came to the Baroness. They promised to post a guard over the outer cabin "every Saturday night — a time when "it was the ship's fashion to spend the evening drinking healths to wives and sweethearts."

The "helmsman and under officers" had wives and children with them aboard ship, and the Baroness had shared her meals with these women and children. She thought this was the reason that the men had rallied to protect her.

The convoy of thirty ships entered the Gulf of St. Lawrence on the third day of June. "It was the birthday of my husband," wrote Frederika. "My heart was filled with a mixture of joy and sadness and with a longing to see him, to hold him in my arms and to deliver over to him our dear children."

7

Winter in Canada

GENTLEMAN Johnny Burgoyne doubtless gave plausible reasons for going back to London — other than the real one, which was to cut the ground out from under Carleton. Certainly the winter quartering of the troops in Canada was beneath Burgoyne's notice, but Riedesel was just the man for the job. He marched and countermarched the troops according to Carleton's orders, seeing that they were provisioned on their way and sheltered on arrival. The arrangements were more for the benefit of the inhabitants than the soldiers, Riedesel saw, but he realized that Carleton had a problem. Many people had sympathized with the Americans and there was no harm in winning them back by kindness, although force would be used if necessary.

The Brunswickers finally settled down in small villages along the Richelieu River between Chambly and Sorel, or along the south shore of the St. Lawrence in the direction of Quebec, the Regiment Riedesel being across the St. Lawrence at Three Rivers. Captain Pausch, artillerist, went to Montreal with his gunners.

Wherever possible, Riedesel commandeered public buildings in a village and made them into barracks. This was so that no private family should have more than four soldiers quartered with them, but families suspected of having helped the Americans got extra German soldiers.

Village or parish government was something new to Germans and they wrote letters home describing this remarkable system. Each town had a captain of militia, and a large town might have two. But the part the Germans found hard to understand was that these captains "have no advantage over their fellows . . . they work like the rest, dress the same" — and receive their office by election. "Their office is more burdensome than lucrative," because militia captains must "provide quarters for soldiers marching through, get vehicles required by the passing regiments, draft inhabitants who may be requisitioned by the generals for labor or teaming, look out for delivery of supplies requisitioned, see that letters of one general to another pass from parish to parish. . . . The government relies on these captains of militia . . . and holds them responsible for whatever happens in their parishes. . . . If there are many refractory people in a parish, their cattle are taken away, their fires quenched and the roofs of their houses torn down — a very severe punishment, because the inhabitants usually have large families which they love dearly. . . . The houses of several rebels who are at present with the hostile army may be utterly demolished pretty soon. . . ."

In front of the captain's house there was always "a tall, peeled pine tree" set up "with a little flag at the top." A German officer with troops to quarter went right to the house with the flag in front and every kind of help was efficiently forthcoming. Yet it surprised the Germans that "Governors do not hesitate to ask these men to their table." Here was a strange idea! How could the election of a man by his fellow townsmen change him so that, although born "a peasant," dressing like his friends and working with neighbors, he was elevated to such a pinnacle that he could eat with a "Governor"?

General Riedesel was quick to see the advantages of the system. He treated captains of militia with the respect due their position, and at Three Rivers during the winter he invited them to his parties.

Canadians had the right to serve under their own officers — and
this annoyed the British sent over to Canada to crush the American rebellion. The "inhabitants," especially in Riedesel's area,
had no enthusiasm for going to war at all: they wanted to stay
home and cultivate their fields. When the recruiting officer came
along, he often found that there were no men at home. "Gone
hunting," the women would say. But there were severe measures
to be taken. Men might come home from hunting rather fast if
the roof were on fire — if they happened to be hiding in the loft
under it.

General Riedesel had anticipated a grim winter, long, lonely
and cold. But the winter of 1776–1777 was so unusually warm
that it was known as "the winter of the Germans." Snow did not
come till the twenty-fourth of November. After that it snowed
hard and often, although rarely for more than twelve hours at a
time. There was snow and ice "four or five feet deep," but the sun
seemed "far warmer in Canada" than in Brunswick or Hesse-
Hanau.

On the last day of December, Riedesel was invited to attend
the first anniversary of the raising of the Siege of Quebec. Several
Canadians convicted of collaborating with Americans were
marched to the cathedral with ropes around their necks. They
attended a solemn High Mass and were required to ask forgiveness
of the King, the Church and God, the alternative being that the
ropes they wore would be used to hang them. All were penitent,
"but they prayed for whom they pleased." There was a Protestant
service in the lower town a little later and at noon guns were fired
from the city walls.

Noon was also the hour of "the great banquet," where "sixty
guests ate for several hours" at the expense of Governor Carleton.
At seven in the evening the ball began. There were ninety ladies
and a hundred and fifty gentlemen, and they "danced with such
ardor that a Mr. Guilard died of apoplexy." No one paid any at-

tention to the poor man. They just hauled him out by the heels and went on dancing.

During the festivities at Quebec, General Riedesel met Lady Mary or Maria Carleton, perhaps for the first time. She and her sister, Lady Anne, had only just arrived from England. These sisters would have been interesting to General Riedesel, if he had known their story.

In 1770, only six years previously, Sir Guy Carleton had been in England, where he visited the Earl of Effingham and proposed to the Earl's second daughter, Lady Anne. She refused him, explaining that she was already engaged to his nephew, Captain Christopher Carleton. Much embarrassed and chagrined, Sir Guy left the Earl's country house and went to London. But on hearing about all this, Lady Mary, the Earl's third daughter, was said to have exclaimed, "If an offer like that had been made to me, I wouldn't have refused such an attractive man."

The remark was repeated to Sir Guy; he returned and proposed to Lady Mary, who accepted. She was twenty-four and he forty-eight.[1] There were some who called Lady Mary a "little blond doll" and said she tried to put on airs because she had been to the Court at Versailles. General Riedesel did not like her very well. "She is too proud," he wrote his wife. "She will not be to your taste. But Mrs. Murray will be just the friend for you. Everyone here who knows you says Mrs. Murray is like you—which is why she is my favorite." The General's prediction was wrong, however. Mrs. Mich Murray, the wife of a Quebec merchant, turned out to be no great favorite with Mrs. General, who liked Lady Mary Carleton quite well.

General Riedesel stayed about two weeks in Quebec, and then went back to Three Rivers to do what he could to enliven the scene for himself and his officers in that area. He began by celebrating the birthday of the Queen of England. There were forty guests invited to dinner, and "Many healths were drunk in champagne to the firing of a small cannon in front of the house.

During the afternoon and evening there was a ball with 37 ladies present who were also at supper." An account of the occasion was written by a young German officer who drove to the party in a sleigh, covering about twenty-one miles in four hours — he had never before experienced such speed. The letter which he wrote home to Germany was published, but unfortunately without his name.

"Miss Tonnencourt," wrote this young man, "enhanced her charm greatly by her jewels," but a girl whose name was published only as R——e, "in her wretched cotton gown, won the preference of many by her natural gentle charm and her fine voice." The young lady with the jewels was the daughter of the colonel of militia.

"Several chansons in honor of General von Riedesel have been written and set to music and are often sung at Three Rivers," the same young German officer wrote. Riedesel gave dinners and dancing parties every week. "I do this partly to gain the affections of the inhabitants," he wrote his wife, perhaps wondering what she would say if she got news of his gaiety. The parties were "also to give the officers a chance to indulge in innocent pleasures and thus prevent them from visiting taverns and getting into bad company."

The Murrays wrote to Riedesel from Quebec: "Your balls at Three Rivers surprise everybody here and have added not a little to the good character you had before acquired among the ladies for they say that no other man could have brought to light thirty-five well-dressed women at Three Rivers." At Quebec they had a contest at the Queen's ball to see which lady's headdress was the highest — with Colonel St. Leger to measure them. "The lovely Mrs. Johnston carried off the prize, as her head was easily three quarters higher than any other in the room." There were also "carioling parties," where "every person carrys his Bottle, Glass, knife and fork and dishpan." Afterwards they would have an informal dance at the Château, wrote Riedesel's friend "Mich

Murray."² It was gay in Quebec; but he would be delighted to come to Three Rivers and bring "the beautiful Mrs. Johnston," who was pleased with General Riedesel's invitation.

By "carioling" Mich Murray meant sleighing.³ Hardly a letter went home to Germany that winter without some description of Canadian "carioles." By November 16 the St. Lawrence was frozen and carioling on the river began. The word itself was French, meaning a light covered cart, but it was spelled by the Germans with variations. In describing it, the Germans explained that it was a "carriage with rockers on which were fastened iron bands." People going carioling "are dressed entirely in furs" and the ladies' furs were "elegant." One of the young German officers promptly bought himself a "minx" cap which he said cost him 7½ piasters, and he had been pricing fur coats. Black martin "without the cloth cover" would be 12 guineas, and beaver cost a guinea a pelt, 12 pelts to the coat. Everybody had "buffalo robes" to cover their knees.

The cold might be "severe" but skies were "often quite serene with not a cloud to be seen. Dressed in furs . . . "you parade over ice and snow amidst perhaps a hundred other carioles, painted in the most gaudy colors, which from the great contrast of the snow has a beautiful effect. The ice is much smoother and better for this amusement before a snowstorm . . . but yet the idea of the water being deep enough under you to float a ship of the line, and the ice so very transparent as fish to be seen under it, has rather an alarming appearance to a stranger. . . . By order of the government, the roads are marked out on the river." Small fir trees were cut and set up to mark the safest ice route, and this was another duty assigned to the captain of militia of each parish. There were sections of the river safe for carioling early in the season, but during "the winter of the Germans" there was no ice bridge all the way across the St. Lawrence until February.

One of the Brunswickers quartered at St. Anne crossed over to Three Rivers and reported: "It is a strange sight for one who drives for the first time three-quarters of a German mile across a river and in many places sees an open, raging torrent not three paces to the left or right of the bridge!" A bridge higher up the river had broken, and great chunks of ice had floated downstream, filling gaps in the newly formed ice bridge at St. Anne. "You drive over fragments of broken bridges . . . the ice seems to buckle beneath you and sends out cracks on either side." Sometimes "you have to rush over open rifts as broad as your hand."

Warm clothing was issued to the troops, "one pair of long blue over-alls such as worn by sailors, which come high up above the hips and . . . fasten under the feet with a leather strap and have five buttons on the outside of each leg from the ankle. One large woolen cap. One capacious underjacket . . . one Canadian over-coat with cape and facings of white sheeps wool. . . ." Blue wool mittens were lined with corduroy. The men were grateful but they also had to pay for the outfit, "33 shillings 9 pence" being deducted from each man at the rate of 5 shillings a month.

The orderly books at last carried a notation concerning "Women." "Provisions may be drawn for the Women of the different Regiments not exceeding 16 per Battalion or 2 per Company, but these Rations are to be accounted and paid for to the Pay Master General in like manner for those of the Soldiers and others." Children were not mentioned.

Riedesel paid a great deal of attention to the activities of rank and file. For instance, there was a game they played called "ten quills." At first he thought it was good exercise and he approved of it. Then he discovered that ten quills was being played for money and that some of the men were losing heavily. A soldier hopelessly in debt attempted to desert. Sternly Riedesel ordered that there should be no more gambling and that the money won at ten quills must be returned.

For the most part, the men directly under Riedesel's influence spent a cheerful, healthful winter. But Captain Georg Pausch, after seeing plenty of action at Valcour Island, was sent with his gunners to Montreal, where he came under General Phillips. "Everyone was obliged to be at parade at 11 o'clock A.M. — the English Artillery as well as my own," Pausch said. "The companies formed in line at the barracks and were taken by companies to the Parade Ground. They were obliged to run, sometimes for half, sometimes for a whole hour." Pausch admitted that this seemed to be good for the men, but they had never done it before; and in spite of his efforts to encourage them, "the quick-step had no good result except to make the spectators laugh."

Many of Pausch's men had dysentery, and in the hospital they grew desperately melancholy. They "talked day and night of fathers, sisters, cousins and aunts. . . . For this disease there is but one remedy in the world, namely peace and a speedy return, and with this hope I comfort my sick daily," Pausch wrote. But many men died of homesickness, he thought.

There was no means of burial in winter, and Lieutenant Thomas Anburey, whose *Travels through the Interior Parts of America* was widely read in England and has been much quoted ever since, visited "a long room" in the hospital where the frozen bodies of the dead were kept, pending burial.[4] The men died "20 or 30" at a time. "The superintendant of this room, an apothecary, being a man of whimsical ideas . . . had placed the dead bodies of these poor Germans in various postures, some kneeling with books in their hands, other sitting with pipes in their mouths, many standing erect against the wall, and as they have their clothes on you can scarcely at first imagine they are dead but upon nearer approach, what with their long mustaches which are put in form, and their ghastly countenances, you cannot picture to yourself anything so horrible, yet at the same time so truly laughable and ridiculous."

If Anburey's so-called sense of humor were typical of the British that Captain Pausch was obliged to live with, it was not surprising that he was so often angry. General Phillips gave a tea party every afternoon, attendance by officers compulsory, it would seem. Pausch, who had men under him unjustly jailed for incivility to the British, often asked for fair treatment, receiving affable promises over the teacups. But the promises were never kept.

Of course it was understood that war had ceased for the winter, but occasionally scouts were sent out to see what the Americans were doing at Ticonderoga. This duty fell to Canadians and Indians, because they knew the forest. Prisoners were brought in, captured at the portage between Lake Champlain and Lake George. These men pluckily told all sorts of lies about a large force at Ticonderoga, well supplied, well clothed and fed. They seem to have been believed.

Actually, however, "everything at the fort" held by the Americans was in the "greatest confusion" — according to Colonel Richard Varick, twenty-three-year old aide to General Philip Schuyler. He was at Ticonderoga in his capacity as muster master, and although a prejudiced observer because of his loyalty to Schuyler and his dislike of Gates, he was a methodical young man who counted carefully. There were "600 stakes" needed to complete the palisade and "still uncut in mid-November." The "barracks on Mt. Independence are not half covered or chimneys built" and "100 of Dayton's regiment, just arrived, are already fallen sick." The commissary was particularly chaotic. Three hundred barrels of flour arrived but the promised root vegetables, potatoes, turnips, beets, "or Sauce as our New England brethren term it" had not been delivered.

There was rum, however.[5] "Three or four hogsheads of Rum are and have been laying on the dock at the store under the charge of the Centinel. . . . All the hogsheads are tapped, one almost out, one half out . . . the Centinel and Guard concerned.

They carried it by Pails full. Captain Ross discovered it this morning by the continual drunkenness of some of his men for two days. . . ."

Colonel Joseph Wood wrote to General Schuyler on November 28, describing living conditions at Ticonderoga: "The old and new barracks are quite full and my regt. is now lying in old, worn out tents that will scarcely keep a drop of water out. The sod houses, as the frost and rain comes on, all moulder away, my people fall sick every moment. What can be done? We have no boards, with the winter coming on fast, we must perish. We have undergone great hardships in Canada, was as Quebec, have had hard service at every place to this and here our fatigue not less. The men have no coats to their backs. I do solicit you, Sir, that you use your influence to have us relieved. The men will not stay longer than their first enlistment." Colonel Wood was not a man who had given up, however. He could "get men to engage for the war, if they had liberty to go home," but furlough had never been granted. He praised his command. "They are good men. They turn out smartly on all alarms." It is hard to blame these men very much for stealing rum!

Most of the garrison at Ticonderoga were militia from Vermont, New Hampshire and upper New York State. They were organized very similarly to the Canadian militia, and they also insisted on serving under their own officers. But instead of serving for a year, each militia band signed up for a term of months, or even weeks — the length of time decided among themselves. They were indispensable, but to say that they presented problems to the high command would be to put it mildly.

When word reached Ticonderoga of General Howe's march toward Philadelphia, the situation grew worse. On February 19, 1777, Major Francis Barber wrote to General Schuyler from the fort: "My regiment cordially consents to remain." He spoke strongly in their behalf: "I beg leave however to mention, as an Argument for our removal, a circumstance peculiar to ourselves. A great majority of this battalion have friends, family and property suffering from the descent of the enemy upon New Jersey, and consequently are anxiously concerned for their native Province and very impatient under events in that quarter."

News that Washington had captured a thousand Hessians at the Battle of Trenton on December 25, 1776, did not reach the British in Canada for three or four months, and then it simply was not believed. In March, Mich Murray, writing from Quebec, told General Riedesel that there was no war news and complained of boredom. "Our Balls, Routs etc. being over, we are becoming dull and stupid," he said. He quoted some prices because General Riedesel, after all the dinner parties, was out of wine. Port was thirty-seven pounds ten shillings the pipe and Madeira was forty-five pounds. He supposed the General would not want to buy any at such cost.

In a letter to the Duke of Brunswick, written in French and intended to be put into cypher, General Riedesel discussed Lord Howe.[6] "He seems to do nothing but play at cards all day long and gambling reigns so universally in this army that most of the officers are ruining themselves. They have pillaged frightfully and made almost a desert out of Jersey." People were criticizing General Howe's "too extending winter quarters," Riedesel said. "The post of Trenton was entirely without forage."

This letter was dated May 6, 1777, and General Riedesel now knew there had been "the disaster at Trenton." If it hadn't happened, he thought, "the spirits of the Rebel Public would have been so low that surely they would have got rid of their leaders in order to submit." But their morale was now "much lifted."

General Burgoyne had just arrived in Quebec after his winter in London, where he had finessed the command out of the hands of Carleton. "The change of Commander in Chief of the Army in Canada has caused much confusion," Riedesel wrote. "General Carleton is annoyed to the point of making remarks against

My Lord Germain, and he will bring public charges against him in parliament. He has written a blistering letter and has complained to the King. . . . General Carleton is already getting on badly with General Burgoyne and complains that the latter demands impossibilities of the Province of Canada."

On June 4, 1777, the Baroness Riedesel's ship was in the lower St. Lawrence. She saw vessels sailing towards them, but the wind was so strong the captain could not ask them for news. Someone said there were soldiers on board and Frederika was suddenly terrified. Her husband's last letters had been full of optimism: the war with the rebellious colonies was bound to be a short one anyway. Suppose it was over and her husband was on one of those ships, going home!

The more she thought about it, the more probable it seemed to the Baroness that she might be left alone in a foreign land. To calm her nerves, she took out her embroidery, which had often proved a solace during the long voyage. She had already made "two purses and seven caps for myself and the children," she said. She had "finished a double night-cap" for her husband, and the best thing to do would be to start embroidering another.

On June 11, after a voyage of almost three months, Madam Riedesel's ship dropped anchor off Quebec. She was "shaking with excitement." The city "appeared quite handsome" in the distance, and it was not until later that she pronounced it "as dirty as possible and not at all convenient because you have to climb a great mountain in going through the streets."

Honors were not lacking. The Baroness Riedesel was "saluted with cannon by all the ships in the harbor." At "twelve noon a boat approached carrying twelve sailors dressed in white and wearing silver helmets and green sashes." They had been "sent to fetch" Mrs. General.

Before she left the ship, the captain came to ask pardon. As the Baroness told it, he had been "seduced through his relations with Madam Foy" and he was sorry that "he had behaved rudely." He was especially sorry right now, because he had found out that his crew could be "pressed" for the British navy in Quebec and he wanted Madam von Riedesel to intercede for him so that he could get his ship back to London. She did exactly that, and it pleased her to be able to do him a favor.

All Frederika looked for, however, was the handsome figure of her German General. He was not in the boat manned by the white-clad, silver-helmeted seamen. He was not on the wharf. But the sailors handed her a letter from her husband. On the last day of May, he had received orders from General Burgoyne to go forward with the army, which was once more poised on the shore of Lake Champlain for a second thrust at Fort Ticonderoga, northern gateway to the rebellious colonies.

Frederika was "grieved and frightened," she said, but she resolved to follow her husband with all speed in the hope of catching a glimpse of him before he sailed away across Champlain. "I seated myself and my entire family in the boat," she said. And then once more she resorted to coals of fire. "I begged permission to take also Madam Foy and her sister. This request was granted and I had the satisfaction of making them ashamed of the trouble they had caused me."

8

"Welcome to the Canadian Continent"

ON THE dock in the lower town, "a little carryall with one horse" was waiting. It belonged personally to Lady Mary Carleton, and she had sent it to bring the Baroness von Riedesel to her house to dinner and to spend the night. A lady's calash could carry two people — or a lady and three children at the most. There was no further opportunity for a generous gesture toward Hannah Foy: perhaps her husband, the commissary, was there to meet her — although Madam Riedesel did not say so. And perhaps it was this same "wife of a commissary" whom Frederika was to meet again — or perhaps another commissary's wife was a lady of equally easy virtue.

General Riedesel had predicted that Frederika would not like Lady Mary Carleton — but such was not the case. "A small blond woman," according to French descriptions, Lady Mary was none the less taller than the small, vivacious Baroness. To judge by her portraits, Lady Maria, as she now liked to be called, had a look not so much of pride as of shyness and great reserve. Madam Riedesel's ready smile, her friendly manner, appealed to Canada's first lady; and Lady Maria won the heart of the Baroness by sending a special courier to General Riedesel to tell him that his wife had arrived safely. This message was sent when their ship was still in the lower St. Lawrence; the dispatching of a carriage to the dock was just another kindly gesture.

The Baroness called her new friend "Mrs. General Carleton" and Her Ladyship liked it. Before long, "Mrs. General Riedesel" found that she was to be called "Lady Fritz" in Quebec, and this too seemed delightful. Conversation at the dinner table took a purely feminine turn: Frederika was relieved to discover that in Quebec, at least, no one was going to "point the finger" at her. "They were surprised to see me dressed English-fashion," she said, and she decided that her London dressmaker must have been a good one for her clothes were much admired. She laughed when they told her that they had expected to see her in "waist-coats, short cloaks and round caps with long ear-laps." That was what the German army women wore when they straggled off the transports in the wake of their men the previous year. Lady Mary and her guests had supposed that a German lady of quality would dress the same.

Canadian women, Frederika took time to observe, were very fond of wearing a long cloak of scarlet cloth. "The rich women wear them of silk and without this garment they never step forth." They also wore "a kind of worsted cap with great colored loops of ribbon and this distinguishes the nobility from the other classes." She was sure that "if a native woman of ordinary rank should dare to wear such a thing, a real lady would snatch it off her head."

Everyone was disappointed when Madam Riedesel refused to spend the night in Quebec. But everyone understood. She must make all possible speed up the river if she was to see her husband again before he embarked on the lake. Ever present in her heart was the fear that her beloved General's next campaign might be his last, and this thought was in the hearts of all the other wives left in Quebec. Captain Pownal of the *Pallas* offered to take the Baroness, the children and the servants up the St. Lawrence that very night on board an oared galley. He could go only as far as

Point aux Trembles, where he would have to turn back; but this was a distance of twenty miles.[1]

People from Lady Carleton's dinner party went along and the Baroness mentioned a Mrs. Johnson — perhaps the "Beautiful Mrs. Johnston" of the high headdress. "We all embarked at six in the evening on the 11th of June," Frederika said. "It was a bright moonlight night and Captain Pownal had a splendid band of music on board." Frederika put her children to bed and then she went on deck "where we all sat up and drank tea together" for the rest of the night. At two in the morning the little girls, their mother and the servants "were all set ashore."

At the village of Point aux Trembles, Mrs. General hired three calashes. They were "a kind of light chaise," she explained, "very small and uncomfortable but very fast." She "could not bring [her] heart to trust one of the children to the servants" so she tied Frederika, aged three, into one corner of her single seat, held Caroline, now a year and three months, in her arms, and had Augusta sit on the floor. Being over five now, Augusta was considered by her mother to be "the most discreet," so she was told to sit on her mother's purse and see that it didn't fly out of the little two-wheeled carriage.

The frugal Baroness was willing to spend money if there was a good reason for it, and she offered the drivers a bonus if they would travel fast. "The Canadians are everlastingly talking to their horses and called them all sorts of names," she said. Since she understood French almost as well as German, and spoke it much better than she did English, she talked French with her driver, who sat on his box just in front of her, his feet on the shafts.

When not "lashing his horse or singing, the driver kept calling out, '*Fi donc, Madame!*' " ("For shame, Madam.")

Pretending to think that the driver was talking to her, "*Plaît-il?*" said the Baroness ("Beg pardon?").

"Oh, it's my horse, the little rascal," said the driver, jovially. He applied the whip awhile, then sang. The Baroness loved to sing, and soon she was joining in with songs of her own. It was a bumpy, often frightening ride; but with French songs, German songs, children's songs, and songs of the Canadian woods and the river, the miles seemed short.

Whenever they came to a village, people ran out of their houses to stare at the three-calash cavalcade. Then they would smile and shout *"Voilà la femme de notre cher Général!"* — for General Riedesel's troops had been quartered along this road and he had done his best to make the burden light for the country people. "The Canadian inhabitants," Riedesel said, "behaved much better than our peasants under similar circumstances."

On the afternoon of June 12 the little procession reached what was probably the town of Batiscan, fifty-eight miles from Quebec. Here the hired calash-drivers would go no farther regardless of the amount of money offered them. Gradually it dawned on Mrs. General that there was just no bridge across a good-sized river which entered the St. Lawrence at this point. She must now go by water, and the boat that they showed her "was made of the bark of a tree!"

"I offered money upon money, I begged and implored for a calash," said Frederika, by no means over her fear of the water for all she had just crossed the Atlantic. "The people pretended to consider these ferries as a regular post route," and they were right. There was a road of sorts, which took a long detour, but the regular route from Batiscan to Three Rivers was by water. "It was horrible weather and I had to cross three rivers which cross each other," said the unhappy Baroness, and it never occurred to anyone that here was a lady who had never before seen an Indian canoe.

"Seated on the bottom of the boat in one corner, I had my three children upon my lap while my three servants sat on the other side," the Baroness said. "We were overtaken by a severe hailstorm" and the three-year-old Frederika was frightened, screamed "and wanted to jump up." And now — for the first time — "the boatman told me the canoe would be overturned by even the slightest movement!" Her mother held the little girl tightly, trying to explain, unable to calm the child, who was by now almost hysterical. Mrs. General "tried not to mind her cries" but she confessed rather apologetically that after this first experience she always hated canoe travel even in good weather.

A bedraggled little group — the lady mistress and two women-servants; Rockel, who must have been longing for his coach and horses; three wet and frightened children — climbed ashore at the town of Three Rivers that same night. Some German troops were still stationed there, and "our officers came out and clasped their hands over their heads," like spectators acclaiming the victory of a prize fighter. They "shouted for joy." All of a sudden the Baroness felt her knees begin to shake, because she "knew from the way the officers behaved how great our danger had been." But just to make sure that she knew, the officers told her that two fishermen had been drowned in a canoe during that storm.

Very shortly the "Grand Vicar," social and spiritual leader of Three Rivers, arrived to call on the Baroness. He found her and the children drying themselves before the fire at the military headquarters, and he sat down for a chat — but not a cheerful one. General Riedesel had been ill, he said, his illness "caused by his distress" at having to leave winter quarters for the front without seeing his wife and children. There had been sad rumors, too, the Grand Vicar declared. "A lady and three children" had been drowned while crossing the Atlantic when their ship went down with all hands. For a long and dreadful period, General Riedesel had not known who the lady was and thought it might be his wife. Then the General heard that his wife had sailed from England but had "become so frightened" that she had herself "set ashore."

After listening to all this, the Baroness "sent ahead an express rider" to tell her husband that she and the children were on their way. She knew he had been ill — he had said so in a letter which he left for her at Quebec. It was because he had left his window open one night, he told her. He had left money for her in Quebec, and some of this the usually frugal Frederika had been spending freely for special services and a quick journey.

The bad weather continued, but Mrs. General set out again at six in the morning. The Grand Vicar very kindly lent her his calash. General Riedesel was said to be at Chambly, where the old stone fort had now been repaired and served as an important base of operations for the coming campaign. There were two ways to get to Chambly. One was by road up the north bank of the St. Lawrence to Montreal, and then southeast through Laprairie and Sorel — the famous Whitcomb ambush route. The other way led across the St. Lawrence to Sorel, and then up the Richelieu River. After her experience in a boat made of bark, it is not surprising that the Baroness chose the Montreal route.

No matter which road a traveler chose, however, the way to Chambly led north from Three Rivers as far as the town of Berthier, where those taking the Sorel and Richelieu River route crossed the St. Lawrence. Lashed into whitecaps by the wind and pockmarked by the rain, this river was the widest the Baroness had ever seen. She drove through Berthier, thankful there was no need to get into a tiny tossing rowboat or a canoe. The land journey proved no pleasure jaunt, however, because the Grand Vicar's calash went so fast that she could hardly get her breath and it jolted so much that she had to clutch her children tightly lest they fall out. "I was completely beaten to pieces," she said, "and at every post station where they changed the horses" she had to get out and walk up and down because her legs were so stiff she could hardly stand and her arms ached almost unbearably.

Having missed one entire night's sleep on leaving Quebec and after traveling almost continuously ever since, she reached Montreal on June 14 in the evening. Setting out very early next morning, she arrived at Chambly on June 15.

As the Baroness drove up to the little clutch of houses, cabins, and huts that made up the town, she saw a group of Brunswick officers and the Riedesel family coachman whom her husband had brought from Wolfenbüttel. "I ran up to him and asked him where my husband was," she wrote.

"He has gone to Berthier to meet you," the coachman said.

"I saw I had chosen the wrong road," she said. Mrs. General remembered, also, that she had left no messages in Berthier. She had just driven on, past the turn that led to the wharf. How would the General know where she had gone? He might ride all the way back to Three Rivers, or perhaps in the direction of Montreal — and the time was so short! Exhausted after this grueling journey, overcome with disappointment, it seemed as though the Baroness could not keep back her tears. But there were the children, equally disappointed not to see their father and already crying. There were the servants, frightened by their first glimpse of a wide, untamed land so different from their own. And there was "the group of officers," now crowding around and offering sympathy. Mrs. General was a fellow officer, at least in her own little army, and generals do not weep. Or hardly ever.

General Carleton rode up and he was kindness itself. She would have to wait only a day, or two "at most," he told her.

"My children and my faithful Rockel kept watch on the highroad," Frederika said. It is to be hoped that she herself tried to get some rest. Carleton was right — a day passed before Riedesel came back. But there had been no need to leave a message, because everybody in every village remembered the German Baroness. On June 16, "from a distance," she saw a calash coming down the road to Chambly with a Canadian riding in it alone. The calash stopped down the road where Rockel and the children were posted, and the "Canadian" got out. "I saw him come nearer and fold the children in his arms. It was my husband!" she said.

General Riedesel was thin and wasted from his illness, and "was so cold on that warm summer day that he had wrapped him-

self in a sort of cassock of woolen cloth bordered with ribbons."
Around the bottom of the coat there was a fringe, variegated
blue and red, and it looked so strange that little Frederika would
not go to her father, but cried and said, "No, no, this is an ugly
Papa; my Papa is pretty." She remembered her father only from
a miniature her mother had with her, a handsome man in a
white wig with brilliant uniform of blue and gold. Augusta "cried
for joy."

"My joy was beyond all description but my husband looked
weak and sick and this terrified me," Mrs. General said. If only
she could look after him properly: see that he ate well and enjoyed the good wine which she had brought — but most of which
she had to leave in Quebec. But here he was on the verge of
setting out on a new campaign.

General Riedesel threw off the Canadian coat, and now little
Frederika saw his uniform and felt better. "She tenderly embraced
him." The baby Caroline was seeing her father for the first time.

Riedesel had not gone all the way to Berthier, after all. At noon,
when he stopped for dinner near Sorel, some villagers said that
a woman had just arrived from Berthier. The General had an
informant brought in. "Is there any news?" he asked.

"Nothing," this village woman said, "except that a German
woman with three children has come through town. People said
she was the wife of a general."

"How many children did you say?" The woman was sure that
there were three. So General Riedesel turned back to Chambly
with a lightened heart. The fleet with which the Baroness left
England was the first to reach Quebec with letters since navigation had been closed for the winter. Lady Maria Carleton's message had said merely that the Baroness had arrived, without mentioning the children, and General Riedesel had begun to worry
about his little girls.

"We remained together for two happy days," the Baroness

wrote. She spoke in praise of the "good houses" with "large rooms" and "nice bed-curtains" in Canadian villages. It was too bad that the partitions were so thin that you could hear everything, but she would have been completely happy if she had been allowed to travel with her husband. "But he would not agree to it." So she "watched the departure of the troops against the enemy" and then turned back along the road toward Three Rivers. She felt "alone and deserted with [her] children, in a foreign land among strangers." This time she traveled slowly, and "at every post station, which carried me farther from the man I loved, my heart seemed to break all over again," Frederika said.

At Three Rivers, Mrs. General was "sad and full of anxiety." Almost her "only society" was the Grand Vicar and his cousin. General Riedesel had already commended the Grand Vicar's cousin to his wife as "a very witty young girl who, I am sure, will please you greatly." Madam Riedesel admitted that the girl was "good-humored and talked pleasantly" and the Grand Vicar "had the same qualities besides being a man of intellect." But as to their being cousins — the Baroness soon learned otherwise, and was greatly shocked by the discovery. She wrote in her journal that it was the custom that vicars should have housekeepers whom they called "cousins," and that "to avoid scandal" these women went away for a while "almost every year, on account of a certain reason." Monsieur Saint-Onge of Three Rivers never became a bishop, although he worked hard to curry favor, she said. He failed of preferment because he never would give up "his 'cousin,' Miss Cabenac" — or so Madam Riedesel believed.

Three Rivers was a pretty town — a bit of Old France in the New World. One small section of it, part of the Rue Notre-Dame, survives unchanged. Low stone houses with dormer windows to light a loft under the steep roof stand close to the roadway. The high gable end of the Ursuline Convent rises at the turn of the street. "Our hospital has been established here," wrote one of the German soldiers, but this was nothing new, for the land had been granted to the Ursulines in 1700 and they had built their hospital soon after. The Germans found Yankees there, for some of the American wounded taken at Three Rivers were still in the hospital. Pay for their care was promised, the promise never kept.[2]

"I found among the nuns several lovely people, with whom I spent many days," wrote Madam Riedesel. They told her that her husband had often sent them "wine and roast meat" and she took this gentle hint and did the same. Often she had her own dinner carried over to the convent so that she could eat with the nuns.

The sisters saw that the friendly German lady was lonely and anxious about her husband — whom they knew and liked. So it occurred to them to entertain her, and the Baroness thought the wine had a little something to do with it when the nuns put on gay peasant dresses and gave her a nun's habit to wear. Then they "danced a dance" which she described as "cossack," and perhaps it was, but since many of the first settlers along the St. Lawrence came from Normandy and Brittany, the dance might have been French in origin.

It was all so entertaining that "I had my children brought in," the Baroness wrote. But little Augusta began to cry when she saw her mother in a nun's habit. " 'Oh, don't become a nun,' " she sobbed, and her sister Frederika joined in. "In order to quiet my children I had to take off my nun's habit quickly," their mother said.

A school was connected with the convent, where "young ladies were taught all kinds of needlework." Lieutenant Anburey, passing through Three Rivers the previous year, observed that the Ursulines were "the most ingenious of any in Canada, making all kinds of fancy ornaments, needlework and curious toys." General Riedesel had supposed that his "oldest daughters" would go to the school, and so they did, Augusta, almost six, and Frederika, not quite three, learning to take the first stitches in formal needlework. This was an art essential to the education of a gentlewoman, its traditions taught from generation to generation.

The Ursuline sisters spoke a beautiful though already slightly archaic French, but the Riedesel little girls seem to have learned none. They spoke English perfectly, however, and their father proudly wrote to the Duke of Brunswick that his children "were everywhere taken for English."

The whole Riedesel family often went to services at the convent. Behind their curtain which concealed the choir from the nave of their church, the nuns sang "so beautifully" that the Baroness could believe she was "listening to the song of angels."

Governor Carleton's headquarters had formerly been at Three Rivers, but Government House had now been turned into a barracks and the Governor lived in Quebec. He owned a comfortable private house in Three Rivers, however, which he had turned over to General Riedesel for his headquarters the previous winter. "You will find my quarters vacant and prepared for you," the General had written in one of the letters his wife found waiting for her in Quebec. "You will find a tolerable garden arranged so you can walk in it."

Wherever he went, General Riedesel planted a garden, even when he had no reason to suppose he would be quartered in one place long enough to reap a harvest.[3] Many of the German rank and file did the same, and he always encouraged them, but the British seem to have looked down on such activities. As the Baroness strolled through her husband's garden she thought of home, for it was laid out European-fashion with a broad gravel walk down the center and narrower grass paths leading out at right angles among precisely oblong beds. The General always indulged himself with a few flowers, but for the most part he planted vegetables — and his wife marveled that they grew so well in a land which she had been taught to think of as cold and desolate. She rejoiced because she would be able to have food at low cost. "Meat, fowl and milk you can have in abundance," the General had written her and this, too, she found to be true. The cost of living was "less than half that in Quebec," just as her husband said.

But at first there was trouble about money. "The officer who had been left behind at Three Rivers was not amiable," was the way Madam Riedesel put it. She referred to Godecke, paymaster for the Brunswick troops. During her brief visit with her husband, General Riedesel had given his wife signed orders so that she could draw upon Godecke. Accordingly she "presented him with an order" from her husband for "one hundred fifty pounds sterling." Godecke refused to honor it.

" 'Is my husband in debt?' " the Baroness asked.

" 'Oh, no,' " Godecke admitted. " 'He has considerable balance.' " But General Riedesel might be killed any day now, and the paymaster thought he ought not to take any chances. He would hate to get in trouble with the Duke of Brunswick for disbursing the funds of a dead man.

"I was exceedingly provoked," said the Baroness, and this was probably an understatement. She told the paymaster that even if her husband was dead she was entitled to a quarter of his yearly allowance.

"True," replied Godecke, "but how about your passage back?" He said this with a sneer, the Baroness thought, and she told him she would never speak to him again. The English paymaster gave Mrs. General the money and told her she could draw on him any time.

This accommodation was greatly appreciated because Captain Arbuthnot, who had brought the Baroness across the Atlantic, had gone to Montreal in behalf of the shipowner, Banker Watson, to buy furs. He had promised to buy some for the Baroness and sell them for her in London. Now that he was indebted to her for keeping the navy's hands off his crew, she knew he would prove a good agent. He was due back any time and she wanted to pay him for the furs. Indications are that Madam's venture in Canadian furs turned out very well.

Meanwhile, the Baroness wrote her husband about Godecke's scornful treatment, and the General sent his paymaster such a scorching letter that the fellow came crawling to Madam, full of "obsequious apologies." She promptly forgave him, and later when he was ill she sent him delicacies from her table. Someone told her that Godecke's letters home were so full of praise of her that his wife was jealous.

General Riedesel wrote to his wife daily, but letters were often long in reaching her. "It is certain that we are more afraid of danger to those we love, if they are absent, than if they are near us," she said, and she worried about her husband constantly.

9

Second Thrust

ONCE General Burgoyne had concluded with Lord Germain that a second thrust across Lake Champlain would bring a quick victory over the Americans, there was no time to lose. Gentleman Johnny sailed for Quebec to take the command away from Governor Carleton before Carleton could advance and win the laurels for himself.

Although everything seemed to be coming his way, there were one or two details that Burgoyne did not like. He was not to be commander-in-chief until he crossed the border from Canada into the Province of New York. And as soon as he met Howe in Albany, and proceeded with him to New York City, Howe would outrank him. Promotions made by Burgoyne in his own army would be scrapped and the men demoted, once they joined Howe. Burgoyne decided not to tell this to any of the officers whose rank he had raised.

General Riedesel was not happy about starting the new campaign without word from Howe. He felt that it was essential to "establish communications with Howe," but, as he wrote the Duke of Brunswick early in June, "Burgoyne judges somewhat hastily and carries out the plan of the ministers. His predecessor

[Sir Guy Carleton] went to work more carefully but safely and made no plan until he was convinced it could be carried out. The results will show who was right in the present situation."

Howe had never received official orders from London to effect a junction with Burgoyne at Albany.[1] The story of what happened comes from two sources: Lord Shelburne, famous for his attitude of conciliation towards the colonies, and William Knox, undersecretary in the colonial department. In a memorandum, Lord Shelburne wrote that "although it might appear incredible," Germain had been on his way to spend a weekend in the country when he called at his office to sign dispatches. The dispatch for Howe had not yet been "fair-copied" and he did not want to wait for it. On Germain's return to London, the Howe dispatch was forgotten and never sent.

The historian, Sir George Trevelyan, did not believe this story. He said that there were so many clerks and secretaries in the war office that such a mistake could not have happened. But a plethora of clerks and secretaries can cause accidents fully as frequently as they can prevent them. William Knox left a notation among his manuscripts that there was "certainly a weak spot" in Germain's defense, "which was the want of an official communication to Howe of the plan and Burgoyne's instructions, with orders for his co-operation."

It is a dramatic story: Lord George Germain's horses waiting at the door; His Lordship dashing out and jumping into his carriage, off for a jolly weekend; the clerks hurrying away to their own hard-earned holiday — not fair-copying orders that might have changed the course of history. But the fact remains that eventually Howe knew that Burgoyne was coming down the Hudson and expected strong support. Washington's secret service, nonexistent at the beginning of the American Revolution, had been improving daily but it was never able to stop all messengers from Canada. Lacking "official orders," Howe continued to enjoy himself in New York with Mrs. Loring,[2] the wife of his Commissary of Prisoners. The commissary himself was having a good time too, getting rich.[3] It was said that he "caused the death of two thousand" American prisoners of war by starving them and selling the food intended for their use.

General Riedesel, although understandably critical of the British, assumed that Howe was at least getting on with the campaign. "In spite of our delays, in spite of inexpert movement" made by the British, he told the Duke of Brunswick that "if General Howe has crossed the Delaware, he will take away the slight advantage the rebels have" as a result of the Battle of Trenton. "If we are so fortunate as to push through to Albany in the month of August, I think the business will be ended entirely this year. But I don't think we will be in Germany in 1778. I admit," Riedesel added, "that intrigues and misunderstandings so obvious as to be publicized distress me greatly and I fear to find much disagreement after we join with General Howe's large army."

Burgoyne left Canada with 8581 men — 4135 British, 3116 Germans, 830 Canadians and 500 "savages."[4] Orders were to "march to Crown Point in two columns, the Germans on the left, the English on the right, Canadians and Savages making up the advance guard. . . ." It would be technically speaking a march, but one hundred miles of extremely rugged country lay between the Canadian border and Ticonderoga so that most of the army were going to get a boatride. Coming out of winter quarters on the St. Lawrence, in Montreal and near Sorel, the army made its way up the Richelieu River and converged upon Cumberland Head, a level peninsula about twenty-five miles north of the present Plattsburg.

Meanwhile, Lieutenant Colonel Barry St. Leger was sent out along the Mohawk River on a "secret" mission that everybody seemed to know about. With a detachment of two hundred and eighty British, three companies of Canadian Volunteers and all the Indians they could get hold of, this expedition was to take Fort Schuyler, induce the neutral Indians (known to be friendly to the Americans) to join them, and enter the Hudson by the portage where the Mohawk made its seventy-foot fall. They would then escort the victorious Burgoyne into Albany — at least according to plan.

Ever since reaching Quebec, Burgoyne had been working on his "Proclamation" or "Manifesto." This was designed to bring all American Tories flocking to his banner and to strike terror into the hearts of the "froward and stubborn generation" of rebels. He began with the recitation of his titles and honors: *By John Burgoyne Esq'r; Lieut. Gen'l of His Majesties Armies in America, Col. of the Queens Regt. of Light Dragoons, Governor of Fort William in North Britain, one of the Representatives of the Commons of Great Britain in Parliament, and Commanding an Army and Fleet employed on an expedition from Canada, &c., &c., &c.*

On the morning of June 19, General Burgoyne reviewed his troops at Cumberland Head. Splendidly attired in scarlet and gold, he read them his Proclamation:

"The Forces entrusted to my command are designed to act in concert and upon a common principle with the numerous Armies and Fleets which already display in every quarter of America the power, the justice (and when properly sought) the mercy of the King . . ."

The present "Rebellion," Burgoyne said, would, unless put down, be "made a foundation for the completest system of tyranny that God in his displeasure" ever allowed. "To the profanation of Religion," the rebels "added the most profligate prostitution of common reason . . ." Carried away by his own eloquence, Burgoyne asserted that there were "multitudes compelled not only to

bear Arms but to swear subjection to the usurpation they abhor."
In the tiny towns and hamlets where this printed "Proclamation"
circulated, Americans would be amused to hear themselves called
"multitudes."

"Animated by these considerations, at the head of Troops in
full power of health, discipline and Valour," Burgoyne was "determined to strike when necessary, and anxious to spare when
possible. . . . With the blessing of God," he was going "to extend
[his army] far" and he wanted "to assure the domestick, the industrious, the infirm and even the timid inhabitants" that he was
"desirous to protect" them "provided they remain quietly in their
Houses; that they do not suffer their Cattle to be removed, nor
their Corn or forage to be secreted or destroyed; that they do not
break up their Bridges or Roads, nor by any other acts, directly
or indirectly endeavour to obstruct the operations of the King's
Troops . . ."

Burgoyne promised to pay for "every species of Provision
brought" to his camp "at an equitable rate in solid Coin." He
did not say how the inhabitants were to get through his advance
guard of Indians in order to bring provisions. Burgoyne himself
had yet to learn what a problem his Indians were going to present.
But he now got around to discussing what he would do to those
"inhabitants" who disregarded his remarks. They were not to
think they were "too far away from the immediate situation" of
his camp. "I have but to give stretch to the Indian Forces under
my direction (and they amount to Thousands) to overtake the
hardened Enemies of Great Britain and America (I consider them
the same) wherever they may lurk."

After many a sonorous sentence, Burgoyne concluded by assuring the "unnatural rebels" that if "the phrenzy of hostility should
remain," he would "stand acquitted in the Eyes of God and Men
in denouncing and executing the Vengeance of the state against
the wilful outcasts." The messengers of justice and of wrath

"awaited them in the Field" and "devastation, famine, and every concomitant of horror" awaited their families at home.

Copies of Burgoyne's Proclamation passed from hand to hand among the colonies. It would be a long time before he learned what the reaction was — if he ever did. Never could he have understood it. But the Americans laughed long and loud; satires and parodies began appearing in the newspapers — with that opening paragraph concerning Burgoyne's titles bringing forth the most derision. In the *New York Journal* for September 8, 1777, William Livingston, Governor of New Jersey, poked fun at Burgoyne as follows:

> By John Burgoyne and Burgoyne John, Sir,
> And grac'd with titles still more higher,
> For I'm lieutenant-general too
> Of Georgie's troops both red and blue
> On this extensive continent,
> And of Queen Charlotte's regiment
> Of eight dragoons the colonel,
> And Governor eke of Castle Will,
> And furthermore when I am there
> In house of commons there appear,
> (Hoping ere long to be a Peer)
> Being a member of that virtuous band
> Who always vote in North's command,
> Directing too the fleets and troops
> From Canada as thick as hops,
> And all my titles to display
> I'll end with thrice et cetera.[5]

Governor Livingston was not much of a poet — but these were grim days, and a measure of a people's courage was that they could laugh.

Burgoyne graciously acknowledged the cheers of his troops as he finished reading his Proclamation, and then, to the booming of cannon, the blaring of trumpets and the unfurling of flags, he went aboard the *Lady Mary*.

General Riedesel embarked next day, but without the fanfare. He had his troops "ready at the appointed time," good organizer that he was. Provisions to last the whole army for six weeks were ready, according to Burgoyne's orders, and all heavy baggage had been left behind. This was to be a quick summer campaign and no one would need warm clothes.

Lake Champlain itself set aside Riedesel's careful plans, at least for a day. "A violent wind arose and blew furiously, the waves beat angrily on the shore." Far out on the lake "Burgoyne's ship and those which set out along with him could be seen from the shore to be in constant danger." Riedesel, with smaller vessels and cumbersome bateaux, "made several attempts to round Point de Ligonier" but failed and "the flotilla" was finally ordered to come about. They reached their campground on Cumberland Head and managed to get ashore safely. Next day they started out all over again. This time the weather seemed favorable at first, but a thunderstorm came sweeping over the lake and hailstones beat upon the soldiers and their wives and children. There was no shelter in the open boats. The storm was followed by such a thick fog that the "musicians" — there were 102 of them — were ordered to beat drums to help the fleet keep together. No one had a reliable chart of these waters, however, and drumming was certainly no protection against hidden reefs and the many small islands that suddenly loomed ahead in this treacherous lake.

At the end of three hours the wind rose again — and now they were too far from Cumberland Head to come about and seek shelter. Women and children bailed the boats, while soldiers rowed and thanked their stars they had learned to row the previous year. They showed "skill with the rudder" Riedesel said; but five vessels were driven off course and presumed lost. They had managed to land on a little island appropriately called "Four Winds," and eventually they found their way to the west shore of Champlain at the mouth of the Bouquet River, where Riedesel and the rest of his "flotilla" were safely anchored.

At the Bouquet River, the army stopped to "bake bread to last four days" and to catch salmon. There was a ferry here and a small settlement called Willsboro. It had been founded by William Gilliland who bought up soldiers' land grants after the French and Indian War and planned to establish a manor. His letters to General Schuyler expressed sympathy with the American cause, but in such flowery terms as to seem two-faced, and Arnold removed him from his lands "to protect him" — and keep him from helping the British.

At the Bouquet River encampment, Burgoyne made another of his speeches — this time to the Indians. After considerable preamble about "the great King our common father," he told the "savages" that they were "too sagacious and too faithful to be deluded or corrupted" by such people as the Americans, and that they "now burned to vindicate the violated rights of the parental power" they loved. Just what the interpreter made of this it would be interesting to know. It seems improbable that all of these words had an Indian equivalent — but the speech continued, paragraph after paragraph. John Burgoyne, playwright and member of Parliament, was in his element; and with appropriate gestures he pointed first to the British, then to the German officers, "chiefs of His Majesty's European forces and of the Princes of his Allies." Toward the end he got around to the subject of scalping.

"In conformity and indulgence to your customs, which have affixed an idea of honour to such badges of victory," General Burgoyne told the Indians, "you will be allowed to take the scalps of the dead when killed by your fire or in fair opposition, but on no account or pretense or subtlety or prevarication are they to be taken from the wounded or even from the dying."

But there were exceptions. "Base, lurking assassins, incendiaries, ravagers and plunderers of the country, to whatever army they belong, shall be treated with less reserve." If the Indians understood any of this at all, here was carte blanche. They shouted *"Etow! Etow!"* at intervals. Burgoyne ordered rum for the Indians and they had a war dance.

The Indians proceeded to burn the houses and mills at Willsboro. They plundered the farms, slaughtered the cattle, taking a flank or two of beef to roast over the campfire and leaving the rest for the crows. Gilliland wrote a very unhappy letter to Schuyler asking to be indemnified, because he had lost an income of over a thousand pounds a year by being taken from his home and sent to Albany.[6] Apparently he felt he came under the heading of "domestick, industrious, infirm and even timid inhabitants," and that Burgoyne would have given him protection.

No farmers "properly seeking the Mercy of the King" came in with provisions, horses and cattle to be exchanged for "solid coin," and this must have surprised the General. He sent "a large detachment of Savages and Rangers up Otter Creek to bring in forage." About ten days later, a notation in Burgoyne's orderly book tells its own story. "No private persons are to buy horses from the Savages as they are destined for the public use of the army." No one asked the Indians any questions about where they got the horses they were selling; they must have found some "base lurking assassins" who had some.

One thousand five hundred horses had been bought in Canada. They "were ordered to be sent overland" to Crown Point, but there was no continuous road — only a series of cart tracks with here and there a section of corduroy laid down by some of Gilliland's tenants. A road of sorts led along the shore of the lake to a distance of a few miles beyond Plattsburg, but then the foothills of the Andirondacks intervened and the track detoured far inland. Weeks went by and finally only a small proportion of this herd of horses was ever seen again.

The army traveled light but German dragoons usually wore "leather pantaloons, high boots, long gauntlets and immensely heavy hats. . . . They carried short, thick guns[7] and wore huge sabers on a belt." Brunswick "jack-boots weighed 12 lbs the pair" and it was said that the hat and saber alone weighed more than an English soldier's whole equipment. But all this was of no consequence usually because a dragoon was a man who rode a horse. Riedesel made his men as comfortable as he could by ordering "long linen trousers, striped blue and white" somewhat like those worn by the French Canadians in summer.[8] But his dragoons still needed horses — and where were they? General Riedesel had at most not more than two, brought by water, and the other officers sometimes had only one. The increasingly unhappy dragoons, awkward on foot and the laughingstock of the British foot soldiers, had none. Real difficulty for lack of horses was yet to come, because the artillery was useless without them.

But on went the Indian advance guard to Crown Point. They "surprised a detachment of the enemy, killed ten and captured an equal number, whom they scalped." Burgoyne gave orders that the inhabitants around Crown Point should be "treated with great consideration" — but it was a little late for that.

Crown Point is a long peninsula reaching far out from the western shore of Lake Champlain as though to touch hands with another point of land coming from the eastern side. This spot, with its narrow water passage, had long been a French trading post with imposing Fort St. Frederick on one side and a barracks with many chimneys on the other, giving it the name of "Chimney Point." In 1759, the French blew up Fort St. Frederick at the approach of Lord Amherst — leaving, however, plenty of cut limestone in usable blocks ready to hand. With these Lord Amherst built a fort which he named for himself and located west of St. Frederick in a position to guard Bullwaga Bay, where ships could take shelter. Ramparts twenty feet thick still stand, overlooking a deep ditch quarried out of bedrock. Grass grows over the great walls and only a footpath leads through what was once a gateway. Within, a wide parade ground comes suddenly into view with two gaunt, gray stone buildings standing roofless, their empty windows like the eyesockets in a skull. Lord Amherst's fort was never completed according to his plan, and in 1773 it caught fire and the powder magazine blew up. General Carleton had urged that the fort be repaired, but in 1775 it was held by only a corporal and eight men. It fell to Ethan Allen and his "hundred odd" Green Mountain Boys and to Benedict Arnold with his Connecticut recruits — each American leader claiming command and credit at the expense of the other. Retreating Americans, in their efforts to destroy the fort at Crown Point, had left it roofless and windowless, and so it remained. But General Burgoyne found it a comfortable spot to camp in summer.

On June 25, 1777, "the Fleet proceeded to Crown Point where we came to anchor," Lieutenant James Murray Hadden noted in one of the memorandum books he carried. "Thursday, June 26, Generals Burgoyne, Phillips and Riedesel came up with the army."

"Magazines were erected at Crown Point," said General Riedesel. "The transport ships were unloaded and returned to St. Johns for more provisions and more ammunition." Heavy artillery had still to arrive.

On June 30, in another of his speeches, Burgoyne made his famous statement, "This Army must not retreat." Next morning the troops embarked for Ticonderoga. Lake Champlain was "in a manner covered with Boats or Bateaux . . . the Music and Drums of the different Regiments were continually playing."

In gala mood, Burgoyne's invincible troops advanced, landed and encamped near Fort Ticonderoga. They were annoyed to find the "ground wooded with no roads. The Indians, getting drunk, advanced too near the Enemy," said Hadden. "This folly terminated in an officer being sent to bring them off, in doing which he was wounded; one Savage killed and another wounded."

This was not quite the way in which Burgoyne intended the siege to begin, and on the third of July he gave out orders, headed "Camp near Ticonderoga":

"It being very apparent that Liquor is sold or given to the Savages, notwithstanding the positive and repeated orders to the contrary, the Commanding officers are to assemble the Suttlers and Women of the respective Regiments and inform them that the first person found guilty of disobedience shall instantly have their liquors and their suttling stores destroyed and be turned out of camp, besides receiving such corporal punishment as a court martial shall inflict."

The next day was July 4. A "feu de joi" was heard coming from Fort Ticonderoga, but the besiegers had no idea why there was a thirteen-gun salute, or that the Americans were celebrating what they called their "Independence Day." British and German "artificers" were "making a road to the top of a high Mountain called Sugar Loaf Hill."

10

Within the Walls

WHEN Fort Ticonderoga was taken from the British during the night of May 9–10, 1775, it gave a tremendous lift to the hearts of Americans. The English still held Boston, and the Battle of Bunker Hill was still to be fought. Washington had not yet taken formal command of the Continental Army at Cambridge, but this amazing victory on Lake Champlain showed what colonists could do. Since Ethan Allen with his Green Mountain Boys and Benedict Arnold with his men from Connecticut had taken the fort, New Englanders rather looked upon the place as their own. And then, only six weeks later, Philip Schuyler was commissioned major general in the Northern Department. Ticonderoga was his.

Command of an ill-fated expedition to Canada fell to Schuyler in July, 1775, and he soon saw that supply would be the insurmountable problem. During his frantic efforts to provision troops on their long march he was stricken with a severe attack of gout, and so did not set out with the men. When the expedition collapsed and the routed army with its sick and wounded retreated, Washington sent Horatio Gates, commissioned major general after the evacuation of Boston, to see what could be done to rally the men. Gates thought he had just been given the Northern Department, and it was a bitter blow to his pride when he received news that he commanded only in Canada. The remnant of the army was already south of the border. The fact that Schuyler had never gone to Canada was held against him, especially in New England where Gates was popular, and Gates lingered at Ticonderoga hoping that his friends in Congress would give him Schuyler's place.[1]

Gates was the highest ranking officer at Ticonderoga when Carleton appeared on Lake Champlain in October, 1776. Arnold sailed under his orders, and it was only after the American fleet was destroyed that Gates remembered that he had told Arnold not to sail too far north. He now declared that Carleton had "fled," and many believed this, including himself. He had announced that he would not serve under Schuyler, and on November 18, 1776, the garrison at Ticonderoga saw him "finally going off" on his way to Congress, which he found in Baltimore and followed to Philadelphia. During February, Washington offered him his old job of adjutant general, but Gates would have none of it. He wanted the Northern Department, and he planned to get it by means of intrigue.

Philip Schuyler might almost be said to have inherited the Northern Department. He was the eldest son in the fourth generation of Dutch settlers, and the owner of thousands of acres of land near Saratoga, in the Mohawk River area and along the Hudson. There were more Indians than white settlers among the forests legally belonging to Schuyler and as a young man he had been sent to trade and live among them. He wrote with youthful fervor of "eyes like an Indian beauty" and an elderly relative explained that "chiefs, to express their gratitude, had exchanged names with Philip Schuyler." The pious old lady recalled that "several Indians assumed his surname."

Schuyler's marriage to "sweet Kitty V. R." was equally pleasing to the Van Rensselaer family and his own, and their marriage was blessed with fourteen children. General Schuyler spoke Dutch, as did older members of his and his wife's family; and his French, learned as a boy while studying with a Protestant clergyman in New Rochelle, New York, was correct and elegant. Although a linguist, Schuyler's bent was for mathematics. His family trained him to be a merchant and he delighted in trade. If high social position and inherited wealth had been all that went into the making of a Tory, Schuyler would never have joined the struggle for American Independence. But it was restraint of trade which caused him to catch fire. With his courtly manners and his business acumen, he was a new breed — a merchant prince who favored government by the people. He and others like him were an enigma to the British.

Schuyler rose to the rank of major in the British army. His service was confined to America, where he commanded a company under Sir William Johnson against Crown Point. Under Bradstreet, he provisioned the garrison at Oswego and fought against French and Indian raiders at Oneida. Under Amherst he was deputy commissary. Leading men he had personally recruited, he campaigned over territory he would some day inherit or purchase.

Philip Schuyler had many faults. He was often hasty and tactless when dealing with men who opposed his plans. There were those who resented his air of command and thought him arrogant. But his most serious blind spot, as far as his service to his country was concerned, was his insistence on New York's territorial rights against the claims of New Hampshire and the future state of Vermont. Schuyler was a "Yorker" of the deepest dye.[2]

Horatio Gates was British-born. His mother was "probably a housekeeper to the Duke of Leeds" and his father was variously described as a "revenue officer, army officer, clergyman, greengrocer." It was condescendingly said of him that he did well to rise as high as major in the British army, "considering his antecedents." He was married in Halifax while on duty in America during the French and Indian War, but he had retired to England on half pay when ordered to join the Royal American Regiment in New York. He had served under Braddock at Fort Herkimer in the Mohawk Valley, and when he came to Fort Ticonderoga as would-be commander of the Northern District, he was paying a return visit. He had done duty there under the British.

Washington himself made an American out of Gates. They had met when Washington was aide-de-camp to Braddock. After the French and Indian War, Washington was living on his Virginia plantation, and wrote to Gates to try to sell him some land. In August 1772, Gates, his wife and his son set sail for America. They bought a plantation in Berkeley County in what is now West Virginia, equipped it with stock, slaves and an overseer, and named it "Travelers' Rest." The life of a Virginia gentleman suited Gates and he played it to the hilt. He was a politician by nature and never missed a chance to make good contacts. Cultivating his acquaintance with Washington, he espoused the American cause and was commissioned adjutant general in June 1775. While in Cambridge, Massachusetts, with Washington, he did a good job supplying the army. At that time and along the seacoast, the problem of supply was easy. Gates departed the scene with a commission as major general and under an aura of success.

Horatio Gates felt no personal animosity toward Schuyler, at least at first. Gates was merely a man on his way up in a hurry, and Schuyler was someone to shove aside. His first move was to get his friend Dr. Potts appointed medical director in the Northern Army in place of Dr. Stringer, Schuyler's appointee. It was easy enough. Charges were brought against Dr. Stringer, who was given no hearing, and the change in medical directors was accomplished through Congress without the knowledge or consent of Schuyler.[3]

It was no surprise to Gates when Schuyler lost his temper. Philip Schuyler was severe in his punishment of looters, often unfair to Vermonters, but fanatically loyal in defense of his friends and subordinates. He wrote to Congress that Dr. Stringer had "come to the aid of the stricken troops on their retreat from

Canada." The doctor had "saved many lives and had brought and supplied his own medicines where none could be had at any price." Congress "had no right" to dismiss Dr. Stringer.

No one could say to the Continental Congress that they "had no right" to do whatever they pleased. Congress "resolved" that as they had "proceeded to the dismission of Dr. Stringer upon reasons satisfactory to themselves, General Schuyler ought to have known it to be his duty to have acquiesced therein." Schuyler's suggestion that he should have been given reasons for Dr. Stringer's "dismission" was "highly derogatory to the honor of Congress," and the President was instructed to tell him to write "in a style more suitable to the dignity of the representative body of these free and independent states. . . ."

The joyful and triumphant Gates was given the Northern Department he so greatly coveted. At the end of March, 1777, Congress ordered Gates to "repair immediately to Ticonderoga," taking with him Brigadier General Laroche de Fermois, one of the least desirable of the French adventurers who plagued Washington, and Major General Arthur St. Clair, Scottish-born Pennsylvania landowner who had served under Lord Amherst. St. Clair brought his little son to Ticonderoga, apparently convinced by Gates that the coming campaign of 1777 would never materialize, that Carleton had "fled," and that a pleasant outing on Lake Champlain was in store.

Gates had been loud in his criticism of Schuyler for staying in Albany instead of at the fort. But now he too found it a pleasant city and settled down. Mrs. Gates had been left in Virginia, whence she wrote complaining letters about lazy slaves and stupid overseers. She was delighted when her husband sent for her to come to Albany. She could visit Dr. Potts's family on the way, he said, and bring the doctor along with her.

Mrs. Gates, it was noted in Albany, "appears to be a gay, lively though not very beautiful woman." "Her air denotes her to be a high-spirited Dame."

Early in May, 1777, General Tadeusz Andrzej Bonawentura Kościuszko was sent to Fort Ticonderoga to design and direct the building of new defenses. He was a romantic and popular figure in the American Revolution, although it is easy to see why he was almost never referred to by his full name. A member of the Polish petty nobility, he had studied engineering and artillery in France. He borrowed money to come to America to offer his services to Washington, and he was one of the few who sincerely believed in the rights of the colonists and paid little attention to serving his own ends. His plans for the defense of the Delaware River were so successful that he was commissioned colonel of engineers in the Continental Army in 1776. Arriving at Ticonderoga, he immediately advocated fortifying "a hill called Sugar Loaf."

Sugar Loaf Hill was west and south of low-lying Ticonderoga, and almost exactly opposite Mount Independence, where the Americans had already begun fortifications. But Sugar Loaf was over five hundred feet higher than Independence. Surveying the terrain further, "We have only one company of artillerists here and need three," Kościuszko said. "We have a good place to make a resistance, but to defeat the enemy will take plenty of courage and more artillerists." Kościuszko would "say nothing" of works built uselessly. "They have a passion for building Blockhouses which are located in some of the least suitable places," he observed. But the thing to do now was go to work on Sugar Loaf.

Kościuszko labored under a serious handicap, however. French was the only language he spoke other than Polish, and his French, judging by his letters, was strange indeed. Laroche de Fermois might have helped out. He had come to Ticonderoga under orders from Gates. He agreed with Kościuszko that the fortifications at Ticonderoga were badly planned, but he was one of the most self-seeking of Washington's foreign volunteers and merely made fun of Kościuszko. The American officers tried to tell Kościuszko that no one, least of all the British, would think of climbing Sugar Loaf with its almost perpendicular cliffs. So what did it matter if it overlooked and could control the fort and Mount Independence as well? Trumbull had urged the fortifying of Sugar Loaf in 1776 and Congress had vetoed it. Now it seemed sufficient to change the name from Sugar Loaf to "Mount Defiance."[4]

James Wilkinson, at this time only twenty, was aide-de-camp to Gates. Kościuszko was "a mere cypher," Wilkinson thought. But he "detected, under his placid silence, more than a little Anguish and Mortification." Before long, Kościuszko asked General Washington to relieve him from a post where he could be of no use.

In 1775, when General Knox of Washington's newly-created artillery hauled the guns from Ticonderoga to Cambridge, Massachusetts, everyone had been astonished at this feat of courage and ingenuity. But from this time forward, the problem was how to re-arm Ticonderoga. In June 1776 General Knox confidently reported that there were cannon to spare at Crown Point. But most of these were put into the ships of Arnold's fleet and in 1777 some of them had been at the bottom of Lake Champlain ever since the Battle of Valcour Island, while others were on board Burgoyne's fleet soon to be turned against Ticonderoga.

Schuyler had written frantically to Congress for guns, but his letters went unanswered. He applied to Massachusetts, whose legislature at first refused and then promised "to furnish what cannon etc. we can." Letters from Schuyler went to Governor Trumbull of Connecticut, to the "president of New Hampshire" and the "New York Convention," begging that guns be sent over the snow — a comparatively easy task. As far as New Hampshire was concerned, Schuyler was a Yorker — let him get his own guns.

Although Gates succeeded in ousting Schuyler on March 25, 1777, it was April 17 before he arrived in Albany. Schuyler had continued his labors in behalf of Fort Ticonderoga until Gates actually took command. By this time, spring thaws had set in and roads were so bad that "a horse sank above his belly" in the mud, and bridge after plank bridge had been carried away by flood water. Some cannon had actually reached Albany, however. A month went by, with Gates now in command, and "most of the cannon" were still in Albany — over ninety miles away from the almost defenseless fort.

General Schuyler's wife and children urged him to resign from the army and "become plain Philip Schuyler, Esq." when Gates took over the Northern Department. Schuyler longed to do just that. But he had been accused of embezzling soldiers' pay in the course of debate in Congress concerning his command, and he could not let this accusation go unanswered. First he put his case before the New York Convention, exhibiting all his accounts, and was exonerated. New York appointed him a delegate to the Continental Congress, where he asked for a hearing on his conduct while in charge of the Northern Department. Schuyler was completely vindicated, and Congress restored his command. On May 15, 1777, he superseded Gates.

It seems incredible that men should quarrel and that Congress should reverse itself in face of mounting danger. Gates had been the aggressor, but Schuyler, because of his attitude toward "men on the Grants," his impatience and his high temper, was not without blame. As for the Continental Congress, regional jealousies made any kind of logical action impossible to them. They were to reverse themselves once more.

"Discomposed and angry," Gates rushed to Philadelphia, burst into the State House and spoke before Congress without invitation and in such a manner that some said he must be drunk. He was "called to order and told he must memorialize." His wife and son, far from being happy over a prospect of his retirement to become plain Horatio Gates, Esq., wrote to tell him that he was "disgraced before all America." His son, who had been courting a girl in Boston who would have none of him, wrote: "Dear Papa, As your son and heir, let me intreat you not to tarnish the hitherto unspotted honour of our family by a mean and servile condescension. . . ."

Schuyler was at Ticonderoga by the end of May, conferring

with General St. Clair, who was in command of the fort. A
wooden palisade had been built around the fort and outside of it
was an abatis made of felled trees, their branches pointing outward. At the old French redoubt, six cannon had been mounted,
but the forward fortifications had not yet been repaired. Most of
the time and effort during the weeks of Gates's command had
been spent in fortifying Mount Independence, across the narrow
arm of Lake Champlain, east of the main post. A bridge leading
to it had just been begun. Iron chains, fastened to stone piers,
were to be sunk in this narrow channel and were supposed to stop
the British fleet. Utterly discouraged, Schuyler told St. Clair
privately that Ticonderoga might have to be abandoned. He rode
back to Albany and sent his muster master, Richard Varick, to
the fort to count and report on men and munitions.[5]

British Lieutenant Thomas Anburey was at St. Johns, Canada
on the fourteenth day of June, 1777. He was about to embark
with General Burgoyne upon the long journey which would
qualify him to write his *Travels through the Interior Parts of
America* . . . and he had been listening to news which he wrote
down as Gospel truth: "The Americans are in great force at
Ticonderoga. . . ." On that same fourteenth day of June, Colonel
Varick was at Ticonderoga — mustering and counting men. The
news which Lieutenant Anburey heard was nothing more than
splendid lies told by American scouts who got caught. Young
Colonel Varick wrote the truth, as he saw it, to General Schuyler.

Being as much a "Yorker" as Schuyler, the twenty-four-year
old Colonel Varick was scornful of New Englanders (and they returned the compliment). "Were New England to be at War half
a Century their troops would not be disciplined under officers
from their own states," he said. "Not a corps on the ground under-
stands the simple manual of arms."

As muster master, "I am at a Loss what to do with the Boys,"
Varick confessed. "They are too numerous for so small an Army
and there are also too many Old Men. General St. Clair is at a

stand what should be done at this time. My Duty will oblige me to Strike some out of the rolls."

Varick described the garrison at Fort Ticonderoga, brigade by brigade:

"I found Colonel Francis's a pretty good corps both with respect to Officers and Men, well armed and pretty well clothed — arms neat and clean.

"Col. Brewer's a small corps, indifferently armed and clothed and not much better officered, the arms neat and clean.

"Colonel Warner's Battalion is very indifferently armed and clothed — the arms were very indifferent and they want Bayonets — though the arms they had were clean.

"Colonel Cilly's Battalion a pretty good one and pretty well officered and armed, which arms were neat and clean — the clothing very indifferent.

"Colonel Scammell's Battalion a very indifferent one having many young soldiers badly clothed, the arms were new and good and clean.

"Colonel Jackson's consisted of about 50 or 60 men badly clothed tho' pretty well armed and arms clean.

"None of the troops have uniforms and consequently make a very Awkward appearance and many are very young lads, some of whom I rejected and would have many others had not the situation of our Garrison forbid the Measure. . . ."

There were only 3300 men. Of these 2500 were Continental troops, presumed to have some training and experience. There were 800 militia, with a hundred more still to come according to a different count.

Colonel Seth Warner, whose troops were "indifferently armed and clothed" had once been proclaimed an outlaw in New York State because of his efforts on behalf of the Grants. But he had put all that aside and was writing to the Committees of Safety in the mountain towns asking for militia. "If forty or fifty head of cattle could be brought on with the militia they will be paid for by the commissary on their arrival," he promised. "I should be glad if a few hills of corn unhoed should not be a motive to detain men at home, considering the loss of such an important Post can hardly be recovered. . . ."

On June 28, Richard Varick left Ticonderoga. There were a hundred and four cannon at the two Posts, Ticonderoga and Mount Independence. The "fleet" had sixty-seven guns. He took with him "young Master St. Clair, who is sent down by the General to prevent the trouble of him in case of an attack." Mrs. Schuyler would look after the boy in Albany. General St. Clair had finally decided that the summer at Ticonderoga was not going to be a peaceful outing after all. His scouts had discovered on June 24 "an encampment of the enemy at Gilliland's Creek." This was another name for "Bouquet River," where Burgoyne delivered his speech to the Indians and "after the meeting" had "ordered them some liquor."

It was not surprising that the American scouts discovered the encampment — and without being caught. As Anburey told it, the Indians "had a war dance in which they threw themselves in various postures, every now and then making the most hideous yells." Some of them "dressed with the skins of bulls with the horns upon their heads, others with a great quantity of feathers, and many in a state of total nudity." There was one, Anburey said, "whose modesty" caused him to smile, "because the Indian rather than be divested of every covering had tied a blackbird before him."

Within the walls at Ticonderoga, St. Clair still thought he would wait for more reports from his scouts. On June 26 he still "did not imagine" the British "meant a serious attack on Ticonderoga." Perhaps "this movement of theirs" was "intended to cover an attack on the Mohawk River . . . or an attempt to penetrate New Hampshire."

On June 30 Henry Brokholst Livingston, another of Schuyler's aides, climbed to the log fort on top of Mount Independence, carrying his spyglass with him. He was nineteen, the youngest of the colonels aiding Schuyler; he was brave, inexperienced and an optimist.[6] Burgoyne had now left Crown Point, and Livingston was watching the approach of a water-borne army.

"We have a fine view of their boats," Livingston told his father, the Governor of New Jersey, in a letter he continued to write for several days. We "cannot see that they have brought many Regulars with them — at least the number of red coats in them is very small. The wind having been contrary for several days has prevented their fleet from coming up. The first fair day I expect to see them. Many Betts are depending, that we shall be attacked in the course of this week.

"Our troops are determined and in great Spirits. They wish to be permitted to drive the Savages from Three Mile Point but Gen'l St. Clair chooses to act on the sane side and to risque nothing. The few Alarms we have had have been of great service in making the Men alert and vigilant — but I am afraid the Enemy will repeat them so frequently as to throw them into their former state of indolence and inattention."

On July 1, Livingston saw "the second division of their army." He began to count the British boats. "The second division, in forty bateaux about twenty men each, landed on the eastern shore of Lake Champlain opposite Three Mile Point." Next day "they received a third reinforcement in sixty bateaux." Young Livingston had just seen General Riedesel's corps take up their position on Burgoyne's left.

"Two Hessians have deserted to us," Livingston wrote. "They both seem very intelligent fellows. They agree that Burgoyne commands the army and under him General Riedesel and the German forces. . . . Their dragoons are not mounted but come in expectation of getting horses at this place."

"We are daily receiving additions to our strength," Livingston told his father. . . . "Tomorrow we shall give the British a 13-gun salute," a "feu de joi," "because it will be the anniversary of the ever-memorable 4th of July, 1776, on which day we broke off connections with slavery and became the free and independent States of America."[7]

On the night of the Fourth of July, 1777, German artillery was being hoisted up Sugar Loaf Hill.

The Fall of Ticonderoga

TO GERMAN eyes, Lake Champlain had looked like an inland sea, and a stormy and dangerous one. Reaches of woodland which the Germans supposed to be on the lake shore turned out to be islands, while some of the smaller islands with pointed fir trees growing above cliffs looked in the distance like frigates. Then suddenly the lake narrowed at Crown Point, and it was not surprising that they thought this was a river.

Riedesel's men were ordered to line up in front of their encampment at Crown Point, leaving their tents standing, at the sound of two guns. At four guns they struck tents, loading them on bateaux along with provisions and ammunition. Then the troops embarked, Brunswickers taking the heavy oars. Slowly they inched southward against the current. Brunswick dragoons were leading the whole army. General Phillips was ordered to the right flank or west bank of Champlain, and he encamped three miles north of the fort. Riedesel landed and encamped his men opposite. "We heard their signal guns," wrote Colonel Varick, from within the walls of the fort.

Now the British fleet approached Ticonderoga, with Burgoyne himself aboard the *Royal George*. This was a new frigate, built at St. Johns the previous winter and carrying thirty-two guns. Next in size was the old *Invincible*; then came the gunboats. On July 3 in the afternoon, the "radeau" came up. Burgoyne's heaviest guns were mounted on this raft, which was to be rowed forward straight at the main defenses of the fort. Since the guns on the radeau outranged anything now mounted on the walls, a blast from the raft would open a breach through which the besieging army would march to victory — so the plans went. But the lake water shoaled off suddenly, the radeau grounded, and its guns proved useless. It was ignominiously towed off the mudbank and the guns taken out of it.

Burgoyne's army is sometimes spoken of as "over-artilleried." He had brought heavy guns for the siege of Fort Ticonderoga, and the maps on which he relied made it appear that he had but to float his guns on waterways *almost* to the Hudson. Lieutenant William Twiss[1] was Burgoyne's chief engineer and he had been Controller of Works at St. Johns when Carleton's fleet was built there. Before coming to Canada he had designed new defenses for the British navy yard at Portsmouth, England. He was now thirty-two and faced with the most difficult task in his career, that of moving Burgoyne's guns. Doubtless he was distressed by the failure of the radeau, but he already had a new assignment.

It was General Phillips who had summoned Lieutenant Twiss on the second day of July. Phillips, "taking command of Brigadier General Fraser's corps and one British brigade," circled west and south around the point of land where Ticonderoga stood. He advanced to a hill, Mount Hope, where his Indians flushed out a few men who had been posted there. The American outpost guard got safely into the fort, but, from the vantage point of Mount Hope, General Phillips discovered Sugar Loaf Hill. He sent for Twiss and asked if a road could be built to the top and a battery established there. Twiss said he could build a road in twenty-four hours.

General Phillips moved forward to the Mount Hope area and

asked for Brunswickers to take his place on the west side of the lake. General von Gall's brigade went over. Germans were sent to Twiss for his working party of seven hundred men, and Twiss found a ledge just below the summit of Sugar Loaf where he could mount a battery.

A road to the west side of Sugar Loaf Hill would be for the most part out of sight from Fort Ticonderoga. But a man with a spyglass or some of the scouts from the fort might have discovered activity in the forest, so the new road was cut through dense underbrush during the night. Bushes chopped off too high, in haste, made men stumble in the dark. These working parties were discovered after all, and fired upon. "A man and a horse harnessed to the carriage of a gun were killed." They soon moved out of range. Then these same working parties barely escaped being fired upon by their own men, because no one had thought to tell the British sentries that cannon would be moving along a new road in the nighttime.

On the fourth of July, at about noon, the British occupied Mount Sugar Loaf with a small force from Fraser's advance guard. They began to raise their battery that night. Two twelve-pounders had already been dragged to the foot of the hill and "most of the cattle belonging to the army were employed." Where the "ascent was almost perpendicular" Lieutenant Twiss slung his cannon in a rope cradle and hoisted them by means of ropes and pulleys fastened to trees on upper ledges. This almost incredible feat was accomplished in total darkness, and the maneuver which would have caught the garrison at Fort Ticonderoga like rats in a trap was still a secret. But on the summit of Sugar Loaf, beyond the ledge where the battery was being installed, someone lighted a fire on the night of July 4 — Indians were later blamed for this. On the morning of the fifth, guns were pointed straight down into Fort Ticonderoga with orders not to fire until the battery was complete.

From that low hill on the east bank of Lake Champlain called Mount Independence, rebel spyglasses were trained on Sugar Loaf, across the lake and due west. A light had been seen during the night and now on the morning of the fifth activity could plainly be observed. It did not take long for the Americans to pick out the two-gun battery "seven hundred feet" above Fort Ticonderoga. General St. Clair called his officers in conference, retreat was decided upon, and plans made in haste.

The American troops were not told what was happening, and even Dr. James Thacher, second in command of the sick, was surprised when he was "awakened at mid-night" on the night of July 5 and told to get his "regiment of invalids into boats." It was three in the morning, Sunday, July 6, before all the bateaux were loaded. They set out "up the lake," south of the bridge connecting Ticonderoga with Mount Independence, under a convoy of armed galleys and a guard of six hundred men. Their destination was Skenesborough, thirty miles away.

"Some of the boats were deeply laden," Dr. Thacher wrote. There were "cannon, tents, provisions, invalids and women" in two hundred bateaux. Dr. Thacher was the only one to mention that there were women with the Ticonderoga garrison. He had reason to be grateful to them for they could help him care for his "regiment of invalids."

"The night was moonlight and pleasant," Dr. Thacher continued. "The sun burst forth in the morning with uncommon lustre, the day was fine, the water surface serene and unruffled." Lake Champlain extends southward, with Lake George about four miles to the west over high hills. "The shore on each side exhibited a variegated view of huge rocks, caverns and clefts, and the whole was bounded by a thick, impenetrable wilderness. . . . We could but look back with regret and forward with apprehension. We availed ourselves, however, of the means of enlivening our spirits. The drum and fife afforded us a favorite music; among the hospital stores we found many dozens of choice wine, and, breaking off their necks, cheered our hearts . . ." with the contents. "At three o'clock in the afternoon we reached our destined port at Skenesboro', being the head of navigation for our gallies." Certain that the chain across Champlain between Ticonderoga and Mount Independence would hold back the British fleet, they went ashore, leaving galleys and bateaux "lying at the wharf" with baggage, provisions and cannon still in them and no guard posted.

All cannon left at Ticonderoga were to be spiked. The American battery on Mount Independence was to keep up a cannonade to cover the sound of marching feet as the garrison crossed the bridge, defiled eastward around the mountain and turned south to join General Schuyler at the nearest fort along the Hudson. Orders were to burn Ticonderoga and explode the powder magazine at the last moment. The Mount Independence garrison was to be evacuated to form a rear guard.

The British battery had been mounted in darkness and now the American retreat was to be carried on at night, with equal secrecy. But a strangely similar accident spoiled the American plans. No one knew exactly how it happened, but in the recriminations which followed it was General Fermois who was accused of setting his own house on fire in his panic, long before fires were supposed to break out. Fermois's flaming hut, on top of Mount Independence, lighted the whole scene like a stage. The American retreat was no longer a secret.

Now all was confusion inside the walls of Ticonderoga. Fuses laid to explode the powder magazine were never lighted. Guns were not spiked; provisions were left behind as well as quantities of paper money, the pay of the garrison. Someone remembered to set fire to the bridge leading to the east shore of the lake, but somehow a fire lighted accidentally will sweep all before it while a fire set intentionally will often smoulder and go out. The bridge was only partially damaged.

Nevertheless, the evacuation of Fort Ticonderoga came as a complete surprise to Burgoyne — at least until the first fire broke out. General Fraser saw it from his post on Mount Hope, north of Sugar Loaf. "At dawn of day [Fraser] unfurled the British flag over Ticonderoga." General Riedesel saw something burning inside the American works on Mount Independence, but thought it merely an accident "to one of the enemy's magazines." It was not until full daylight revealed an empty fort that he knew what had happened. He "embarked his men," sailed southward toward Ticonderoga, and "took possession of Mount Independence," which was on his side of the lake. General Fraser, leaving only a picket behind him at Mount Hope, set out in hot pursuit of the Americans, giving orders for the rest of his brigade to follow him. Fraser's detachment crossed the damaged bridge single file and plunged into the forest — Riedesel later following with methodical caution.

Burgoyne was still on board the *Royal George*. With no one to hinder their efforts, men from the British fleet made short work of the iron chain and the stone piers in the lake at the narrows at Ticonderoga. Before noon, their gunboats and even their frigates had a free passage to Skenesborough; they had a favoring wind.

Dr. James Thacher admitted rather apologetically that he wrote up his diary a few days late. But he had by no means forgotten what happened on Sunday afternoon, July 6 on the American side. At Skenesborough, "Here we were, unsuspicious of danger; but behold! Burgoyne himself was at our heels. In less than two hours we were struck with surprise and consternation by a discharge of cannon from the enemy's fleet, on our gallies and bateaux lying at the wharf. By uncommon efforts and industry they had broken through the bridge, boom and chain, which cost our people such immense labor, and had almost overtaken us on the lake, and horridly disastrous indeed would have been our fate.

It was not long before it was perceived that a number of their troops and savages had landed and were rapidly advancing toward our little party. The officers of the guard now attempted to rally the men and form them in battle array . . . but in the utmost panic they were seen to fly in every direction. . . ."[2]

Dr. Thacher ran to one of the bateaux and seized his medicine chest, "carried it a short distance" and then took out such instruments and supplies as his pockets would hold. "A small rivulet named Wood Creek was navigable" for light craft from Skenesborough to Fort Anne, the next American post on the Skenesborough route to the Hudson. A few of the sick men got into boats and escaped that way.[3] Dr. Thacher followed the creek on foot for twelve miles and arrived at Fort Anne at five next morning. This fort was an old Indian trading post, really no more than a blockhouse surrounded by a palisade fence.

Ebenezer Fletcher, sixteen years old and a fifer, left Fort Ticonderoga on foot, with the American garrison under General St. Clair, right after the invalids set off in boats.[4] "Early on the morning of the 6th of July, orders came to strike our tents and swing our packs," he said. "It was generally conjectured that we were going to battle but orders came immediately to march. We marched some distance before light. By sunrise, the enemy . . . pursued us so closely as to fire on our rear. A large body of the enemy followed us all day but kept so far behind us as not to be wholly discovered."

This was Fraser's advance guard, who continued their pursuit of the Americans all day Sunday "without any provisions." Fraser's men "happened to kill a cow in the woods," but they had no bread; and the cow, "divided up among so many, was of little use."

The Americans marched as far as Hubbardton, a settlement in the woods north of Lake Bomoseen, with only nine families living in the entire township. Here, on a partially cleared hilltop, St.

Clair halted for two hours. Then he and the main part of his army marched for Castleton, six miles ahead, leaving Seth Warner in charge of a rear guard with Colonel Ebenezer Francis of Medford, Massachusetts, in command under him. As young Richard Varick had recently reported, Colonel Warner's battalion was "indifferently armed and clothed," but Colonel Francis had "a pretty good corps. . . ." The two officers decided to send some of their men "to bring off the settlers." Although families soon came hurrying over the rough cart tracks from their solitary farms, driving their oxen with wagons full of household goods in pathetic disarray, there was really no time for this attempted rescue.

On Monday, "the morning after the retreat, orders came very early for the troops to refresh and be ready for marching," young Fletcher said. He was in the rear guard because he was recovering from measles and could not march very fast, he explained. "Some were eating, some were cooking and all in a very unfit posture for battle. Just as the sun rose there was a cry, 'The enemy are upon us.' Looking around, I saw the enemy in line of battle.

"Orders came to lay down our packs and be ready for action. The fire instantly began. We were but few in number compared to the enemy at the commencement of the battle and many of our party retreated into the woods. Captain Carr came up and says, 'My lads, advance, we shall beat them yet.' A few of us followed him in view of the enemy. Every man was trying to secure himself behind girdled trees which were standing in that place." Sixteen-year-old Ebenezer Fletcher "made a shelter" for himself and discharged his piece. He reloaded and took aim again, but this time his gun misfired. He had raised his gun once more when he "received a musket ball" in the small of his back. The question arises, had he turned his back to run away? But he showed no embarrassment in telling his tale. He and the men Captain Carr had rallied were nearly surrounded. Young Fletcher's uncle, who was nearby, "carried me back some distance and laid me down behind a large tree," he said. Fletcher was taken prisoner and sent back to Ticonderoga, but afterwards escaped. Someone stole his silver shoe buckles, and he was much distressed, because in the colonies silver shoe buckles were a mark of distinction. But he felt much worse when someone stole his fife.

After the first surprise and confusion, Warner and Francis each rallied his men, and the Battle of Hubbardton lasted for two hours. Colonel Warner ordered a charge which broke the British line, and they fell back. They re-formed under cover of the forest and made a bayonet charge. Warner's were the men "without bayonets," as Varick had reported, yet they broke this first charge and it took a second to make them give ground. Warner sent messages to St. Clair at Castleton for help, and it was said that some of the militia were on their way — but they were too slow. Colonel Francis's men began to break or, as Quartermaster Cogan, who was on the scene, put it, "some behaved and some did not." Colonel Francis was killed "at the head of his men."

General Fraser had come very close to being routed, and had sent urgent messages to Riedesel to bring up reinforcements. Riedesel arrived just in time to observe disorder among the Americans as Colonel Francis fell. Lieutenant Anburey said that General Riedesel got to the field of action at Hubbardton "a considerable time before his men." Anburey was sure that he heard the German General "pouring forth every imprecation against his troops for their not arriving." Riedesel's excited German may have sounded like prodigious swearing to Anburey's English ears, and perhaps it was. But Riedesel's Brunswick troops "after a rapid march of a quarter of an hour" had "arrived, terribly heated, upon an eminence from which could be seen the contending forces."

Riedesel could tell that Seth Warner (whom he called "Colonel von Werner") was about to surround Fraser's left wing, so he ordered his company of jaegers to advance and attack while the rest of his men circled toward the Castleton Road to keep Warner from retreating. He "ordered a band of music to lead the jaegers" so that the Americans would think a whole army was coming. Anburey said the Germans "began singing psalms on their advance" and that Fraser's men "thought from the noise they made that a reinforcement had been sent back from the main body of the American army."

The Brunswickers came on, singing "and at the same time keeping up an incessant firing which totally decided the fate of the day," said Anburey. Burgoyne commended the Germans less enthusiastically, and by degrees he managed to forget who really won the Battle of Hubbardton.

Two hours after the fighting was over, British officers gathered around the body of Colonel Francis. They were reading the papers taken from his wallet when they "heard a bullet whizz by." The captain who held the papers jumped up — then fell, crying out that he was wounded. Smoke from a gun could be seen still hanging in the air but "the fellow, as soon as he had fired, made his escape." This was a strange sort of war, reflected Anburey. Men seemed as ready to fight for "an individual as . . . over an army of thousands." A Captain Ferguson got Colonel Francis's watch, which he said he bought from a drummer boy who had stolen it. This was considered an acceptable way of looting the dead, and when he met Colonel Francis's widow in Boston, months later, he gave it to her.

General Fraser put his advance corps in a state of defense behind some "log works." No provisions had come up, so he sent men out "to shoot some bullocks that were running in the woods." The soldiers cooked their steaks over campfires but had nothing to eat with their meat until it was discovered that one of the men had brought along a strange sort of loot from Ticonderoga. It was gingerbread, sent from home to one of the Americans in the garrison. This was passed around, General

Fraser sharing some of it. Apparently gingerbread was an unfamiliar confection to these particular soldiers, received as a sort of joke and found to their surprise to be very good eating.

The valiant American rear guard had been sure that St. Clair would reinforce them. Men who were with him at Castleton said they could hear the sound of battle six miles away. Now it was assumed that St. Clair would return to attack Fraser; but instead he left Castleton, marching through Dorset, taking time out only to send Schuyler a dispatch — in "great need for provisions," he said. When night fell on the field of Hubbardton, wolves came out and fed upon the bodies of the dead.

On July 10, Burgoyne, comfortably at his ease in Philip Skene's house at Skenesborough, issued one of his General Orders which he composed with so much evident relish:

"On the 6th day of July, the Enemy were dislodged from Ticonderoga by the mere countenance and activity of the army and driven the same day beyond Skenesborough on the Right and beyond Hubarton on the left, with the loss of all their artillery, all their armed vessels, a very great quantity of Ammunition, Provisions and Stores and the greater part of their Baggage."

Burgoyne made no mention of the battery on Sugar Loaf Hill. He complimented everybody except Twiss, the artillery and the "Artificers," who had built the road and hoisted the guns. It was so much more dramatic to say that the Americans ran from the "mere countenance" of the army!

Burgoyne's arithmetic, in his next paragraph, required a little explanation. "On the 7th Brigadier General Fraser, at the head of little more than half the advanced corps, came up with a party of near 200 of the enemy, strongly posted, attacked and defeated them with the loss on the enemy's part of their principal officers, 200 men killed on the spot, a much greater wounded and about 200 made prisoner." Surely General Fraser was to be congratulated for disposing of so many more men than he encountered. But the 200 taken were not the same as the 200 supposedly killed. Colonel Nathan Hale of Hampstead, New Hampshire, got lost in the woods with a company of militia. Mistaking Fraser's foragers out looking for bullocks for a much larger force, he surrendered himself and his men, most of whom were said to be "invalids." Hale was a veteran of Bunker Hill with the reputation of a brave officer, but he died while prisoner of war, unable to clear his name.

After giving a polite nod to General Riedesel for reinforcing Fraser at a crucial moment, Burgoyne proceeded to commend "Lt. Col. Hill who on the 8th, at the head of the 9th Regiment" was attacked near Fort Anne by more than six times his number and repulsed the enemy after a continuous fire of three hours. In consequence of this action, Fort Anne was burnt and abandoned and a party of this Army is in possession of the country on the other side. . . ."

Dr. James Thacher, having arrived safely at Fort Anne, had the American version of the story to tell. "On the 7th instant, we received a small reinforcement from Fort Edward by order of Major General Schuyler and on discovering that a detachment of the enemy under the command of Colonel Hill had arrived in our vicinity, a party from our fort was ordered to attack them in their covert. The two parties soon engaged in a smart skirmish, which continued for several hours, and resulted greatly to our honor and advantage. The enemy being almost surrounded, were on the point of surrendering when our ammunition being expended and a party of Indians arriving and setting up the warwhoop, this being followed by three cheers from their friends the English, the Americans were induced to give way and retreat."

Young Dr. Thacher was curiously lucky. "One British surgeon with a wounded captain and twelve or fifteen privates were taken and brought into our fort," he said. "The surgeon informed me that he was in possession of books etc. taken from my chest at

Skenesborough, and singular to relate, some of the British prisoners . . . had in their pockets a number of private letters from a friend in Massachusetts which were now returned to me." The genial, much liked little doctor (he was "small of stature") married Susannah Hayward of Bridgewater, Massachusetts, at the end of the Revolution, so perhaps she was the "friend" whose letters he prized. "Fort Anne being a small picket fort of no importance, orders were given to set it on fire and on the 8th we departed for Fort Edward, situated about thirty miles to the southward." The abandoning of Fort Anne had been determined in advance by Schuyler, and it was also planned to give up Fort Edward, but not before as many obstacles as possible had been placed in Burgoyne's path. Axe-men were already out felling great trees so that their branches interlocked across Wood Creek. Bridges were being cut and the only road obstructed.

Schuyler was able to use the wilderness itself against Burgoyne, but the wilderness also worked against St. Clair and his men. "Warner, if hard-pressed, will go to Rutland," he wrote Schuyler. And Warner was certainly hard-pressed. They were "hurried at an unmerciful rate through the woods . . . obliged to kill oxen belonging to the inhabitants" whenever they could get them. Before the oxen "were half skinned" the men had to "take a bit and half roast it over the fire then before half done was obliged to march. . . . The Indians took and killed a vast number of our men on the Retreats."[5] Warner reached Bennington and finally marched on to Rutland with only ninety men. St. Clair headed for Fort Edward on the Hudson, and heard that Burgoyne was at Skenesborough, so turned and made for Rutland. He "wandered in the woods" for a week, and finally joined Schuyler with only fifteen hundred men.

General Riedesel was "detached to Castleton with five battalions of the left wing . . . for the purpose of making the rebels believe that the army intended to march in that direction and of giving the loyal inhabitants a chance to join the army" — so he wrote to the Duke of Brunswick, after reporting the news of Ticonderoga and the story of his saving Fraser's men. He "twice asked permission to scatter" the remnant of "Colonel von Werner's men" at Rutland, only "ten hours away." But "Burgoyne will not allow me to do it, pretending that he does not wish me to go so far away from the army." So Riedesel put in his time surveying the possibility of an immediate foray "to the flatlands of the Connecticut river," to confiscate all the horses in that vicinity. He prepared a memorandum which Burgoyne "seemed to like very much."[6]

Riedesel was back in Skenesborough on July 22, writing in French for General Burgoyne's perusal: "The great and rapid successes have suddenly carried the army forward, where of necessity we must advance often. . . . The equipment of the army is of such a kind that our boats are indispensably necessary and from the moment we separate ourselves from them we shall lack everything. Misery will follow. Without transportation of provisions, half the army would be out foraging, the men overcome with fatigue and battalions so weak they are no better than a company . . . The army can move only very slowly and in small companies for lack of resources for transporting all that is indispensable."

"I suppose there are but two sides to choose. We must always remain with the army locked close to a river and not leave it until we have the means of transporting the boats to another, so as never to lack more than 8 days subsistence."

Riedesel now gave his objections to being "locked to a river":

"The army cannot advance except very slowly. We can never profit . . . from the advantages that the hasty retreat of the enemy would furnish us with, nor increase the panic terror which the Rebels feel for the forces of the King."

Numbering his paragraphs carefully, Riedesel said that, second, "The Inhabitants of the country, now much intimidated, would submit voluntarily in a short time and the army would be furnished with everything if they should see appearing, here and there, some detachments; but as the army cannot spread out," the Americans "had everywhere small detachments of their own to keep the people under surveillance." These so-called "detachments" were the local militia, raised by the people for their own protection, and supplied from their own farms and those of their neighbors! General Riedesel had a good deal to learn.

But he proceeded to his third point: "The country into which our army has advanced will recover courage, they will raise new armies, they will succeed in overrunning the country with little Detachments, and some good Rebel could undertake some blow against our communications which could incommode the army more and more as time goes on."

Riedesel now launched into his argument concerning horses. "In order to prevent all these inconveniences it would be necessary to have a mobile army, that is to say, to get hold of some horses sufficient to transport the most essential equipment of the officers, to distribute horses to carry tents and ammunition and to have some horses to set aside for the artillery and the provisions.

"According to my idea, it is very pernicious to transport equipment and tents in Canadian carts, for the carts spoil the roads and cannot get through bad roads without difficulty." The thing to do, Riedesel thought, would be to abandon most of the carts and use "bat horses." This term, much used in the British army, came from the French *bât*, meaning pack saddle, or provisions. Bat horses "go through everything," Riedesel said, "marching on the flanks of the army, instead of crawling along behind," and the men would always have tents and ammunition right at hand. A few carts would still have to be used for heavy provisions and the artillery.

"There is scarcely an inhabitant who has fewer than two or three horses," General Riedesel continued, and a good many of the "inhabitants" would have felt flattered to hear this. It would have come nearer to the truth to say that in the Green Mountains and the rugged Berkshires there was "scarcely an inhabitant." But Riedesel had been told that "on the other side of the Connecticut there are no troops and the country is full of good horses." He "subjoined a calculation" of the number of horses he thought Burgoyne ought to have — beginning with his own Dragoons, who needed 336. He came up with a total of 1147 horses which he thought that his company of Dragoons, "Peters's corps and that of Jessups" [American Loyalists, both of them] could go out and bring in, "under a good officer of the rank of major."

General Riedesel loved horses and had owned many fine ones. He had just bought a horse from an "inhabitant" and paid a good price for it, and his fourth, rather long argument, seems to indicate a slightly troubled conscience. He thought the farmers could get along just as well with oxen. They used horses "only to carry grain to the mill or to take a ride" — and anyway Burgoyne was to pay for the horses, or promise to pay. "Lacking horses," the inhabitants "will not be able to carry news to the rebels so fast and so frequently," and "this small bleeding is less punitive than they deserve, for their treason and bad conduct toward the King. . . . So this action can be defended and justified before God, before the King and Parliament, because the essential interest of the army and of the service of the King is so clear."

12

The Baroness at Fort Edward

THE days had been passing slowly for Mrs. General Riedesel, left behind at Three Rivers in Canada with her children. At first letters came regularly from her husband while Burgoyne's army moved southward along Lake Champlain. Riedesel had nothing but encouraging news as he sailed or encamped. There were no armies in the field against him, no American fleet on the water and not so much as a skirmish with country militia to mar the advance.

As the distance increased, letters were delayed. There was the cold fear in her heart, as Mrs. General read cheerful, reassuring words, that the man who wrote them might not still be alive when his letters reached her. And she loved him so much. But this was all part of being the wife of a soldier, and the Baroness Riedesel smiled confidently before her servants, telling her children that "Papa" was well and that they would see him soon. To her husband she "wrote and urged and implored him to let me come to him," she confessed.

Burgoyne sent triumphant messages back to Canada when the British flag flew over Ticonderoga. He left nine hundred men to hold the fort and the post on Mount Independence, but this did not trouble him, because he was sure that Carleton would send a detachment to relieve these men so that they could rejoin his army. There was a surprise in store for Burgoyne, however — Carleton wrote that "because the post has been taken out of my hands" there would be no sending forward of additional forces. However, some horses previously contracted for were on their way. And a lady was crossing the lake.

This was Lady Christian Henrietta Caroline Acland, daughter of the first Earl of Ilchester. She was twenty-seven years old, never used her real name but preferred to be called "Lady Harriet," and she had come to Canada in 1776 with her husband, Major John Dyke Acland, a member of Parliament. When her husband was wounded in action against the retreating Americans at Chambly, she had "nursed him in a miserable hut" on the Richelieu River. Now Major Acland was wounded again, shot through both thighs by the Americans at Hubbardton. He was carried back to Ticonderoga, and Lady Harriet, who had been staying in Montreal, set out at once to go to him. She was "the most amiable, delicate piece of quality," the impressionable General Gates was to say when he met her. She was also rugged, and this time she was not going to be left behind when her husband once more recovered and re-joined Burgoyne's army.

Madam Riedesel soon heard that Lady Acland had been allowed to follow the army. Her own letters asking to come became increasingly urgent, and she began to pack. There was food to be prepared for the journey; and hams and sausages must be taken to the General, who was surely not eating properly without his wife to look after him. The children's clothes must be ready and nothing forgotten, because this would not be a journey where missing items could be supplied from shops along the way. There was the difficult problem of what to leave behind and how best to protect furs and winter clothing which everyone was certain would not be needed. Frederika Riedesel was an artist at packing chests and boxes, as one of her husband's aides discovered, long later. Her summons to join her husband came in August.

Burgoyne remained in the vicinity of Skenesborough throughout the month of July. His decision to advance upon Albany by
way of Skenesborough and Wood Creek was a fatal move, and
Colonel Skene, commanding the American Loyalists in Burgoyne's
army, was blamed for it. Philip Skene needed a good road to insure the increased success of his gristmill, lumber mill and iron
foundry. This private kingdom of his would have to pay him well
if he was ever to liquidate his debts and support his son, who had
been sent to New York to learn to be a gentleman but who had
learned instead to be a spendthrift. Colonel Skene was delighted
to have the British army "cutting a road" to Fort Anne big enough
to "bring up their cannon." He assured Burgoyne that all the
tenants on his lands were brave Loyalists who would join the
British army.[1]

Skenesborough, the Whitehall of today, is now on the Champlain Canal. Steep cliffs crowned with spruce and pine overlook
the town, which was marked on early maps as a post on the
regular water route from Champlain to New York. Named for this
Scotsman, who was "Lt. Governor of Crown Point and Ticonderoga" and "Surveyor of His Majesty's Wood bordering on Lake
Champlain," Skenesborough was literally his private property. His
various grants amounted to eighty-eight square miles. On taking
out his land patents, Skene had promised to settle a hundred
families but he never intended to sell any land: what he visualized
was a feudal empire, with himself as overlord. Negro slaves worked
his iron mines near Crown Point. Tenants were given three years'
free rent as an inducement to settle in his mountainous wilderness, but they owed him their work in return for implements,
building materials and the provisions he sold them. They soon
owed more than they could ever pay.

Skene had labor troubles even among his slaves. Having rented
them out to some of his settlers, he was astonished to hear that
they had refused to work. They said that this was because he had

"promised to wive them" and had broken his word. He wrote urgently to his New York agent to buy and send up the Hudson, "a Negroe Wench. . . . If she can make up clothes and wash so much the better. And young. I saw one by Advertisement in Gaine's paper that would answer." And again he wrote, "I want a Negroe Wench, hear they are cheap in a Guinea ship. If from the Congo, should be glad of one pregnant to a good Negroe. Let her be young with good teeth and limbs. . . ." In this same letter, he negotiated for "a stallion as advertised to be sold at the Coffee House if he is handsome. . . ."

Colonel Skene was a man after Burgoyne's own heart. Burgoyne was a guest in Skene's stone mansion which, thanks to Schuyler's stern measures against looting, was still furnished handsomely. When Skene talked about the hundreds of loyal tenants ready to spring to arms, Burgoyne set himself to one of his favorite tasks, the writing of a proclamation.

"*Instructions to* GOVERNOR SKENE
"*Headquarters, Skenesborough House*   *July 15, 1777*

"You are to consider persons who shall take the Oath of Allegiance and sign the declaration hereto annexed, as the First Objects for protection. Such, however, as shall decline signing, shall remain unmolested Provided they strictly comply with the Manifesto.

"You are to Require from every Township an immediate Return of the Names of the Inhabitants who are with the Rebels, distinguishing those who have been Compelled and those who engaged Voluntarily.

"You are also to Require Return of the numbers of Horned Cattel and Waggons and Carts in each Township and also of the Grain and Mills to grind it. All Cattel and Corn faithfully returned will be paid for in solid coin, at a reasonable price. . . .

"All persons bringing in firearms shall receive a Guinea for every one that shall be in Repair and such Persons as shall enlist in any of the Provincial Corps will be allowed besides that Gratuity, to keep their Arms for their own use.

"Persons so enlisting will also be permitted to choose their Corps and to name the space of time they are willing to serve.

"You will inform the People in General of my powers to Compell and my inclination to Protect. . . ."

Just in case that "power to Compell" was not entirely clear, Burgoyne brought up the matter of his "Five hundred Savages from the Upper Nations."

"Inhabitants of the Several Townships" were invited to send "10 persons or more from each Township" to hear this "Manifesto" read.

Burgoyne had moved forward, but General Riedesel was still at Skenesborough, trying to expedite provisions, when he wrote his wife that she might join him. The country was "secure," he said: a fine new road was being built and all the bridges repaired, all the way to Fort Edward twelve miles below the southern end of Lake George. Hard on the heels of the General's letter came the aide-de-camp he had sent to bring his family across the wilderness. Captain Willoe was English, especially appointed to Riedesel by Lord George Germain. He was young, naïve, very fond of children and soon to become the much-loved friend of little Frederika and her sister, Augusta; and as soon as Caroline could talk she called him "Lo-lo." Two days after Captain Willoe reached Three Rivers, the Baroness was ready to set out. Accustomed by now to army delays, Captain Willoe must have been astonished at Mrs. General's efficiency.

Two boats carried the little family of travelers from Three Rivers across the St. Lawrence and up the Richelieu. One of the boats belonged to General Riedesel, and there were troops on board, commanded "by the good Sergeant Bürick." He took charge of Mrs. General's baggage, not only on this journey — he "kept an eye on it" all through the dangerous days ahead.

The Baroness did not mention the date when she left Three Rivers, so it is not easy to figure out just how long the journey lasted. "Night overtook us and we found ourselves obliged to land on an island," she said, but this was surely not the first night. It would have been easy enough to land anywhere along the banks of the Richelieu, so on this particular night they must have been on Lake Champlain. "The other boat, which was more heavily laden and was not so well manned, had not been able to keep up." So they had "neither beds nor candles, and what was worse, nothing to eat. . . ."

On the island where they landed they "found nothing but the four walls of a deserted, unfinished house." Bushes grew inside the house walls, and the Baroness covered them with the ample wool traveling cape she had brought along. There were cushions in the boat, so she sent her servants for these and felt satisfied that she had made a reasonably comfortable bed.

Outside the walls of the abandoned house a soldier lit a camp-fire and put a pot on to boil. The Baroness "looked wistfully at it" and asked the man what he was cooking. "Potatoes," he said. Before long they began to smell so good that Mrs. General and her children felt desperately hungry. Still, the man "seemed so happy in the possession of them" that she tried not to ask for any. Finally she broke down and wanted to know if she could have "just a few." The soldier gave her half — "maybe a dozen," she said — and "at the same time handed me two or three short candle-ends he had in his pocket." This gave Mrs. General "great joy," because her children had been afraid to go to sleep in the dark. She gave the soldier "a thaler — which made him as happy" as she was.

The second boat finally arrived with Captain Willoe on board. But he looked pale, and he was evasive when Madam Riedesel asked him what the matter was. He spoke of a storm that threatened, and said he'd like to break camp and find another island. This made very little sense to Mrs. General, who assured him that she liked it where she was. She was surprised to hear him ordering fires to be lighted which were kept burning all night. It seemed as though Captain Willoe and some of the men were unnecessarily noisy as they clumped around the abandoned, roofless house, knocking at the bushes with sticks.

The Baroness and her family slept well, nonetheless. Provisions were unloaded from the boat that had arrived late, and they had a good breakfast cooked over campfires among the rocks down by the lake shore. Captain Willoe looked weary and admitted he hadn't slept. Mrs. General asked him why he had seemed so anxious the night before and laughingly chided him for being so noisy and restless during the night. He was forced to explain. One of the men in the laggard boat had happened to mention the name of the island which they had chosen for their camp: it was Isle aux Sonnettes, or "Rattlesnake Island."

"We made haste to finish our breakfast," said the Baroness. Now that she had been told this news she said she saw "skins and slime of these nasty creatures everywhere," and she remembered that she had heard of German soldiers who had died as a result of rattlesnake bite. There were no rattlesnakes in Brunswick, Germany.

They "ferried over Lake Champlain and came at noon to Fort John," Mrs. General said. "We were received by the commander with much kindness and courtesy. It was this way everywhere, because my husband was so much loved by the English and the inhabitants of the country." Madam Riedesel forgot that the sight of a pretty woman and her nice children would be wonderfully welcome to a man exiled at some remote outpost. As to the "inhabitants," there were varied experiences in store.

Wolf's Island was to have been the next stop, but there was no going ashore. A thunderstorm came up which was "the more terrible" because the thunder echoed and reverberated along the rocky shores of the lake. It seemed to the Baroness "as if we were lying at the bottom of a caldron surrounded by mountains and great trees." They had left the small boats which carried them up the Richelieu and had been put aboard a frigate, for which they were thankful because they felt sure that a bateau would have been swamped by the waves.

Next day they reached Ticonderoga, but passed it by with scarcely a halt except to arrange for transportation across the portage to Lake George.

"Captain Anstruther, an exceedingly good and amiable man who commanded the 62nd Regiment, undertook to do the honors" at Fort George. Mrs. General and her family reached the southern end of Lake George "about noon"; Captain Anstruther ordered the best meal he could in view of the fact that the Americans had successfully evacuated Fort George well before any of Burgoyne's army got there and had most inconsiderately carried off all provisions. In any case, Mrs. General's presence in this burnt-out, barely habitable post made dinner a festive occasion.

The Americans had built a "military road" from Fort George to Fort Edward, on the Hudson.[2] On evacuating, after the fall of Ticonderoga, they had done a good job of cutting bridges and throwing trees to obstruct it, but a "new" road had just been built. "In the afternoon, we seated ourselves in a calash," said Madam Riedesel, "and reached Fort Edward on the same day, which was the 14th of August."

The Hudson at Fort Edward was not the mighty river that Madam Riedesel was to cross and recross in days to come. Here it was but a small stream, having an island in the middle of it where once a wooden barracks stood, a hospital for the wounded of the French and Indian wars. This building had now been torn down, the beams and boards carried off to build houses in a tiny settlement. Ford Edward itself stood on the east bank of the Hudson.

Built by the French, it was once star-shaped with a central tower like a European castle.[3] In spite of this ambitious design, Fort Edward was never built of stone, however. It was only a log fort, and no one had repaired it. "There is nothing but the ruins of it left," General Schuyler had written to Washington on July 26, 1777. "I have frequently galloped my horse in on one side and out the other. But when it was in the best condition, with the best troops to garrison it and provided with every necessity, it would not have stood a two days' siege after batteries had been opened on it. It is situated in a bottom on the banks of the river, and surrounded with hills from which the parade may be seen within point-blank shot." Fort Edward was built to withstand Indian arrows but not Burgoyne's guns, and Schuyler was explaining to General Washington that it must be abandoned by the Americans when the proper time came.

It was a pity that the Baroness Riedesel could not have seen the village of Fort Edward and the farms around it before General Burgoyne had moved forward with his army. Lieutenant William Digby, of the "53rd or Shropshire Regiment of Foot," who was by no means a poet, was almost lyrical when he described the scene on July 29. "Our tents were pitched in a large field of as fine wheat as I ever saw, which in a few minutes was all trampled down." Next day Digby's regiment "moved on farther to rising ground about a mile south of Fort Edward and encamped in a beautiful situation." They could see "the most romantic prospect of the Hudson's river interspersed with many small islands. . . ." There was "a fine plain around the fort which appeared doubly pleasing to us who were so long buried in the woods." Albany was "about 46 miles away," Digby thought. "The land improves much and no doubt in a little while will be thickly settled." He and most of the others, the Germans especially, who had come through from Skenesborough, had begun to wonder why the rebels would fight over such a wilderness.

Digby left Ford Edward just in time to carry away a pleasant impression. On July 30, Burgoyne's orders present a different picture of the newly acquired post. "Each regiment of the Line will turn out 20 men, burn and bury old meat, rubbish and every other nuisance in or near the camp, under the direction of the Provost. This is not confined merely to the ground where the troops are encamped on, but extended to every nuisance and unwholesome thing about the camp." It was a standing order that "new and clean Necessaries are to be made in the rear of every cantonment and encampment every week and the old ones filled up"; and that "at least six inches' depth of Earth should be thrown into the Necessaries in use every morning." But the men had been living in the swamps south of Skenesborough from July ninth to the twenty-second, clearing Wood Creek and building a causeway. There was no way of building new "Necessaries," and dysentery was epidemic by July 29 — when they got orders to move to high ground beyond.

A great disappointment was in store for the Baroness Riedesel when her calash jounced over the new road into the tiny town of Fort Edward. Her General was not there to meet her! The little girls probably cried. But Augusta, just six now, Frederika, three, and Caroline a little over a year were already referred to as "the little ladies." They were big girls now, as their mother doubtless reminded them. And the Riedesel family found that everything had been made ready for them in a little house down by the river. It was known as "the Red House" and there was a large yard around it and a big barn close by where the children could play. "I had only one room for my husband, myself and my children," wrote Mrs. General. "My women servants slept in a kind of hall." Other rooms in the little house were occupied by General Riedesel's aides.

Every one of the few houses in the little town of Fort Edward was crowded with people. If the Baroness noticed it, she made no comment. Crowded towns were common enough in Europe, and perhaps she had yet to learn that Americans liked to spread out in their great half-tamed country, each man in the midst of his own woods and fields. These people who were huddled together in Fort Edward had come in from outlying farms because of Burgoyne's Indians. Of course not all escaped. Neighbors found nine members of the Allen family tomahawked and scalped, having been surprised inside their house at dinner. One man had been killed while trying to get a horse from the barn so as to ride for help; another lay dead and mutilated at the door where he had been defending the women. Two little children, who had hidden under a bed, had been dragged out and tomahawked. Neighbors buried the dead — some of them standing by with guns ready while others dug a common grave. Another family, by the name of Barnes, was wiped out before reaching Fort Edward.[4]

On the twenty-seventh of July, Jane McCrea was visiting a family friend, Mrs. Sarah McNeil. Jane was engaged to a former neighbor, David Jones, a Loyalist who had enlisted in Burgoyne's army at Crown Point and who was now a lieutenant under General Fraser. Jane was about twenty years old. Her father had been a Presbyterian minister, but both parents were now dead and she lived with her brother John, not far from Fort Edward but on the other side of the Hudson. John McCrea had been a colonel in the American army during the expedition to Canada the previous year.

Jane McCrea crossed the river to visit Mrs. McNeil just before the Americans withdrew from Fort Edward.[5] It was said that she and Lieutenant David Jones had managed to exchange letters across the lines, and that they planned to be married as soon as Burgoyne's army occupied the town. She could then go forward with the troops along with other officers' wives. But Burgoyne's Indians were traveling in advance of Fraser's advance guard.

The story of Jane McCrea has been told many times with imaginary details. It was said that Lieutenant Jones sent a party of Indians to escort her to him and that, at a signal, she came out of Mrs. McNeil's house "in bridal array" — that she was an unusually beautiful girl with hair of a "golden-red." Much effort has recently gone into the winnowing out of facts, and it seems clear that Indians were marauding and that they broke into the McNeil house. A Negro servant and her child hid in the cellar, but Mrs. McNeil and Jane were dragged out and the young girl put on a horse. Mrs. McNeil was "very corpulent and unable to mount a horse," so they made her walk.

One first-person account survives, that of Samuel Standish, written when applying for his pension for service in the Revolution:

"We were marching to Fort Edward and, while there, with others, were called on to relieve a guard on a hill north of the Fort. Went and relieved the guard, had not been there long before we heard an Indian scream and instantly was fired upon by them. We ran towards the river and the Fort and before I arrived I met three Indians coming from the river between me and the fort, who all fired upon me but missed me, when I was taken up the hill near a spring, was there stripped of my hat, coat and handkerchief and pinioned by them and after a short time I saw a party of Indians coming with two women. They came up the hill to a spring and seemed to be in a quarrel. They shot one of the women and scalped her. This woman I knew to be Jennie McCrea."

It is said that Lieutenant David Jones recognized Jane's red-gold hair trailing from the small, circular piece of her scalp which hung from a pole as a trophy in the Indian camp. The Indians had hidden her body beside the road, but when she was found, her brother, who was in the American rear guard, was allowed to give her burial. Mrs. McNeil was unharmed, but she had not seen the murder. And the Indians, finding themselves less praised for their exploit than they expected, said that Jane had been killed by a bullet from the gun of a retreating American, before they scalped her. Burgoyne called them to account, but as he had already said that they could scalp the dead he let them go with a reprimand.

The story of Jane McCrea had tremendous impact upon the American so-called "rebels." It spread by word of mouth, and many who were loyal in their hearts to Great Britain were grieved and angered to the point of changing sides. Others, who had been apathetic, feeling that one government was about as good or as bad as another, now became actively, genuinely rebellious because of this tragedy.

The Baroness Riedesel never mentioned Jane McCrea in her letters or journals, or, if she did, the story never reached the printed version of her *Berufs Reise.* Some of the horror of war her husband and his devoted young aides succeeded in keeping from her, but Burgoyne exchanged several letters with American officers on the subject of Jane McCrea and it seems probable that Frederika Riedesel heard about it. Her heart must have contracted as she thought of her own little girls, and it is safe to say that her respect for Burgoyne was not greatly increased. Even among his men, it was hinted that Burgoyne was afraid of his own Indians and dared not punish them.

General Riedesel came to the Red House at Fort Edward on the fifteenth of August and stayed until the sixteenth. "On that day, he was obliged to rejoin the army," to his wife's "great sorrow." The General's new post was Fort Miller — which was just another blockhouse surrounded by palisades, built originally for the protection of fur traders' goods. There was not a "trace left of any fortifications," General Schuyler had written to Washington, as he prepared his gradual retreat down the Hudson.

General Riedesel had gone forward to direct the sending out of a detachment, mainly of Germans, but with a few British troops and American Loyalists. Burgoyne had liked Riedesel's plan of a foray into the hinterland to seize horses, but he had put off doing anything about it while at Skenesborough. Now he could see that the difficulty of moving artillery was going to be so great that horses were a prime necessity. Colonel Skene was going on the expedition with one of Burgoyne's proclamations in his pocket. The response at Skenesborough had been disappointing, but Skene still said that he knew where there were great numbers of Loyalists.

The German dragoons were still slogging along in their cumbersome boots, entangling their great sabres in the underbrush and getting themselves more and more laughed at by British fellow soldiers.

They were going to a place called Bennington. Philip Skene said that at Bennington there was an American army depot with provisions, ammunition, and plenty of horses. Everything was to be had for the taking. The German dragoons were going to walk to Bennington, but they were sure they would come back on horseback.

13

Bennington

GENERAL Riedesel had prepared a blueprint for Burgoyne's ill-fated attack on Bennington when he wrote his memorandum at Skenesborough with its plan for seizing the horses of the inhabitants. Later, however, he pointed out that what was true on the twenty-second of July was no longer true on the sixteenth of August. In July "the inhabitants of the country were much intimidated," he had said, but he accurately foretold that they would "recover courage." They had more courage than the invaders realized. What the Americans needed was time to organize, and this Burgoyne gave them while he built roads and causeways and struggled with his guns.

The small towns of Vermont and New Hampshire had Committees of Safety, like the larger towns and cities all over the country. Hampered by distance, by pitifully small numbers of fighting men and by lack of weapons, they nevertheless went to work in their own defense. Charlestown, New Hampshire — often referred to as "Number 4" in colonial documents — was an American military base. Indians once had taken captives from this pioneer town. Now American militia trained on the village green, and a military road had been built in the direction of Crown Point. So General Stark sent a messenger with a letter to Colonel

Bartlett, chairman of the Committee of Safety at Charlestown. On the seventeenth of July Colonel Bartlett replied:

"I expect to march tomorrow or next day. We are detained a good deal for want of Bullet Molds as there is but one pair of them in town. . . . I am afraid we shall meet with difficulty in procuring utensils to cook our victuals in, as the troops have not brought any. . . . There is four pieces of small cannon at this place that looks good but wants to be cleaned out and put on carriages . . . there is people here that says they can do it. As there is very little rum in store, if some could be forwarded to us it would much oblige us."

Seth Warner was in Manchester, Vermont, on July 20, when he appealed to "all officers in the several counties. . . . The frontier is where there is a body of Troops sufficient to stand against the enemy," he wrote — and he had only five hundred men. He sent messengers riding southward, from town to town, because "the counties farther south need not feel safe" now that Ticonderoga had fallen. All troops "are desired to bring Kittles and materials for cooking. This Express is to alarm the Inhabitants as he goes through."

On July 24 the Assembly of New Hampshire voted to raise three battalions and place them under the command of General Stark and send them to Vermont "to oppose the ravages of the coming forward of the enemy." Colonel Warner sent a major to show the troops the best road to Manchester.

Scouts were dispatched to keep an eye on Burgoyne. One Josiah Farnsworth, "duly sworn," said that he and his brother had gone to Skenesborough "on Sunday last" — which would have been the twenty-seventh of July. He had heard Colonel Skene say "he would cut a road out towards Fort Edward if the Cut but stood a day." And Farnsworth declared on oath that he "saw the Indians cut both hands off three prisoners lately taken and afterwards hanged two up by the heels on a tree and roasted them, the other they let go. . . ." When the "Deponent heard the cries of those that burned" he "came away," he said. He couldn't swear to what "he heard some say," that "the Indians afterward ate the flesh of them they roasted." But when New Hampshire and Massachusetts militia began to come in, and when their own Green Mountain Boys began to assemble, it must have been good news in Farnsworth's home town of Granville, only about ten miles southeast of Skenesborough.

Lead was the most difficult item for the Americans to get hold of. Stockbridge, Massachusetts, sent in "all their town stock" and sent express riders to other towns, who took "weights from sundry clocks" until most of Berkshire County had to tell time by the sun.[1] At Bennington "the Dishes, Plates and Spoons" had all been "melted into ball." The "powder left at Pittsfield" would not have been "sufficient to make an Alarm," and there were "no Select men or Committee men but what is gone forward. . . . A few Squaws could take the whole town," for they had no arms or ammunition. Mr. Williams of Pittsfield wrote to the Commandant of the Armory at Springfield, Massachusetts, where Washington had located a factory for the making of arms: "Notwithstanding the Order you have received from His Excellency General Washington not to deliver arms to the Militia, yet I am confident you will judge it for the good of the Service upon this emergency to Deliver out, and if you cannot think of a more proper Person, I will be accountable, if you send 100 Stands which I will endeavor to forward to whom you shall direct at Bennington or elsewhere. . . ."

The news that Stark and Warner were gathering an army was brought to General Schuyler, who had retreated to Stillwater, in the vicinity of Saratoga.[2] Kościuszko was with him, able to make himself understood because of Schuyler's knowledge of French, and together they had looked over a high plateau — where an American army could encamp, entrench and block Burgoyne's further progress down the Hudson. But, on the last day of July,

General Schuyler made one of his tactless blunders caused by his "Yorker" blind spot. He sent Major General Benjamin Lincoln of the Continental Army to Manchester, Vermont. "Colonel Warner is on the Grants with a small body of Continental troops and some militia, and expects reinforcements in a day or two by General Stark with a body of Militia from New Hampshire," Schuyler told Lincoln. "You will please to repair to Manchester, the place where the above troops are collecting, and take command of the whole."

General Lincoln set out according to orders — a fat man whose girth had not been reduced by war's privations. After his arrival on the Grants, his almost daily letters to Schuyler were most unhappy ones. On August 6 the tall, broad-shouldered Stark, his face as angular as though chipped from granite, rode into Manchester at the head of his men. Not all had arrived, but he expected a total of fourteen hundred militia. Lincoln had ambled off to Bennington, but had left orders for Stark to join Schuyler, at Saratoga, at once. Stark said that "by his instructions from the New Hampshire Assembly," he was free to join Schuyler or not, just as he pleased. Stark had no commission in the Continental Army, having resigned in a quarrel over promotions.

At Bennington, General Lincoln found "a considerable quantity of flour and several hundred bushels of salt which may draw the attention of General Burgoyne and induce him to send a party this way in order to destroy them and distress the inhabitants." He thought the thing to do would be to "send the flour to Stillwater, if it is wanted in the army, escorted by ye troops marching that way." It seemed to have escaped his attention that there were no troops marching that way, but he did notice that Stark "seems to be exceedingly soured and thinks he hath been neglected and . . . is determined not to join the Continental Army till Congress gives him his rank there-in."

On August 8, while General Lincoln was in Bennington trying in vain to get his new command to obey his orders, Burgoyne sent an order to General Riedesel which Riedesel obeyed with alacrity. Everything was to be arranged with Colonel Baum of the dragoons "so that he may march tomorrow." Burgoyne had just been to Fort George, and "from this place," at the southern end of Lake George, he had "collected all the Sacks he could hear of, to be delivered to Lt. Col. Baum to carry flour. . . ."[3] On August 9, Lieutenant Colonel Baum marched from Fort Edward to Fort Miller, with the dragoons. Here he was to receive more troops for his detachment for the Bennington expedition, from General Fraser's advance guard.

Ordered for Baum's detachment were 200 Brunswick dragoons, "Captain Fraser's Light Company of 50, Col. Peter's Provincial Corps, 150 men," and 56 men from the Canadian Volunteers — plus 100 Indians.[4] But on August 10 Baum was delayed, "the Provincials and Indians intended for him being gone to Stillwater." One hundred Germans were ordered from Breymann's corps to make up the deficiency. Some Provincials and Indians also joined Baum, but not as many as first ordered.

Taking a large sheet of sturdy writing paper and folding it vertically down the middle, General Riedesel had written out Baum's orders to the left of the fold, leaving a right-hand column blank for Burgoyne's comments or corrections.[5] "You are to proceed by the route from Batten Kill to Arlington and take post so as to secure the pass from Manchester. You are to remain there till the detachment of Provincials under Captain Sherwood shall join you from the southward. You are then to proceed to Manchester, where you are to take post so as to secure the mountains on the road from Manchester to Rockingham; hence you will detach the Indians and light troops to the northward toward Otter Creek. On their return and also on receiving intelligence that no enemy is in force in the neighborhood of Rockingham, you will proceed by road over the mountains to Rockingham, where you will take post. This will be the most distant post on the expedition." By modern roads, this little town of Rockingham, on the Connecticut River, would be about eighty-five miles away. Apparently neither Riedesel nor Burgoyne had any idea of the distance, so this was to be such a rapid foray that the troops would take no tents.

From Rockingham, Baum's detachment was to "descend by the Connecticut River to Brattlebury." And from that place, "by the quickest march," they were to return "by the great road to Albany." From Rockingham to Brattleboro on present-day roads the distance is about twenty-six miles. Here the "great road to Albany" goes west, on approximately the present route 9, to Bennington, a distance of about forty-one miles. Considering the rugged mountainous country, and the state of the primitive, stony dirt roads of that day, with their steep grades and sharp turns, Baum and his men would have had quite a ramble even if no enemy had been in force.[6]

"During your whole progress, your detachments are to have orders to bring in to you all horses fit to mount the dragoons under your command," the orders went on, "or to serve as bat horses to the troops; they are likewise to bring in saddles and bridles as can be found." "The number of horses requisite, besides those for the mounting of the dragoons, ought to be 1300." Written in, on the right side of the page, this was Burgoyne's estimate of how many horses the detachment was to bring in. Riedesel had already said that the dragoons needed 336. "If you can bring more" than this total of 1636, Burgoyne wrote, "so much the better."

But this was not all. The narrow roads were not only to be choked with horses, but Baum's "parties were likewise to bring in waggons and other convenient carriages, with as many draft oxen as will be necessary to draw them, and all cattle fit for slaughter. . . ."

Baum would have Colonel Skene with him, to help him "distinguish the good subjects from the bad." But he was to "make hostages of the most respectable people . . . to insure . . . the

delivery of horses and cattle, waggons and harness." "Good" inhabitants were to be paid for their horses and cattle, but not in
money — they were to get paper receipts, which they must later
bring into Burgoyne's camp. Of course "bad" inhabitants got
nothing, but Baum was to "use all possible means against plundering." The Indians were to be paid for horses brought in.

"The dragoons themselves must ride and take care of the horses
of the regiment. Those horses which are destined for the use
of the army must be tied together in strings of ten each in order
that one man may lead the horses." Baum was to use unarmed
men of Peters's corps and inhabitants he could trust to "conduct"
the horses. At this point it seems to have occurred to the Generals
Burgoyne and Riedesel that Baum was going to have his hands
full with all those horses, cattle and wagons. He was to send back
detachments of them from time to time.

Then there was the possibility of the detachment's being attacked. In their progress down the Connecticut River Valley they
would have the "defile of the mountains" behind them. Baum
was "always to bear in mind that the corps is too valuable to let
any considerable loss be hazarded on this occasion," and a retreat
through the mountains "might be difficult." He was to "endeavor
to be well informed of the force of the enemy's militia in the
neighboring country." This was written on the right, or Burgoyne's
side of the ledgerlike page. On Riedesel's side was written, "It is
highly probable that the corps under Mr. Warner, now supposed
to be in Manchester, will retreat before you." It was "Mr.
Warner" now, not "Colonel. von Werner." Both Burgoyne and
Riedesel were underestimating the Americans.

On August 10, "His Excellency General Burgoyne changed the
route first intended for the detachment and ordered . . . [it] . . .
direct to Bennington." He had heard that Bennington was a depot
for ammunition, lead, horses, and flour.

On August 11 Baum marched out, not forgetting the flour bags.
He took post on the Batten Kill, a sizeable stream emptying

into the Hudson but finding its way there in a most devious manner.

On the twelfth he proceeded to Cambridge, New York, leaving the Batten Kill to its wanderings, as he moved southward down a fertile valley. His "advanced guard fell in with and defeated a party of Rebels; took 8 prisoners, 1000 bushels of wheat, 150 bullocks and several other articles," which he sent back to Burgoyne's camp.

"The accounts you have given me are very satisfactory," Burgoyne wrote, dating his dispatch August 14 and sending it by courier. He wanted to know if the road to Cambridge, New York, would be "practicable for a large corps with cannon." And he added, "You will please to send to my camp as soon as possible Waggons and draft cattle and likewise such other cattle as are not necessary for subsistence. Let the waggons and carts bring off what flour and wheat they can. . . ."

Baum had now heard that there were militia at Bennington, and he wanted orders. Burgoyne told him "to possess Bennington" if he could; if the enemy were too strongly posted, he was to "take such post as you can maintain until you hear from me. I will either support you in force, or withdraw you."

Meanwhile Stark continued his argument with Lincoln. From the point of view of good discipline, his refusal to co-operate and place himself under Lincoln's orders was shocking. His stubborn attitude turned out, nevertheless, to be a powerful stroke of luck for the Americans. Writing politely to Schuyler, Stark explained that he had consulted with Colonel Seth Warner "of this state" — namely, Vermont, a state the "Yorker" Schuyler refused to recognize, as Stark well knew — and everyone was of the opinion that Stark's men were too tired to march to Stillwater to join Schuyler. They were going to Bennington. "Fifty Indians have been seen this day [April 13] at Cambridge," Stark added. "I have sent 200 men to oppose them doing any mischief."

Baum was now on the road to Bennington. Most of the "defeated party of Rebels" encountered by Baum on the road to Cambridge were now on their way to Bennington too — via Arlington, or by North Hoosic, or just by way of trails of their own. They were sniping at Indians as they went, hoping to save their own scalps so as to fight another day. Reaching Bennington before Baum did, they spread the news of his approach.

Baum arrived at the Sancoik mill at "8 in the morning" on August 14. He was feeling pleased. He had been told of "a party of the enemy being in possession" of this mill. Writing with his paper placed on the head of a flour barrel, he had "the honour to report" to General Burgoyne that the rebels had "abandoned the mill at our approach but in their usual way fired from the bushes and took their road to Bennington. A Savage was slightly wounded." So much for the vaunted marksmanship of the frontier! Baum was a little annoyed, however, because these rebels "broke down the bridge, which has retarded our march above an hour."

In the mill Baum found "78 barrels of very fine flour, 20 barrels of salt and some pearl and potash."[7] He had ordered "30 Provincials" to guard the loot at the Sancoik mill, and also the bridge — when it was repaired. Five prisoners, taken at the mill, told Baum that there were 1500 to 1800 men at Bennington "but are supposed to leave it at our approach." Baum promised to "fall on the enemy to-morrow early" and he made a casual comment: "The Savages cannot be controlled. They ruin and take everything they please."

The Sancoik mill belonged to a Loyalist, so Colonel Skene stepped in to order other Loyalists to get the mill going. "Mr. Bull will have the department of grinding as he is a good miller," Skene reported to Burgoyne. "He is to grind as fast as possible and take receipts for all flour delivered to wagons or carts." The "solid coin" which Burgoyne had promised would be forthcoming — sometime.

On the morning of August 14, as Baum crossed the bridge, now at last repaired, and set off down the road to "fall upon the enemy," he saw "about 700 of the enemy" coming toward him. He stopped and loaded one of his two four-pounder brass cannon and had a shot at them. They retreated. They were an advance party sent out to look for the enemy — and one look was enough, it seemed. Baum imagined that he was only three miles from Bennington, but he was eight miles away. A Loyalist told him that the rebels were well fortified at the town, so he "took post" as advised by Burgoyne.

The post was at the summit of an extremely steep little hill. Below it wound the Walloomsac River, and Baum placed a gun at the bridge over it, just in case some rebels might dare again to approach. He then sent to Burgoyne for the promised reinforcements.

The fifteenth was a rainy day and Stark's main body remained in camp — not in the town of Bennington but on David Henry's farm, about a mile an a half below Baum's post. The Americans spent the day throwing up breastworks and sending out scouting parties, which now and then fired a few shots to keep Baum where he was. Next morning, Baum saw "several bands of armed men near his camp." Skene told him the bands were Loyalists.

"On Saturday, August 16, at twenty minutes past three in the afternoon, the battle began in earnest, we being on every part of them." So wrote Peter Clark of Lyndeboro, a farmer, justice of the peace, and a rebel. He commanded sixty men, and he said that the "Battle held about ½ an hour," as near as he could tell, "and was equal to Bunker Hill excepting there was not so many cannon. The enemy had two brass field pieces, we had none. . . ."

Jesse Field, a man from Bennington "belonging to Captain Dewey's Company of Militia," was sent "across the river, nearly against" or opposite Baum's hilltop post, and then "over the hills and forded the river again below the enemy and came up in their rear from the southwest. . . ." When they came in sight of the breastworks which Baum had thrown up, they halted, "because some of our party did not come on so quick as they ought to have done," Field said. He heard firing from the Americans sent around the hill to the north. "My God, what are we doing — they are killing our brothers!" an officer exclaimed. Just then the order came to advance.

"We pressed forward and as the Hessians rose above the works to fire, we discharged our pieces at them and we kept advancing and about the second fire they left their works and ran down the hill to the south and southeast. We followed on over their works and pursued them down over the hill. The day was very warm, they were in full dress and very heavy armed, and we in our shirts and trousers and thus had much the advantage in pursuit. Some were killed in their works, many killed and taken in going down the hill and others on the flat upon the river."

From the top of the hill, inside the "Hessian" Baum's entrenchments, a Tory or Loyalist volunteer on the British side told how things looked to him on that same fatal sixteenth of August:

"We were all ready when we saw the rebels coming to attack us and we were on such a high bank that we felt perfectly safe and thought that we could kill any body of troops sent against us before they reached the place we stood upon. We had not expected however that they would approach us under cover but supposed we should see them all the way. We did not know that a little gulley that lay below us was long and deep enough to conceal them. . . . The first we saw of the party coming to attack us, they made their appearance right under our guns. . . .

"Several of us leveled our pieces at once. I took as fair aim at them as ever I did at a bird . . . but we had to point so much downwards it made a man but a small mark. We fired together but to our surprise, they all sprang up the bank so that they did not give us time to load and came jumping into the midst of us

with such a noise that we thought of nothing except getting out
of the way of their muskets as fast as possible. I saw all my com-
panions going over the wall on the other side and I went too.

"We had open fields before us and we scattered in all directions. . . . I looked back and saw a raw-boned fellow running
like a deer only a short distance behind me and gaining on me at
every step."

The young Tory threw away his gun, which "was only a useless
bother for it was discharged and had no bayonet, and although a
valuable one," he thought his "pursuer would stop to pick it up."
But the rebel threw away his own gun and kicked off his shoes,
because he could run much faster barefoot. So could his Tory
neighbor, for that matter, but the Tory wore silver buckles which
held his shoes on tightly. He could not get them off.

The Tory youth had been heading for a thick wood — or so he
thought. But what he had seen was the tops of trees along the
Walloomsac River. He came to a "frightful precipice." There was
no time to change course; he jumped — and landed deep in the
mud on the edge of the river. He never forgot the sound he
heard — *Splat! Splat!* as he hit the mud. And then, close by him,
he heard that sound again. "The fierce fellow" had jumped after
him. Now they were both stuck in the mud. The Loyalist was up
to his knees, but it was a relief to see that "the rebel had no
pistol. . . . Neither of us made any progress although we wasted
almost all our remaining strength trying to get out of the mud."
But the Tory youth thought that those buckled shoes of his had
kept him from sinking as deep as his enemy. Now if he could just
get them off! With a mighty heave he broke the straps. His feet
"slipped smoothly up through the clay," and although those shoe
buckles were of solid silver he "did not regret them." And being
"still dreadfully afraid," he ran downriver as fast as he could.

Baum had asked for reinforcements on August 14, and on the
fifteenth, at eight o'clock in the morning, Lieutenant Colonel

Heinrich Breymann got orders to march. He was to take "the reserve of the Advance Corps," a battalion of grenadiers, one of chasseurs, one rifle company and two six-pounder cannon. General Riedesel himself offered to go out with Breymann, but Burgoyne would not allow it. Brigadier General Fraser thought Breymann ought to have more than the "seven or eight hundred men" given him, and wanted the entire Advance Corps to go; but "this was rejected because the Advance Corps was too considerable to be risked. . . ."

Breymann marched at nine. Because of the scarcity of carts, Riedesel "put two boxes of ammunition on the artillery cart. Each officer carried 40 rounds in his pouch."

The distance Breymann's corps had to travel was twenty-five miles, but he himself figured that he made only "½ an English mile an hour." There were those who said that Breymann was intentionally slow because he was jealous of Baum. This may be true, but in any case there were others reasons for delay. On the night of the eleventh horses in Burgoyne's army down by the Hudson kicked their shed to pieces in terror because of a violent thunderstorm. Two days later the ford on the Batten Kill was flooded, so as to be almost impassable, and boats forming a bridge over the Hudson filled, broke the chains binding them together and sank. On the fifteenth, when Breymann set out, it rained all day. The road leading to Bennington wound between steep hills where trout brooks coming down each slope had turned to roaring torrents. Shallow fords had suddenly become deep, with water spreading and flowing outward all over the road. The road itself was a quagmire.

"Each gun and ammunition cart had to be dragged up every hill, one after another," Breymann said, and he lost count of the hills. "One artillery cart was overturned and with the greatest difficulty gotten back on its wheels again. . . . Our guide lost his way and, after a long search, Major Barner" had to hunt up "an

Inhabitant who was able to put us again on the right road." It was night when Breymann halted seven miles short of Cambridge, New York.

The artillery horses had had no food all day. They were so weak they could no longer drag the guns, and Major Barner "went forward and took horses from the Inhabitants." An overloaded ammunition cart broke down. And then, from a more or less easterly direction, a mud-spattered horseman rode up with a message: Colonel Skene wanted help in holding Sancoik mill. Breymann sent him sixty men.

The sun shone during August sixteenth. The hillsides steamed with moisture, and it was unbearably hot. At "twenty minutes past three in the afternoon," when the Battle of Bennington began, Breymann was not in sight. To be sure, Baum could see very little in spite of the height of land he had chosen for his post. The Walloomsac was a narrow ribbon winding below — widened now because of the rains. But the road, which followed the river, was hidden by thick forest; on the surrounding hillsides there were only occasional clearings.

No one knew that the German and British reinforcements were coming — least of all the Americans. "Our men were scattered all over the field of battle, some resting, some refreshing themselves, some looking up the dead and wounded, and others in pursuit of plunder," Jesse Field said, continuing his story of what, happened as he saw it that day. "I did not pursue more than half a mile, though some went farther, probably near or quite down to the mill."

It was "perhaps an hour after sunset" when Field heard the report of cannon, and news soon came that "we were attacked by a body of Hessians. . . . We went down upon the side-hill north of the road. The Hessians were marching up the road, their cannon in front, clearing the way."

When Breymann reached Sancoik mill, it was four in the

afternoon. "I positively declare that I did not hear a shot fired," Breymann said. Colonel Skene told him that all was well — but with Baum all was over. Breymann crossed the bridge, and just beyond he said he saw "a considerable number of armed people, some in jackets, some in shirts. . . . I showed these to Colonel Skene who assured me they were Royalists and rode up to them and called out but received no other answer than a discharge of firearms. . . ."

Field was among the men in shirt-sleeves. "Our men kept collecting in front and on their right," he said. "Our party were on the side-hill within 12 to 20 rods of them, generally behind trees, and kept up a constant fire. The road appeared full of men and it was like firing into a flock of sheep. They kept firing but with little success. The battle continued till dusk when they retreated and were not pursued far."

Field and his friends, apparently without orders and entirely on their own, did a good job of frontier fighting but it was fortunate nonetheless that Colonel Seth Warner now arrived from the town of Bennington with fresh men. "We had another battle much harder than the first one," wrote justice of the peace Peter Clark. This was no half hour affair. The battle "continued till dark but finally they were obliged to flee before us and leave behind them two more brass field pieces, small arms and other things."

"We do not know how many we have killed," Peter Clark wrote nearly two weeks later. "Our Scouts daily find them dead in the woods. . . . All this week we have been vendueing the plunder that we took from the enemy which if justice is done there will be considerable to each man." One man, Thomas Hooper of New Boston, "belonging to our company that was wounded in the fight, died Monday morning." But "the wounded Hessians die 3 or 4 in a day. They are all in the Bennington Meeting House which smells so it is enough to kill anyone to be in it. The weather has been so hot it has been bad for the wounded."

Back at Fort Edward, General Riedesel sat down to write a difficult letter to the Duke of Brunswick. First, in regard to his plan, he pointed out the lapse of time. He had suggested a foray for horses on July 22, and Baum's expedition did not set out until August 11. Then there was the matter of the route taken—Burgoyne had changed it. As to the Battle of Bennington:

"All who were present testify that Baum and the troops did well. He had thoroughly beaten the enemy when he was forced through want of ammunition to retreat. . . .

"General Burgoyne has publicly praised the men," Riedesel wrote, "but notwithstanding this I cannot divest myself of the sorrow which I feel at this event, especially since the expedition was planned contrary to my wishes. . . . But aside from the great loss of so many brave men of Your Highness, and the boasting of the rebels, this affair will not be of much consequence."

Months went by before the list of Germans — dead, wounded or prisoners of war — was complete, but out of a total of 374 Germans under Baum, only 9 rejoined Burgoyne's army. Breymann's reinforcement numbered 643 men; but the only Brunswickers to return were Captain von Schlagenteuffel and 29 dragoons.[8]

14

The Road to Albany

"THE unlucky affair at Bennington," the Baroness Riedesel called the battle which marked the turning of the tide against Burgoyne and his army. She was not a military strategist — just a woman who loved her husband. The General was troubled because of his fondness for his men, and his grief at losing so many. That the whole army was now in a perilous position was none of Mrs. General's business; the thing for her to do was to be her own "frolicksome" self and divert her husband's mind from sad thoughts. She told of "the joy of seeing him on August 18th" and of "spending three happy weeks with him in perfect peace" at the Red House in Fort Edward.

"The surrounding country was magnificent. We were encircled by the encampments of the English and the German troops," and at night campfires gleamed on all the hills overlooking the Hudson. In the morning the Germans were awakened by notes on the tuba, while the fife and drum aroused the British. "When it was beautiful weather we took our meals out under the trees. When it rained, we laid boards on top of casks and ate out in the barn." There were usually four or five of the General's aides, known as his "family," at the long table with his wife and children. At the Red House, the Baroness ate bear meat for the first time and found it delicious.

Lady Fritz loved to entertain, and although she was "sometimes hard put to it to find enough to eat," she gave little dinner parties several times a week. The General had a cook who was an accomplished forager, and it was not until sometime later that the Baroness discovered that the large sums he said he paid to "inhabitants" went into his own pocket while the inhabitants got nothing but mysteriously vacant hen roosts and empty pigsties.

The matter of finding suitable guests was not easy. Fort Edward was just a country town, a former trading post, with no Tory gentry to speak of. It was fun to have lots of men at a party — Frederika loved it; but a few ladies made things more festive, and only the wives of officers were of a sufficiently exalted station to be received by a Baroness.

Lady Acland and the Major were among the first to dine with General Riedesel and Lady Fritz. Major Acland, cured of his wound, had rejoined the army with Lady Harriet on the sixth of August at Fort Edward, and the Baroness owed them a debt of gratitude. "Upon the arrival of milady Acland at the army," she wrote, "General Burgoyne said to my husband, 'General, you shall have your wife here also.' Whereupon he immediately dispatched Captain Willoe for me."

Major Acland was not much of a favorite with the Baroness, however. Lady Harriet "loved him very much, but he was a plain, rough man and got drunk almost every day."

Also at Fort Edward were Major and Mrs. Harnage and Lieutenant Reynels and his wife. General Burgoyne was a widower, his wife having "sunk into a decline" before he left England. She had been Lady Charlotte Stanley, sixth daughter of the eleventh Earl of Derby, and their marriage was a romantic elopement. She had died by the time Burgoyne reached Canada.

General Burgoyne was not living in the town of Fort Edward. He had gone forward to a comfortable farmhouse on a ridge overlooking the Hudson. It was known as "Duer's house"; it was new and not entirely completed. William Duer was now a delegate from New York to the Continental Congress, where he was at work on the problem of making his country, not the "states of America," as young Livingston had called it, but the United States. The Americans had driven off all of Duer's cattle, but Burgoyne found his house delightful.

It was some time before Madam Riedesel discovered that General Burgoyne was not alone at Duer's house, but living with "the wife of a commissary who is his mistress," she said. Here was a social predicament. The wife of the commissary was entitled to be asked to dinner because of her husband's rank. And Mrs. General Riedesel naturally wanted General Burgoyne to grace her dinner table. But she was not going to have a lady of easy virtue in her house or even in the barn where the long boards were laid over casks to make a table.

The Baroness never mentioned Burgoyne's mistress by name. But in speaking of her as "the wife of a commissary" she seemed to assume that everyone would know the lady in question. Was this, then, her old friend Hannah Foy? Certainly Hannah had no great objection to being seduced. Her sea-captain friend, whose "intimacy" dated from Bristol days, had gone back to England. There were witnesses enough to her conduct on shipboard so that her husband might have heard tell of it, and he might have left her free to look for new adventures. Burgoyne was not in Quebec when Hannah arrived, but he had been in Bristol more than once. Perhaps she had already caught his eye.

In justice to Hannah, however, it should be remembered that there were several commissaries in Burgoyne's army, and his mistress could have been the wife of any one of them: especially a mysterious "Mrs. Higgins," wife of a deputy-commissary, later to be entrusted with secret messages from Burgoyne to Clinton.[1] Burgoyne's mistress was a gay lady, fond of singing and of champagne, Mrs. General Riedesel said. Had she been properly married to the commander in chief, she and the Baroness might have been friends.

Burgoyne's "General Orders" were a little less oratorical than usual after the Battle of Bennington. He said that "upon the whole the Enemy have severely felt their little success" but he wished to warn the troops "against the impositions of a treacherous enemy, many of whom in the very hour of swearing allegiance to the King, fought against his troops." What he needed, in other words, was an army of Americans willing to line up and be shot at, in the conventional manner. He warned his men "against expending ammunition too fast, by which conquering Troops were obliged to retire with loss." He cautioned about delay. "The loss of two hours may decide the turn of an enterprise, and it might happen in some cases, the fate of a campaign."

Four weeks now went by, after the "incident at Bennington," before Burgoyne moved in any direction.

General Riedesel went on writing to the Duke of Brunswick to tell him the news as it was brought to Burgoyne's camp. The Bennington affair would be of little consequence, because "Lt. Colonel St. Leger has captured Fort Stanwix with many cannon and a strong garrison. It is also said that General Clinton has won a battle near the Highlands. The army of Arnold has evacuated Stillwater and, it is rumored, is in Albany." But there were one or two things wrong with Riedesel's information.

It was true that St. Leger had arrived before Fort Stanwix, called by the Americans Fort Schuyler. This log-palisaded blockhouse on the Mohawk River stood on the present site of Rome, New York. But St. Leger had invested not captured the fort, and Arnold had not gone to Albany — he was on his way to Stanwix to raise the siege.

St. Leger invested Fort Stanwix on August 3. On August 6, the American General Herkimer had attempted to raise the siege but was ambushed and defeated at the Battle of Oriskany, a brief but bloody engagement in which Herkimer himself was killed.

Arnold reached the town of Herkimer on August 20, with eight hundred men. He had come as a volunteer in charge of volunteers.

It was not Arnold but General Schuyler who had retreated from Stillwater, to take post at Half Moon or "Camp Van Schaick," a fort on the Mohawk River, about four miles from the point where the untamed Mohawk took its seventy-foot leap into the Hudson.² Two men had somehow managed to get out of Fort Stanwix one dark night. They crept through the camp of besiegers and encircling Indians, and reached General Schuyler with the news that food and ammunition were almost gone; the fort must soon surrender. Schuyler called a conference of officers. He personally favored sending help, but was outvoted — on the grounds that his force was too small. Losing his famous temper, he declared that he would "beat up for volunteers next morning." Arnold, one of the officers at the conference, had volunteered on the spot.

One move Schuyler made without asking advice. As head of Indian affairs in Northern New York, he was able to hand Arnold one thousand dollars, partly in wampum belts, to distribute judiciously among the Oneidas.

On his way, Arnold was delayed at Fort Dayton (now the town of Herkimer). He presided over the trial of two Tories, brought in under sentence of death for recruiting for the King of England behind the American lines. Arnold granted them a reprieve. One of these prisoners named Hon Yost was said to be half-witted, and was dressed in tattered Indian garments. The fellow was related to General Schuyler, but this particular cousin had gone native among the Indians.

Arnold must have suspected that Hon Yost was more crafty than crazy; and the American commander had an inspired idea. Why not send Hon Yost to the "savages" besieging Fort Stanwix, with a message that a great host was marching against them? Hon Yost was sure that he could do that, and more: he would pretend to have a vision and make direful prophecies, because the Indians not only revered a madman but were especially impressed by one with hallucinations. Arnold gave Hon Yost a few wampum belts which might help the scheme along.

Hon Yost was pleased both with his reprieve and his assignment, but Arnold took Yost's brother as a hostage just in case the "madman" should just slip away never to be seen again. The Americans marched cautiously forward, not unduly hopeful that this plan would succeed. But St. Leger's "savages" were impressed by the act Hon Yost put on, and also by the gift of wampum; so they told St. Leger of an approaching enemy as numerous as the leaves on the trees and urged that everybody run for their lives. St. Leger was indignant, but panic spread among his troops. They fled, leaving tents standing, abandoning provisions and ammunition, throwing away their knapsacks so that they could run faster. St. Leger's own Indians fell upon the stragglers, gathering in scalps and loot. St. Leger's idea now was to march eastward to join Burgoyne, but he was hustled along the trail to Montreal and his guides seemed suddenly to have forgotten all other trails.

The siege of Fort Stanwix was lifted on August 22. Arnold then made a rapid march to rejoin the main American army. He brought the promise of some Oneida braves who would join the Americans, because Schuyler had finally agreed to fight fire with fire.

There had been a band of Stockbridge Indians with the American forces for some time. Young Livingston told how they brought five British prisoners into Fort Edward on July 21 — "the enemy not knowing we had Indians, were decoyed, thinking them their own." These Stockbridge Indians were known as "tame" because they lived peaceably with their American neighbors. It was Schuyler's hope that the Oneidas would remain neutral if given enough wampum and trade goods, because they were anything but "tame" and he was reluctant to enlist them. But Gates continually asked for Indians "who would be of infinite service to this army to assist Col. Morgan's Corps as spies and guides."

"Some of the Oneidas, Tuscaroras and Onondagas arrived yesterday afternoon in Albany," Schuyler told Gates on the fifteenth of September. "This day will be spent in the usual ceremony of mutual congratulations which they will not dispense with. . . . We shall, however, strive to procure some of them to join you but cannot advise that you depend on them for guides as they are unacquainted with the part of the country you are now in." Schuyler was as good as his word, for about ten days later "three Tories were just now brought in by the Oneidas," wrote Colonel Benjamin Warren from the American camp at Stillwater.

Next day "the Indians brought in 27 Regulars and Hessians, also Tories who were given them to buffet." This cruel game of running the gantlet did not seem unfair to Benjamin Warren, for he had lost men under him "when the Indians crawled up . . . killed a sentry, killed and scalped a sergeant." On Warren's march to Stillwater the Indians "crept between our rere and the body of our troops and killed and scalped an inhabitant who was watching his pigs." But Warren showed concern when a British officer was "killed and scalped by the Oneidas." They said the officer "was offered but refused quarter," and Colonel Warren hoped this was true.[3]

Although General Schuyler sent Indians to Gates, Schuyler was no longer in command of the Northern Department. The fall of Ticonderoga had aroused great resentment against him, especially in New England. "Is he *never* there!" exclaimed John Adams, on learning that Schuyler had left the fort shortly before the attack. Schuyler was removed from his command by order of Congress on June 29, but did not learn of it until the tenth of August. He continued to send out axmen to block roads, to cut bridges and to carry off the planks from bridges to build shelters at Stillwater. By his orders, Fort George was successfully evacuated and stripped, and even after he knew that he had been superseded he remained at his post continuing his efforts to block Burgoyne's march until his successor appeared on the scene.

"I am far from insensible of the indignity of being ordered from the command of the army at a time when an engagement must soon take place," he wrote to Congress. For a while no successor was appointed, although General Nathanael Greene of Rhode Island "was spoken of." He was one of Washington's most brilliant generals, but he had offended Congress. Eventually Schuyler's successor was — Gates!

Sadly, Schuyler wrote that now perhaps the militia from New Hampshire and Vermont would come to join the handful of Continental troops. They might be willing to serve under Gates.

Schuyler retained control of the Indian Department and on August 19 Gates came to Stillwater, the campground which Schuyler had chosen. Burgoyne, meanwhile, lingered in the vicinity of Fort Edward, and the American militia marched unopposed to Stillwater, tremendously heartened by their victory at Bennington.

General Riedesel was optimistic at this point: "As soon as our provisions and the necessary bateaux, which are transported by land, shall have reached us, the army will advance and will soon be in Albany," he wrote to the Duke of Brunswick. An attempt was made to bring one of the Canadian-built gunboats from Lake George and float it in the Hudson, but the attempt failed, "the road being in so many places hilly and rocky." Bateaux to carry provisions were brought forward from Fort Anne to Fort Edward and "there launched on the Hudson" but they moved downstream only about six miles before they grounded opposite Fort Miller. They had to be unloaded, hauled up on shore and carried "two or three hundred yards on rollers pushed by fatigue parties," then "put again into the river." Rafts and scows were built on the banks of the Hudson just below Fort Miller. Burgoyne rode from

point to point — from Fort Anne to Fort George — from Fort
Edward to Fort Miller — issuing orders.

On August 19 all but fifty of Burgoyne's five hundred Indians
went back to Canada. They had been the first to arrive back in
Burgoyne's camp after the Battle of Bennington, and it had
seemed then as if they might just keep on running. However, they
had a few horses to sell and some plunder they wanted to pack
up and take with them. Their chief made a formal speech of farewell. On first joining Burgoyne's army, the chief said, the sun
shone clear and bright, foretelling conquest. But "clouds were
now rising, dark and gloomy . . ." For once the speechmaking
was brief, because there was very little Burgoyne could say in
reply — and the Indians were in a hurry.

Philip Skene did not seem to realize that he was out of favor
because his hundreds of "loyal inhabitants" had failed to appear.
He made up "an Account of Money spent on Private and Public
Service" and presented it to Burgoyne.[4] He wanted fifteen pounds
for "Mr. Tyler sent on Express . . . from Lt. Col. Breymer
for himself and horse lost by riding express the night of the 16th
August" and for "Mr. Browning who went and brought intelligence from Bennington." Then there was the matter of Captain
Lane, a Loyalist, "stripped by the Indians." Two pounds ten
shillings were what his clothes cost. And now that the Indians had
gone, an item was due "To 2 Horses, Bridles and Saddles Delivered to the Indians at Skenesboro by order to go on Private
Service never returned, $100." Also "1 Horse, saddle and Bridle"
had been supplied to "Joseph Brant, a Mohawk Indian dispatched
with letters from Duer's: $45."

There were two particularly significant items on Colonel Philip
Skene's bill. On the third of July "Mr. Kean" and on July 7 "Mr.
Hume" and "Mr. Stalker" were sent "to New York with Dispatches." Their setting out was billed to General Burgoyne at
10 pounds 10 shillings each, and there was no indication that

they ever returned. Skene's bill lengthened as time went by and was never marked paid.

Burgoyne ordered "a corps of marksmen to be formed, consisting of one non-commissioned officer and 16 men from each of the five British regiments." They must be "robust men of good character" and according to Burgoyne's order they were to "act with the Savages." Everyone knew they were to replace the Indians, and they had orders to make "the Inhabitants who had called themselves Tories but who went over to the enemy pay dear for their late successes at Bennington."

On August 28 Burgoyne got the news that Colonel St. Leger had been "obliged to retire" from the Mohawk River.

Burgoyne's first bridge of boats across the Hudson had been strung along above the Saratoga rapids, but a better crossing point had been found below the Saratoga Falls two miles above the present Schuylerville. Intrenchments three hundred feet long, with embankments six feet high, were thrown up to guard the new bridge. Behind the entrenchments a wooden platform was built for cannon.

Now General Riedesel had lost his optimism and was becoming more and more uneasy: he did not like the defection of the Indians, nor news of failure at Fort Stanwix, nor the fact that the "inhabitants" were by no means flocking to Burgoyne. The delays worried him. There was no word from British-occupied New York, and the problem of supply was increasingly acute.

The General decided to send his wife and children back to Canada, but he counted without the courage and the persuasive powers of Mrs. General. "Upon my urgent entreaties," as she put it, she received permission to follow the army. Part of her baggage was sent back because she knew as well as her husband did that a rapid march must now be made. There were "about thirty Carts . . . loaden with Baggage said to be the Lieutenant General's," but these were headed toward Albany. They contained his wine, his dress uniforms and the belongings of his mistress. Burgoyne was making himself the exception to his own rule.

General Riedesel acquired oxen and one cart for his personal baggage. He had a carriage built at Fort Edward by the blacksmith, the "collar-maker" and the "wheelers" who marched with the troops. The new calash was composed of parts of broken-down forage carts and a carriage belonging to an inhabitant in no position to protest. It was large, covered, with seats inside for Lady Fritz, the children and both maidservants. They carried a small chest of clothes, a bottle or two of wine and quite a few provisions.

Once more Mrs. General, who had been the busy housewife, ordering bears' paws to be cooked in the kitchen, superintending her children's lessons in their one-room apartment, became the army wife with a moving job on her hands. The weather had been hot and humid in the valley of the Hudson during July and August. Neither Mrs. General nor her husband liked hot weather. They had been marching south and now they were going south still farther. Back to Canada went the General's blanket coat which had made him look so strange and unmilitary. Traveling cloaks went back to lighten the load of baggage, but the General's wine would have to follow the army. It would seem that nothing could be more unwieldy to carry than a large quantity of wine, but the decision to take it probably saved the whole family from illness because of polluted water.

The Baroness now spoke enthusiastically of Albany. It was a fine city with enough good houses to provide comfortable quarters for all officers — or so she had heard. "We cherished the sweet hope of victory and of coming into the Promised Land," she said.

It had rained the day before, but on Saturday morning, September 13, the sun shone brightly when Fraser's corps led off across a bridge of boats.[5] Fraser started at seven, and three hours later Riedesel and his rear guard of Germans crossed the Hudson. No longer the laughingstock of the army, the Brunswick dragoons were mounted at last; they rode proudly, as they had been trained to do — but there were only some twenty men. When they left Canada there had been 246 dragoons, 8 musicians, 29 servants, 33 noncommissioned officers and 20 officers.

"I followed the army in the midst of the soldiers who were singing songs," Mrs. General wrote. The British troops called her "Red 'Azel," as well she knew, although she may not have understood enough English to realize they thought her name was Hazel. They were respectful and she could tell that this odd name meant that they liked her. As for the Germans, she was their Baroness — symbolic of everything good and beautiful that they longed for when they thought of home.

Frederika Riedesel crossed the Hudson on a swaying, groaning bridge, its roadway built of logs laid over boats. She was mercifully oblivious of the fact that history is full of fatal river crossings.

After crossing the Hudson, "we passed through boundless forests[6] and magnificent tracts of country, which, however, were abandoned by all the inhabitants who fled before us," wrote Lady Fritz. It was assumed that the rebels were going to run again, and the British felt supremely confident as they carried with them an American flag captured at Fort Anne, "a very handsome one of 13 stripes alternating red and white with thirteen stars in a blue field, representing a new constellation." But later with knowledge born of experience, the Baroness explained what had happened to the inhabitants west of the Hudson. They had "reinforced the army of General Gates. . . . Every one of them was a soldier by nature and could shoot very well. Besides, the thought of fighting for their fatherland and their freedom had inspired them with still greater courage."

The Baroness was wrong about the Americans' being soldiers

by nature, although she meant it as a compliment. They were farmers and tradesmen, men and boys who wanted nothing so much as to get the fighting over with and go home. "Camp life" was "irksome to them."[7] But for the first time, Mrs. General understood that this America was not just a rebellious colony but a "fatherland."

Meanwhile Mrs. General Schuyler had been busy at the family summer home on the southern edge of a little town then called Saratoga (now known as Schuylerville).[8] Apparently, Catherine Schuyler rarely put pen to paper, but she told her husband's aide, young Henry Brockholst Livingston, just what to say when he wrote to General Schuyler. The American's letter could have been written by Mrs. General Riedesel, so similar was the content:

"Mrs. Schuyler sends you by the Bearer, five Gallons of Wine, one half Gallon of Brandy, 1 pound of Tea, 10 Wine glasses, a piece of Cheese, a Loaf of sugar, some smoked Tongues, a bundle for Mr. Lansing, some Chocolate, Coffee and Ruske.

"Mrs. Schuyler, in consequence of your letter, is packing her Effects and preparing to move down. She is not at all pleased with leaving Saratoga so soon, as she had proposed to stay here several days. The Alarms we have had have but little Effect on her. She is uneasy for you and has enjoined me to entreat you not to expose yourself unnecessarily. There were a few Indians discovered yesterday afternoon . . . and a constant firing all last night by the Sentries who saw, or pretended to see Indians. I will take a strong Guard with us and not dismiss them till we are free of all Danger. *P. S.* There are two bottles of Porter put up in the greens." It was August when Mrs. Schuyler finally decided to leave the farm, which everyone spoke of as hers because she loved it so much. Ripe wheat was standing in her fields and she personally set fire to it before she set out for Albany.

In September Mrs. General Riedesel's calash rolled into Saratoga, past the church and the three or four small houses that made up the entire town. The bridge across the Fishkill, which the retreating Americans had destroyed, had been repaired, and just across it stood Mrs. Schuyler's house with its Dutch door, its many windows, its air of hospitality. Burgoyne had taken it for his headquarters.

Lady Fritz rode on past blackened wheatfields and then through heavy forest. Three and a half miles or so beyond the Fishkill, there was another clearing and a good-sized house at the foot of a hill. Madam Riedesel was delighted to hear that she could have a room for herself and the children, her maidservants sleeping in a "kind of entry" in this house under the hill.

Burgoyne's orders were now headed "Sara Toga"; the city which has since been called Saratoga would eventually be located eleven miles away from where he was posted. The health resort and the race track at Saratoga Springs were all part of a distant future; but Indians, for generations, had visited this region's mineral springs, whose waters were supposed to cure their ills. Burgoyne's Indians now brought him trout from Saratoga Lake. His officers said that "Schuyler's house" was "the best" that they "had yet seen in that part and much superior to many gentlemen's houses in Canada." Spacious rooms opened left and right upon a center hall, and below was a huge vaulted cellar divided into kitchens and storage rooms with space for hams and sides of beef. Above-stairs there were comfortable bedrooms for a large family and accommodations for servants up under the roof. Mrs. Schuyler had made no attempt to save her furniture. It was more important to send men to dismantle the gristmill and sink the stones deep in the millstream in the hope that they would not be discovered and the mill put into commission for Burgoyne.

Scouts from Burgoyne's army had seen American soldiers at Schuyler's house "guarding bullocks." But before Burgoyne got there, all the cattle had been driven off, and the general in the

American camp at Stillwater, twelve miles south, was now Gates, not Schuyler. Varick, Schuyler's aide, wrote indignantly that General Gates had taken Mrs. Schuyler's favorite cow to supply milk for his own table. Varick planned to get that cow sent down to Albany.

General Burgoyne was disappointed to find wine cellars empty and rows of wrought-iron meat-hooks in the cellar bare of hams or beef. But he found Schuyler's house perfect for entertaining, and gave supper parties every night. He had brought plenty of champagne with him, which his mistress liked as well as he did. But Lady Fritz was certainly not at the parties, nor was Lady Acland.

On September 15, at about midnight, Lieutenant Digby returned to his tent on the high ground south and west of Saratoga. He had been ordered to stand to arms, but the alarm was over and he had just dropped asleep when he "heard a great noise of fire, and on running out, saw Major Acland's tent and markee all in a blaze." Lady Acland camped with the troops and the marquee was hers. Before Lieutenant Digby got there, she had crawled out under the back wall of her large canvas shelter, but her husband thought she was still inside. He was badly burned when he rushed into the marquee trying to save her. The accident was caused by a Newfoundland dog the Aclands had brought along on the campaign, who became "restless" and knocked over a table with a lighted candle on it.

Burgoyne continued a gradual advance, mending roads and building bridges over creeks. The meadow land beside the Hudson was marshy and the high ground farther west heavily wooded, intersected with ravines and brooks. Two roads for the two columns of Burgoyne's army were to be built and at the same time a bridge was to be repaired, wrote General Riedesel. "The spot occupied by the British army" had had an American encampment on it only the previous day. The Americans were even now only about five miles away, and "Burgoyne himself sallied out to reconnoiter."

On the morning of the sixteenth a combination work and reconnoitering party marched out. The detachment consisted of half of Fraser's light troops, the 2nd Brigades of the 9th and 62nd regiments, with six guns, all from the right wing, together with the Regiments Specht and Hesse Hanau from the left wing. Along with them were two groups of men ordered out for fatigue duty, each group having one hundred men and their bridge-building and road-making tools. They "left camp accompanied by Burgoyne, Phillips, Riedesel and Fraser."

The column of the right wing under Major Acland crossed a bridge as soon as it could be repaired and marched to a road "leading to Dovogat's house." This house was "about fifty rods from the Hudson." The left column, under von Gall, crossed the same newly repaired bridge and "took the road leading to Sword's house." This house was on the south bank of a brook and "about fifty yards west of the Hudson." Both houses were only two and a half miles from the army's main camp, and "about 800 paces away from each other through dense woods." Because of the delay in repairing the bridge, this two-and-a-half-mile march represented the entire day's work, and at about eight o'clock in the evening everybody went back to camp.

James Wilkinson, aide to General Gates and now a lieutenant colonel, had been camping at Dovogat with 170 men. His evidently not too tidy camp had been made on the night of September 12 (not on the sixteenth as Riedesel supposed). He had climbed the heights overlooking the Hudson near Saratoga, and had been watching Fraser's advance corps "come within three hundred yards of him." From now on, Burgoyne's every move was watched — although he saw no enemy.

On September 17, the British army started out again, taking the two roads that had been built for them. This time Fraser's light troops and the English regiments made up the right wing,

while all the Germans went left. Behind came "the heavy artillery
. . . the stores and all the baggage." The right wing was on high
ground, the line extending from Dovogat's house "back to Sword's
house." Fraser was forward "among the hills" and the Germans of
Specht's regiment were down on the Hudson where the bateaux
with freight had arrived and anchored. "The Americans had destroyed all the bridges and Burgoyne could advance no farther,"
wrote General Riedesel, who kept a careful account of each move
and of the disposition of the troops.

On the eighteenth Burgoyne "caused a road to be cut through
the woods." The road along the Hudson "had been entirely destroyed by the Americans," and as the left wing with the heavy
artillery and baggage were to pass this way, Riedesel superintended
the repair work himself.

"A deserter reported that the Americans had left their camp at
Stillwater and were coming to attack the British army." This was
not true — Gates had not moved, but Arnold, with about fifteen
hundred men, had been sent out again, to harass the British.
Riedesel saw men on the east bank of the Hudson, but "all un-
necessary firing was forbidden" because ammunition must be
conserved. He and his work party continued to build a bridge
which he called "Bridge Number One." The men on the east
bank of the Hudson disappeared, and "toward four in the afternoon four regiments of the enemy with banners could plainly be
seen." It was Arnold again — but for once he was cautious and
withdrew "because the ground was unfavorable for a skirmish."

Not bothering with her carriage, and wearing trousers, Lady
Fritz rode astride one of the horses her husband had left with her
and gaily set out over the road her husband was building. She
arrived in time to have breakfast with the General at the campfire. "Very often I also took my noon meal with him," she said,
and whenever he could General Riedesel "rode over to my quarters
to eat with me."

The men "slept on their arms," not carrying their tents. On the nineteenth of September, Burgoyne's army formed to march again, this time in three columns. Riedesel placed Regiment Hesse-Hanau on the hills around Sword's house with orders to "defend the road leading into the woods behind this house." They were to stay there until the left wing had passed and then they were to form a rear guard. The signal gun echoed among the hills — but not until eleven in the morning. The advance guard with pitifully few dragoons and a hundred light infantry pressed forward. Next came Regiment Riedesel, a detachment of men for the working party, the artillery for the left wing and then Regiment Specht. They crossed Bridge Number One and marched only a short distance before they came to a marshy creek. Riedesel ordered the regiments to "send out patrols as far as possible, called for his working party, and set to work on Bridge Number Two.

"Towards one o'clock in the afternoon musketry fire was heard in the distance. It seemed to come from "the second" or middle column of this three-pronged advance. But the three columns were now separated by dense woods, marshland and a sluggish creek with a meandering course. The workers went on building their bridge. General Riedesel ordered Regiment Rhetz to close in next to Regiment Riedesel. He ordered two companies to ford the creek and take post on the other side, but "half an hour later the sound of firing ceased."

General Phillips was in command of the heavy artillery and he was with Riedesel. He offered to go to look for the "second column" and "investigate the cause of the late firing." He dared not go "through the woods by the nearest way" but backtracked along his own march and then picked up the trail of the second column and began to follow it.

"As soon as the bridge was done," Riedesel fired a signal gun to let the officers of the troops strung along behind him know that they could come forward. But General Riedesel had scarcely gone six hundred paces before he came to another creek without any bridge! So he stopped to build one, "Bridge Number Three" in his report. Two twelve-pounders were brought up to defend Bridge Number Two, and Regiment Rhetz brought up a six-pounder to defend the working party. Bridge Number Three was close to the Hudson; it would soon prove to be the farthest point south on the riverbank that Burgoyne was to reach.

Around two in the afternoon "Major Bloomfield of the artillery" arrived, to find General Riedesel sweating profusely in the sweltering heat by the river and urging on his tired working party. General Phillips had sent the major for "a few guns from the artillery train," all of the guns being behind Riedesel waiting for bridges. Riedesel ordered the guns back along the road, but had scarcely got them rolling when he and his men heard new volleys of musket fire over on their right, in the woods away from the river.

Riedesel dispatched Captain Willoe to see if he could find Burgoyne, who was with the middle column, and to ask if there were by any chance any orders. He posted men to guard bridges One and Two, because "here were the artillery and the supply train," practically stuck in the mud. And now "some Indians came running through the woods and across the mountains" to say that the enemy was coming.

15

The Battles of Saratoga

"FREEMAN'S Farm" was on high ground on the west bank of the Hudson, overlooking marshland and the river. With immense labor, Freeman had cleared twelve or fifteen acres in front of his house on land sloping east and south. A log cabin first served as shelter for the pioneer family, but by 1777 a frame house of sorts had been built, the log house had become a barn, and there were other log buildings. Farmer Freeman sold his place to Isaac Leggett but the "inhabitants" had fled. They were Quakers, now living in Albany, and it was said that Arnold had questioned them closely as to whether they had supplied Burgoyne with provisions. They claimed they had not, and when Arnold seemed to doubt them, daughter Mary had spoken up with spirit: "If thee knows better than I, why did thee question me?"

Isaac Leggett had been extending the clearing in the forest. He had hacked out heavy undergrowth and girdled tall trees with fire so that they would fall victim to his ax more easily. On September 19, these great trees were to be chipped and scarred with cannon ball and canister.[1]

Morgan's Rifles had just been sent to Gates from Washington's army. They were to serve as scouts, and on the morning of the

nineteenth of September they left the American camp to find out
exactly what Burgoyne was doing. General Riedesel was laboring
mightily to build bridges and drag the artillery train through the
marsh by the river. Burgoyne was advancing in a remarkably
carefree manner on higher ground. Morgan met "Canadians and
Indians in the middle ravine south of Freeman's cottage," and
drove them back. Burgoyne's right wing was reinforced about
halfway between the ravine and the farmhouse. The Battle of
Freeman's Farm, also called the First Battle of Saratoga, had
begun.

The American Major, Henry Dearborn, twenty-six-year-old
veteran of Bunker Hill and of the sieges of Quebec and Ticonderoga, marched out to support Morgan. He sent for reinforcements — and Colonel Joseph Cilly, veteran of the Battles of Long
Island, Trenton, Princeton, and Ticonderoga, brought out his
battalion; Major Alexander Scammel, who had seen service in
Canada and at Ticonderoga, came up with his brigade. These
were all New Hampshire men — men Burgoyne was sure had,
every one, run away for good after Ticonderoga and Hubbardton.

At one o'clock in the afternoon the battle began in earnest.
Freeman's Farm, with its fairly level acreage, came as close to
being a proper battle field as anything General Burgoyne had
seen in America. He was "at the head of his troops," and whatever his faults, he had courage. Four English regiments led by
Burgoyne himself made up the column of the center on the
heights, separated by two miles' distance from the column on the
left, when Riedesel heard "the sound of musket-fire" but thought
nothing of it. Fraser's column was on the right, out of sight if not
as far away. At first, the firing sounded as casual and unimportant
to Burgoyne as it did to Riedesel. But brigade after American
brigade was marching out against Fraser, and this time nobody
was running away. The engagement soon involved the column led
by Burgoyne.[2]

General Riedesel's aide, Captain Willoe, was sent to find out what the shooting was about. His appearance on the field of battle at that particular moment was just a matter of chance. General Phillips had arrived with his guns, but the American General Ebenezer Learned had been sent out with New York troops under Arnold's command and three other American brigades were fighting "about 60 rods west of the cottage on a plain, or level ground." So General Burgoyne would be obliged, he said, if General Riedesel, "after reinforcing his position near the river as much as possible," would take the rest of his troops and attack the flank of the enemy "near a place called Freeman's Farm."

Riedesel had already anticipated the first part of these orders when Captain Willoe brought them to him "in less than an hour." He had cut through the woods with Regiment Riedesel, two companies from Regiment Rhetz, and two cannon. Sending a patrol ahead, he "plunged into the underbrush in the direction the firing was coming from." To his astonishment, "on coming out of the woods near a house they call Freeman's Farm, [he found himself] directly on the Flank of the two armies engaged, and the left wing [of the British] began just then to fold. Quickly making up his mind, he formed the seven companies" and burst from cover, "drums beating." The Americans were "attacked and overthrown all in the same instant," as Riedesel told the story.

Riedesel left Captain Georg Pausch, artillerist, to post two guns on the road by the river and then to follow. Pausch threw down stone walls so that an enemy coming up in the rear would have no place to hide, and then he dragged two more guns through the woods in Riedesel's wake and reached the foot of Freeman's small plateau "under a shower of bullets. The 21st and the 9th Regiments were about to abandon the field of battle," he said; "nevertheless, I continued to drag my two cannon up the hill. . . ." He saw General Phillips, whose guns were all out of ammunition, "exhorting the English regiments to face the enemy. . . . English captains and other officers and privates and also Brunswick

Chasseurs . . . grasped the ropes" of Pausch's guns; "the entire line faced about and by this faithful assistance, my cannon were soon on top of the hill. I had shells brought up and as soon as I got the range, I fired 12 or 14 shots into the foe who were within pistol range.

"Presently the enemy's fire, though very lively at first, ceased." Pausch "advanced about 600 paces, sending a few shells into the flying enemy and firing from 12 to 15 shots more into the woods where they had retreated. Everything then became quiet and about fifteen minutes later, darkness set in."

General Riedesel made it clear, in his account and in his letters to the Duke of Brunswick, that he and his German troops had once more saved the British from defeat — as they had done at Hubbardton. And as before, Burgoyne once more claimed a glorious victory and brushed off German help as of little consequence. It never occurred to either general, apparently, that the Americans "withdrew at nightfall" because they were out of ammunition and that they had gone only a short distance, to their camp, where Kościuszko had designed redoubts for them in which they could bide their time.

The British "occupied the field of battle" and this, to them, meant victory. "Our small party of Indians had a fine time next morning, plundering and scalping the Americans left on the field," wrote Pausch. But when he went out "to count the dead" he got shot at, and a German surgeon found "a fellow [who] levelled a gun at him when he came near."

On the morning of September 19 (the day of the battle of Freeman's Farm), the Baroness got up early, put on her riding habit with the trousers which so astonished the inhabitants, and set off down the road that her husband was building. She had breakfast with him, took a look at "Dovogat's house," which would be Burgoyne's next headquarters, and then watched the bridge-builders. The noon meal was usually eaten around two o'clock, but at one o'clock she heard the spattering of musket-fire off in the woods. "I could hear everything," she said. The sound of ax and hammer continued as the bridge-builders went on with their work. When General Phillips set out, she could hear the guns rumbling down the road and the General's lan-gauge as he urged on the horses. But then firing broke out again, and Mrs. General was ordered to the rear with only time for a quick farewell to her husband.

"I was an eye-witness of the whole affair," said Lady Fritz. She stood in the dooryard of the house under the hill and on the heights beyond she saw dense clouds of smoke following every boom of cannon. "I knew my husband was in the midst of it, and I was full of grief and anguish. I shivered at every shot." Figures could be seen off among the trees, men in red coats showing up clearly. And then men in brown, green or blue came forward. Those Americans seemed to disregard the importance of a uniform. A knot of men in red moved slowly toward the house under the hill. Then there was a straggling line. They were the wounded coming down the new road.

They brought Major Harnage to the house and put him in his room, which was next to Madam Riedesel's. The walls were very thin and she could hear him moan. He had been shot through the abdomen, and "he suffered exceedingly," Frederika said. Mrs. Harnage was with him; she tried to help the surgeon, but when Lieutenant Young, a boy of nineteen, was brought in, there was no one to comfort him. Madame Riedesel sent in some broth for him and he asked to see her. "I went to him at once and found him lying on a little straw because his camp equipage was lost." She brought him pillows and a mattress and visited him every day, discovering that his parents were people she had known in England. He was their only son. "He had bled considerably and they wanted to take off his leg, but he could not bring his mind to it and now mortification set in. . . . Finally, they attempted the amputation of his leg but it was too late and he died a few days afterward." Lady Fritz promised to write to his people.

A hospital for the wounded was set up in a barn in the marshy valley where Riedesel had been building bridges. The artillery park was there, and bateaux were tied up along the bank of the river, provisions still aboard. This area was Riedesel's responsibility, and he was constantly anxious lest the Americans should raid it. But they had destroyed so many bridges below Saratoga that they, themselves, were cut off from return.

It was decided to fortify the position at Freeman's Farm with a series of earthworks. This was a most uncomfortable post because the Americans were so close that they could be heard "cutting trees and making works," and British pickets were constantly fired upon. Then there was the noise at night. "The two first nights this noise was heard, General Fraser thought it was the dogs belonging to the officers" — for Major Acland was not the only one to bring a dog along. "An order was given for the dogs to be confined within the tents; any that were seen running about, the Provost was to hang them." Lieutenant Anburey told of this and it seemed to him a good idea, for he was getting very little sleep. But "the noise like the howling of dogs on the right of the encampment" continued and it was "imagined that the enemy set it up to deceive us while they were meditating some attack." A detachment of "Canadians and Provincials" was sent out to reconnoiter. They found great packs of wolves "that came after the dead bodies; they were similar to a pack of hounds, for one setting up a cry, they all joined, and when they approached a corpse" — either unburied, or only half buried — "their noise was hideous until they had scratched it up."

Burgoyne kept his army at Freeman's Farm for three weeks. Forage for the horses became scarce and the American scouts were so alert that "we were always obliged to send out a heavy guard with our foragers," Riedesel said. "Some soldiers and women, having strolled in front of the encampment about 3 or 4 yards to gather potatoes, were fired upon by a party of the enemy. Several were killed and about 26 taken prisoner."

Nobody worried about the women, but Burgoyne issued a special order to make it clear how he felt about the men. "The General will no longer bear to lose men for the pitiful consideration of Potatoes or Forage." He figured that twenty men "could have cost the lives of some hundred odd of the enemy," and he warned that "the life of a soldier is the property of the King. . . . The first soldier caught beyond the advance Sentries of the Army will instantly be hanged. . . ."

General Riedesel was always at his forward post in the marshland, with the artillery, or on the field at Freeman's Farm during these three weeks. Every day Lady Fritz left her comfortable room³ and rode forward to be with her husband. Major Griffith Williams, in command of the British artillery, was one of the older officers in Burgoyne's army. He was a rough soldier with no pretentions to elegance like so many of the officers in this elite army, but the Baroness liked him and he was devoted to her. He offered to have a house built for her own use, just behind the lines.

"How much would it cost?" she asked.

"Oh, not more than five or six guineas," Williams told her.

"I took him up on it," said Mrs. General. "They called it a 'blockhouse,' and for such a building large trees of equal thickness are chosen, which are joined together, making it very durable and warm, especially if covered with clay." Major Williams promised Mrs. General a chimney with a good fireplace. The whole house would be twenty feet square and Lady Fritz watched the building of her new home with pleasure and anticipation. Here was a house "I could steadily occupy," she said. "My husband could live in it with me," and still "be very near his camp."

Already, "nights were damp and cold" and she was worried because he had been sleeping on the ground before his campfire.

Burgoyne wrote to tell Brigadier General Powell, in charge at Ticonderoga, about the battle at Freeman's Farm.[4] "I take the first opportunity to inform you we have had a smart and very honorable action and are now encamped in front of the field which must demonstrate our victory beyond the power of even an American news-writer to explain away." But Burgoyne's letter was intercepted by the Americans and never reached General Powell.

On September 21, Burgoyne's advance guard "appeared before" the American lines and the Americans "gave them three huzzahs and immediately thirteen cannon." It puzzled the British, who had no idea that the Americans were celebrating a foray behind Burgoyne's lines. An American detachment had "taken Tye Landing and the Mills and French Lines"; they had captured 293 of General Powell's men and liberated 100 American prisoners.

Powell's letter to Burgoyne came through. He had managed to hang on at Ticonderoga. The Americans had taken Fort Independence, looted then abandoned it, and had disappeared "over the mountain." It was anybody's guess where they were now.

Burgoyne did not tell rank and file about this letter because it meant that communication with Canada was cut off. To "avoid the delay in getting provisions from Canada" he reduced the bread and flour ration and ordered the deputy paymaster to issue "one hundred and sixty five days' Forage Money to the officers of the army." He did not say how the officers were going to spend the money where no shops existed, no "inhabitants" remained, and where large enemy scouting parties daily tightened the ring around his camp.

Most of Burgoyne's Indians had left, but there were now "in all near one hundred and fifty with Gates. They were the ones who intercepted the messengers with dispatches from General Burgoyne to General Powell. As time went by, it looked as though all the tribes south of the Canadian border would either "take the Hatchet" on the American side or stay at home and remain neutral.

In Albany, a German-American set himself to a propaganda task apparently entirely his own idea:

"I am in no public office in the army," he explained in a long letter written in German and in English and addressed to all the Germans in British service.[5] "I am a free tradesman, a shoemaker by profession, yet I live better than most of your nobles in Germany." The German-American was "amazed" at the German soldiers "for believing us to be Barbarians. But my dear Countrymen, believe not the English that tells you so. Come and see us here as friends — even Blood Relations you will find here. You'll not repent it, depend on it, for we want all sorts of tradesmen, who can get employment immediately, and even if they have no trade, they may get employment and live better with half the labor in this country than in Germany. . . . They call us Rebels but believe them not, we are bold to call God and the world to witness that we are not. We do not pretend to anything but what God has allowed to all men — freedom. . . .

"I hope as soon as you receive this you will come over to us, and if not, leave the ugly name Rebel out of your thoughts. . . . Here the poor laborer can go fishing and hunting where and when he will as well as the rich. . . ."

The WELLWISHER, as he signed himself, wrote out his letter in English to give to Gates. Copies in German he distributed by methods best known to himself among Burgoyne's German troops. He offered to pay for "arms and accoutrements," just as Burgoyne had offered money to Loyalists, and he extolled the advantages of joining the American army. The Germans would have to ponder all this. But eventually, Gates was to write, "The Germans desert to us in shoals. . . ."

On October 7, the Baroness Riedesel rode out to the Freeman's Farm campground as usual. She was to move into her new house the next day, and she "rejoiced at" the sturdy little cabin, smelling of fresh-cut logs — so clean, so snug and soon to be so warm with a fire on the hearth.

"General Fraser, and, I believe, Generals Burgoyne and Phillips were to have dined with me [the seventh]," she said. She was feeling gay.

There seemed to be "considerable movement among the troops" and Mrs. General asked her husband what was up. "Just a reconnaisance," he told her, and this was no surprise because "it often happened." After breakfast at the campfire, Lady Fritz mounted her horse and rode slowly back to her house under the hill.

Suddenly, around a bend in the road, came "savages in their war dress, armed with guns." It never occurred to her to be afraid of them. She called out to know where they were going. "War! War!" they shouted. "They meant they were going to fight and it overwhelmed me. I had scarcely got back to my quarters when I heard skirmishing and firing, which by degrees became constantly heavier until finally the noise became frightful. It was a terrible cannonade and I was more dead than alive."

It was true that Burgoyne had ordered a "reconnoitering expedition." But at ten o'clock in the morning, when the troops were ready, they had been issued rum and five days' rations. "General Burgoyne with fifteen hundred men and eight cannon" started out "accompanied by Generals Riedesel, Phillips and Fraser." The troops were a mixture, "drawn from all the regiments except the 47th." Previously General Riedesel spoke of fifty Indians. Now he said there were a hundred and fifty, who "with a corps of Provincials crossed to the right flank in a wide circuit through the woods."

Burgoyne was once more using his favorite "three-pronged formation," placing himself in the center, Riedesel on the left near the river and General Hamilton on the right.[6] In a conference with the high officers, General Riedesel had proposed the night

before to return "behind Batten Kill" — or back to the vicinity of
Fort Edward. But Burgoyne had sounded his old war cry, BRITONS
NEVER RETREAT, and this morning he led his "reconnaisance in
force" south and westward, hoping to outflank Gates and attack
the Americans in the rear. All efforts to find out just what sort
of camp the rebels had fortified had failed — the underbrush was
too thick, at times the fog had been too heavy — but of course
according to precedent the rebels would run.

"Toward three in the afternoon the jaegers discovered a small
party of Americans near a house that lay a little way in advance
and was separated from them by a ditch" — so General Riedesel
said in his account of this day's events. The Americans, instead
of running, "grew stronger and stronger and Burgoyne, supposing
they meant to oppose his farther advance, fired his two twelve-
pounders at them but without producing the least effect. On the
contrary, they continued to increase in numbers." This was the
beginning of the Second Battle of Saratoga, also known as the
Battle of Bemis Heights.

"At four o'clock in the afternoon" (and here other German
officers take up the story) "the Americans attacked the left wing,
composed of grenadiers under the command of Major Acland,
who were posted in the wood." Major Acland was beaten back.

"Lt. Col. Specht had been assigned to the center under Burgoyne, with three hundred Germans." When Acland retreated,
Specht's flank was exposed. He ordered two regiments, Specht
and Hesse-Hanau, "to form a curve supporting the artillery. Specht
maintained his ground long and bravely." Then suddenly, "the
right wing under Lord Balcarres" moved off. He had "been
called back by mistake," and now Specht's right flank "was
equally exposed" and "balls struck within their lines from three
different sides. Three of their captains fell and their two cannon
were taken." Reidesel called what happened "a retreat," but
Captain Pausch said that "each man for himself, they made for
the bushes."

Brigadier Fraser, always commanding the advance guard, had been stationed "more to the right with one half of the English grenadiers, the light infantry and the 24th regiment." He saw that the center, or middle prong of the main army, was about to crumple — so he ordered the 24th Regiment to reinforce them, and he rode at the head of that regiment on his gray horse.

Back at the house on the Hudson, opposite the field of battle, the table had been set for dinner. Lady Fritz was still expecting her husband and her guests, Generals Fraser, Burgoyne and Phillips. She tried to shut out of her mind the terrifying roar of cannon from the nearby hill as she concentrated on her wifely duties. With all those generals coming, it must be a good dinner! The room was a pleasant one, rather large, with a low ceiling and a big fireplace where meat was turning on a spit. Even the cook who was such a rascal had not been able to get meat lately, but they had saved a shoulder of pork for just such an occasion. A long trestle table was set up before the fire with benches and various assorted chairs pulled up to it. General Riedesel's camp kit included a good many plates, cups, knives and two-pronged forks. Nothing was elegant from the point of view of a Baroness, but Mrs. General achieved a homelike atmosphere wherever she went. She would have been happy — if only those guns would stop.

"About three o'clock in the afternoon, in place of the guests who were to have dined," a litter came to her door. They were bringing General Fraser, "mortally wounded."

"The table was taken away and in its place they fixed a bed for General Fraser. I sat in the corner of the room, trembling. The noise kept growing louder. The thought that they might bring me my husband, in the same condition, tormented me incessantly," the Baroness said.

"General Fraser spoke to the surgeon, 'Conceal nothing from me. Must I die?'" The wound was abdominal, as Major Harnage's had been. By a miracle Major Harnage was recovering; but there was no hope for General Fraser. He suffered greatly and "amidst his groans" the Baroness heard him speak of his wife — and of "poor General Burgoyne." Prayers were read, and General Fraser asked that he be buried "next day at six o'clock on top of a hill which was a sort of redoubt." Burgoyne always called this "the great redoubt."

"The Americans advanced with more vehemence and in greater numbers" after General Fraser was carried from the field," said General Riedesel in his account written for the Duke of Brunswick. The forward "detachment was nearly surrounded when General Burgoyne determined to retire to the great redoubt."

Now the British were back on their first battle field, Freeman's Farm. "Scarcely had the troops been posted in the redoubt, than the enemy came to attack it with great fury." Everyone recognized the man on the black stallion. It was Benedict Arnold, fighting like a crusader against Saracens or like a Norseman gone berserk. He rallied the men, but they could not take the redoubt with its abatis of felled trees — branches pointing outward in the style of their own American breastworks. Arnold rode in the open across Freeman's clearing, under a hail of bullets; then he and the men who had gathered under his leadership "attacked Breymann's corps in front and on both flanks." Breymann was killed, and his men broke and ran. Arnold's horse was killed, and Arnold's leg was crushed — either by the fall of his horse, by a bullet, or by both. His comrades carried him from the field.

Captain Georg Pausch was on the scene with his artillery and wrote down what happened to him at the Second Battle of Saratoga. On the morning of October 7, he was ordered to get two six-pound cannon ready with ammunition carts to go with them. At ten he crossed to the right wing of Burgoyne's army, and it took him three quarters of an hour "to march from one wing of our army to another." He arrived at a deserted log house, which had a hole cut in its roof. Here "all the adjutants, engineers and quartermaster generals were gazing through their spyglasses" trying to get a glimpse of the enemy. But "nothing could be seen." Pausch posted his "two six-pound cannon on a somewhat elevated piece of ground" about twenty-five paces apart and fifty paces "in advance of the front." Major General Williams "of the English artillery" came up and posted two twelve-pound cannon in front of the log house. "After being made ready, they were loaded.

"An English officer arrived in haste, saying there were no cannon on the flank of the left wing and that I must immediately send one of mine." The Americans were not the only ones to protest orders — Pausch said he would not give up a gun. He would either take his two guns or stay where he was, "one cannon being no command for a subaltern, to say nothing of a captain." He reminded the Britisher that "they had four six-pound cannon of their own." The officer disappeared.

Half an hour later, Pausch "noticed a few patrols in the woods and on the height to the left of the woods." Then the "enemy's advance guard, who were in the bushes, engaged our jaegers, chasseurs and volunteers. The action extended all along the line, the enemy appearing in force." He was "serving his cannon," while the Americans marched out "at a double quick, and in squares, two strong columns" of them. They were reinforced "and advanced madly and blindly in the face of furious fire." The troops behind Pausch were gone. He never knew how long they had left him alone with his guns, but when he saw "great numbers" of Americans advancing on him he looked back where he supposed "our German infantry" was — and there was "not a man to be seen. They had all run across the road into the field and thence into the bushes and had taken refuge behind the trees."

Captain Pausch managed to get back to the log house, "where the two 12-pound cannon stood dismounted and deserted." Major Williams had been taken prisoner while directing the firing of these guns, and it was said that the hard-bitten old artilleryman wept at the loss of his cannon.

Pausch "presently came across a little earth-work, 18 feet long by 5 feet high." It had been thrown up by Burgoyne's advance picket, and Pausch posted his two guns here "and began to fire alternately with balls and with shells." He realized that he must have hit some of his own men "who were in the bushes" because the Americans "without troubling them, charged savagely upon my cannon hoping to dismount and silence them. In this they twice failed, being frustrated each time by the firing of my shells."

An English lieutenant of artillery came up and asked Pausch for ten artillerymen and one subaltern to serve the abandoned twelve-pounders left in front of the log cabin. But Pausch said he couldn't spare any men. Two of his detachment were killed, "three or four wounded, a number had straggled off." All the infantry he had commanded were "either gone to the devil or run away." Moreover, "I had no desire to silence my own cannon, which were still in my possession, and thereby contribute to raising the honor of another corps.

"Three wagons of ammunition were fired away by my cannon, which became so heated that it was impossible for a man to lay his hand on them. In front, and also to the right and left of my guns, I had conquered for myself . . . a pretty good fort. But the fire behind us was coming nearer. Finally the Americans were "repulsed in our rear. . . . I could see the road on which I had marched to this second position, as far as the plain and the clearing." The road was open — and here was a chance to retreat. Pausch and three of his men dragged one of the guns, "while a subaltern followed with the other cannon" still on its carriage. They got both guns on carriages and "marched briskly along the road, hoping to meet a body of our infantry" and make a stand. But "some ran in one direction, others in another" and Pausch "found the road occupied by the enemy. They came towards us on it, the bushes were full of them, they were hidden behind trees, and bullets in plenty received us." Pausch called to his remaining men to save themselves; he "took refuge behind a fence on the right of the road with the last of the ammunition wagons" and the horses. He saved these "with the help of a gunner," and here he "met all the different nationalities of our division, running pellmell. . . . In this confused retreat, all made for our camp and our lines. As soon as it grew dark, the enemy desisted from their attack."

One of Burgoyne's cannon was never fired before being captured and turned against him. All the "cannon with the exception of two howitzers fell into the hands of the Americans."

"We had been told that we had gained an advantage over the enemy," said Mrs. General Riedesel. But she knew better. She "could see by the downcast, sorrowful faces that the opposite was true." In the house where she lived "the whole entry and the other rooms were already filled with the sick, who were suffering from camp sickness," for that scourge of armies, dysentery, had broken out with great violence. Now the wounded were being brought in, and there was no place to lay them.

"I no longer knew which way to turn," Frederika said, "but finally I saw my husband coming and then I forgot all my sufferings and thanked God that he had been spared to me. We went outside and ate a hasty meal.

"Before my husband went away again he drew me to one side and told me that everything might go badly and that I must make ready to leave, but by no means to let anyone know what I was doing."

16

Mrs. General in Command

MRS. GENERAL had been critical of the fact that the women in Burgoyne's army knew all his plans. It was a matter of principle with her never to ask questions and never to repeat anything she knew concerning troop movements, so now she pretended that she was getting ready for the move to the log cabin which Major Williams had built for her behind the lines. She packed as though about to begin housekeeping there next morning.

"Milady Acland occupied a tent" in the field close to the house under the hill. "She slept in the tent but spent her days in camp" just as Lady Fritz had been doing, and she had come back to her tent when the action began on the heights of Saratoga. Toward evening "someone came to tell her that her husband was mortally wounded and in the hands of the enemy." Lady Acland "wept and we comforted her," said Mrs. General.

"She was the loveliest of women. I spent the night first comforting her and then looking after my children. As for myself, I could not go to sleep, as I had General Fraser and all the other wounded gentlemen in my room and I was afraid that my children would cry and disturb them." The little girls were huddled together in a corner on their camp mattress.

"General Fraser often sent to beg my pardon for making me so much trouble. About three in the morning they told me he could not last much longer. I wrapped my children in blankets and went with them into the entry." General Fraser died about eight o'clock. "After they had washed the corpse, they wrapped it in a sheet and laid it on the bedstead. We came back into the room and had this sad sight before us all day."

"Officers that I knew kept coming in, and the cannonade began again. Retreat was spoken of but not the least movement made toward it. About five in the afternoon" Mrs. General "saw the house" that Major Williams had built for her "go up in flames. So the enemy was close."

Orders came that General Fraser was to be buried at six o'clock that evening, the eighth of October, "at the great redoubt," in accordance with his last wish. This was a gallant gesture which Burgoyne could not resist, but it made Mrs. General angry. She did not believe that General Fraser would have wanted to postpone retreat if he had known what the situation was, and her husband shared her feeling.

"Precisely at six o'clock the corpse was brought out." Madam Riedesel was living so near that she had but to step out of the house to watch the cortege of "all the generals and their staffs" winding up the steep hill to the great redoubt. Drums beat the long roll as the procession mounted slowly. At the top of the hill the English Chaplain, Mr. Brudenel, read the service for the dead. Cannon balls "soared continually over the party or landed among them" with a vicious thud, sending up sprays of dirt. "Many cannon balls sped through the air not far from me," said Mrs. General, "but I had my eyes fixed on the hill, where I distinctly saw my husband in the midst of the enemy's fire."

General Burgoyne himself described the scene. "The incessant cannonade during the solemnity, the steady attitude and unaltered voice with which the chaplain officiated, though frequently covered with dust which shot threw up on all sides of him, the mute but expressive mixture of sensibility and indignation on every countenance, these objects will remain to the last of life upon the mind of every man who was present."

At first, the Americans had no idea what was going on at the great redoubt. When they saw that it was a funeral, they no longer loaded their cannon with ball but fired "minute guns in honor of the dead." But no one on the redoubt noticed this.

"The order had gone forth that the army should break up after the burial and the horses were already harnessed to our calashes," said Mrs. General, speaking for herself and the other officers' wives. "Major Harnage dragged himself out of the barn used as a hospital" and got into his wife's calash, "determined not to be left behind under a flag of truce." He saw the Baroness "in the midst of danger" and ordered the Riedesel servants to take the three little girls and get into the family calash. She "begged to stay, being determined not to set out before the troops."

"Well, then your children must go," Major Harnage insisted. "He knew how to take advantage of my weak side," Mrs. General admitted. "I gave up, got into the calash and we drove off at eight o'clock that night."

Darkness fell, and campfires were lighted in Freeman's clearing where Burgoyne's army had been encamped so long. Tents and marquees had been left standing and a rear guard fed the fires so that the Americans would think that troops were still there. But Burgoyne's army was at last beginning to move back up the Hudson, and "a great silence had been ordered" along the pitch-black road. There had been a heavy fog during the day; now there was no moon, there were no stars. And before long, it began to rain.

"We traveled continually all night," said Mrs. General. Little Frederika was afraid and began to cry, and her mother had to "hold a handkerchief over her mouth lest our whereabouts should be discovered.

"At six in the morning a halt was called at which everyone

wondered." It was now October 9. General Burgoyne sent orders to have "all the cannon ranged and counted, which worried all of us as a few good marches would have placed us in safety," Mrs. General added. Burgoyne "gave as his excuse that he wanted to refresh the troops and give time to the bateaux, loaded with provisions . . . to come abreast."

General Riedesel "was completely exhausted and seated himself, during this delay, in my calash. . . . He slept nearly three hours with his head on my shoulder. In the meantime, Captain Willoe brought me his pocketbook containing bank bills, and Captain Geismar brought his beautiful watch, a ring and a well-filled purse and begged me to keep all these for him."

It must have been about nine in the morning when "at last the army began its march" again. They moved at a snail's pace for "scarcely an hour" when another halt was ordered — this time because the enemy had been seen. It was only a scouting party of "about 200 men," and Mrs. General thought these Americans could have been taken prisoner "had not General Burgoyne lost his head."

Lady Acland wanted to cross into the enemy's camp to find her husband, and Mrs. General told her to make Burgoyne give her a pass.[1] So Lady Harriet sent one of her husband's aides, Captain Lord Petersham, to Burgoyne to ask for a flag of truce and an escort to Gates's lines, but at first Burgoyne refused. "I told her she should insist on it," said the Baroness. "She did, and finally got permission to go."

Confronted with a drama much to his liking, General Burgoyne sat down to write, dating his letter October 9:

"Lady Harriet Acland, A Lady of the first distinction by family rank and by personal virtues, is under such concern on account of Major Acland, her husband, wounded and a prisoner in your hands, that I cannot refuse her request to commit her to your protection.

"Whatever general impropriety there may be in persons acting in your situation and mine to request favors, I cannot see the uncommon perseverance, and every female grace and exaltation of character of the Lady and her hard fortune without testifying that your attentions to her will lay me under obligation."

Burgoyne sent Chaplain Brudenel with Lady Acland, to carry this letter.

Anburey said that Burgoyne "had not even a cup of wine to offer" to Lady Harriet Acland, "but from a soldier's wife she obtained a little rum and dirty water." This does not mean that Burgoyne had drunk all of his wine. He himself was still at Dovogat's house, his headquarters ever since the battle of Freeman's Farm, but his baggage was already in retreat. He did give Lady Acland "an open boat," and she set out with her "waiting-maid and the Major's valet de chambre, who had a ball in his shoulder," a wound he got while searching the battle field for the Major.

They put off into the Hudson, and Lady Harriet "herself hailed the sentry" at the first American outpost. The sentry was cautious — he told the lady to stay where she was and wait. It was about ten o'clock that same night, according to the American General Wilkinson, when he was "advised from the advanced guard that a bateau under a flag of truce had arrived from the enemy with a lady on board. Major Henry Dearborn was ordered to detain the flag till morning, the night being exceedingly dark." But Dearborn invited Lady Harriet to come ashore, built a fire for her in a log hut his pickets used, and "her attendants followed with her bedding and necessaries." Lady Acland "took tea. . . ."

"Next morning before sunrise" Lady Harriet floated on down the river to Stillwater, where Gates received her "with all the tenderness and respect to which her rank and condition gave her claim," as Wilkinson later wrote. By "condition" Wilkinson meant that Lady Acland was pregnant and was expecting her child soon.

Gates was as fond of composing long wordy letters as Burgoyne was, and he sat down to write a reply which he dated October 12:

"I had the honour to receive your Excellency's letter by Lady Acland. The Respect due to her Ladyship's Rank and the Tenderness due to her Person and Sex, were alone Sufficient Recommendations to entitle her to my Protection; considering my preceeding Conduct with respect to those of your Army whom the Fortune of War has placed in my Hands, I am surprised that your Excellency should consider that I could consider the greatest Attention to Lady Acland in the Light of an Obligation. . . ." Gates was telling the truth about his treatment of prisoners. He had sent doctors to Bennington to look after the wounded of both sides, and Burgoyne's wounded, which the British general had abandoned after the Second Battle of Saratoga, were being cared for along with the Americans. Chaplain Brudenel returned to Burgoyne with the letter from Gates.

"We spent the whole day in the pouring rain, ready to march at a moment's notice," wrote the Baroness Riedesel on the ninth of October, the day she had advised Lady Acland to leave. "The Savages had lost their courage and they were seen going home, in all directions. My maid-servant did nothing but curse her fate and tear her hair. I told her to compose herself or she would be taken for a Savage but she tore off her bonnet and let her hair hang down over her face." But "my good Lena," the children's nurse, who had come all the way from Germany, "said nothing although she was just as frightened.

"Toward evening, we came at last to Saratoga, which was only half an hour's march from the place where we spent the whole day. I was wet through and through and there was no place where I could change my clothes so I sat down before a good fire, undressed my children and we lay down together on some straw." The Riedesel calash must have crossed the bridge over the Fishkill, and perhaps the Baroness found shelter in some very crowded house among the three or four in town. General Phillips came during the night and Lady Fritz asked him why the troops had halted.

" 'My poor woman, I am amazed at you,' " Phillips said. " 'Here you are, soaked to the skin and yet you have the will and the courage to go on in this weather. I wish you were our commanding general! He halts because he is tired and intends to spend the night here and give us a supper.' In this latter achievement, General Burgoyne was very fond of indulging," said Lady Fritz caustically. "He spent half the nights in singing and drinking and amusing himself with . . . his mistress . . . who liked champagne as well as he did." Although Burgoyne was unable to offer Lady Acland any wine, it would seem he had now caught up with his supply. Burgoyne was spending one more night at General Schuyler's house, the best place he and his officers had so far found in America.

"On the 10th, at seven o'clock in the morning, I drank some tea by way of refreshment and we now hoped from one moment to the next that at last we would get under way again," said Mrs. General. She knew that her husband had "pledged himself to cover the retreat and bring the army through." But it was nearly noon when "an English officer brought me some excellent broth which he shared with me, as I was not able to refuse his urgent entreaties. Then we set out upon our march but only as far as another place not far from where we had started.

"The commissaries had forgotten to distribute provisions among the troops. There were cattle enough but not one had been slaughtered," and the excuse on the part of the commissaries was that no orders had been given. "More than thirty officers came to me who could endure hunger no longer," said Lady Fritz. "I had tea and coffee made for them and divided among them all the provisions with which my carriage was constantly filled." In spite of the "confusion and disorder," the Riedesel cook had been foraging; and he probably found conditions favorable to the art of stealing. Mrs. General was supplied with "sheep, poultry and pigs," but at last even her provisions gave out, and in despair she called to Captain Lord Petersham who was passing: "Come and see for yourself these wounded officers who are in need of everything!" She admitted that she spoke "passionately." She told him to tell Burgoyne, and in about fifteen minutes Burgoyne arrived in person. He told Lady Fritz that "a general was much to be pitied when he was not properly served or his commands obeyed," and he thanked her "very pathetically for having reminded him of his duty."

Mrs. General politely begged Burgoyne's pardon "for having meddled with things which I well knew a woman had no business with. . . ." She explained that it was just because she had nothing more to give the wounded officers. Burgoyne thanked her again, but she knew perfectly well he never forgave her "for the tongue-lashing."

Once more, "The horses were harnessed to our calashes ready to leave. The whole army clamored for a retreat," and General Riedesel again promised "to make it possible if no more time were lost." But now Burgoyne "gave express orders that provisions should be properly distributed." Burgoyne seated himself at table.

"About two o'clock in the afternoon, the firing of cannon and small arms was heard and all was alarm and confusion." General Riedesel sent an aide with a message for his wife, telling her what to do. She jumped into her calash with her children, gave Rockel his orders, and they galloped down the road. The tiny town of Saratoga was soon behind them and they reached a house on a bank overlooking the Hudson, where they were to take shelter. Just as they turned in at the dooryard Lady Fritz saw "five or six men with guns, on the opposite side of the river." These men took aim and fired.

Gates had sent this detachment across the Hudson on October

8, the day after the second battle of Saratoga. There were only nine hundred men, but they were to "make a show of field pieces," and at night they "arranged a long line of fires to indicate a large army." They had a battery on the riverside just opposite the house where General Riedesel had told his wife to take shelter. "We saw a number of officers on the stairs and on the east side of the house on the hill . . . apparently surveying our position and works," said Ebenezer Mattoon, the American officer who had been sent out to help block Burgoyne's retreat. Guns "were levelled with such effect as to disperse them."[2]

When Lady Fritz saw the men take aim, "almost involuntarily, I threw the children on the bottom of the calash and myself over them," she said. "At that instant the villains fired and shattered the arm of a poor Englishman who was already wounded" and was trying to take shelter in the house. The Baroness and her children now piled out of the calash and got safely under cover. "Immediately after our arrival a most frightful cannonade began, and became so heavy that we were finally obliged to take refuge in the cellar. I laid myself down in a corner not far from the door. My children lay down upon the earth with their heads in my lap and in this manner we passed the whole night."

The American Captain Benjamin Warren, whose retreat from Fort Edward had been harassed by Burgoyne's Indians, told how it was when it came to be Burgoyne's turn to retreat.[3] On Friday, the tenth of October, "the greatest part" of the American army "marched up to give them the fatal blow." They found the road "strowed with wagons, baggage, dead carcases, Ammunition, tents, etc., much of it as damaged as they could for want of time; houses and buildings mostly burnt as they retreated and the bridges also though our carpenters repaired them as fast as we marched."

On Saturday, October 11, Captain Warren arrived at Saratoga village just at sunset. He had seen a great column of smoke rising at the southern edge of the town and the smell of burning wood hung in the air. The British "burnt Schuyler's house, just as our people got there," he said.

The Baroness did not sleep at all on the night of her arrival at the house on the north side of town. The cellar where she and her three little girls had taken refuge was full of the wives of soldiers and their children, who cried in the terrifying darkness.

Worst of all, however, was "the horrible stench. The women and children, being afraid to venture forth, had soiled the whole cellar. . . . Next morning the cannonade began again, but from a different side." The Baroness was too good a general in her own right not to realize that this meant that Burgoyne's army was encircled, but the house where she had taken refuge was not at the moment under fire — so she saw an advantage and made the most of it: "I told everybody to go out of the cellar for a little while so I could have it cleaned or we would all be sick," she said. The army women obeyed Mrs. General without question, and she selected the strongest and healthiest among them and "at once set all hands to work."

Mops and brooms may have been left behind by the owners of the house, or perhaps they had to be improved from rags and birch twigs. In any case, Mrs. General found tools for her working party and had the cellar thoroughly cleaned as a German woman knew so well how to do. Next, she "fumigated" by "sprinkling vinegar on burning coals." Then she "ordered everybody out," including the working party, and "for the first time surveyed our place of refuge," she said. "It consisted of three beautiful cellars splendidly arched."

Mrs. General organized the people whose care she had taken over. The "most dangerously wounded of the officers" were brought in and laid in the cellar farthest from the entrance. The women and children were told to stay in the second section of the cellar, and all the rest were allotted places in the vaulted space nearest the door. "Each person had found the place prepared for him" in the cellar "when a fresh and terrible cannonading threw us once more into an alarm."

They closed the cellar entrance, but "many people who had no right to come in threw themselves against the door." Mrs. General had just sent her children into the space under the stairs and they would have been crushed if a mob had broken in, for the stairs were flimsy and badly built. "With arms outstretched" Lady Fritz held that door. Afterwards she could not understand how she did it, except that "God gave me strength," she said.

"Eleven cannon balls went through the house" and the people in the cellar "could plainly hear them rolling over their heads." Upstairs, surgeons were at work amputating a soldier's leg when a ball came through the house, table-high. The patient's "comrades ran off," but they came back to find that the cannon ball had taken off the soldier's other leg. The poor man was still alive.

"I, myself, was more dead than alive," said Mrs. General, but this was not on her own account but out of anxiety for her husband. As often as he could, he sent her an aide with a message to say he was all right.

During the day the "ladies" who had taken refuge in the cellar "sat together." They were Mrs. Harnage, wife of the major, and Mrs. Reynels,[4] whose husband was "the good lieutenant who shared his broth" with Lady Fritz on the road back to Saratoga. Under the circumstances, the Baroness had relaxed her stern German-Lutheran principles slightly: "The wife of the commissary" was now included among the "ladies," but she was still not mentioned by name.

Someone came to the cellar and spoke to one of the ladies. Lady Fritz saw the whispering and thought they were "glancing her way with exceedingly sad expressions." Suddenly she was sure that her husband had been killed and she "shrieked aloud." But "a moment, later, it was Mrs. Reynels who was "called from the room." Lieutenant Reynels was not dead, but a cannon ball had

taken his arm off at the shoulder. They brought him into the
cellar and laid him down as gently as possible, but "during the
whole night we heard his moans which resounded fearfully
through the vaulted cellars." The lieutenant died toward morning.

"My husband came to visit me, which lightened my anxiety
and gave me fresh courage," said the Baroness. People tried to
make themselves a little more comfortable in the cellar, and Mrs.
Harnage and Mrs. Reynels "made a little room in a corner by
hanging curtains from the ceiling." They wanted to fix up a corner
for Lady Fritz and her children, but she refused. She "had some
straw brought in, laid her camp bed on it and slept in the little
cubby-hole under the stairs. Her maidservants slept "not far off."
Suppose, in the course of a cannonade, this farmhouse should
catch fire over their heads! Mrs. General wanted to stay near the
door where she and the children would have a chance to escape,
even if it meant dashing out into gunfire.

"In the night, I was often terrified lest a stealthy and secret
retreat might have been ordered. My husband would have to
march away. When this fear overwhelmed me, I crept out of my
cellar to reassure myself, and if I saw the troops lying around the
fires, for the nights were already cold, I would return and be able
to go quietly to sleep."

All the men in the cellar were wounded, but there were three
English officers still able to move about. They had places opposite the cubbyhole where Lady Fritz and the children slept, and
they promised her that "in case of hasty retreat" each of them
would take one of her little girls on his horse. One of General
Riedesel's horses stood "constantly saddled" for the children's
mother. They would all try somehow to keep together.

The three children were afraid in that dark cellar, but they
were the daughters of a general and they knew they must not cry
the way the children of soldiers did. But little Frederika sometimes cried in her sleep. One of these three wounded officers "discovered a great talent, however. He could imitate very naturally

the lowing of a cow and the bleating of a calf." When three-year-old Frederika cried, he would "imitate these animals," and the little girl "would be still and we would all laugh."

The only water available to Burgoyne's troops "was from a very muddy spring." The men were so desperate that they "got water out of the holes the cattle made with their feet," and since it rained a great deal they "tried to catch water in their caps." More water was soon desperately needed for the wounded in the farmhouse, but when men went down to the Hudson with a pail they were either killed or wounded by riflemen from across the river. Mrs. General called for volunteers among the army women. Jane Crumer, the wife of a sergeant, set out across the meadow and not a shot was fired at her. After this, she brought water to the farmhouse whenever it was needed, "and they never molested her," said Mrs. General who had now learned two new things about Americans: they loved their "fatherland" and they "respected women."

The difficulty in keeping reasonably clean troubled Lady Fritz — she who put cleanliness next to godliness. On the third day in the cellar, some of the wounded lent her their "corner." Her three devoted British officers stood guard for her, discreetly turning their backs while she "changed her linen." The valuables she had promised to take care of — Captain Willoe's wallet, Captain Geismar's "beautiful watch and ring" — worried her. "I fastened them inside my stays, as I was in constant terror lest I should lose some of them and I resolved never again to undertake such a commission," she said.

"Our cook saw to our meals," wrote the Baroness, as casually as though she had been at home in her husband's ancestral castle. "But he cooked almost entirely without water and in order to quench thirst I was obliged to drink wine and even give it to the children." In spite of her love of cleanliness she did not seem to realize that wine would be better than water taken out of horse-tracks or even river water.

Fortunately, although much baggage had been "strowed upon the road," General Riedesel's wine had been saved in the retreat. "It was the only thing he could take," Lady Fritz said, and "our faithful Rockel," using the privilege due the family coachman, came to her in great anxiety: " 'I fear the General drinks so much wine because he dreads falling into captivity and is therefore weary of life.' " The Baroness reassured Rockel the best she could.

But Lieutenant Reynels had died, Mrs. Harnage's husband was still suffering from his wound, and "it seemed too much to hope that I should be the only fortunate one," Frederika said. She nevertheless prayed earnestly for her husband, who "lay outside by the watchfires at night" — and nights were "damp and cold." This alone might kill him, she thought, even if enemy bullets passed him by. She "constantly busied herself with the wounded" so that anxiety would not become unbearable.

There was a "Major Plumfield" who had "a small bullet go through both cheeks, shattering his teeth and grazing his tongue."[5] This wound became so horribly infected that the discharge from it "almost choked him"; he could not eat, "could hold nothing in his mouth." Lady Fritz gave him "a bottle of Rhine wine" and told him to keep some of it in his mouth all the time. This cleared up the infection and the major's wound healed.

"One day a Canadian officer came into our cellar who could hardly stand." Mrs. General thought he must be ill or gravely wounded; although there seemed to be no mark on him. She "finally got it out of him that he was almost dead with hunger," and she gave him her dinner.

"Finally . . . [Burgoyne] . . . spoke of surrender." Mrs. General Riedesel ought to have been called into the conference, for she had acted the part of commanding officer in her sphere.

17

Troops of the Convention

IT TOOK General Burgoyne's army almost four days to retreat eight miles. The ground where he was surrounded and besieged was not of his choosing — he just intended to halt on the small plateau a little west and north of Saratoga Village.

"We began to entrench ourselves, all hands being ordered to work . . .," wrote Lieutenant Digby, the young Britisher who thought that "a determination was made to fall nobly together rather than disgrace the name of British troops."[1]

"The men worked without ceasing during the night and without the least complaint of fatigue. Our cannon were drawn up and ready to receive" the Americans "at daybreak. Next morning their cannon and ours began to play on each other.

"We were obliged to bring our oxen and horses into our lines where they had the wretched prospect of living but a few days, as our grass was all gone and nothing after but the leaves of trees for them. Still they continued firing into us from batteries they erected during the night and placed their riflemen in the tops of trees but still did not venture to storm our works. At night, we strengthened our works and threw up more."

Burgoyne divided his troops into three camps, forming three different fronts, one facing south toward the Fishkill where lay the ruins of General Schuyler's house, one facing east toward the Hudson, and the third looking westward. Here the ground was high and heavily wooded, but there was no hilltop Burgoyne could have fortified. American troops on the east bank of the Hudson had been reinforced, General Stark was circling north and west; Gates moved forward to Freeman's Farm and then to Saratoga village.

On October 12, the same young Britisher wrote: "Our cattle begin to die fast and the stench is very prejudicial in such a small space. A cannon shot was near taking the General, as it lodged quite close to him in a large oak tree." Burgoyne had set up his marquee in a slight hollow in the midst of his men, and it was said that a cannon ball carried the leg of mutton off his dinner table. "I believe that the general's greatest wish, as indeed it ought to be, was for them to attack us," said Digby, but the Americans "acted with greater prudence well knowing what a slaughter must have been made upon them.

"In the evening, many of our Canadian drivers of wagons, carts and other like services found means to escape from us." On the morning of October 13 the American cannon "reached our post . . . the bulk of their army was hourly reinforced by militia flocking in to them. . . . Our lines were infiladed or flanked by their cannon. . . ."

Lieutenant Anburey took post at "a small redoubt" built of logs, breast-high, with "angles which faced the enemy. . . . A man risked his life if he ventured in day time to look over the works." To relieve the boredom, the men would hoist a cap on a stick for the "Yankee marksmen. . . . Instantly there would be one or two shot fired at it and as many holes through it. . . ." Only the "angles" in this redoubt were safe from riflemen, who could be seen coming out each morning and climbing into trees overlooking the outpost. Anburey and his men were forbidden to fire at them because of the shortage of ammunition, and if the British moved about they were picked off like quail in a clearing. Men became so stiff from sitting huddled in the "angles" all day that they could scarcely walk when darkness came. Anburey's horse had dropped a colt and he had become fond of the little thing, but now he had to shoot it because it was starving. Wolves were again heard close to camp. If cattle strayed, wolves got them.

"Surrounded by the enemy and obliged to pass a marshy ravine and to ascend a steep hill to reach them," Burgoyne could not attack the army under Gates, but Gates could easily cross the Hudson "to attack our rear." The "moment for retreat was past," Riedesel wrote, on October 13, 1777.

The German General would have felt still more bitter about Burgoyne's failure to retreat in time if he had known of the real situation among the detachments of American troops who held the escape routes. The American General John Fellows sent in a report from Batten Kill. "I have received one load of ammunition and that is all dealt out." Many of the troops were "destitute" of ammunition, "some flints being especially wanting." A detachment sent to Fort Edward captured "a few score of men" and "seven barrels of rum," but no provisions or ammunition.

The worst news of all for the Americans just now was that the "laboratory" for making ammunition in Albany was "at present standing still owing to the want of lead for musket cartridges and grape for canister. . . ."

But Burgoyne was unaware of all this. General Riedesel took up the narrative. On the thirteenth at a later conference, Burgoyne "stated that he saw no mode of attacking the enemy." The only possible retreat would be for each individual to make his way as best he could through "almost impassable forests." There "were only five days' provisions left . . . the defeat and dispersion of the army was not only probable but certain.

"After a short pause, intended to leave the officers time to reflect on what he had told them, General Burgoyne solemnly declared that he alone would be responsible for the present situation of the army, as he had never asked any advice, but required a submissive obedience to his commands." General Riedesel "could not but approve of a public declaration so well calculated to convince everybody." He had his aide, Captain Heinrich Urban Cleve, take careful notes of all the proceedings, write this account of them, and then he not only "begged all British officers to testify" to what Burgoyne had said, but had them sign Cleve's narrative.[2]

After his dramatic "short pause," Burgoyne "then laid the following queries before the council of war.

"1. Whether military history offers precedents of any army having capitulated in such a situation?
"2. Whether capitulation under such circumstances would be dishonorable?
"3. Whether the army really was in such a situation as to be obliged to capitulate?"

The staff thought hard, like a class of history students anxious to please the professor.

"On the first question it was generally answered that the situation of the Saxon army at Perna, of General Fink at Maxen, and of Prince Maurice of Saxony had been less forlorn than that in which our army was placed; and that nobody could have blamed the generals who should have capitulated at that juncture in order to save their armies." Someone (and it could have been Riedesel) remembered that "the King of Prussia cashiered General Fink, but chiefly to gratify his personal resentment." This last was not quite what General Burgoyne wanted to hear, but the "answer to question two, based on the answer to question one, was that the capitulation could not be dishonorable."

On the third count, "all the officers replied that if General Burgoyne could see any possibility of successfully attacking the enemy, they were ready to sacrifice their lives . . . but that their ground was untenable. . . ." General Burgoyne "then pulled out of his pocket the draft of propositions to be made to General

Gates. This was unanimously approved. We found it very much to our advantage — provided the enemy would agree to it."

They "sent a drum" into the American camp on October 13, with a note which read: "Lieutenant-General Burgoyne is desirous of sending a Field Officer to Major-General Gates upon a matter of highest moment to both armies. He requests to be informed at what hour General Gates will receive him, tomorrow morning." Next day, Major Kingston appeared with a much longer letter in Burgoyne's best style:

"After having fought you twice, Lieutenant-General Burgoyne has waited some days in his present position, determined to try a third conflict against any force you could bring against him.

"He is apprized of the superiority of your numbers and the disposition of your troops to impede his supplies and render his retreat a scene of carnage on both sides. In this situation he is impelled by humanity, and thinks himself justified by established principles and precedents of state, and of war, to spare the lives of brave men upon honourable terms; should Major-General Gates be inclined to treat upon that idea, General Burgoyne would propose a cessation of arms during the time necessary to communicate preliminary terms by which, in any extremity, he and his army mean to abide."

The cease-fire went into effect at once and in the sudden silence everyone breathed a deep sigh. The wounded crawled out of the cellar. The women and children went back to husbands and fathers in camp — or sought in vain for a man who was dead or missing.

Mrs. General Riedesel took quarters aboveground after what seemed the longest days of her life. "I had a good bed made up for my husband in a little room, while my children and I and both my maids lay down in a little parlor close by." The General fell into the deep sleep of total exhaustion.

About one in the morning a messenger came who wanted to

speak to General Riedesel. Mrs. General awoke and told the man to go away. But "I had to admit him, he was not to be denied," she said. "I finally agreed to wake my husband, the man gave his message, and I observed it did not please him. He lay down again and went back to sleep."

Next morning General Burgoyne reconvened the conference with his officers, and read General Gates's proposals aloud:

"General Burgoyne's army being exceedingly reduced by repeated defeats, by desertion, sickness etc., their provisions exhausted, their military horses, tents and baggage taken or destroyed, their retreat cut off, they can only be allowed to surrender prisoners of war."

Burgoyne's "officers unanimously declared that they would rather die than submit to such dishonorable conditions. . . . The suspension of hostilities ceased in consequence. . . .

"My husband went back to his post and I to my cellar," said Mrs. General. "A large amount of fresh meat was distributed to the officers . . . and the good woman who constantly kept us supplied with water made us a capital soup." But Lady Fritz "had lost all appetite." The wounded officers that she had been taking care of came and told her "it was absolutely necessary" that she should eat, and declared that they would not touch their own food until she had some with them. "I could no longer withstand their friendly entreaties," she said, "and they assured me it made them happy to be able to offer me the first good thing they had enjoyed."

General Gates had been writing joyful and triumphant letters to John Hancock, President of the Continental Congress, telling of "the great success of the Arms of the United States in this Department." He sent not so much as a line to General Washington, to whom the news of the victory at Saratoga was vitally important. But Gates owed his appointment entirely to Congress, as well he knew. He wrote an understandably gleeful letter to his

"Dear Betsy," telling his wife that "The voice of fame ere this reaches you will tell how greatly Fortunate we have been. . . ."

And then, on the lower Hudson, the Americans captured "thirteen British men, one furiner & Six of the Tories, one of which is a noted Vilin and has once before bin our Prisoner; his Name is Tailor." Daniel Taylor was an officer sent out by Sir Henry Clinton from Fort Montgomery, on the Hudson. He was disguised as a "country man" and was driving a cart. Clinton had just captured the fort, and he wrote a letter to Burgoyne on thin silk, dated October 8, 1777. "Nous y voila and nothing now between us but Gates," it said. "I sincerely hope this little success of ours may facilitate your operations. In answer to your letter of the 28 September by C.C. — I shall only say, I can not presume to order or even advise for reasons obvious. I heartily wish you success, & that etc." The letter was put into a hollow silver ball, made in two parts and threaded to screw together. The ball was lead coated to make it look like a bullet.

Taylor was captured at New Windsor, just below Newburgh. He had fallen in with a patrol from Webb's Connecticut Regiment, who were wearing red coats taken from a captured British transport, so that Taylor thought he was among friends. He spoke unguardedly, and these men offered to "take him to Clinton." Unfortunately for Taylor, he found himself in the presence of General George Clinton, then the American Governor of New York, instead of Sir Henry Clinton, second in command to Howe. Taylor panicked and swallowed his silver bullet — and apparently everyone saw him do it. Dr. Moses Higby was called, and recovered the bullet by forcing Taylor to drink "Tartaremetic." Taylor was court-martialed and hanged on October 14.[8] News, although slow to travel, reached Gates, not only concerning the message in the bullet but also that Sir Henry Clinton was taking the forts on the Hudson, one after the other, and burning American ships in the river.

"On the 15th of October in the morning, General Gates sent

new proposals of capitulation in which he acquiesced to all that General Burgoyne had stipulated, except some immaterial things." This was "to the surprise of everybody," General Riedesel said, but it did not take anybody very long to guess the reason. In his sudden willingness to agree to everything, Gates had tipped his hand. Clinton must be coming.

A council of war was called, and it was agreed to send two commissioners to "Arrange minor articles and prepare a Convention for the signature of the two respective generals." They went to work in the American camp, with General Gates, and by eleven o'clock that evening they had a paper which he signed, and the British commissioners gave their word of honor that Burgoyne would sign it too. But that very night, "a man calling himself a Royalist asked to see General Burgoyne. He said that he had heard third hand that General Clinton had taken . . . Fort Montgomery, that he had advanced as far as Esopus [the old Dutch name for Kingston] eight days previously and that according to all appearances he ought now to be in Albany."[4]

General Burgoyne "and several other officers were excited over this good but very vague news," General Riedesel said. "They wanted very much to break the treaty which had just been arranged and on the morning of October 16" they had another council of war to vote on it. Eight favored breaking the treaty, fourteen said it was as good as signed and could not be broken without breaking faith. The same majority "decided not to place faith in what the Royalist said. Even if Clinton had been at Esopus within the last four days, the supply of food was too short to wait for his help." But "in order to drag on negotiations" Burgoyne wrote Gates another letter, accusing him of having detached troops, saying the action was against good faith, and demanding to "send two officers to see and count the army of the enemy." He also said that in the treaty the word "capitulation" must be changed to "convention."

It was true that Gates was in a panic over Clinton's advance.

British General Vaughan burned Esopus [Kingston] on October 16. "They drove off the Inhabitants who remained in town to the River and fired on them, avowing they would shew no mercy." The Americans assumed that either Clinton or Vaughan was now headed for Albany, and there Mrs. General Schuyler was packing her family silver and a few clothes and some provisions in chests. She looked at the spacious rooms, their walls lined with family portraits, and wondered if she would ever see her home again. The Schuylers had built and lived in one of the most beautiful houses in Albany, or anywhere in the colonies, now the "States of America."

Burgoyne must have been "astonished" all over again when Gates refused to let him count the American army. That army was "four times larger" than it had been when Burgoyne arrived at Saratoga; Gates made this statement "on his word of honor," and he gave Burgoyne an hour to think it over, "after which he would take measures." Unfortunately, however, he agreed to amend the treaty to read "Convention" instead of "Capitulation," and to call Burgoyne's army "troops of the Convention" instead of "prisoners of war." Gates had lost the battle of the conference table, just as surely as Burgoyne had lost the battle of Saratoga.

General Burgoyne put on his handsomest dress uniform and mounted his horse. Doubtless he now had fewer than thirty carts loaded with personal baggage, but he had enough to support his dignity. General Riedesel, having taken too literally the orders to send back superfluous belongings, could not compete. But he gathered his aides around him and made the best appearance he could for the honor of the Duke of Brunswick. There was no one he could send back to the house above the river except "a groom" to escort his wife.

"We saw the British army piling their arms, the piles of arms extending from Schuyler's Creek northward nearly to the house on the hill," said Ebenezer Mattoon, who was posted across the river. "They were along the ground west of the road then traveled. . . ." General Gates's marquee was on "a level piece of ground about 150 rods south" of the ruins of General Schuyler's house and "a little south and west of this there is a rising ground, on which our army was posted in order to appear to the best advantage. About noon on the 17th [of October] General Burgoyne with a number of his officers rode up near to the marquee, in front of which General Gates was sitting, attended with many of his officers. The sides of the marquee were rolled up so that all that was transacted might be seen.

"General Burgoyne dismounted and approached General Gates, who rose and stepped forward to meet him. General Burgoyne then delivered up his sword to General Gates, who received it in his left hand, extending his right hand to take the right hand of General Burgoyne. After a few minutes' conversation, Gates returned the sword . . . the other officers did the same. Then all repaired to the table and while dining, the prisoners were passing by." This was the surrender as the American Ebenezer Mattoon saw it.

Mrs. General, weak from hunger and very nervous, did the best she could to prepare herself and her children for surrender. Now, at least, there was water so they could all bathe, and there was privacy for changing linen. She got out the good clothes she had saved for a triumphant march into Albany, and dressed herself and her children for a very different occasion. The little girls were scrubbed clean, their hair washed and combed. Augusta, now six, promised to take care of her sisters. Three-year-old Frederika would be sure not to cry; and Caroline, no longer just a bundle in blankets, would sit on her mother's lap in the calash.

Jane Crumer, the woman who had brought water to the people in the cellar, came to say good-by. And the men and women she had helped so greatly crowded round; someone told her to hold out her apron, and "everyone threw a handful of money in it."

She "received over twenty guineas," and as she followed the army, plodding along with the other women in their assigned place among the baggage, life would be a little easier for her. She could buy food and even a pair of shoes.

But now it was time to go. "I seated myself in my dear calash," said Lady Fritz. She and the children were all frightened as Rockel took up the reins and they drove down the road and "into the camp of the enemy." Then came a surprise. The Americans "all greeted me, even showing compassion in their faces at seeing a mother with her little children in such a situation.

"When I approached the tents, a noble-looking man came toward me, took the children out of the carriage and kissed them. Then with tears in his eyes he helped me to alight. 'You tremble,' he said. 'Do not be afraid.' "

" 'No,' " said Mrs. General, " 'for you are so kind and have been so tender toward my children that it has given me courage.' He then led me to the tent of General Gates, with whom I found Generals Burgoyne and Phillips, who were on an extremely friendly footing with him."

Lieutenant William Digby of the grenadiers described the surrender through English eyes. "About ten o'clock, we marched out according to treaty, with drums beating & the honours of war, but the drums seemed to have lost their former inspiring sounds, and though we beat the grenadiers' march, which not long ago was so animating, yet it seemed by its last feeble effort, as if almost ashamed to be heard on such an occasion." Tears (though "unmanly") forced their way to Digby's eyes.

One of the Germans told how the American army looked to him:

"We passed the hostile camp, in which all the regiments along with the artillery were drawn up under arms. Not one of them was properly uniformed, but each man had on the clothes in which he goes to the field, to church or to the tavern. But they stood like soldiers, erect, with a military bearing that was subject to little criticism. All their guns were provided with bayonets and the riflemen had rifles. The people stood so still that we were greatly amazed. Not one fellow made a motion as if to speak to his neighbor; furthermore, nature had formed all the fellows who stood in rank and file so slender, so handsome, so sinewy, that it was a pleasure to look at them. . . ." One of the German officers was "grieved that he cannot enroll any recruits from this people.

"The officers of the regiments in General Gates's camp wore very few uniforms and those they did wear were of their own invention. All colors of cloth were usable, brown coats, with sea-green facings, white lining, and silver sword knots; also grey coats with straw [colored] facings and yellow buttons were frequently seen . . . other officers on the other hand were in their ordinary clothes. . . .

"There were men with snow-white wigs with mighty long bushy hair at the sides and thick lamb's tails behind. There were glistening black Abbot's wigs which especially set off red and copper-colored faces. There were also white or gray English Pastor's wigs, whose horse or goat hair was done up in a dangerously high roll standing up in the air. You think such a man has a whole sheep under his hat. . . . They have a great respect for wigs. . . . The respected wearers of these various wigs are in part between their fiftieth and sixtieth year and . . . they sometimes cut a droll figure under arms. . . . But you recognize at first glance the earnestness which has led them to seize their guns and powder-horns and that — especially in engagements in the forest — it is no joke to oppose them and that they can cold-bloodedly draw a bead on anyone. . . .

"There were also regular regiments in the hostile army who could not yet be properly uniformed because of lack of cloth and time. These had standards with all manner of emblems and mottoes, some of which seemed to us very caustic. Still I must say in praise of the enemy regiments that there was not a man among them who showed the slightest sign of mockery, malicious delight, hate or other insult; it seemed rather as if they wished to do us honor."

General Gates, "a man between fifty and sixty," who "wears his thin gray hair cut round," was "very lively and friendly." He "wore spectacles because of his weak eyes" and stood at the door of his tent inviting all the "commanders of brigades and regiments" in, and "offering them all sorts of refreshments."[5]

"All the officers remained to dine with General Gates," said Mrs. General Riedesel but it was very evidently a party for men only. The Baroness, who was so apt to be anxious about proper social behavior, began to feel her cheeks grow hot. Mrs. Harnage and Mrs. Reynels were nowhere to be seen nor was "the wife of the commissary." Lady Fritz had never been at a surrender before and "the thing was so entirely new to me!" she said.

At this point "the gentleman who had received me so kindly on first driving into camp, came up and said, 'It may be embarrassing to you to dine with all these gentlemen. Come into my tent and bring your children. I will give you a frugal meal, I am afraid, but you would be a welcome guest.'

" 'You are certainly a husband and a father, since you show me so much kindness,' " said Lady Fritz — inviting the gentleman to tell her his name. He was "the American General Schuyler." Since American officers wore all sorts of clothes, she did not think it strange that he was out of uniform. Superseded by Gates, not yet vindicated by the court-martial he had asked for, Philip Schuyler was too much of a gentleman not to appear in order to congratulate his successful rival. But at the moment he was plain Philip Schuyler.

"Never have I eaten a better meal," said the Baroness. There was "smoked tongue, beef-steaks, potatoes, good bread and butter." The last "good bread and butter" she had eaten was in Canada. "I was content, I saw that all around me were the same, but what rejoiced me most was that my husband was out of danger."

"As soon as we had finished dinner, General Schuyler invited me to be his guest at his house in Albany. General Burgoyne would also be there. I sent and asked my husband what I should do. He sent me word to accept the invitation and as it was two days' journey from where we were and already five o'clock in the afternoon, he advised me to set out . . . and to stay over night at a place about three hours' ride away." General Schuyler sent "a French officer" as escort for Lady Fritz, perhaps because he had already discovered that she spoke French better than she did English.

18

Overland Journey

DAYS were growing shorter now that it was October, and darkness had fallen before the Baroness reached the house on the Hudson, partway to Albany. She was not entirely happy to see her escort turn back, leaving her alone with her children and the servants.

At the house was "a mortally wounded Brunswick officer" with a "French doctor" who was taking care of him. The "wounded man praised the good nursing of the doctor and the doctor may have been a good surgeon," but as far as Lady Fritz was concerned, he was "a young coxcomb." The doctor was delighted when he found that this most attractive German lady could speak French — and the Baroness soon wished she had not let him discover it.

"He began to entertain me with all kinds of sweet speeches and impertinences, among other things, that he could not believe that I was a General's wife, because a woman of such rank would not follow her husband into the army. I ought therefore to stay with him, he said. It would be better to be with the victors than with the vanquished.

"I was beside myself with his insolence but dared not let him see the contempt I felt because I had no protection. When night came, he offered to share his room with me." Lady Fritz an-

nounced that she would sit up in the room with the wounded
German officer. Whereupon the doctor "distressed" her "still
more with all sorts of foolish flatteries."

Suddenly the door opened and there was General Riedesel and
one of his aides. "Here, sir, is my husband," said Lady Fritz, with
a glance meant "to annihilate the Frenchman." The doctor "withdrew, looking very sheepish. Yet afterwards, he was so polite as to
give up his room to us."

The next day the Riedesels arrived in Albany. It was a pleasant
little city built on the natural terraces formed by the Hudson in
centuries past. Here and there a church steeple pricked through
trees now nearly bare of leaves. There was a large open square
where the militia drilled and paraded in times of peace, but the
grass had been worn away by the more purposeful drills of war-
time. General Riedesel and his aide rode down the cobbled street
close to the river, sending the cook with the camp gear to the
public square where the baggage was to be guarded by "ten or
twenty militia." The cook was to find a bed for himself. The
General, his aide and a few militia escorted Mrs. General's calash
as it jounced along over the stones, past warehouses and docks
which were for the most part empty and deserted, now that there
was no trade with British-held New York. Then the pitifully thin
horses struggled through mud as paved city streets gave place to
a country road.

They came to well cultivated fields, barns and stables, then
vegetable gardens where the harvest had been gathered. Set among
formal lawns and flower gardens was a tall brick mansion with
small-paned windows, bars painted white, and at the edge of the
roof a delicate white-painted balustrade. The Baroness did not
describe the Schuyler mansion, with its wide entrance hall and
handsome staircase, its drawing-room, wainscoted, paneled and
carved. She spoke only of the "friendly reception" Mrs. General
Schuyler and her children gave the family from Germany. "They

treated us as people would who could forget their own losses because of the misfortunes of others," said Lady Fritz. She was thinking of the blackened ruins of Mrs. Schuyler's country home, but perhaps she did not even know how close this town house in Albany had come to being looted and burned by Clinton.[1]

Schuyler had sent Colonel Varick, his former aide and now his secretary, to ride through to Albany to tell Mrs. Schuyler how many guests to expect. She and her servants had been preparing rooms: a chamber for General Riedesel and Lady Fritz, a small one for the children and the maids, and the great formal bedchamber for Burgoyne. "Even General Burgoyne was deeply moved at their magnanimity," the Baroness said.

General Schuyler had gone to look at the ruins of his Saratoga home. Nothing remained but the log "necessary," behind the house, and he dispatched orders to Albany for carpenters and blacksmiths. Later, Burgoyne sent him "two British soldiers who are masons by trade and prisoners" to help with the rebuilding of the house.

Meanwhile, young Varick wrote to Schuyler from Albany: "On Saturday, Burgoyne mentioned with tears in his eyes, his situation — that he had received so much civility from you and again repeated by Mrs. Schuyler, whose property he had destroyed."

Drying his eyes, Burgoyne retired to Mrs. Schuyler's guest chamber overlooking the Hudson to write a letter to Sir William Howe. Among the many concessions he had won from Gates was permission to send an officer to Howe with dispatches, unopened and uncensored. So, in a letter marked *Private*, Gentleman Johnny told his real thoughts: "The treatment of the officers and troops in general is of so extraordinary a nature in point of generosity that I must suppose it proceeds from some other motive than mere kindness of disposition."

Burgoyne was proud of the treaty or "Convention" he had

made with Gates, and he had good reason to be — for it was a masterpiece. His army was to march to Boston and then have "Free passage to great Britain, upon condition of not serving again in North America during the present contest." In case Howe could not see the beauty of this any better than Gates, Burgoyne spelled it out. It would "enable the Mother Country to send forth the force at home in proportion to what she will receive from their return. . . ." If Howe liked this idea, he was to "order transports and convoy to Boston without delay."

On the other hand it might be better to send the whole Convention army to New York and there exchange Burgoyne's troops for a few American prisoners. Burgoyne arranged for this alternative in the next article of his Convention, but if Howe liked the idea, "I confide in your justice and friendship not to leave me unexchanged," he wrote. "My honor and in great measure my life depend upon my return to England." He planned to see the King personally and to exert his oratorical gifts in his own behalf in Parliament, where accusations would surely be made against him.

General Burgoyne wrote two letters, both headed "Albany" and both dated "October 20, 1777."[2] One was his "official" letter, in which he said: "General Riedesel exerted himself to bring up a part of the left wing, and arrived in time to charge the enemy with regularity and bravery." This was during the battle of Freeman's Farm when Riedesel sent to know what the shooting was about. In describing the Second Battle of Saratoga, Burgoyne complimented his foe General Benedict Arnold, who led the enemy when they stormed the lines "with great fury." Arnold was "wounded, but unhappily the entrenchments of the German reserves . . . were carried."

But in his letter marked "Separate and Private" Burgoyne told another story:

". . . For your private consideration, I have to add to the circumstances of my public letter . . ." There were "the scandalous defection of the Indians; a desertion or timidity worse than deser-

GENERAL BARON VON RIEDESEL

These two paintings, copies of German originals, are the property of Mrs. Kenneth Bullard and are reproduced with her kind permission. Photographer: George Bolster, Saratoga, New York.

THE BARONESS VON RIEDESEL

Augusta, Countess Reuss

Frederika, Countess Reden

Caroline
(unmarried)

Amerika
Countess Bernsdorf

Charlotte
m. Major von Schoeni

THE FIVE RIEDESEL DAUGHTERS

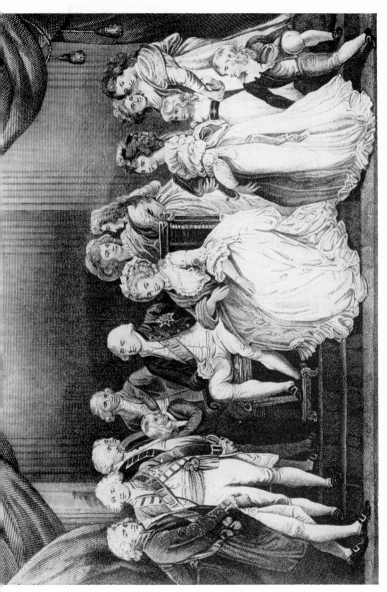

George III and Family

As the Baroness Riedesel saw them. "All the royal children . . . all beautiful as pictures." (from the Emmet Collection No. 3510, Manuscript Division,
New York Public Library.)

GENERAL JOHN BURGOYNE BY SIR JOSHUA REYNOLDS
(from the Frick Collection, New York City.)

GENERAL SIR GUY CARLETON

First Lord Dorchester, Governor of
Canada. (Courtesy of the Public Archives of Canada)

GENERAL SIR FREDERICK HALDIMAND

Governor of Canada. (Abbey Photo
Service: Courtesy of the Public Archives of Canada)

MAJOR GENERAL WILLIAM PHILLIPS

from the Frick Art Reference Library)

THE BRIDEGROOM

Friedrich Adolphus von Riedesel
as "Captain of Hussars"

GENERAL PHILIP SCHUYLER

Commander Northern Department, American Army. (Emmet Collection No. 2613, Manuscript Division, New York Public Library)

GENERAL HORATIO GATES

"The Superseder", Northern Department. (Emmet Collection No. 3586, Manuscript Division, New York Public Library.)

GENERAL WILLIAM HEATH

In Command of the Prisoners in Cambridge. (Emmet Collection No. 3546, Manuscript Division, New York Public Library)

Castle at Lauterbach

(A photograph of this sketch was very kindly sent by Baron Dr. von Galera from Lauterbach)

St. James's Palace Mall

Where they "Point the Finger" at the Baroness and her little girls. (Reproduction from Salaman's *London Past and Present* courtesy of Prints Division New York Public Library)

QUEBEC

Engraved at Augsburg and "published in Germany about 1775," this picture is captioned in French and German: "A
... of Canada in North America ... it was the capital of New France but the English took it in 1759 ..."

FRASER'S FUNERAL AT THE "GREAT REDOUBT" AT SARATOGA

This picture was sketched either by Lt. Anberey or a friend who was also at the Battle of Saratoga. It was afterwards engraved in London, the engraver using his imagination.

BARRACKS OF THE PRISONERS OF SARATOGA

At Charlottesville, Virginia. Here is another illustration from Anburey's *Travels in America* done at the scene but embellished by the London engraver.

Plan of Boston

As the captive Troops of the Convention looked out over Boston from Prospect and Winter
Hills, there was but a small town to be seen.

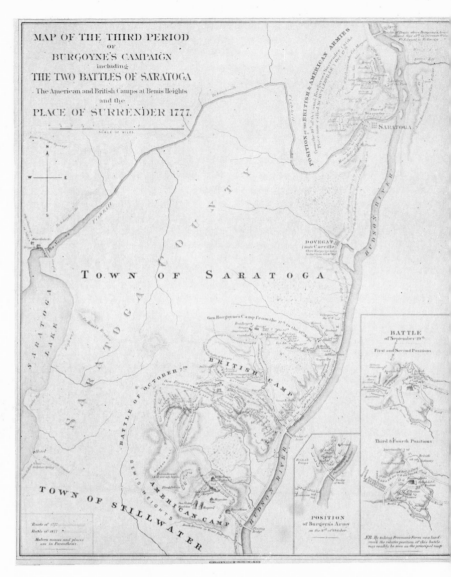

BURGOYNE'S POSITIONS AT THE BATTLES OF SARATOGA

This map comes from *Battles of Saratoga* by Mrs. Ellen Hardin Walworth — a paperbound book published in 1891 and sponsored by the Saratoga Monument Association. New roads have been built, but this map remains one of the best to be found.

tion of the Provincials and Canadians, a very few individuals excepted; and a strong disposition on the part of the Germans to be prisoners rather than endure hard blows." So much for Riedesel's troops, who had saved him twice.

"Had all my troops been British, I in my Conscience believe I should have made my way through Mr. Gates's army. At Saratoga, destitute as I was of provisions, I was not without resources to have opened a passage to Ticonderoga had my whole army been in a temper for hardy enterprise — even British troops declined. The utmost that the officers gave me to hope from the complexion of their men was that they would fight upon *that* ground if attacked. The Germans fell short of that — it was notorious that they meant to have given one fire and then to have clubbed their arms."

Letters were being written in more than one of Mrs. Schuyler's upper chambers. General Riedesel also had a report to make, and although he passed on the blame as was only human, the tone of his letter was very different:

"The army has been the victim of poor planning by the War Ministry in London," he said, writing in French to the Duke of Brunswick. There was the matter of Howe's failure to meet Burgoyne, but there was also pride. "The army has been the victim of our own vanity, encouraged by the taking of Ticonderoga, so that in order to achieve a great renoun in England the whole army has been risked." He spoke of the impossibility of so large a force leaving bases so far behind and penetrating a wilderness with no knowledge of the terrain.

But Riedesel wasted few words in vain regret or recrimination. He spoke of his men: "A soldier is worse off than a commander — and all that they have suffered has been in vain." Almost worse than defeat was the utter confusion and lack of system. German regiments were scattered, some in Canada, some prisoners of war, some among the "Convention Troops," as they were to be called. General Riedesel begged to be relieved of his command.

"What troubles me even more than the sad situation is the regret and embarrassment that all this will cause Your Serene Highness," he said.

The Duke of Brunswick had already gone on record as doubtful of the practicability of Burgoyne's plan, and he had no intention whatever of dispensing with the services of so faithful an officer as Riedesel. But of course his reassuring letter would be a long time coming, and Madam Riedesel would have a hard time cheering her unhappy General.

The rest, the good food and above all Mrs. Schuyler's warm-hearted welcome were what Lady Fritz needed most after her long ordeal and to prepare her for difficulties ahead. Even the children had playmates for a little while. Doubtless twelve-year-old John Bradstreet Schuyler found little girls of six, three, and a year and a half much beneath his notice. But there were Philip Jeremiah Schuyler, aged nine; Rensselaer, aged four; and Cornelia, only ten months old. They were a lively family, and it was said that one of them, probably Rensselaer, burst into Burgoyne's bedroom, where the great man himself lay in the canopied bed, his aides on mattresses on the floor around him. "Surrender!" Ren shouted. "You are all my prisoners." The little boy was "very arch and forward," and his mother apologized for him.

Burgoyne lingered on as a guest of the Schuylers', where they served "a table of more than twenty covers for me and my friends," he said. These guests gave Mrs. Schuyler "no small trouble," but Burgoyne behaved "with Great Politeness."

General Riedesel and his family left the Schuylers' hospitable home as soon as they could, because the General was anxious about his troops — who were already marching overland.

Mrs. Schuyler gave the Baroness a letter to the oldest Schuyler daughter, Angelica, who, with her sister Betsy, was living in Boston. Angelica had eloped with John Barker Church in July.[3] "This match was exceedingly disagreeable to me and I had signified it to him," General Schuyler said. "But as there is no undoing this Gordian knot . . . I frowned, I made them humble themselves, forgave, and called them home." Angelica's husband had gone to Boston to make his fortune building and buying shares in privateers. Angelica would surely enjoy knowing the Baroness Riedesel, her mother said, and she was right. But she spoke of her daughter as "Mrs. Carter," not "Mrs. Church." John had taken the name of Carter when he left England in haste because of a duel, and not even his wife knew his right name at this time.

The "mortally wounded" Major Acland was in Albany, not wounded mortally at all but getting well fast. The Baroness parted with Lady Acland with real regret. General Schuyler was to send his aide, Colonel Livingston, and his own coachman, horses and sleigh to carry the Aclands to New York. On his return, Colonel Livingston was to be captured by Tories — but he was to escape.

General Arnold was also in Albany, also recovering from a wound — a hero to the British as well as to the Americans. But he had fought his last battle for his country at Saratoga; within three years he would be despised even by the British, and in America the name of Benedict Arnold would be forever linked with treachery.

General Riedesel need not have hastened across the Hudson to catch up with Burgoyne's defeated army. The progress of the Convention Troops toward Boston was painfully slow. On October 18, the day after the surrender, they were herded down to Stillwater to be ferried over the Hudson at the wide stretch of calm water just above the rapids. But there were not nearly enough rafts to carry so many men, and only the British crossed the first day. The Germans encamped in the rain, on the west bank. The Germans were to take a different route to Boston in any case, so that the small towns the prisoners passed through would not be swept completely bare of provisions.

At first, the younger British officers had a sort of cross-country junket, at least according to Lieutenant Anburey. "After we had crossed the river, we purchased some liquor and fresh provisions of the inhabitants," he said. "This purchase convinced us of the value of the precious ore as the Americans received our guineas with much cordiality and gave us paper dollars in lieu, at the rate of nine for a guinea." He said that the "real" rate of exchange was "four and two thirds dollars." Now he wished he had not "greatly despised and converted to all manner of uses the many reams of paper dollars taken at Ticonderoga."

"We were two days crossing the Green Mountains," said Anburey. The route assigned to the British prisoners led through what is now called the Berkshires — and the wonder of it is that they did so well. "The roads across were almost impassable" — and when they reached the top of the pass "there came a heavy fall of snow. After this, it was impossible to describe the confusion; carts breaking down, others sticking fast, some oversetting, horses tumbling with their loads of baggage, men cursing, women shrieking and children squalling."

At one time, Anburey was assigned to "the baggage guard" where the women and children were. "Exclusive of being covered with snow and riding about after bat men to keep them together . . . my attention was directed to a scene which I did not think possible for human nature to endure," he said. "In the midst of the heavy snow storm, upon a baggage-cart and with nothing to shelter her from the inclemency of the weather but a bit of oilcloth, a soldier's wife was delivered of a child." She and the infant arrived safely in Boston at the end of the march. "It may be said that women who follow a camp are of such masculine nature that they endure hardships but this woman was quite the reverse, being small and of a very delicate constitution."

It was now, in the vicinity of Williamstown, that Anburey encountered "that indelicate custom they call bundling," as he put it. He thought, however, that the American's point of view was "innocent." Arriving at "a small log hut," Anburey found that his servant with his camp mattress had lagged behind. But American featherbeds were "remarkably good," he had observed — "neat and clean." Since there were only two beds in the log hut, "I inquired which I was to sleep in," he said, assuming of course that he had a right to one or the other.

" 'Mr. Ensign,' said the housewife, 'Our Jonathan and I will sleep in this and our Jemima and you will sleep in that.' "

Anburey seems to have been embarrassed as well as surprised. He offered to sit up all night, but the father of the family "immediately replied, 'Oh la! Mr. Ensign, you won't be the first man our Jemima has bundled with, will it, Jemima?'

"When little Jemima, who bye the bye, was a very pretty black-eyed girl of about sixteen or seventeen archly replied, 'No, father, by many, but 'twill be the first Britainer.' I did not go to bundle with her," said Anburey, although he was "gravely tempted." He would be "in the same room with her father and mother, my kind host and hostess! I thought of that — I thought of more besides — to struggle with the passions of nature; to clasp Jemima in my arms — to — do what? you'll ask — why to do nothing! For if amid all these temptations the lovely Jemima had melted into kindness, she had been an outcast from the world — treated with contempt, abused by violence — No, Jemima, I could have endured all these things to have been blessed by you, but it was too vast a sacrifice when you was to be the victim." After these pious reflections, Anburey added that "great" must be the "virtue" or "cold" must be "the American constitution when this unaccountable custom is in honorable repute and perpetual practice."

Apparently Anburey never saw the "bundling board" which Jemima's father would have fastened securely down the middle of the bed.[4] High, thick and tightly clamped in place, it protected virtue while Jemima and her friends also modestly kept their clothes on. Although there were tales of ardor and the circumventing of bundling boards, in all probability Lieutenant Anburey need not have been so worried.

Starting out a day later, the Germans were at last ferried across the Hudson and marched to Schaghticoke. They, too, had eyes in their heads where girls were concerned; they wrote accounts which were published in Germany and read not only by the families of men hired by George III but by Germans wondering if America might be a good place to live some time.

"We received provisions from the Americans," the Brunswickers wrote. It was fresh meat, and they had "tasted almost nothing but salt pork the whole campaign." They marched only three miles on the east bank of the Hudson before dark, because the river crossing had taken so long. Schaghticoke was "a village inhabited by Dutchmen, rich but very avaricious people. . . . From here on, we found a great quantity of apples from which in New York and all New England they make an incredible amount of cider. . . .

"Here they first stole our horses, a trick which did not cease the whole march. To comfort us, they said that we had either stolen them ourselves or must have bought them from the Royalists who stole them. . . . We could not understand however, how they pretended to reclaim horses born and bred in Canada and even German horses."

But even if the Yorkers and all the New Englanders were horse thieves, one young German who was writing home had great admiration for the girls he saw along the way. "The womenfolk in this whole extensive region . . . are slender and straight, fleshy without being stout. They have pretty little feet, very solid hands and arms, a very white skin and a healthy complexion without having to paint. I have hardly seen one with pockmarks, but smallpox innoculation has long been in use here. Their teeth are very white, their lips pretty and their eyes very laughing and animated. At the same time, they have natural good manners, a very unconstrained manner, a frank, gay face and natural boldness.

"They think a great deal of cleanliness and of good footwear. They dress very decently, but then, any clothes would become them. . . . They curl their hair every day, do it up in a moderately high tuft in front and a chignon at the back. Generally they go bareheaded and at the most put on a tiny heart-shaped cap or other such trifle on their heads; now and then a rustic nymph lets her hair fall free and ties it with a ribbon.

"If they go out, they put on a silk wrap and pull on gloves no matter how miserable a hut they live in. They know how to drape themselves very neatly in their wraps so that one little white elbow peeks out. Then they put on their heads a Corsican or other well-made sun-hat from beneath which they can peep out very roguishly with their mischievous eyes.

"In the English colonies, the beauties have fallen in love with red silk and woolen wraps. Dressed in this manner, a girl runs, springs and dances along and offers a friendly 'good day' or mayhap according to the nature of a question, gives a pert little answer. Dozens of these pretty girls stood by the road everywhere and let us pass in review, laughed at us mockingly now and then or now and then coquettishly extended an apple with a curtsy. We thought at first they were city girls, or at least those of class 2, but lo! they were the daughters of poor peasants [whose] fathers one recognized as such by their garb."

Although the Germans were sure they recognized a "poor peasant" when they saw one, these men in homespun and leather "had incredible stores of grain. Great heaps of it lay in bays covered with temporary roofs," and barns were filled with hay, so that there was no place for the plodding prisoners to sleep except in the fields. If some "peasants" lived in log huts, others had well-built farmhouses "the interior fitted up with very good furniture . . . even to mirrors with gilded frames and very good pendulum clocks."

The Germans were sure that there was "petticoat rule throughout America." They did not seem to notice that there were sheep as well as cattle on nearly every farm, and that hardly a house was without a spinning wheel and a loom, so they concluded that "wives and daughters made a display beyond the income of most men. The last penny from his pocket must be yielded for this purpose — there is no help for it." There was something extremely puzzling about this situation, from a German point of view. "The women do not get it by stamping their feet, do not bite or scratch their husbands, do not fall in a faint or feign illness — Heaven alone knows how they go about it so that their husbands submit so patiently to this taxation."

General Riedesel's men had seen but few Negroes in their lives, but they did not have to wait to travel south to observe slavery. From the Hudson "to Springfield [Massachusetts] one finds few habitations without a Negro family dwelling in a separate cabin. . . . The children are well fed, especially while still young, and their slavery is very bearable. The Negro is much like the Peasant's hired man. He can go to war in his master's place, hence you never see a regiment in which there are not a lot of Negroes and there are well-built, strong, husky fellows among them. Here also are many free Negro families who dwell in good houses, have means, and live quite in the manner of the other inhabitants. . . ."

Days grew short, nights were bitterly cold, and in front of the Germans the Berkshires now rose like a wall. They crossed at Great Barrington — where they "never saw a ruder, more spiteful people." Not even the officers were allowed "to stick their noses inside the door" of any of the houses and had to "lie in stables which had not been cleaned out and in barns." The Germans plunged into deep forest immediately on leaving town. Then the road began to rise with incredibly steep grades and it was hard to imagine that carts had ever used it. These woods were known to be full of bears and it seemed as though the men (and women and children) from Brunswick might be following a bear-track. It began to rain.

Just as they thought the so-called road would never emerge from the forest, they came out upon a ridge in the tiny town of Blandford. Now the rain changed to sleet and snow. "The wet clothes froze like armor on the body and one grenadier froze to death on the march." They reached Westfield, where "the nature of the weather softened the hearts of the inhabitants and they took us in." Westfield was "a really nice town."

The Brunswickers used their eyes while marching through Springfield, Massachusetts. They praised "a small but well-built arsenal." Springfield "was now an important munitions center of the Americans. . . . We found there several parks of artillery . . . with, among other things, twelve brand-new four-pound French cannon. The storehouses were crammed full. In all the houses, workmen of every sort were staying, who are making ammunition wagons, gun carriages, muskets, etc." They saw "wagons as good as can be made in England . . . and order reigned in everything."

On plodded the Germans, giving Massachusetts towns a good or a bad mark, as the case might be. Palmer was "a wretched village," Brookfield had "good houses and rich inhabitants," Worcester was "a thriving little city."

General Riedesel, the Baroness and the three little girls had stayed only three days with the Schuylers. When they left, Lady Fritz said that the Schuylers "acted as if they were very reluctant to part with us." The little girls hated to leave the first friends they had made among the Americans. But Burgoyne would stay in Albany one week more, his "suite and visitors" entirely discomposing "the economy of the family."

Now the Riedesels discovered that their "knave" of a cook had lost all their campaign equipment. He said the wicked Americans stole it, but eventually they found out that he himself had sold it. "The British officers each gave us something — one gave a pair of spoons, another some plates," said Mrs. General. "We used these borrowed things for a long time" and "it was at great cost" that they finally acquired anything more.

Mrs. General had her "calash covered with coarse linen which in turn was coated with oil" to keep out the rain. "I do not know whether it was my carriage that attracted the curiosity of people to it but it certainly looked like the kind of wagon they carry rare animals around in," she said. Sometimes, as they traveled through the small towns, the crowds pressed so close that Rockel would have to pull up the horses and come to a halt. Lady Fritz was good-natured about it. She thought the crowds would "tear off the linen covering in their eagnerness to see what was inside," so she would get out and talk with the people. "I must say, they were very friendly," she remarked, "and were particularly delighted by my being able to speak English." She no longer believed that Americans ate cats, but she seemed surprised to discover that "English was the language of their country."

It was a long, hard journey. "God supported me," said Mrs. General, "and I lost neither my frolicsomeness nor my spirits."

But General Riedesel, as he rode forward to help his officers try to find shelter for his men, or as he rode beside his wife's calash, was surveying in his mind's eye the ruin of his military career. He expected to be called home in disgrace. He never supposed he would be given another command and a chance to redeem his reputation; and, as his wife put it, "he was gnawed by grief." The constant halts made him so angry "he could scarcely endure them." And one night he was ill "from an emetic he had taken," doubtless the army doctor's prescription for a broken heart.

The noise "our American guard made, who never left us but were continually drinking and carousing before our very door," kept the General awake. He sent a message for them to be quiet, "but they redoubled their racket."

So Mrs. General went herself to talk to the guard. "I told them that my husband was ill and begged they would be less noisy. Immediately, all became still. . . ."

19

The Baroness in Cambridge

O N THE twenty-third of October, at one in the afternoon, the cannon on Fort Hill, overlooking the city of Boston, began to roar, sending up a dense cloud of smoke. The guns on Dorchester Heights replied. Boston citizens might have been alarmed at first, for they had not forgotten the hungry, humiliating days of occupation and they constantly feared a return of the British fleet. But this was a thirteen-gun salute telling a joyful story. Rumor of "the capture of General Burgoyne and his whole army" had reached Boston the day before — but nobody believed it. Now a courier, breathless from his six-day journey, confirmed the news.

In Cambridge that night, "the colleges were beautifully illuminated."[1] There was a bonfire on Cambridge Common, and a constant popping and banging as the Americans troops stationed in Cambridge answered the fire of cannon on the Common. "Prominent gentlemen of the town and army" got up a dinner and drank toasts until morning. Tory newspapers announced that the news of Burgoyne's surrender was all a hoax, but the courier had seen it with his own eyes.

Major General William Heath's headquarters in Boston were "illuminated," and for the moment he was a happy man as he went about putting lighted candles in every window. He was

251

forty years old, "of middling stature, light complexion, corpulent and bald-headed." Since 1632, when the first William Heath had taken up land in Roxbury, Heaths had tilled their fields. The present William was much more of a country squire than a general. But he had a passion for American self-government, and he had been a member of the Massachusetts General Court when Gage dissolved it. At seventeen he had joined the Ancient and Honorable Artillery Company of Boston. Later he helped to organize the Minute Men, and he was one of the few "embattled farmers" at Lexington who knew how to fire a cannon. He received his rank of Major General after the Battle of Bunker Hill, but he had proved no strategist when New York City was taken and now most of his duties concerned civilian defense. General Heath was honest, incorruptible and fearless. He could keep records, and Washington needed such men.

Heath's mood of elation over the American victory at Saratoga lasted only until he got the news that Burgoyne's surrendered troops "were coming this way." As he was commander of the Eastern Division, they would be under his care, and he must have them guarded, housed and fed. It was gratifying that everyone from Washington on down thought that Heath could handle the problem, but it would have been better still if someone had been willing to help him.

Heath had responsibility, but he hated to assume military authority over civilians.[2] Everything he attempted to do he put before both "Houses of the Assembly" in Boston. The Massachusetts legislature felt no kindness toward their uninvited guests. The "best men of the militia" were ordered to report for guard duty, first of all. But the drafted men were allowed to hire substitutes, and a great number "of Lads and old men" appeared. There were far too few of them, even if they had been good soldiers. Those who came shuffling into line would desert as soon as they felt like it and, in vain, Heath begged for more and better guards.

The barracks on Prospect Hill in Somerville and the Winter Hill barracks on the road to Medford had been occupied by American troops. They would now shelter Burgoyne's army, the British on Prospect Hill, the Germans on Winter Hill. But the buildings were in bad repair, carpenters hard to find and lumber in short supply. The American troops had been far from comfortable in the barracks and people were unable to see why Burgoyne's troops were entitled to anything very much better.

But the greatest difficulty was in getting houses for the officers. It was decided that they should live in Cambridge, because in Cambridge was "Tory Row," a street lined with large mansions, the country homes of Boston Tories who had departed with Gage or earlier. The finest house had belonged to Major John Vassall, a Tory, who fled in 1775. His mansion had been Washington's headquarters. It would be "suitable" for General Burgoyne, but when "the lady who lives in Vassall's house was asked to move out for General Burgoyne she answered very short, that she was burnt out of Charles Town, she supposed by his orders. She would move out in a moment for General Washington, but not for *him*."[3]

In order to survive a winter on those hills overlooking Boston, Burgoyne's troops would need firewood for their small iron stoves. In the mansions on Tory Row in Cambridge, fireplaces in every room consumed great quantities of wood. Even before the Revolution firewood had been scarce around Boston, and small schooners brought it in from Maine or Nova Scotia. The British blockade had stopped these little ships and the countryside for miles around had been scoured for wood. People stole out in the night to cut trees not their own, and farmers tried in vain to save their apple orchards. Now these prisoners were coming, and if Massachusetts citizens had anything to say about it, they would get firewood last if at all. Produce and forage for horses were also in short supply — and again who could blame New Englanders if they wanted to supply themselves and their own troops first?

Burgoyne's troops arrived in Cambridge, Massachusetts, on Friday, November 7, 1777, and Hannah Winthrop, wife of a Harvard professor of mathematics, described them:

"I never had the least idea that creation produced such a sordid set of creatures in human figure," she told her friend Mercy Warren of Plymouth. "Poor, dirty, emaciated men, great numbers of women who seemed to be the beasts of burthen, having a bushel basket on their back by which they were bent double. The contents seemed to be pots and kettles, various sorts of furniture, children peeping through gridirons and other utensils. [There were] some very young infants who were born on the road.

"The women were barefoot, clothed in dirty rags. Such effluvia filled the air while they were passing, had they not been smoking all the time, I should have been apprehensive of being contaminated by them.

"After a noble-looking advanced guard [these were Americans] General Johnny Burgoyne headed this terrible group on horseback. The other Generals also — clothed in blue cloaks.

"Hessians, Waldeckers, Anspackers, Brunswickers etc. etc. followed on. The Hessian Generals gave us a polite bow as they passed — not so the British. Their baggage wagons were drawn by half-starved horses.

"But to bring up the rear [was] another fine, noble-looking Guard of American Victorious Yeomanry, who assisted in bringing these Sons of Slavery to terms. Some of our wagons, drawn by fat oxen, driven by joyous looking Yankees, clos'd the Cavalcade.

"The Generals and other officers went to Bradish's where they quarter at present. . . . The Privates trudged through thick and thin to the hills where we tho't they were to be confined but what was our surprise when in the morning we beheld an inundation of these disagreeable objects filling our streets. How mortifying it is! They are in a manner demanding our houses and colleges for their genteel accommodation. Did the brave General Gates ever mean this? Did our Legislature ever intend the military should

prevail over the civil? Is there not a degree of unkindness in loading poor Cambridge, almost ruined before, with this great army
seeming to be let loose upon us? And what will be the consequences, time will discover.

"Some polite ones say we ought not to look upon them as
Prisoners, they are persons of distinguished rank. Perhaps too, we
must not view them in the light of enemies. I fear this distinction
will soon be lost. Surprising that our General should insist on the
first University in America being disbanded for their more genteel
accommodation and we poor oppressed people seek an asylum in
the woods against a piercing winter. . . ."

Mrs. Winthrop had heard that General Heath had been trying
to get the use of Harvard dormitories for the Convention Troops.
This was true, but he tried in vain. Harvard had been evacuated
for Washington's army, the students going to Concord — which
was the "asylum in the woods" Mrs. Winthrop had evidently disliked. The Harvard buildings had been much damaged by the
troops, "noble American Yeomanry" though they might be, and
Harvard voted not to let their property be wrecked again. The
legislature had left everything to Heath, while denying him any
power of eviction — the students got an extra vacation while
the wrangle lasted — but the Harvard overseers finally refused to
hand over anything "but a wooden dwelling."

"It is said that we shall have not less than seven thousand persons to feed in Cambridge and its environs — more than its inhabitants," Mrs. Winthrop continued. "Two hundred and fifty
cord of wood will not serve them a week. Think how we must be
distressed. Wood is risen to five pounds ten shilling per cord and
but little to be purchased.

"General Burgoyne dined Saturday in Boston with General
Heath."

Heath had "sent one of his aides for him and the other officers"
to escort them into Boston, by way of Roxbury, and Hannah
Winthrop saw Burgoyne riding through Boston "properly at-

tended." She heard that after dinner he "walkt on foot to Charlestown Ferry, followed by as great a number of spectators as ever attended a pope."

Burgoyne "observed to an officer with him, the decent and modest behavior of the inhabitants as he pass'd," and said that if he "had been conducting prisoners through the City of London, not all the Guards of His Majesty could have prevented insults."

General Heath said in his *Memoirs of the American War* that in Boston, "before the dinner was done, so great was the curiosity of the citizens of both sexes and of all ages and descriptions to get a peep at General Burgoyne that the streets were filled, the doors, windows, the tops of houses and fences were crowded." As Heath with Burgoyne and his staff walked out after dinner, Burgoyne turned to Phillips and Riedesel and said: "There is the former residence of the Governor." A man in the street heard him and remarked in a loud voice, "And on the other side is the riding school." This was Old South Meeting House, where the British during the occupation had chopped up and burned the pews and used the building for a place to exercise their horses.

Before that dinner, there had been business to attend to. The parole for officers to sign, fixing the limits where they were free to go, was shown to them. Perhaps it might have been better to have shown the officers this document after dinner, when they were mellow with wine, for they made a great fuss about it. They were not to be allowed in Boston! Many besides Burgoyne had lived in Boston previously, and they wanted to pick up where they had left off — living in fine houses, frequenting the best taverns, acquiring mistresses and above all gambling at cards.[4] They liked the idea of living in Cambridge no better than Cambridge liked having them. The officers did not sign the parole until three weeks later.

One other point was brought up, before dinner. General Phillips, second in command to Burgoyne, suggested to General Heath that he "should delegate to General Burgoyne the power of seeing your orders executed." The British regarded Heath as a farmer — which he was — and therefore a peasant, which he was not. The American General's reply astonished them: All officers were to keep discipline in the rank and file; but as to command — Burgoyne would take orders and Heath would give them.

At first, Burgoyne spoke noble words about not separating "his lot from that of the army." But long before the parole was signed, he let slip the mask of fatherly commander and amiable good fellow. Complaint after complaint was delivered to General Heath. "I cannot speak with satisfaction upon what has passed and still passes here," he said. "The officers are crowded into the Barracks, Six and Seven in a Room of about Ten Feet square and without Distinction of Rank." It was "distinction of rank" that mattered, and Burgoyne never got around to mentioning that the troops had no blankets, nor even straw to sleep on, and little firewood.

Eventually, General Heath had to order "all the wood on Charlestown wharves to be confiscated for the prisoners," much as he hated to exert military authority. He sent a colonel to Cambridge "to take up proper houses for the officers," but Colonel Chase was to use persuasion, not force. None of this made any sense to Burgoyne, who felt that his personal sufferings were great:

"I and General Phillips after being amused with promises of Quarters for eight Days are still in a dirty, small, miserable tavern, lodging in a Bed Room together, and all the Gentlemen of our suite Lodging upon the Floor in a Chamber against, a good deal worse off than their Servants have been used to.

"The only Prospect that remains to me Personally is that I shall be permitted to Occupy a House without a Table, Chair or any one article of Furniture for the Price of an Hundred and fifty pounds Sterling till the first of April, but the same Sum is to be paid tho' I should embark in ten days." Burgoyne had already turned down two houses as "exceedingly inconvenient." He said he did not blame Heath or other officers, "They do what they can."

But the "Supreme Powers of the State are unwilling or unable to enforce their authority and the Inhabitants want the Hospitality or indeed the Common Civilization to assist us without it, the publick Faith is broke and we are the sufferers. . . ." Heath sent this letter of Burgoyne's to the Continental Congress.

Congress had ratified the Convention of Saratoga and awarded a gold medal to Gates. Apparently only one man in America understood the second article of the treaty, which Burgoyne had "privately and separately" explained to Lord Howe. This man was General George Washington. "I do not think it is to our interest to expedite the passage of the prisoners to England," he wrote to General Heath, "for you may depend upon it, that they will immediately on their arrival there, throw them into different garrisons and bring out an equal number. Now if they sail in December, they may arrive time enough to take the place of others, who may be out in May, which is as early as a campaign can be entered upon."

Washington was at Whitmarsh, fourteen miles from Philadelphia. He had suffered defeat at Brandywine, well-conceived plans had gone wrong at Germantown, and he would soon be wintering at Valley Forge. But Washington did not suggest that the treaty be repudiated. He noticed that nothing had been said about supplying the prisoners with provisions for their homeward voyage and he suggested that Heath refuse to do this so that Clinton would be forced to put supplies aboard the transports before they left New York. This ought to cause just enough delay so that bad weather would set in and sailing ships would wait till spring before attempting the Atlantic.

Congress finally came to its senses and began looking for a way to nullify the whole agreement between Burgoyne and Gates, whose glory was now growing dim. They leaped upon the phrase in Burgoyne's letter, "the publick Faith is broke." This "charge was not warranted" they said, and indicated that Burgoyne planned to "disengage himself." Sensing what was up, Burgoyne's tone became milder.

It seems strange that a linen-covered calash containing a German Baroness and three children should have escaped description from Hannah Winthrop's sharp quill pen. Perhaps Mrs. General Riedesel slipped into Cambridge after dark or after the troops had passed. It is not at all surprising, however, that Lady Fritz should be fully as critical as Mrs. Winthrop. "This filthy place," she called Bradish's Tavern, otherwise known as "The Blue Anchor," just off Harvard Square. It was not the sort of inn that a Cambridge citizen would have recommended to a friend, to be sure, but it was the only one willing to take the prisoners.

Long and loud were the protests of Burgoyne and his officers but they consoled themselves at Bradish's by giving a dinner in honor of British royalty. "I believe it was the birthday of the Queen of England," said the Baroness, not too sure. "They drank a great deal of wine" — of this she was certain, pledging King, Queen and country, absent friends, wives and sweethearts, confusion to the enemy, and so on, from noon till after dark. The Riedesel children's nursemaid must have been busy with little Caroline, because Augusta and Frederika watched the whole performance with fascinated eyes.

The dinner was over at last. The guests staggered off for a long nap before supper, and they must have laid in plenty of wine because there was some of it left. Augusta and Frederika watched the servants putting it away in a closet under the stairs. When everyone had gone, the two little girls went over to the closet, got out the wine and sat down on the floor to "toast the Queen." Their mother found them, much later, flushed, excited and yet strangely sleepy. She thought they had caught some terrible disease. Frederika "had spasms and I was entirely at a loss to know the cause when Nature helped her and she vomited and then I saw that it was the wine. I blamed the little girls greatly" but they said that "they too loved the King and Queen" and wanted to "wish them happiness."

After a day or two at Bradish's Tavern, the Riedesels were given quarters in a house nearby. It was a tiny cottage, once owned and occupied by Judah Monis, Harvard's first teacher of Hebrew. A "peasant" owned it now, the Baroness said. She and her husband had "only one room up under the roof," while her servants slept on the floor and her husband's "menservants in the entry." She had some straw put under her "field bed," but straw was extremely hard to come by and had to "serve for a long time."

"Our host allowed us to eat in his room where the whole family ate and slept," said Lady Fritz. "The man was kind, but the woman, in order to revenge herself for the trouble we were to her, played the trick . . . of combing out her childrens' hair, which was full of vermin, every time we sat down at table." Putting it mildly, she added, "It very often entirely took away our appetites." They begged the woman to stop but she said it was "her room" and she "liked to comb her children's hair at this time." They dared say no more for fear of being put out in the street.

Three weeks went by. The Baroness had her servants scrub and clean the room under the eaves and the entry, and doubtless she would have had the whole house cleaned if her landlady had allowed it. This little cottage in Cambridge was less habitable than the cellar at Saratoga, but no cannon balls were coming through the walls and General Riedesel was not in danger. Lady Fritz did not complain.

General Burgoyne finally accepted quarters in the "Bishop's Palace." This house was built by the Reverend East Apthorp, Church of England missionary to Cambridge, founder of Christ Church. People in Cambridge gave the house this name because of the luxurious style of the mansion — it was not the sort of house a Puritan parson would have cared for. At the beginning of hostilities between the colonies and the mother country, the Reverend East Apthorp thought it best to depart; he sold his house to John Borland, a Tory merchant, who added a top floor for his family slaves. Cambridge patriots looted Apthorp's Christ Church, taking the organ pipes to melt into bullets. Then John Borland also departed. Once richly furnished, the Apthorp house at 10 Linden Street had now been looted along with the church, and General Burgoyne was in the market for secondhand furniture for which he paid (or promised to pay) handsomely. He complained, of course.

General Riedesel's turn came at last: General Heath found a house for him on upper Brattle Street — then called Watertown Road. This house had been built by Richard Lechmere, once the owner of many acres of farmland now part of the city of Cambridge. It was a simple, unpretentious country farmhouse, built for comfort, but with the quiet elegance of good paneling, fine hand-wrought hardware and stenciled walls.[5] General Riedesel hired from the American commissary "2½ dozen chairs, 2 bedsteads with beds, one night chair, 2 bureaux and 2 looking glasses." To furnish the downstairs rooms, they had "one large breakfast table, 4 other tables, one tea board and 1 large kittle."

The Baroness loved this house. "It was one of the most beautiful in Cambridge," she said. She was also impressed by Tory Row, but not primarily because of the imposing architecture. "Never have I chanced upon such an agreeable situation," she said. "Seven families who were connected with each other, partly by family relationships and partly by affection, had here farms and gardens and magnificent houses and not far off plantations of fruits. The owners of these were in the habit of daily meeting each other in the afternoon, now at the house of one, now at another and making themselves merry with music and dancing — living in prosperity, united and happy until, alas, this ruinous war

severed them and left all their houses desolate. . . ." The Baroness
Riedesel resolved to do what she could to restore at least a sem-
blance of gracious living to Cambridge.

"General Phillips was ever our kind and welcome friend," she
said. "We saw much of him. Our house was constantly full of
Englishmen." The other Englishmen were young captains and
lieutenants, described by Hannah Winthrop as "prancing and
patrolling every corner of the town, ornamented with their glitter-
ing side-arms, weapons of destruction." One of Burgoyne's
Articles of Convention allowed all his officers to keep their side-
arms, and greatly did the Cambridge citizens resent this.

Lady Fritz discovered that it was an English custom to pay a
first courtesy-call and hope to be asked to come again. If no such
invitation was forthcoming it was assumed that the hostess did
not want to continue an acquaintance. She had been surprised
when nice young men whom she had made welcome failed to
return to her house. She "soon learned of this convenient custom"
she said and chose "those whose company was the most agreeable." But she was so happy when cheering and welcoming homesick young officers that she almost always said, "Do come again."

"None of our gentlemen were allowed to go to Boston," said
Lady Fritz, and she must have listened patiently to many com-
plaints. But she had no trouble in getting a pass from General
Heath for herself, calash and coachman, to go to call on Mrs.
Carter, daughter of General Schuyler.

John Carter (or John Barker Church) was an ardent American
patriot, although he never gave up his British nationality and
returned to England, eventually, to become a member of parliament. Angelica would one day have a fine house in London
and entertain royalty. A letter from her John to one of her
father's aides during the winter of 1777 reveals a young man
not quite thirty learning to be a good husband to a girl of
twenty-one. "I entreat you to purchase for Mrs. Carter, one or
two of the best cookery books, as she is a young Housekeeper and

wants to gain Experience." John Carter did not insist that his
wife be too serious, however. He also sent for "a set of strings for
her guitar" and powder for her hair. If there were any "Hysong
tea" to be had in Albany, it must be bought for Mrs. Carter, "be
the price what it will."

The Baroness found "Madam Carter as gentle and good as her
parents. I dined at her house several times," she said, and many
prominent Bostonians would remember Lady Fritz. But she had
not one good word to say for Angelica's husband. It would appear
that the young man had a macabre sense of humor, and that he
delighted in shocking the somewhat literal-minded Baroness.

"When the English General Howe had burned many hamlets
and small towns, this miserable Carter" proposed that the Americans "chop off the heads of our generals, salt them down in small
barrels and send them over to England — one barrel for every
hamlet or little town burned down." John Carter "was wicked and
treacherous," asserted the Baroness, "but this barbarous suggestion
was fortunately not followed.

"The city of Boston, throughout, is pretty but it is inhabited
by violent patriots and full of wicked people," Madam Riedesel
declared. "The women, especially, were so shameless that they
regarded me with repugnance and even spit at me when I passed
them by."

One of General Riedesel's young officers, Ernst Johann Schuler
von Senden, from Wolfenbüttel, tried to explain the American
attitude.[6] "It is natural that they have completely wrong ideas
about German women if they look upon the soldier-women in
camp as typical. . . ." These poor women "run around in rags as
they own nothing else." They were so dreadful to look at that
"an order went out [apparently from a superstitious city council]
that these wenches were not to show themselves outside of camp
for fear the pregnant women in Boston should be marked" —
and bring forth an ill-favored child! But the optimistic von Senden
was sure that "when it becomes known that the German *Generalin*

is a pretty and educated woman," this "judgment" would get "a little correction."

The Baroness invited the Carters to dinner at her house in Cambridge, and they came often. Whether she knew it or not, John Carter (Church) also played cards with British officers. Word from Burgoyne written to Riedesel explains: "I did not understand you, my dear General, in what you mention'd in your note about Carter. But Anstruther, who is just now come in to dinner, tells me of Carter's gambling — I was not of the party nor out of my house all day yesterday which was lucky, for I hear the little man carried off money in all his pockets. . . ."

On the third of June, 1778, the Baroness Riedesel gave "a ball and a supper in honor of the birthday" of her husband. It was a grand affair. The terrace and gardens were "illuminated" and there was a "magnificent supper of more than eighty different dishes" prepared by that "knave" of a cook whose thievery had yet to be discovered. He must have raided all the barnyards in the township of Cambridge, with great success.

Madam Riedesel had met Boston people at the Carters' house and she asked them to her party. Not one of them came except the Carters, and she was hurt. But she felt much worse when "Burgoyne, who was expected, sent an excuse after keeping every body waiting for him until eight o'clock in the evening." Nevertheless, she had fun at her party.

"We danced considerably," said Lady Fritz. It grew late — and then it was early in the morning of the next day. They remembered that it was now "the birthday of the King of England" so they resolved they would not separate till the King's health was drunk. All joined in singing " 'God Save the King' and all eyes were full of tears.' " The Baroness looked around the circle of officers, young and old, thinking of their own land. "Even the Carters could not shut their hearts against us," she said.

The two oldest little girls had been allowed to stay up to see the illumination. They too sang "God Save the King" and perhaps their mother let them drink a toast in carefully watered wine.

Then the company separated, and on coming out of the lighted house and the torchlit gardens into the dark road, they saw that the "house was surrounded." Barefoot men had silently arrived, carrying guns. On nearby hills, barrels of pitch were burning.

There was constant fear among the people of Boston and the neighboring towns that Burgoyne's troops would break out and march to join Clinton in New York, ravaging the country as they went. The militia had been called out lest the Reidesels' gay party meant "a mutiny" among the prisoners of Saratoga.

20

Peaceful Cambridge

GENERAL Riedesel visited his troops every day. He insisted that the men get out in the open and drill in front of their barracks, using any sort of stick of wood they could find in place of the guns they had given up. He appointed a guard from each regiment, consisting of one noncommissioned officer and sixteen privates under the command of a lieutenant, to see that order was kept among the men and to avert quarrels between the men and the local militia. "Theft or marauding" was to be punished promptly, and restitution made to citizens who brought forward provable claims. Gambling was forbidden to the Germans under severe penalties, but the men could play tenpins — though not for money.

Toward the end of November, 1777, General Riedesel wrote to General Heath asking for a separate commissary or "store" on Winter Hill, and this was immediately granted "so that the common complaint of the British being amply supplied" while the Germans were "destitute" might be removed. Riedesel tried desperately to get straw for his men to sleep on. The barracks were built on the ground with no excavation under them and the winter of 1777–1778 was intensely cold. But straw seemed to have vanished from the earth and he had to let his men sleep on bare boards so that the little straw he found and paid a fancy price for could go to the wounded in hospital. The cold was much worse in Cambridge than in Canada, Riedesel said, but he was surprised to find that his men were comparatively healthy.

Schuler von Senden described "Winter Hill, three miles from Boston. . . . The barracks where we are stationed are flimsily built, offer but little shelter against the impending cold. But they are better than what we have had up to now. Each room beds twelve to eighteen men; otherwise they are unfurnished, without tables, chairs, or cots. In each there is a small stove at which four or five men at the most can warm themselves at one time. . . .

"I can easily discern the city of Boston with its suburbs, Cambridge and Charleston, separated only by a bridge. In fact, it is easy to observe every ship in the harbor. Only one English mile from us, I can see Bunker Hill where such bloody battles took place at the beginning of the war and only a short distance away is Prospect Hill where the English prisoners have a camp exactly like ours.

"We are rapidly growing accustomed to our life here. . . . For the first month the food was good, but now it is deteriorating and at times we receive the notorious ships' biscuit instead of bread, and salt fish instead of meat. After only a short time we made our barracks homelike and we feel quite comfortable, considering the circumstances. . . . The treatment of the troops is not bad. To be sure . . . one may leave camp only on a pass, but every so often each of us receives one in order to buy necessaries. . . ."

Von Senden said that only about a hundred Germans deserted while the troops crossed the mountains from Saratoga into New England, and he considered this a good record because "our people, particularly as far as clothes go, are in wretched condition." General Riedesel was doing what he could about this. He sent Captain Willoe, that trusted young aide who brought Madam Riedesel to Fort Edward, back to Canada with a letter for Governor Carleton. "Our troops, from officers down to privates are without clothes, shoes and other necessaries," the letter said. Along with the request for winter clothing, General Riedesel commended Captain Willoe's bravery in action and hoped that His Excellency would look after Willoe's future and give him a promotion. Then day after day the German troops on Winter Hill watched for the coming of sailing ships from Canada. But the clothing ships never came.[1]

Riedesel managed to buy some cloth. He set the women to making caps and mittens, and he ordered the long skirts of the soldiers' coats cut off, the material to be used to patch what was left of their uniforms. At inspection time, officers praised the regiment with the neatest patchwork. The German women also worked in the hospital, and were paid for their services, but only after Riedesel had wrangled with the British for several months in their behalf (the Germans being allowed by treaty between the King and the Duke of Brunswick to run their own hospitals, the British government to pay the expenses).

If Burgoyne ever went near his troops on Prospect Hill, it was not a matter of record. Disorders in the British camp were frequent but they were all laid to the discomfort of the soldiers. General Howe had refused to give ships carrying firewood a safe-conduct through the naval blockade, so there was always a shortage of fuel and all the troops suffered from the cold. British soldiers constantly slipped off to Boston, sometimes bringing women back to the barracks with them. Apparently their own officers made no objection. The American militia were supposed to prevent it, but the "lads and old men" who guarded the prisoners were weak, inefficient — and all too often open to bribery.

General Burgoyne's first thought was to get back to England as soon as possible; his obsession was his personal dignity. On January 4, 1778, he wrote angrily to General Heath: "As to your allotment of a convenient Transport for my passage, if it is from Yourself, I am to thank you, Sir, for a sort of Insult which the most haughty man in Office would be ashamed of in any other Country." He explained that he must have a "Frigate, together with the Transports" — the frigate for himself and the transports for the common soldiers.

General Heath replied mildly: ". . . When the transports arrive to receive the troops, they will enter the harbor, and if you find by the Convention that a Frigate is to enter for the particular reception of yourself, she will not be prohibited. But if it is rather uncommon for ships of war to bear flags of truce and if consenting to it in the present case should appear rather to be an act of politeness and generosity than otherwise — I leave it to your own reflections whether you have made choice of the most happy expressions to obtain it. . . ."

Great Britain was to pay for the keep of the prisoners. Nothing so far had been paid, and General Heath had used all the money that Congress had sent him. "The expense of the Troops of the Convention only, is about $20,000 a week for provisions and fuel," he wrote in desperation to Henry Laurens, President of the Continental Congress. Then there was the matter of pay for the "regiment of guards" and "the great expense of transporting stores." Burgoyne seemed to think that these bills need never be paid, but Congress "resolved" that neither he nor his troops should leave any debts behind them. Burgoyne was "much chagrined."

"General Burgoyne somehow communicated to Viscount Howe the subject of the Frigate," said Heath, who was trying in vain to keep his prisoners from getting or sending news. Howe said the transports had been delayed. He thought a frigate could never get into Boston Harbor, and Burgoyne began to campaign for permission to go home alone to England, leaving from British-held Newport.

So far, both Howe and Burgoyne unintentionally helped the United States Congress in detaining Burgoyne's troops, but Congress was still looking for an excuse to break the treaty altogether. They wanted to know where the colors of the regiments were.

Burgoyne said he had left them in Canada, and this may have been true. At this point, no one knew where the German colors were except General Riedesel, and no one seems to have asked him. Arms were to have been surrendered in good condition at Saratoga, but many of the Convention Troops had smashed their muskets before piling them on the bank of the Hudson. This was in violation of the treaty but hardly important enough to nullify it. The troops allowed to go to Canada had promised not to fight again in North America, but Congress had heard that Carleton had enlisted them. This was a fact but, as yet, proof was lacking. Things looked bleak for the lawyers in Congress.

At last a courier arrived with a letter for General Heath, marked "Confidential." On the eighth of January, 1778, Congress had resolved to hold the Convention Troops "until Great Britain ratified the Convention of Saratoga." Great Britain could not ratify the treaty without recognizing the United States as a nation with a right to negotiate. So the lawyers had thought of a way to keep Burgoyne's army waiting for quite a while.

As President of the Congress, Henry Laurens had wanted General Heath to get the news in confidence in case it might cause trouble among the prisoners. But "people in the streets" knew it long before Heath did, much to his dismay. The people believed that "a meeting was planned": that arms had been smuggled into the barracks on Prospect Hill. This "meeting" would be between escaping prisoners and the British, either at Newport or New York.

Serious trouble began early in January, when Colonel David Henley, in charge of prisoners under Heath, reported that there had been "mutinous behavior" at the British barracks. A prisoner had thrown a stone at an American "Centry," which "deprived him of his reason and near his life." The prisoner took the gun away from the unconscious guard and other guards called for help. "Colonel Gerish directly, with 200 men, made search for the villain and the Centry's piece, upon which the Prisoners arm'd themselves with clubs etc." Colonel Gerish gave the order for his men to fire, "but on discovering some of his own party in the barracks, he countermanded those orders and rushed upon them in a brave manner, with fire-locks clubbed—drove them from barrack to barrack till he made them sick of their Frolick, taking some prisoners and confining them." So Henley's report read.

Next morning Colonel Henley took a hand. The prisoners "assembled," refused to "disperse," behaved with "their usual insolence, and rescued" one of Colonel Gerish's prisoners taken the night before. At this point Henley lost his temper. But as he wrote it up in his report to General Heath, he was "acting with resolution" when he personally "gave orders to disperse" and "they did it with so much reluctance and insolence" that he "ran a British soldier through the body and pushed with such force that it may prove fatal to him."

Burgoyne said that "insults and provocations, at which the most placid dispositions would revolt" were "daily given to the officers and soldiers" of his army. Colonel Henley was "indecent, violent, vindictive" — he was guilty of "intentional murder" — and Burgoyne made "a demand for prompt and satisfactory justice."

General Heath ordered a Court of Inquiry for Colonel Henley.[2] He also promised Burgoyne that he would look into all complaints, such as "the conduct of a number of [British] officers at Bradish's Tavern, of prisoners being rescued from the guards, sentinels abused and insulted at their posts; passes counterfeited; robberies committed in the environs of the barracks. . . ."

The Court of Inquiry agreed that Colonel Henley was entitled to a court-martial, and General Burgoyne himself appeared against him. Day after day, the courthouse in Cambridge was packed. To the amazement of one of the German officers, "every male person can attend such a court and everyone is permitted to take notes . . . not even the humblest is refused admittance."

But of course there were no women allowed. In the "oval building with great church windows all around, reaching to the roof, the President, General Glover, sat on a chair like a professor's." In front, seated at a large rectangular table, sat Colonel Henley, "the accused," with Lieutenant Colonel Tudor as Judge Advocate. General Burgoyne was seated at the same table, with Generals Phillips and von Riedesel as his assistants.

It was "a long and tedious trial," said General Heath. "General Burgoyne . . . said everything which he judged proper, which, although novel in Courts Martial was yet permitted."

"General Burgoyne has several times shown himself a great orator and drawn tears from the whole court," said the German observer, who was probably one of Riedesel's aides.

Lieutenant Anburey published what he said was a verbatim report of Burgoyne's speeches, and they were certainly long and tedious, especially when he took time out to air some of his personal grievances against General William Heath. Basing his case on the accusation of "intentional murder," Burgoyne's eloquence included passages referring to Colonel Henley's hands "imbrued with blood" or Henley's "thirst for blood," along with sarcasm directed at the Provincial rebel lawyers and their methods of defense. Burgoyne's oratory helped to get Henley acquitted of all charges.

The affair had provided free entertainment for most of the male population of Cambridge and doubtless for their wives over the dinner table. It had occupied Burgoyne's mind, and he had enjoyed the center of the stage — small, provincial and rebellious though his audience might be.

Hannah Winthrop, who should have been a modern columnist, wrote her report to Mercy Warren. "The British officers live in the most luxurious manner possible, rioting on the fat of the land, stalking at large like Lords of the Soil. General Burgoyne has been allowed a Court Martial on a Continental Colonel for doing his duty . . . interrogating and aiming to intimidate witnesses on our part, encouraging those of his own, displaying his Parliamentary eloquence, Spouting forth his Contempt of America, sometimes by insidious, ironical compliments, at others by direct abuse. . . ."

The Henley trial ended on the twenty-seventh of February, 1778, and on March 19 General Burgoyne at last got leave from Congress to go to England. He was not exchanged — he was free to go only on parole, but this news was "joyous to the General" as Heath put it.

Burgoyne was less than joyous when he was reminded that he was not to leave Cambridge until all his personal bills and all the accounts for provisions for his army had been paid. At first, Congress insisted that the bill be paid in gold, the gold to be forwarded to the treasury and used to pay for munitions bought in France. Patiently, but with an undercurrent of desperation, General Heath pointed out that large sums of money were owing in Boston and that his task of getting in more provisions would be almost impossible unless current bills were paid. Finally Congress agreed to accept "specie" for part of the bill, which Heath could use to satisfy creditors. The rest of the debt could be paid in provisions for the future use of the prisoners, these provisions to be forwarded from Newport or New York "by vessels bearing flags." As a "pledge for any deficiencies, a box of gold" must be deposited with General Heath. Burgoyne wrote many haughty letters, but finally agreed to all demands.

Heath gave Burgoyne a farewell dinner in Boston and this was the second time, while a prisoner, that Burgoyne was allowed to go into that city. "If you will give me a memorandum," said Burgoyne, grandly, "I will forward to you any foreign necessaries you may want. . . ." How about wine? Some tea, perhaps — or sugar? Heath replied that he preferred to go without luxuries along with his fellow countrymen.

Burgoyne called on Madam the Baroness von Riedesel, who

could be haughty, too, when she chose. She had asked him to her house many times, "but he invariably excused himself on various pretences." He now "made me a great many apologies, to which I replied that I would be extremely sorry if he had gone out of his way on our account."

Lady Fritz had nothing to say, this time, concerning Burgoyne's mistress. According to the Convention of Saratoga, he had been allowed to send back to Canada "all Canadians and persons belonging to the establishment in Canada," and "many other followers of the Army who come under no particular Description." It would seem that Burgoyne's mistress could have gone if she had wanted to. If Burgoyne had a companion, commissary's wife or otherwise, to share his bed at Bishop Apthorp's house, apparently no one was so indiscreet as to mention it.

On April 7, 1778, "General Burgoyne, attended by several officers" arrived in Newport, Rhode Island.[3] Along with him was "a rebel commissary," come to get the money promised in cash. Writing without fear of censorship at last, Burgoyne said he had paid "Sums which altogether amounted to 27,000 pounds sterling." The rest of the sum of one hundred thousand pounds must go to Boston "by the Hands of the Paymaster . . ." But to Burgoyne's dismay, he had discovered that the whole military chest at Newport was "only £156,000." So he took out 47,000 pounds sterling and said that 27,000 of this "was indispensable to discharge the agreement with General Heath" and the remaining "20,000, tho' a mere pittance, will be some immediate resource in point of subsistence."

Burgoyne would have "refused all demands," he said, "if it affected" only his own departure. But Heath had informed him, quite truthfully, that there would be no more food for the prisoners unless money and provisions were supplied at once.

On the tenth of April Burgoyne made "a tour of the island attended by General Pigot and other officers" to look at Newport's defenses. That night there was an "Assembly attended by about 40 ladies and 100 gentlemen." On April 15, Gentleman Johnny "embarked on the *Grampus,* which, with a fleet of about 30 sail, immediately got under way. No salute was given or other compliment paid to him...."

General Burgoyne would not be seen riding with the King in London. He would not even be allowed to see the King. There would be lonely hours during which he prepared his statement of what had happened to him among the rebels of North America, and gradually it would dawn upon him that no move whatever was being made for his exchange. His ungrateful sovereign wanted him left a "prisoner of the Convention" — on parole.

General Phillips was now in full charge of the Convention Troops. Burgoyne had left with him the means of writing secretly to Lord Howe, and had described how the secret writing was to be done. "I cut the enclosed Cyphers and left the counterparts in his [Phillips's] hands; the one is for a shorter, the other for a longer correspondence. Your Excellency will immediately perceive the method of using them is to write the secret part in the interstices, and then fill the Vacuities so as to make them seem Part of an indifferent letter. The Person who receives has only to apply the interstices and consequently reads the secret Part. They are meant to be applicable to each Page, and when the second Cypher is to be used, two strokes are to be put under the date."

These "masks" were usually cut out in an hour-glass shape or an oblong, but it sounds as though Burgoyne had cut some very fancy holes in his papers.[4] General Phillips wrote pathetically once or twice to say that he had received no letter that made any secret sense when he laid his cut-out masks of paper over them. Phillips began to realize that the British High Command had forgotten him and his Convention Troops — or at least, that he was on nobody's mind particularly. He wrote to Sir Guy Carleton, who was in Quebec. There were American prisoners in Canada, why not send some of them in the "clothing ships" and arrange an exchange so that Burgoyne's former army could go to New York and fight again from there? But the clothing ships did not come, and relations between the unhappy prisoners and the equally unhappy "inhabitants" grew daily worse.

On June 17, 1778, Lieutenant Richard Brown, an English officer, was "riding out of the lines with two women" when the American guard ordered him to halt and show his pass and that of the women. Lieutenant Brown, "when repeatedly challenged," did not stop, and the guard shot him.

"Murder and death has at length taken place," wrote General Phillips, who was a man of choleric disposition at best. Boredom and frustration concerning his career and his situation as a forgotten prisoner had made his temper almost uncontrollable these days, and he let himself go in his letter to General Heath:

"An officer, riding out from the barracks on Prospect Hill, has been shot by an American sentinel. I leave the horrors incident to that bloody disposition, which has joined itself to rebellion in these Colonies, to the feelings of all Europe. I do not ask for justice, for I believe every principle of it has fled from this Province.

"I demand liberty to send an officer to Gen. Sir Henry Clinton, by way of the head-quarters of Gen. Washington with my report of this murder."

Inquiry into the shooting of Lieutenant Brown had already begun when Heath received Phillips's letter. There were witnesses who confirmed the guard's account, and he was exonerated. But the patient General Heath was angry. "Were it even certain that the shooting of the officer was an act of the most deliberate, wilful murder, why should you charge these free and independent States with a bloody disposition and with rebellion, and this state in particular as void of every principle of justice?" he wrote Phillips. "Although I ever had and still have a personal regard for you, and wish in every respect to treat you with the utmost generosity; that duty which I owe to the honour and dignity of the United States will not allow me to pass unnoticed such expressions as are contained in your letter. . . ." The demand of liberty for an officer to proceed to Sir Henry Clinton was denied. Heath promised that a copy of Phillips's letter should go to Clinton, however — and also to Congress. And he restricted General William Phillips to his "house, gardens and yard" in Cambridge, with the exception of "the direct road to the quarters of the troops on Prospect and Winter Hills." Phillips refused to sign a parole accepting these limits and Heath put a guard at his house.

General Heath reminded Phillips that France had "acknowledged the independency of the United States." French ships were arriving daily in Boston Harbor "with goods and stores." This was a bad time for Phillips to be talking about rebellious colonies, but every letter he wrote was in an angry vein and his blood pressure must have reached a new high point every day. Eventually, he refused to communicate with Heath at all, and appointed Riedesel to carry on all correspondence.

General Riedesel had troubles of his own. It was spring and his men were escaping from the barracks and deserting. He had one of his aides write out a polite report in English for General Heath. Congress had "resolved" and Washington had confirmed the ruling that "no officer of the Continental Army should receive or enlist soldiers of the Army of the Convention." But "facts had come to light" which convinced Riedesel that "provincial officers do enlist German troops. . . ." There were houses in Watertown where German soldiers could go to enlist, and the American guards on Winter Hill would not stop a man who said he was going there.

Riedesel had sent a noncommissioned officer to the tavern in Watertown to look for Grenadier Dohlenberg, "deserted from the barracks." Instead of hunting down Grenadier Dohlenberg, arresting and returning him, an American Captain Merket, who was busy recruiting at the tavern, blithely offered to enlist Riedesel's noncommissioned officer — to no avail, to be sure.

Worse followed! "A patrol of the garrison of Cambridge took up five men, by name Christian Crone, Andrew Entrott, Henry Schmidt, Anthony Staderman and William Büttcher," who were found roaming the streets at night. They were confined forty-eight hours in the guardhouse on Prospect Hill; but they had not "committed any riot," so they were to be returned to their barracks. When Riedesel sent his aide, Lieutenant Du Roi, to get them — the men were gone. They had been "released," having been found "innocent," and "by some accident" had disappeared. At least that was the story told to Du Roi. But a sergeant of the guard let slip that "the men had been sent . . . to Bunker's Hill in order to be carried over to Boston, as they had enlisted in the Continental Army." Everyone promised to help General Riedesel find his five men, but somehow they were never seen again.

At last, Riedesel had a little luck. "Yesterday afternoon," he wrote on the last day of May, "I met three men in Continental uniform, two in a calash and one on horseback riding before. Upon looking a little nearer, I perceived them to be German, and Brunswick soldiers."

General Riedesel rushed into the street and shouted to the men to halt. But "the man on horseback rode off." The two in the calash obediently pulled up, and when he ordered them out of the carriage they stepped down. Riedesel ordered them "into a neighboring house to examine them nearer." (He did not say what the householder might have thought of this.) One man was a Bennington prisoner of war, the other a Brunswick soldier "included in the Convention." Riedesel ordered the Brunswick man to take off the Continental uniform and give it to the man captured at Bennington, who was to deliver it and himself to the Cambridge guard. Then, gathering in his own man, who was presumably wearing some sort of clothing, he took the Brunswicker back to Winter Hill.

After questioning this man, Riedesel knew who had been causing all the trouble. "A certain Colonel Armand clandestinely persuades our troops to desert and enlists them publicly in the American service," he discovered. Writing to General Heath, Riedesel declared that "numbers of our men (half of them in Col. Armand's uniform) and half still in the Brunswick uniforms were swarming in the town of Boston." He did not see how Heath could be unaware of this.

General Heath knew Colonel Armand all right. He was the Marquis de la Rouerie of the French Guards, a rich young man with a taste for adventure. He had been with Washington at Valley Forge, had hoped to go with Lafayette on a winter expedition into Canada, and for this purpose had recruited volunteers for a regiment at his own expense. The expedition could not be organized quickly enough to follow upon the heels of Burgoyne's defeat, and was given up. But "Armand," as he liked to be called, was in Boston recruiting for his private little army, passing out gaudy uniforms of his own design, and there was little or nothing that General Heath could do about him — except give him Riedesel's letter, and write to General Washington for advice.

However, Heath had a word to say to General Riedesel. "I cannot but express surprise that in the public road you should stop men cloathed in the uniform of the United States, to strip or confine them under guard. . . . I shall by no means allow of the taking up of men cloathed in the Continental uniform in any place where an officer of the Convention may happen to see them. You will therefore please immediately, Sir, to set at Liberty the Person whom you stripped . . . without offering him any abuse or punishment."[5]

Riedesel replied that the deserter had confessed to receiving thirty dollars for his enlistment, and "had testified so much repentence for his crime" that he had been released and pardoned. But "he has since disappeared and I know not what has become of him."

Colonel Armand wrote a letter which Riedesel considered frivolous and impertinent — and so, of course, it was.[6] But Armand, although he wrote English very badly, had a good time composing it. "In the first days I was in Boston, good many of the Germans came to me for being enlisted," Armand said. "General Heath I consulted, told me he could not grant me such leave. I had the mortification of seeing all those brave men dispers'd. . . . I have been informed that a good many of them . . . have enlisted in the Militia. I don't suppose your intention be to make me responsible for what the Militia does. . . . In fine, Sir, of all your deserters from your camp, I haven't seen the twentieth part of them. I am positively ignorant where they have gone. . . . I have the honor of assuring you that Last Campaign, my Corps was almost composed of these brave men I made an essential point to love them better than any others. If I had some this campaign, they would be happier under my orders than in any other Regiment."

It was not surprising that General Riedesel suffered from severe headaches and that his wife had difficulty in cheering him up! She encouraged him to plant a garden, and he got some of the best gardeners among the prisoners to help with it. The land was fertile on Brattle Street and they planted some strange American produce such as the pumpkin.

On June 18, 1778, General Phillips — still refusing to make peace with Heath, still under house arrest — wrote to General Riedesel. There was a party at the Riedesels' and he could not be there.

"I do sincerely give you my congratulations on the return of Madam de Riedesel's birthday," General Phillips wrote. "It was the peculiar order of Providence to give her to the World for your happiness — the Worthiest Woman, best wife and most amiable Companion and Friend.

"I shall drink her health in a Bumper of Claret at my dinner."

21

Marching Orders

AMERICAN land forces and Admiral d'Estaing, Commodore of the French fleet, had worked out a plan to liberate Newport, Rhode Island. It was good strategy and, in the opinion of German officers engaged in the battle, the Americans were fighting well. But then on August 11 "a terrible storm arose" which "lasted three days." In Boston, "the strongest trees were torn up" and some "of the barracks demolished." In other words, there was something very like a hurricane in New England in August 1778, and the French fleet "was dispersed."[1] The land army hung on desperately, but naval support was necessary and a retreat was ordered. Tory newspapers said that "the wrath of Heaven" had descended upon the rebels and the utterly discouraged Americans could not help wondering if this were true. It took steadfast faith to believe that so many defeats could ever add up to victory.

A very battered French fleet limped into Boston harbor, "12 sail of the line and 4 frigates." D'Estaing's flagship, the *Languedoc*, was dismasted; she lost her bowsprit and rudder and had to be towed into port. The *Marseilles* lost her foremast, and the *Caesar*, a seventy-four, driven clear of the squadron, was much battered when "she fell in with a British 50 gun ship" and fought her "for near three glasses." When other British ships hove in sight, the *Caesar* broke off the engagement and somehow managed "to make Boston lower harbor" on August 22. Count d'Estaing determined to bring the remnants of his whole squadron to Boston. He "came up to town" and John Hancock politely invited him to breakfast and to bring his officers.[2]

The French count accepted with pleasure John Hancock's kind invitation for himself and three hundred officers. Mrs. Hancock sent servants "in all haste to milk the cows on Boston Common." Most of the cows belonged to her neighbors but there was no time to ask permission and nobody complained. This was a hungry French fleet that had arrived in Boston, a city already host to hungry Convention Troops.

Some of the Convention Troops had already been sent to Rutland, Vermont, to relieve the burden of providing food for them in Boston. In New York, Clinton was also hungry, so he had stopped sending provisions to the prisoners. He was asked to provide passports for "American vessels, to transport provisions," but refused. When "passports were not granted within three days after application" and "measures were not taken by Clinton to send supplies to Boston," Congress resolved "to remove the prisoners to such part of the United States as they may be best suited in."

General Phillips railed in vain against the use of the word "prisoners" in connection with the Troops of the Convention. It was all beside the point: his men could march or starve. They must pay the bills now owing, since Burgoyne's departure, and officers must pay their board and lodging bills. But they had used up all their cash paying gambling debts, and it was a blow to learn that a debt to a landlady, although not a debt of honor, must be honored.

There was another reason for removing the Troops of the Convention from Boston, besides shortage of food. As early as March, writing from Valley Forge, Washington had warned: ". . . If they remain within reach of that part of the Enemy who are at Newport, I think it more than probable that they will make an effort to rescue them. . . ."

On the first day of September, 1778, the French officers were just sitting down to dinner with General Heath when signal guns began to boom. Mr. John Cutler, who was "posted in the steeple of the Old South Meeting House, [had seen] about twenty sail." Count d'Estaing, instead of sitting down at table, "immediately put off for the squadron."

The German troops, looking out over Boston from Winter Hill, saw that "alarm flags were hoisted on all their buildings and spires. Everyone who could carry or obtain arms hastened to the city. The people of the neighboring townships came riding into the city on horseback. . . . Governor Hancock had the forts around the city occupied. Meanwhile, it grew dark and the alarm fires shone from the heights."

The British ships decided that the entrance to Boston Harbor was too well fortified to approach at that time, but on October 11 there came another alarm. General Heath now advised Boston citizens "to pack up their effects and remove women and children." This, too, proved a false alarm; but it buoyed up the hopes of the prisoners. "General Howe attempted a landing to rescue the captive troops," wrote Madam Riedesel.

The news that the troops were to march into the distant "Province of Virginia" was greeted with deep dismay. "I have heard from *particular* channels . . . and make no doubt that the troops will be marched away," wrote General Phillips to Riedesel. "Patience, perforce, *mon Général. Si nous avions attaqué le 20ᵐᵉ septembre, ceci n'aura pas arrivé.*"[3] So there had really been a plot, and the words "We will have to be patient, my General, if we had attacked on the 20th of September, all this would not have happened" referred to some plan not carried out.

Phillips was putting every obstacle he could think of in the way of the departure of the troops in the hope that rescue might still come. He refused to pay the provision bill first because he was named as "debtor," and next because the Convention Troops had been called "prisoners"; then, when these matters had been politely explained or corrected to please him, he objected to the words "the United States" on the grounds that there was no such nation. At this, Heath's patience was at an end. He replied briefly: Phillips would pay or no one would eat. So Phillips sent to Newport for fifty thousand pounds sterling.[4]

But there had been changes in the British high command. Howe had now gone home to England, although Madam Riedesel did not know it and perhaps none of the other prisoners did. Clinton, after taking charge of evacuating Philadelphia, was in New York waiting for word that his own request to be relieved had been accepted. Instead, he found himself made commander in chief. He informed Congress that he would no longer subsist the Convention Troops, and Congress replied that this effectively broke the Convention of Saratoga. The troops were now prisoners of war, without any further quibbling, and they were going to be marched to Virginia where they would live in a more comfortable climate and where food was much more plentiful. Officers would pay their bills or go to jail.

Phillips received a polite letter from Newport promising not fifty thousand but ten thousand pounds. Then, a day later, came word that the paymaster "must detain" even the ten thousand pounds "in consequence of arrival" of orders from New York. The paymaster was "afraid it would not be hereafter" in his power to obey Phillips's "commands in this way, so much as he could wish." Now Phillips realized that Clinton had cut off his cash.

General Phillips was desperate. He wrote to Clinton suggesting a "cartel" — the Saratoga prisoners to be exchanged for American prisoners in Clinton's hands. He described how healthy all the prisoners were and what a fine fighting force they would make, because they were so angry over their treatment by the Americans.

At the same time, Phillips wrote to Washington to say that his poor, unhappy troops were so weak and ill that they could not possibly march as far as Virginia. This letter, with line after line of heavy-handed flattery, also suggested that he, personally, ought to be allowed to go to New York "to see his friends" before beginning an "exile" in faraway Virginia.

General George Washington, a gentleman from Virginia, replied with an icily polite "no" to all of Phillips's suggestions. Clinton said he would see what he could do about a cartel, and so Phillips had to pin his hopes on that. It seemed to escape everyone's attention that Clinton had nowhere nearly enough American prisoners to exchange for Burgoyne's army. Many Americans had died, "in the sugar-house and on prison-ships" in New York Harbor. "Twenty or thirty die every day — they lie in heaps, unburied," testified an American in 1777. Of "30 hale and hearty men" from Litchfield, Connecticut, only 6 survived imprisonment.

Phillips and Riedesel "determined to borrow on their own credit as much money as possible in and around Boston." Interest was excessive and John Carter (Church) was one of those who advanced cash. "All the officers who had money were obliged to lend it for the use of the troops who, in this manner, received their pay in hard cash," General Riedesel said. Those officers who needed money applied to him and he gave them enough to buy horses for their long journey. "This was fair because they had several month's pay due them." Riedesel did not neglect to write to Clinton to remind him that the advance must be repaid.

"Tho' the Rebel General has ordered us to march, it's a doubt with me whether the inhabitants will let us go, as we are all drowned in debt," complained one of Phillips's younger officers. There were no such remarks from the Germans. They had not dared to go to the clandestine cockfights held in country barns which had so delighted the English. They had searched for moderately priced lodgings, and if they gambled they knew they had to keep it dark because of Riedesel's wrath at such proceedings. One of the German noncommissioned officers did yield to temptation, lost money at cards and stole a silver gorget belonging to his regiment to pay his debts. Riedesel hoped that General Heath would not have to be told.

General Riedesel listed the supplies his troops would need before they began their southward march, and sent the list to Clinton. They should have one thousand and fifty blankets and the same number of nightcaps. Material to make "Waste coats with Sleaves" and dark blue cloth for "Trowsers" was needed along with "6587 yards of yd.-wide Linen for mattresses and Bolsters." General Phillips asked Clinton to "grant the same to the British," but "Sir Henry Clinton was pleased to grant" only five hundred blankets, and no nightcaps.

It was in the month of November in 1778 that the order was finally received to go to Virginia, wrote the Baroness. "My husband fortunately found a pretty English carriage and bought it for me, so that I could travel easily." Much was said about the cruelty of the Americans in sending the prisoners on the march so late in the year, but the delays had been caused by either Phillips or Clinton. Mrs. General said only that she was "sorry to leave Cambridge." As always, she had made a home for herself, her husband and children, in the place the fortunes of war allotted to her. This time she really loved the farmhouse. She had set her maids to work waxing the wainscoting, scrubbing the wide floorboards and polishing the small-paned windows.

Then there was the garden. "Almost all our soldiers understood gardening and were besides glad of the opportunity to earn something," wrote Lady Fritz. "My husband had often a kind of nervous and anxious feeling by which he was never easy unless he was walking or working in a garden. When the grief of being in captivity, the unpleasant situation of our troops, the lack of news from home, all threw him into a despondency," the garden was there, just beyond the house, "to divert him." General Riedesel bought "a small provision cart" for his wife, which would follow after the "pretty English carriage" along the march. She had already laid in their harvest — the turnips, potatoes, cabbages — which would keep well in the deep cellar under the Cambridge house. Now she loaded the provision cart with as much of their own produce as it could carry.

One morning, some townspeople waited upon Madam the Baroness with a bill "amounting to one thousand rix thalers." It must have been a dreadful shock to her, for she had been most careful of her money. Well aware of what her husband thought of people who went into debt with no idea of how to pay, she had been feeling pleased with herself because she owed nothing. She asked to see the bills, of course — and it was the knave of a cook, "whose receipts I had luckily taken daily," who had "paid nothing whatever. My husband had him arrested."

But the cook "slipped off." On the sixth of November, "Major General Gates, with his lady, suite, etc.," arrived in Boston. They lived well and the Riedesel's cook saw an easy mark. He hired himself to Gates. He was soon found to be "too expensive," however, and his next job was with Lafayette, who told the Riedesels that their ex-cook "would answer only for a King."

"My husband wished him well because of his skill at cooking, which was very great," said Lady Fritz. "But the scoundrel hated me, because I watched him."

The Baroness said that it was while she was preparing for the march south that she discovered what had become of the German regimental flags. They were supposed to have been surrendered at Saratoga, but General Riedesel had given her to understand that they had been burned. Now he told her that only the staves had been burned — he still had the flags. But he thought it would be too difficult to try to keep them safely hidden on a long cross-country march through rebel territory. The Baroness "summoned a trustworthy tailor from among the German troops" and shut herself up "with the right honorable tailor" who helped her "make a mattress in which we sewed every one of the flags."

Captain O'Connell, one of Riedesel's aides, "under pretense of some errand, was sent to New York and passed off the mattress as his own."

The voluminous correspondence between the Convention Generals and General Heath show that many had been the requests for a pass and a flag of truce for prisoners to go to New York on one pretext or another, and they were almost all refused. But General Gates was now in charge, having been "appointed by Congress to the chief command in the Eastern Department in the room of the Hon. Major Gen. Heath." Gates had been up to his old tricks, undermining the reputation of men too busy doing their duty to bother with politics, and he began giving orders by the eighth of November. He was still generous to the enemy, and it was he who gave Captain O'Connell leave to go to New York. O'Connell got through safely with his mattress full of flags.

The Troops of the Convention began their march on November 9, 1778, the British going first, in three divisions. On the tenth the "foreign troops began to march, escorted by one captain, three officers and one hundred of the militia from New York state." The wagons "for the transportation of baggage failed to appear" and "drivers of wagons passing in the road were forced to take their baggage." This caused no little indignation on the part of some wood carters and farmers who had set out with produce for the Boston market.

It surprised and touched General William Heath to have the Massachusetts legislature, with whom he had had many an argument, send him an official letter of thanks for being "tenacious of the civil rights of the community and of the honor and safety of these Free and Sovereign and Independent States."

Not realizing what a difficult problem the presence of Burgoyne's captive army had been, Gates supposed he was still a great hero in New England. But he was already out of favor with the hungry Bostonians, and soon his lavish mode of living annoyed them greatly. By the end of the year, John Carter, who was ardently pro-Schuyler, fought a duel with Gates's son Bob —over General Schuyler's right to be called "the Hero of Saratoga." Young Bob missed, and Carter fired in the air.

Angelica Schuyler Carter was probably not in Boston. On September 9 her husband had written that Angelica and their "little son" were visiting her parents, the Philip Schuylers in Albany.[5] Angelica's sister Betsy had returned earlier; perhaps she had already begun to feel the attraction of her future husband, Alexander Hamilton.

Of the "ladies" who had taken refuge in the cellar at Saratoga, the Baroness Riedesel was the only one to make the march south. Mrs. Harnage stayed behind in Cambridge with her husband, who was still suffering from his wound. She had a child, but the baby did not live. Her husband was finally exchanged, and they went back to England together, to their "children at home, both daughters requiring a mother's care."[6] The widow of Lieutenant Reynels "with her two children" was also allowed to go home "where this unfortunate lady hath two more children."

The Riedesels hoped that General Gates would call on them, and on November 21 General Riedesel wrote to him for permission to go to Boston for himself and Madam Riedesel, "to take leave of you," he said. "I take the liberty to request an officer to conduct Madame Riedesel upon the road and a guard to escort my baggage and that of persons belonging to the staff of the Brunswick troops," he added.

Gates did not grant the pass to Boston.[7] His genial mood had vanished. But he sent Robert Troup, one of his aides, to escort the Baroness at least part of the way. It was little Augusta who chose Captain Edmonston from among her father's aides. He promised the little girl not to leave her and the family along the way — "a promise that he faithfully kept," the children's mother said.

Rockel, who had been coachman for the General's wife from

the day she set out from Germany, was still her man, but now he drove American horses hitched to "the pretty English wagon." Rockel was growing old, Mrs. General said. When the road was bad, which was often, he would just sit on the box and shout "Captain!" Edmonston would then get off his horse to give a heave to a mired wheel or lead the carriage horses over a particularly shaky bridge. "I did not like to have him do this," said Lady Fritz, but Edmonston "was amused and begged me not to notice it."

Colonel Robert Troup, the American escort, was twenty-one years old, a law student when the American Revolution broke out and destined to become a judge and a power in the Genesee Valley of upper New York State. He was already a veteran soldier, having served under Washington at the Battle of Long Island and under Gates at Saratoga. He had been a prisoner of war aboard a British ship in New York Harbor and in Provost Prison, and his rank of colonel had been given to him in recognition of both his sufferings and his bravery. He was earnest and amiable, holding no grudge against either the British or their auxiliaries. The Baroness never knew how much he did for her in protecting her against the enmity of civilians who saw a German lady and her children traveling — in what seemed to them like luxury — across their devastated country. Serious damage would not be evident until they reached New Jersey, but Connecticut was feeling poor, her inhabitants truculent.

A total of about 4145 prisoner troops and officers were on the move. For the first time since they had left Canada, women and children were allowed to ride in wagons — by General Heath's orders before he was superseded. Either by hiring or commandeering, three hundred and eighty-four farm wagons with drivers were obtained in Cambridge for the transportation project.

Mrs. General did not set out with the troops, and when she left her husband rode on horseback alongside of his wife's carriage as far as Watertown, then turned back. There were still unpaid bills, and both he and General Phillips would have to stay in Boston until everything was cleared up. Finally, as Phillips wrote to Clinton, "My last requisition for money on Rhode Island succeeded so far as to release Major General Riedesel and myself from Cambridge," and Riedesel left on the twenty-eighth of November. Phillips was anxious about catching up with the troops but he need not have worried: they traveled at a snail's pace.

Lieutenant August Wilhelm Du Roi of Brunswick's Prince Frederick Regiment kept a journal of the march south from Cambridge all the way to Charlottesville, Virginia.[8] "We were all frightened at the prospect of the long march," wrote Du Roi. "But in order not to discourage the men, the officers had to hide their feelings and pretend to be pleased with the change." His pleasure was not all pretense, as many of his journal entries showed. Each day he noted the distance marched and the things which surprised, pleased or annoyed him.

The Germans marched eleven miles the first day. Du Roi was astonished to find that "the villages or townships in New England are often 4 or 5 miles long and the houses on the road placed at such a distance that all the ground belonging to one estate surrounds the house." This was far different from the European walled towns he was used to, where peasants went out to till the fields each morning and returned at night.

It was good the towns were no closer together for one reason, however. "Although our escorts treated us rather well and had allowed our men to walk as they pleased during the march, we had to submit to being marched through all the villages with fifes and drums. They never missed a chance to show us that we were miserable prisoners, subject to the authority of adventurous peasants, who were set to watch us."

The Germans were to cross the Connecticut River at Enfield, Connecticut, and here the Massachusetts drivers with their wagons turned back. There had been "almost a riot" at Wilbraham, where the drivers — especially those who had been forced into service — declared they were going home; threats by the militia plus promises of extra pay had induced them to go on as far as the Connecticut border.

Lieutenant Du Roi felt impelled to sum up his impressions of Massachusetts:

"The province . . . is particularly well cultivated although the houses are of light structure. They are regularly and tastefully built, very clean inside, comfortable and roomy. They are also well furnished. . . .

"The girls mature very early; I have seen quite a number of them hardly 17 years old and as big and developed as they would ever be. . . . However, they get old very early and a woman of 30 often looks like one 50 years old. The people are very fond of luxury, especially the women, which fondness shows itself in their dress and in their houses. However, the way of living in regard to food is very poor. No German stomach can put up with it.

"The men are very industrious, especially in business, but they are selfish and not sociable. The women are exceedingly proud, negligent and very lazy. The men have to do all the outside work, as milking cows, etc. The woman in New England is the laziest creature I know, and not much good for anything."

Flatboats, seventy feet long and capable of carrying from fifty to sixty men, ferried the troops from Burgoyne's army across the Connecticut. Du Roi estimated that the river was over half a mile wide and they told him it had a swift current. The English divisions had crossed ahead of the Germans and he heard that one of the ferryboats had been carried four miles downstream by the current and two men had been drowned trying to get ashore.

After they crossed the Connecticut, the German division marched "as far as Suffield, a little town with well-built houses where we were all well received," said Du Roi. "We noticed a

great difference in the behavior of these people from those of the
Province of Massachusetts who at all times treated us badly and
showed themselves very ill-mannered. Our officers gave the Belles
of the town a ball in the evening. Everyone, even the clergyman's
wife, came and we danced till daybreak."

General Riedesel, riding hard, caught up with his wife's carriage and joined her little army of aides-de-camp and servants.
They crossed the Connecticut together and went to Hartford
instead of Suffield. It was December 5, and Colonel Troup was
having trouble with their transportation problem. He was "much
embarrassed to procure wagons," because Mr. James Bull, who
was in charge, said he had been "hired to expedite the march of
the Convention Troops through this state" but nobody had told
him about any General Riedesel or any Mrs. General either.
Colonel Troup had to pull his rank and order Mr. Bull to get
wagons or answer for his conduct to General Gates, Commander
of the Eastern Division. Bull then promised wagons "by 9 tomorrow."

The Riedesels were enjoying Hartford, however. They had
hardly settled themselves, at a clean and comfortable inn, before
a party of Continental officers galloped up. They recognized one
man among them — General La Fayette. "La Fayette was so polite
and agreeable that he pleased us all very much," said the Baroness. "He had many Americans with him who were ready to jump
out of their skins with vexation at hearing us talk French all the
time." She thought the Americans were afraid Lafayette might be
telling her secrets and that she would "alienate him from their
cause."

As a matter of fact, it distressed the Baroness to see a French
nobleman consorting with peasants and rebels, and she did do
her best to "alienate" Lafayette. "He spoke much of England and
the kindness which the King had shown in having him taken

sight-seeing," she said. "I could not keep from asking him how he found it in his heart to accept so many marks of kindness from the King when he was on his way to fight against him."

La Fayette "appeared somewhat ashamed," Lady Fritz thought. " 'It is true that such an idea passed through my mind on the day the King offered to show me his fleet,' " he said. He made an excuse to avoid "the embarrassment of having to refuse." Some people in England had actually "accused him of being a spy," and he "went immediately to America."

The Baroness heard her husband ask their guest if he had dined. The French officer said no, he had not been able to get anything to eat, and Lady Fritz was almost in a panic when she heard her husband invite La Fayette to dinner. Her provision wagon was not in Hartford — it had lagged behind — and "I knew he loved a good dinner," she said. "Finally, I managed to glean, from what provisions we had on hand, enough to make him a very respectable meal."

22

The Long Road

THE journal of August Wilhelm Du Roi, Lieutenant and Adjutant in the service of the Duke of Brunswick, continued the story of the long road southward, at first comparing what he saw with familiar sights in Europe. The Farmington River at Simsbury was like the Oder in Germany, except that it was not navigable "on account of many rocks and cliffs." He misunderstood the names of many of the towns he passed through, but he put down an approximation of what he heard; he got a few of the names right, so the route of the German soldiers can still be traced.[1] They soon entered rugged country and passed through part of what is now the Housatonic State Forest. Hills from thirteen hundred to nineteen hundred feet high surrounded them, and their primitive cart track followed more or less the route of the present U. S. Highway 44.

"Our expectations and every idea of a bad road were surpassed," said Du Roi. They scrambled down "a very steep mountain," then clawed their way up again "over another, still higher and steeper." Sometimes, rocks "three or four feet in circumference lay in the middle of the road. It was cold and water coming down the mountains was frozen, which made the ascents and descents difficult for the men and almost impossible for the horses." The column was continually halted because of broken wagons, so that the prisoners were often unable to reach the towns where barns had been requisitioned for their shelter and food gathered in for them. Darkness fell, and they bivouacked in the forest.

Leaving four wagons broken down in the woods, the weary Germans finally emerged at a Connecticut village which seems to have been Norfolk. They were welcomed warmly. "The clergyman of that place had a concert and a ball today," said Du Roi; the date seems to have been November 22, which was a Sunday. "An affair of this kind is not considered wrong here at all, as it is at home."

When the troops came into Salisbury, in the northwestern corner of Connecticut, Du Roi said this was "a very good township where we found many nice people and good quarters. The place is situated in a pleasant part of the country, which had induced many rich people to settle here." The Germans asked for "a day of rest," which was granted. "A ball was given and we had a very pleasant time. Twenty-five Belles of rank were present and the ladies danced very well until morning."

Du Roi thought that rich Americans came to Salisbury just for the view — and yet he visited the ironworks, where the money was made. "A smelting furnace" was "laid out well and on a large scale," he said. "All establishments, which have been erected to supply the necessities of war and its continuation, have developed exceedingly well, considering the short time of their existence, and it is astonishing how people who had been completely ignorant of these matters succeeded so well." But iron was discovered in Salisbury in 1632. Du Roi had been passing through country where copper had been mined also, and processed secretly, in defiance of a British law. General Knox, who had taken the Ticonderoga artillery to Boston, was at Salisbury, superintending the casting of cannon.

But no matter how superior he still felt, Lieutenant Du Roi was impressed with the colonies. Connecticut fared better than Massachusetts in his estimation. "The inhabitants are better-mannered and not so haughty as those in Massachusetts. They were very nice to us. There was quite a number of them who were for the King and would tell us so as soon as they were alone with us. The women are more inclined to work and take an interest in their housekeeping."

It is not surprising that the Baroness Riedesel found the march less entertaining and far more tiring than her young fellow countryman, Du Roi. He could ride horseback all day and dance all night, apparently. But Lady Fritz had to sit in her carriage, hope and pray it wouldn't turn over — and worry about what she and the children would have to eat, because her provision wagon was forever breaking down. Her account of the march was brief, not very explicit, and many of her experiences were unhappy.

"One day we came to a pretty place," she wrote, but what that place was called she did not say. It seems to have been east of the Hudson; perhaps it was in the Berkshires, because "our wagon had not been able to follow us and we could endure our hunger no longer," she said. "Observing a quantity of butcher's meat in the house in which we put up, I begged the hostess to let me have some. 'I have several kinds. There is beef, veal and mutton,' the woman said.

"My mouth already watered at the prospect," Lady Fritz remembered. " 'Let me have some and I will pay you well,' " she offered.

"Snapping her fingers almost in my face, the woman replied, 'You shall not have a morsel of it. Why have you come out of your land to kill us and waste our goods and possessions? Now you are our prisoners and it is our turn to torment you.' "

The Baroness kept her temper. "I pointed to my poor children, almost dead with hunger." The woman was adamant, "but finally Caroline took the woman by the hand and said to her in English, 'Good Woman, I am very hungry.' "

The woman took Caroline into another room where she "gave

her an egg. 'I have two sisters,' Caroline said." So the woman gave her three eggs.

" 'I am still angry,' declared the woman, 'but I cannot resist a child.' She became more gentle after that," said Lady Fritz, "and brought out bread and gave us milk.

"I made tea for ourselves and the woman eyed us longingly, for Americans love tea very much. . . . I poured out a saucer of tea for her, and this completely won her over." The woman now invited the Baroness into her kitchen and went down cellar to get a basket of potatoes for her. The husband was sitting in the kitchen before the fire, "gnawing at a pig's-tail." He "reached out this tidbit to his wife," and she gnawed on it for a while and then gave it back to him.

"I saw this singular mutual entertainment with amazement and disgust," said Lady Fritz. In fact, she probably stared so that the man thought she wanted a turn at the pig's-tail. He handed it to her.

"What should I do? Throw it away and not only hurt his feelings but lose the lovely basket of potatoes?" She thought desperately: she dared not risk a plain no thank-you. She took the pig's-tail, "pretended to eat it and quietly threw it into the fire." Considering how much a New Englander hates to waste anything, this might have been a wrong decision, but the Baroness and her host and hostess "had now made our peace. They gave me my potatoes and I made a good supper of them with excellent butter. Besides this, they moved us into three pretty rooms with good beds."

Du Roi reached the province of New York before Mrs. General Riedesel got there. He went through a town "about 2 miles long" called Amenia. "The houses were very poor and, like Canadian houses, built of logs put one on top of the other. Some of them were no better than the huts of Indians. Since the Congress thought it probable that many of our men might want to desert

to New York City a closer watch was kept over us and patrols
were placed on both sides."

As a matter of fact, the reason was a little different. The troops
were now approaching the place, just below Newburgh, where
they were to cross the Hudson. Clinton had sailed up the Hudson
once to a point over thirty miles north of Newburgh, and with a
little enterprise he could sail again and liberate Burgoyne's army
— so Phillips hoped and the Americans feared. No rescuers appeared, however; and news came that Clinton's offer of a cartel
had been refused.

Lieutenant Du Roi heard that General Washington "had come
to . . . see the German division march through" Fishkill. He told
his men, "and we marched in particularly good order." The General sent one of his adjutants to Brigadier Specht, inviting him
and his suite to dinner. Lieutenant Du Roi was included in the
invitation and went to see General Washington.

"He shook hands with us according to the custom here, and we
sat around the fireplace for half an hour, drinking toddy — a drink
made of whisky and sugar. The General was very pleasant, wished
to be able to facilitate matters for Brigadier Specht on the march,
and was quite satisfied that we did not complain of anything. . . .

"General Washington is a man of medium height, well built,
well educated," said Du Roi, putting physique first. "He has rather
a large nose but not out of proportion." Du Roi was acting as
interpreter for Specht, who did not speak English, and he mentioned with gratitude that Washington "speaks very distinctly."
He thought that Washington "expresses himself rather more sincerely than complimentary but is, however, quite polite. In short,
he impresses you as a good man who can be trusted. He has
nothing very extraordinary or great about him, which I expected."

General George Washington "departed next day," and the
Baroness Riedesel did not see him, which was a pity. Her opinion
of him would have been interesting.

The German troops crossed the Hudson a little below Newburgh. Behind them rose the mountains they had just left, their crests now powdered with snow. The men must have looked back in amazement at the high pass they had followed through the forest, and they must have looked ahead with equal amazement at the Hudson, which Du Roi thought was "seven miles wide at this point." Could this be the river they had bridged with boats above Saratoga only three months ago? A "two-masted vessel which held 150 men" crossed the Hudson "in about 12 to 16 minutes" — if the wind was right. It took "four or five hours before the division and all their baggage was taken over."

It was sometime in December before the Baroness reached the Hudson. "We were quartered at the house of a boatman," she said. The room they were given had no glass in the windows "so we hung our bedclothes over the empty window casements and slept upon straw because our baggage wagon had broken down and we had no beds."

Lady Fritz described her landlady as "a perfect fury," a "wicked woman" and an "antiroyalist." Forced by a storm to stay three days at the boatman's house, the Baroness and her party were finally told that they must cross the Hudson, regardless of the weather — and "in a little boat with one sail." It was all the wicked landlady's doing, in order to get rid of her guests, the Baroness was sure, but when the boatman said he would sail the boat himself, she agreed to go.

They all got into the skiff: Colonel Troup, Colonel Edmonston, Lady Fritz, the three children, the womenservants, a footman — and Rockel. The boatman had a boy to help him. They shoved off, and then the boatman jumped ashore! Gray water flecked with whitecaps lay ahead of them and they had no one to handle the skiff except the boatman's boy helper, who was completely incompetent. "We were driven hither and thither upon the river for more than five hours," said Mrs. General. It was a terrible experience. Her husband had gone on ahead and was all unaware of her danger. But at last they reached the west bank of the Hudson, and "waded up to the knees across a morass" to a house.

Men liked the Baroness. Daughter of an army officer and wife of a general, she expected and received protection with a touch of gallantry from officers, respect and services from rank and file. With civilians she just exerted her natural charm and got results. But the women she encountered in rural America she looked upon as peasants, and ordered about as befitted a Baroness among her husband's serfs — pleasantly but firmly. When results were unfortunate she was puzzled, sometimes angry, but more often hurt. Just across the Hudson, however, came the exception which proved the rule: it was the woman who was "kind" and the man who was surly.

The man, "who had just come in from the field in his rough clothes, his dirty linen and wearing a long beard, looked so much like a bear that we trembled before him." Finding the adjutants Troup and Edmonston drying themselves by the kitchen fire, he "seized them by the arms, called them nasty royalists" and wanted to know if it wasn't enough that he harbored them, without their invading his privacy.

"The following day, which was Sunday, the "kind wife" invited the Baroness to drink coffee with her after dinner. "Scarcely had I seated myself than in came the husband, looking much more respectable, for he had shaved himself and put on his Sunday linen." But remembering how truculent he had been, Lady Fritz got up to go.

The man shut the door and barred her way. "Are you afraid of me?" he asked.

"No," said Lady Fritz, with that spark which never deserted her. "I am afraid of no one, not even the devil whom you so much resembled yesterday."

"But today I look much better?"

"Yes," said the Baroness, "but I'm going to leave before you behave badly again." Lady Fritz was never egotistical, so she was surprised that she had not "vexed but pleased" the man.

He took her hand and urged her to sit down. "I am not as bad as you think," he said. "You please me and if I had no wife I would marry you."

At Sussex Court House, just beyond the northern boundary of New Jersey, Colonel Robert Troup left the Riedesels. He had been ordered to Morristown, and "A Captain Brown, sent by General Lord Stirling," took his place. Colonel Troup had become devoted to the Baroness. He hated to part with her and the children, and wished he could have stayed to make their journey easier.

Writing to General Gates on the third of January, 1779, Troup told of his experiences.[2] "You cannot conceive of the difficulties we have met with on the road," he said. "The people of almost every house we stopped at seemed to take pleasure in making our stay with them uncomfortable. I am sorry to add that the women were most impolite to Madame de Riedesel. They could not banish from their minds the notions they had imbibed of the cruelties our prisoners have received. Some were afraid of being plundered by us and others of being killed.

"One young girl, who had been lately married, cried and gnashed her teeth near two hours because I requested her to let Madame de Riedesel sleep in her bedroom where she had a few gowns, petticoats, pots and trammels.

"Indeed, such has been the incivility of all ranks and degrees to us that I have suffered the most painful anxiety."

But General Riedesel wrote to Gates also. "I cannot sufficiently express my thanks for the politeness and attention which Colonel Troup has shown to Madame de Riedesel and me upon the journey and the trouble he has given himself to alleviate the difficulties which naturally and unavoidably occur on such a journey."

General Riedesel had courteously forgiven an incident which

roused his ire at the time when it happened. The militia guard, which escorted his baggage from Hartford to the New York line, went home without waiting for another guard to take their place. They left the baggage "at Colonel Morehouse's" without a guard and someone — Colonel Troup, being a Yorker, was sure it was the Connecticut militia — "broke open some of the boxes and plundered them of several dozens of wine, a great number of spermaceti candles and five dozen packs of cards."

Colonel Troup added some current news in his letter to Gates. Mrs. Washington would soon join the General at Philadelphia. (She had visited him even when he was at Valley Forge the previous year.) General Lee had been found guilty of cowardice by the court-martial which followed his failure to obey orders that would have crippled or perhaps captured Clinton at Monmouth, during his evacuation of Philadelphia. Lee had fought a duel "the other day" with Colonel John Laurens, aide-de-camp to Washington.[3] (This was John Laurens — son of Henry Laurens, who had just resigned as president of the Continental Congress.) Colonel Laurens had been at Monmouth. In the duel, Lee had been "slightly wounded in the body" and "intended to have another pass as soon as he recovers."

Now Colonel Troup rode away and slowly but more or less steadily the Convention soldiers moved southward. Lieutenant Du Roi found more formidable rivers in his path than he had ever seen before and he could no longer compare them with rivers in Europe. They had to wait a day because the Delaware was too rough, and then they crossed "on big flatboats" at Frenchtown, where the river was "half a mile wide" with banks "very high and beautiful." Summing up New Jersey, Du Roi's report was generally favorable. It was "very hilly and woody," he said. He thought so because the route had been carefully planned to keep the prisoners in the northern part of the state — away from New York City with its temptation to escape; away from the parts of New Jersey ravaged by war and empty of provisions. There were "good pastures, cornfields and orchards." It met with Du Roi's approval that there should be "a good many people here who take sides with the King" and he heard that they were "badly treated" by their rebel neighbors. But he was growing a little tolerant and remarked that the "inhabitants are industrious but poor. They have suffered too much from the war."

The bridge over the Schuylkill aroused German admiration. It was "built by General Sullivan and was 228 paces long, resting on 9 wooden pillars with many stones being sunk to keep the pillars in place because of the current.

"Our good Captain Price" who had been sent with some Continental troops as an escort for the prisoners from the Hudson into Pennsylvania, left them near Valley Forge. Perhaps it was Captain Price who pointed out and told them of Valley Forge. "The place is fortified . . ." Du Roi wrote. "Huts had been built in three weeks, and the camp looks like a badly built town. It is remarkable that the [American] army could stand these quarters for a whole winter without many of the necessities of life, as shoes and stockings etc.

"Every one of the officers was sorry to lose Captain Price," said Du Roi, "I especially, because I was very much attached to him, we got along so well." But now Price and his Continentals were gone and the Pennsylvania militia who were to take their place failed to appear. The prisoners "marched seven miles without escort." They could all have escaped — but where would they go? At last "an old Colonel" met them, and he had a letter to Lieutenant Du Roi. "He asked me to tell him for heaven's sake what was he expected to do!" So with the aid of some crudely drawn maps, and with a more or less southerly direction in mind, the troops marched to Lancaster, Pennsylvania, by their usual slow stages.

It was not surprising that Lieutenant Du Roi, German in spite of his French-sounding name, liked Lancaster the best of any American city. His men had quarters "in well-kept barracks, two stories high" and the officers were entertained in private homes. Lancaster had "1000 houses, most of them built of stone in the very best taste four or five stories high," he said. "In front of the houses is a sidewalk made of brick for pedestrians. This is kept very clean."

Du Roi's journal became a tourist guide to Lancaster for the year 1778–1779. There were five churches with steeples, and one of them was "a magnificent building entirely of brick. There were "decorations" inside, and an organ. The clergyman's name was Helmuth, he was German-born and "a very nice, educated gentleman."

The houses were "very clean inside and the way of living is exactly like that in Germany." Everywhere he went, he heard German as well as English spoken, and all this made it the more heartbreaking for the German prisoners. "Our hopes of being hospitably received by our countrymen were cruelly deceived," wrote Du Roi. Although "there were a few nice people among them," for the most part the militia escort had to compel people to give an officer a room.

Du Roi was forced to a conclusion: "On the whole, we were ashamed of being Germans, because we never had met with so much meanness in one spot as from our countrymen."

They reached the Susquehanna, "a mile and three quarters wide," found the current too strong and the weather "too stormy to cross" at Wright's Ferry, so they encamped, in the rain. When the wind went down they boarded flatboats, with long oars "fastened to the boat with iron." Today, a high concrete bridge crosses the Susquehanna to a tiny town called "Wrightsville" on the western bank. From the bridge, a road cuts down to water level, and from there can be seen the "little islands and cliffs" which the Germans found so beautiful but terrifying, as their heavy boats swept along just barely out of reach of the rocks. It took the first German division eight hours to cross the Susquehanna.

Pennsylvanians were still inhospitable, and Du Roi sarcastically remarked: "It really does credit to the character of the Germans that our countrymen were the only ones who treated us mean and at the same time tried to get something out of us and cheat us." When the prisoners reached Hanover, Pennsylvania, the German inhabitants redeemed themselves, however. "They received us very well indeed, which reconciled us a little with our countrymen. All the German maidens came to a ball and danced with our officers, in spite of its being Christmas and a holy day."

The march now led through wide, fertile fields, beautifully cultivated. Snow fell at intervals, and the going was bad; but the German troops found real roads which, though muddy, were vastly superior to the cart tracks they had followed across the mountains. They circled north and westward of Philadelphia and Baltimore. This was a great disappointment to the young officers, who had hoped to see the cities. But Du Roi's size-up of Pennsylvania was most favorable: "Pennsylvania is a very flourishing state, not very hilly. It has the most beautiful estates . . . all the houses are fine and big, also the barns and stables. There is no other country with so many beautiful houses. The inhabitants are also mostly German, and there are quite a number who cannot even understand English, let alone speak it. They are very industrious and consequently rich. . . . However, they do not live extravagantly; on the contrary they are inclined to gather more riches. . . ."

Du Roi encountered Quakers here, and was pleased with them. "Men as well as women dress very plainly, choose however the finest and best material, being magnificently dressed, in this way. They are very kind to strangers . . . We found many nice, good girls among their women, who were in many ways not so shy as others. Almost all the Quakers are wealthy people who never let anyone belonging to their sect be reduced by poverty. . . ."

There was more in praise of Pennsylvania, but the Germans soon crossed into Maryland — which they found thoroughly detestable. Maryland "belonged to a man named Baltimore," he thought; anyway, that was what they told him. Nobody owned his own house; it was this Mr. Baltimore who owned all the houses. Maryland was a land of badly cultivated fields and miserable huts, but Du Roi understood that nobody was going to pay taxes to Mr. Baltimore after this and so Maryland would improve. It sounded as though the good Lieutenant Du Roi had been listening to rebel talk!

Snow fell on Du Roi and the Prince Frederick Regiment in December, and the weather was still colder in January, when the Riedesels came along in their carriage. Madam Riedesel spoke of only one encounter with Pennsylvania Germans, but it was a pleasant one. "We were lodged and well fed," she said, and the "patriarch of the family" told her his life history, which she considered astonishing. He had been the son of a coachman of Count Görtz in Germany. Running away from home at the age of twelve, he had reached America as an indentured servant. His master, "taking a fancy to him, had him well educated" and after the German lad had worked out his indenture his master "gave him some land to cultivate. . . . He was very active and industrious," and soon able to buy the land. So the master "gave him his daughter for a wife," as Lady Fritz put it and this German, now an old man, had nine sons, all of them farmers and landowners. He told the Baroness that his only regret was "the thought of having left his father, to whom, however, he often sent money."

Count Görtz was "a neighbor and friend" of the Riedesels, and this was why the coachman's son "took such good care of us," said Lady Fritz. Looking out across the fields, she could see that this man and his nine sons owned, together, as much or more land than most German counts could lay claim to.

The Riedesels crossed the Potomac among "dangerous ice floes," and a "great quantity of snow" came down as they prepared to cross the "Blue Mountains." The mountains were beautiful, the country was "picturesque," but Mrs. General was cold and, although she hated to admit it, frightened. Four of her servants rode on horseback in front of her carriage to make a path for it in the snow. "Often we were in danger of our lives along these breakneck roads."

But worst of all was lack of food. General Riedesel had ridden forward to try to find a place for his family to live in Charlottesville. Mrs. General and her little private army of servants, and her escort, Captain Edmonston, now traveled with the troops, at the end of the last column. By the time they reached a town or hamlet where food might be bought, everything was gone.

They were "a day's journey from Charlottesville" when they "had nothing left but tea and none of us could get anything but bread and butter. A country peasant whom we met on the road gave me only a handful of sour fruit. At noon we came to a house where I begged for something to eat. They refused me with hard words, saying they had nothing for dogs of Royalists. Seeing some Turkish meal [corn meal] I begged for a couple of handfuls so I could mix it with water and make bread."

"The woman answered me, 'No, that is for our Negroes who work for us. But you want to kill us.' Captain Edmonston offered her two guineas for it because my children were so hungry. But she said, 'No, not for a hundred would I give you any. If you die of hunger, so much the better.'" At this point Captain Edmonston wanted to take the corn meal by force, but the Baroness "entreated him to keep calm."

"We will find better people farther on," she said. But they did not come to so much as a hut. "The roads were horrible, the horses completely worn out, and my three children, exhausted by hunger, looked very pale," their mother said. "For the first time, I lost heart."

Captain Edmonston could not bear the sight of the little girls, too brave to cry, too listless to play or talk to him as they had done so gaily all along the way. He went "from man to man" among the wagon drivers to see if anyone had anything to eat.

But they were just as hungry and just as destitute. At last, a driver gave him "a piece of old bread, a quarter of a pound's weight," which had been considerably gnawed at because it was so hard no one could bite a piece out of it.

When Captain Edmonston brought the children this rock-hard hunk of bread, their "eyes sparkled," their mother said. She started to give it all to the youngest, but little Caroline would not take any until her sisters had some. Augusta and Frederika said that Caroline could have it all, but their mother carefully divided it three ways.

But Frederika Riedesel was no longer "Mrs. General" — she was just a mother with nothing to give her hungry children except stale bread. She began to cry. "If I had at any time refused a piece of bread to the poor, I would have thought that God wanted to punish me now," she said.

Captain Edmonston "was so upset" that he hastily rode off. He gave the wagon driver a guinea for this piece of bread, which had been the driver's last, and which he had so "gladly shared." When the driver turned back to recross the Blue Ridge Mountains, Captain Edmonston "bought him a large stock of bread for his return journey."

23

The Baroness in Virginia

IT WAS snowing hard on the seventeenth of January, 1779, when the German troops reached Charlottesville, Virginia. They had crossed a river which they believed was called the "Rapid Anne." They were out of provisions, but they thought they were coming into a sunny winter paradise. Instead, they found themselves on a high, windy plateau, and "after having gone through all the hardships of the march, we reached the climax of bad things," said Lieutenant Du Roi. "Never shall I forget the day which was terrible in every way. Never have I seen men so discouraged and in such despair."

Huts, 24 feet long by 14 feet wide, intended to house 18 men, stood close together, with no space between them. There were 4 rows of cabins, 12 to the row, set in squares. All around were great trees. The huts were built of logs, notched at the ends and laid up without nails. Logs "a hand wide" formed the roof, and in one side of each cabin "a hole is made in which a door is fastened, in about the way we fix a door in pigpens" back in Germany, Du Roi said. There was "not a single nail used except five or six in the doors." Du Roi did not realize that nails were a luxury and very scarce in Charlottesville.

There were no windows in the cabins, but windows would have been "superfluous because fresh air and rain had free passage through the walls," which had not yet been chinked with clay. There were no chimneys. The fire was built in the middle of the dirt floor, and "most of the huts did not even have a roof."

Thomas Jefferson, writing to Governor Patrick Henry, described the difficulties in Charlottesville. "The barracks were unfinished for want of labor; the spell of weather the worst in the memory of man, no stores of bread laid in, the roads, by the weather and the number of wagons, soon rendered impassable and not only the troops themselves were greatly disappointed but the people of the neighborhood were greatly alarmed at the consequences which a total failure of provisions might produce."

Du Roi said that some of his men preferred to camp in the woods, where they could protect themselves against the cold better than in the roofless huts. But next morning the sun shone and "the men started right away to improve their dwellings although they lacked almost all tools." They filled the spaces between the logs with clay, and later, when Schüler von Senden painted a water-color picture of the huts, he quite rightly gave them orange stripes between brown logs. The color of the clay was bright orange around Charlottesville.[1]

Du Roi's journal would not be complete, of course, without his summing-up of Virginia. He discussed slavery, not entirely condemning it but saying that no slaves were now being imported, "the prices are so high." Virginia horses were very fine but also high-priced. And the agricultural product which impressed him the most was "peaches — so prolific that whisky is made of them and pigs eat them." Du Roi deplored the wood ticks and the rattlesnakes.

"The freemen in Virginia are a lazy lot," he said, "who expect their slaves to do all their work." But the "wealthy and educated people of rank, 'gentlemen,' . . . are hospitable to the highest degree towards strangers." However, he added, it is best never to join a gentleman at cards — he never plays for small stakes.

"The women are a great deal more industrious. A gentleman's

wife considers it highly honorable to do some of the work herself. . . . It is considered a thing to be ashamed of if all the cotton and linen goods needed in the house are not woven at home, the women supervising the slaves' weaving. . . .

"The women here deserve to be highly respected for their industrious tendencies. They are quite the opposite of those in New England, and although not as pretty as those, as a rule they are much more polite and better mannered, also more courteous to strangers." Some sharp-tongued New England girl must have been hard on Du Roi, refusing to go out and milk the cow for him!

General Riedesel was already in Charlottesville, having difficulty finding a house for his family.[2] The English prisoners had got there first and had taken all the best quarters. But by paying them well, he persuaded a Major Irving and two other officers to move out of "Colle," and let him have it. Colle was the name of an estate on one of the small, conical hills that make the environs of Charlottesville unusual and charming. Across a narrow valley, another slightly higher but similar hill rose, crowned by a white house with columns. This was Thomas Jefferson's much-loved Monticello, begun in 1763 when he "levelled off the northeast corner of the mountain."

Colle belonged to Signor Philip Mazzei. Formerly a physician, Mazzei came to Virginia through the influence of Benjamin Franklin and others, bringing with him 10,000 cuttings from the vineyards of his native Tuscany, and also cuttings from vineyards in France, Portugal and Spain. Tuscan vineyard workers also came in the vessel he chartered, and Washington had welcomed him in Williamsburg.

Jefferson and Mazzei became friends and Jefferson helped him procure Colle, then gave him land adjoining Colle for the "4,000 olive trees, lemon trees, . . . seeds, grafts and small plants" to be tried out in Virginia. Jefferson and Mazzei were collaborators in agricultural experiments. Mazzei was an ardent patriot, and in

1779 he went to Europe as financial agent for the state of Virginia. When the Convention Troops descended upon Charlottesville, Colle was for rent but Mazzei had not yet left town.

Major Irving and his friends had paid a fancy price for the rent of Colle. They particularly liked it because there was forage for their horses, they said. The horses were already pastured there, and a long correspondence ensued while they wrangled over terms with Riedesel.[3] But Riedesel outranked the major and also paid him off. Fourteen years later, Thomas Jefferson wrote to Albert Gallatin about Mazzei's agricultural experiments and a few lines from that letter have often been quoted: "Mazzei rented his place to General Riedesel, whose horses in one week destroyed the whole labor of three or four years." But General Riedesel was an ardent gardener. From his correspondence with the English major, it looks as though it must have been Major Irving's horses, not Riedesel's, that ruined Mazzei's vineyards.[4]

"This spring the weather set in remarkably mild," wrote Jefferson in his *Garden Book* on February 8, 1779.[5] All the fruit trees were in blossom on this day when Madam Riedesel's battered English carriage rolled into Charlottesville, after a journey of over seven hundred miles. The "mountains," shaped like giant anthills, where Monticello and Colle and other country homes were built, were misted over with green. Peach trees were aflutter with pink and white blossoms. The road led "through a beautiful wood" which was part of Jefferson's estate and had been stocked with deer.

Then the road wound upward to Colle and just one thing marred the idyllic scene. This was the smell of putrid meat. Preparations for the reception of the troops at Charlottesville had gone badly all along, and there was no co-operation on the part of the weather. Snow had fallen on the unfinished barracks while "oxen and swine" were being slaughtered to feed the troops. Then the weather suddenly turned hot, and "salt was very scarce. They cut the meat into quarters," Mrs. General explained, "placed it in a vault in the earth and scattered ashes between the pieces instead of salt, which answered equally well." But because of the heat "all the top layers were spoiled. The meat was brought to us on a wheel-barrow but we were often obliged to throw the whole of it away, although sometimes we could wash it, salt it, and hang it up in smoke."

Mrs. General reached Colle in the morning of an unseasonably hot day, and dealt first with the meat situation. She found that "two heads of cabbage could be brought in from the garden," and Mr. Mazzei, owner of Colle, let her have "the head, neck and giblets of a ram." This would make a good stew, Mr. Mazzei said. And he would give her "half a putrid ham." Rejecting the ham and proceeding with the stew, Lady Fritz "had scarcely enough for dinner to satisfy us alone." Her family consisted of herself, her husband, their three children "and a minimum of five servants." Then, just before dinner, "eight German officers rode up." Lady Fritz burst into tears.

But she was still Mrs. General. Hastily drying her eyes, she welcomed her guests and asked them all to dinner. This was exactly what they came for, and they accepted with alacrity.

The reason for Mazzei's frugality in supplying the Baroness with food was that he was on the verge of sailing for Europe, and he intended to sell off all his possessions — farm produce included. It took him three days to make an inventory, and he told in his own words what went on:[6]

The General "bought the vegetables in my garden, the chickens in the coop and such other things as he had to buy . . . together with some trifles that his wife desired. There were six coops, for besides having chickens and geese, I had two kinds of ducks and two kinds of turkeys. There were three vegetable gardens, in each of which there was a spring giving an abundance of fresh water."

Mr. Mazzei's auction lasted four days, "beginning early in the morning" and ending late at night with almost no time out for meals. People came from forty miles around, and when it was over, the Riedesels had no furniture "except logs to sit on and logs with boards across for a table."

"During that time," wrote Mazzei, "the General and his wife boarded at my house; afterwards I was their guest."

He had squeezed every cent of profit he could out of the Riedesels, but Lady Fritz served good meals to him, his wife and his daughter. He constantly quarreled with his wife, who had agreed to a divorce, and he spoiled his daughter outrageously. It was not surprising that the Riedesels "looked forward to their departure."

"In March," wrote Jefferson in his *Garden Book*, "it set in cold." The Blue Ridge Mountains, which he could see from his window looming grandly across a plain, "were covered with snow and the thermometer [was] below freezing" at Monticello.[7] "This killed all the fruits, which had blossomed forward. The weather then again became mild till a thunderstorm on the 15th of April and wind at the North West brought on again severe frosts."

Lady Fritz used stronger terms. "We had heavy thunderstorms lasting for five or six days at a time," she said. As for that "north west wind," it was "a tempest which tore more than a hundred trees in our neighborhood up by the roots."

In the night someone beat upon their door and shouted that the new stable they had been building was about to blow down. General Riedesel rushed out, summoning all the men on the place to help prop it up. This left his wife alone in the house with the children and the women servants. The wind rose to a terrifying, sustained roar and "a great piece of the chimney fell into the room. The whole house rocked."

General Riedesel decided that the Mazzei house was not likely to stand many more such gales of wind. He drew some plans, perhaps with Jefferson's advice, and "we had built for us a large house, with a great drawing-room in the center and upon each side of it, two rooms." The house "cost one hundred guineas and was exceedingly pretty," said Lady Fritz.

It was easier said than done to build, however, even with one hundred guineas to spend. The General had "2000 nails" promised to him by Colonel Harvie, who was in charge of the prisoners. But on the first of May, Colonel Bland had taken over and Colonel Harvie had never produced the nails. Riedesel's carpenters were at a standstill, he told Colonel Bland. There were "no nails to be had in Fredericksburg or Richmond," but he had heard that the American quartermaster had some in stores at the barracks — he would like "about 6000." But there were not six thousand nails at the barracks.

Jefferson, in writing to Patrick Henry, must have referred to General Riedesel when he told of "the officer who is building a house for the accommodation of his family. . . . Independent of brick work, for the carpentry . . . I know he is to pay fifteen hundred dollars. The same gentleman, to my knowledge, has paid to one person thirty-six hundred and seventy dollars for different articles to fix himself commodiously." On April 29, Jefferson put in his personal records, "sold my pianoforte to General Riedesel who is to give me £100."

This present to Lady Fritz made her very happy. She was a fine musician, and it had been a very long time since she had touched a piano. There were many musicians among the German prisoners. Captain Geismar, for example, had apparently managed to bring his violin safely through a disastrous campaign and across the long miles from Cambridge to Charlottesville. He accompanied his general's wife when she played her piano and sang arias from the operas.

On April 11, 1779, Thomas Jefferson received an invitation which read: "Major General Phillips sends his compliments to Mr. and Mrs. Jefferson and requests the favor of their company at dinner on Thursday at Two o'clock to meet General and Madame de Riedesel. Major General Phillips hopes Miss Jefferson will be permitted to be of the party to meet the Young Ladies from Colle."

"Miss Jefferson" must have been Martha, just about six and a half years old. Mrs. Jefferson was younger than the Baroness Riedesel by two and a half years but she had been married at eighteen, had had a son, and was widowed at nineteen. Martha was her oldest child by her second marriage. Like the Baroness, Mrs. Jefferson knew the grief of losing children. Martha's little sister Jane had lived only about eighteen months; another son had survived scarcely a month. There was a baby, named Mary, now not quite a year old. The auburn-haired, hazel-eyed Mrs. Thomas Jefferson had great charm and was a fine musician, both on the harpsichord and the piano.

Six-year-old Miss Jefferson often played with the young ladies from Colle: Miss Augusta Riedesel, who would be eight in August, Miss Frederika, five, and Miss Caroline about three. It is to be hoped that they all behaved themselves like proper "young Ladies." But their mother said nothing about it in her book, nor did she mention the musical evenings at the Jeffersons which were so much a part of their social life.[8] However, when the Jeffersons left Charlottesville early in June General Riedesel wrote to them as follows:

"The good fortune which I have had in making your acquaintance and all the kindness which I have received from you during your short stay at Monticello moves me to present these lines of felicitation on your new post. . . . My only regret is that we shall be deprived of your society, which has thus far made our stay at Colle so pleasant. Madame de Riedesel joins her felicitations to mine. . . . She is only saddened that, in going to Monticello, she will no longer find there, her good friend, Madame Jefferson. . . ."

Jefferson had just been elected Governor of Virginia. "I thank you for your kind congratulations," he replied, "tho' condolences would be better. . . ." Everyone knew how much he loved Monticello. He spoke of the "loss of the agreeable society . . . of which Madame de Riedesel and yourself were an important part," and of Mrs. Jefferson's "regret on her separation from Madame de Riedesel."

General Phillips was living at Blenheim, a long, low frame house built by Colonel John Carter for his son, Edward. Set on a hilltop in the midst of a plantation employing 1500 slaves, it was one of the finest houses in the area — but it was very much out of repair. In design, Blenheim was built for hospitality, having a large drawing room in the center and living quarters left and right of it, one side for the family and the other for guests. Phillips complained, of course. He was paying "30 golden guineas a month" for the place and it was in terrible shape. Plantation work-parties had been living in it.

Riedesel was building his new house with American dollars and doing very well. But Phillips had bad luck. The dollars sent him by the British agent in Fredericksburg were "of bad emission" and had to be returned. It had seemed to the British a smart move to break down the American currency by circulating counterfeit paper dollars, but General Phillips was very angry to find himself a victim of the scheme. He would have to try to borrow money "from Col. Harvie and Mr. Jefferson" and "become a Beggar once more for a little Port Wine — a Dozen" would greatly oblige him. General Riedesel would please send them over. And if the Riedesels "had any oil, send me as much as will dress a salad for you on Thursday," Phillips wrote.

Many were the dinner parties exchanged between General Phillips and the Riedesels. The irascible Phillips could be calmed, amused and made to forget his troubles when Lady Fritz played her new pianoforte for him and sang his favorite songs. She was outspoken to her husband's superior officer, telling him not to complain so much and to moderate his language in front of Americans, who would only laugh at him. Phillips was devoted to her. Writing in French, he suggested to General Riedesel that he proceed according to his wife's ideas because "she has more beautiful eyes than you do and permit me to respect her orders instead of yours." When he heard that one of the Baroness's trunks had arrived broken open, he wrote that she didn't need fine clothes to make her any more charming.

The Baroness herself explained how she and General Phillips planned their meals. "Every week we killed, by turns, an ox and two pigs. Very soon we wanted for nothing." Meals alternated: a dinner at Blenheim, a dinner at Colle; but the Baroness set the better table because she had made friends with the colored people living around her and they "brought us everything we needed in the shape of poultry and vegetables." Besides all this, there were wild turkeys, which "weighed over fifty pounds and were perfectly tame." After a while, the turkeys "all flew off into the woods and we gave them up for lost." Then back they came, the hen turkeys followed by broods of chicks, much to the delight of the three little girls.

The Riedesel children were well and happy on their Virginia plantation. Augusta was a serious child with fine eyes and a rather determined chin. Frederika was fair and looked much like her father. Her light blue eyes were gentle. Caroline was a pretty blond baby, learning to speak English and German with a word or two of French, as the case might be. The children could have had an even better time in the woods and in the gardens if their mother had not been "in constant terror of rattlesnakes." It took more than rattlesnakes to scare little girls of their experience.

It was a treat for the children to get into the new "chariot" their mother had chosen, take along provisions for a picnic and drive to the barracks about ten miles away. Twisting and turning, the road led past Monticello, past the northern edge of Charlottesville, and out from among the steep little hills into rolling country. Their father took that journey on horseback nearly every day.

The drive to the barracks was not always without excitement.

One day the horses went through some rotten logs in a bridge. The front wheels of the carriage were smashed, but by a miracle the chaise stayed upright at the edge of the gaping hole where the poor horses struggled and floundered. The harness broke or they would all have been pulled into the bed of the creek.

General Riedesel had "laid out upwards of 200 pounds sterling in garden seeds for the German troops only," wrote Thomas Jefferson. "Their poultry, pigeons and other preparations of that kind, present to the mind the idea of a company of farmers rather than a camp of soldiers." The men had cleared all the ground along "the top and brow of a high hill," and they could see the long line of the Blue Ridge Mountains, majestic against the sky.

Lieutenant Du Roi had become one of General Phillips's aides and was sent on various errands, but Schüler von Senden was at the barracks most of the time and wrote of what went on there. They told him that in those mountains "there are panthers, bears, wolves, elk, stags, wildcats, opossums, marten, skunks, rabbits and raccoon." The Germans were fond of taming small animals and one of the sights at the barracks which the Riedesel children looked forward to was a tame raccoon described by von Senden as "something like a badger but can climb trees rapidly."

The soldiers' gardens were all neatly fenced and "all the things in the gardens at home were also found in the gardens here," von Senden said. And there was a strange new plant, "a kind of pea with a yellow blossom, the leaves of which remind me of our clover leaves. When the blossoms fall off, the stalks growing out from the base push pods into the earth for a distance of 1½ inches, each containing two or three large peas. They are tasty." Von Senden was carefully describing peanuts.

Strawberries grew wild, and were larger "than our garden strawberries at home." As the season advanced melons grew "without any care whatever."

But garden palings were important, because "cows and pigs

usually run around freely although they seldom stray farther than a mile and a half." This was far enough for them to make pests of themselves. Cows wore bells, "so that they can be found more readily."

When it was not the day for the children to go out in the carriage, the Baroness rode horseback. She astonished the inhabitants by her costume — somewhat like a Hussar's, with high jack boots. Her *embonpoint* was commented upon. It was a very thin Mrs. General who had been driven down out of the mountains in February — but during the last few months she had enjoyed good food. The word *embonpoint*, moreover, was not then a euphemism for overweight but a term of sincere admiration. Inhabitants meant that Mrs. General was well stacked and they said that she was also a handsome lady.

General Riedesel "took considerable satisfaction in busying himself in his garden," his wife wrote. But he refused to wear a hat because he was tormented by severe headaches and a hat seemed unbearably heavy.

"I was engaged in putting to rights my new house," Lady Fritz related, "when I heard a noise out of doors. I ran to the window and saw my husband being carried into the house by some men. His face was blue, his hands white, his eyes fixed and great drops of sweat stood upon his forehead. I was more dead than alive with fright and the children uttered piercing shrieks."

The surgeon attached to Regiment Riedesel was living at the house and "happened at the moment to be in." The men laid the General down, and the surgeon "tore off all his clothing and at once opened a vein." Everyone said that General Riedesel had had a sunstroke, but the blue color of his face which his wife observed does not bear this out. He also experienced temporary loss of speech. The diagnosis made no difference, however, because bloodletting would have been the treatment no matter what the illness. General Riedesel regained consciousness and "gazed upon me with a loving look and took my hand," his wife said. "He soon regained his speech, but was weak and ill a long time."

Frederika Riedesel was as close to panic as she had ever been during her whole experience in America. "My God, what would have become of me and my little children in the midst of captives, so far from home and in an enemy's land?" she wrote. She had many loyal friends, from General Phillips on down. Not a German officer in her husband's "family" but what was devoted to her — she could have counted on Jefferson or on any American officer she had social contact with; but she had a special reason for her feeling of terror. She was expecting another child.

24

The New Yorkers

THE weakness that came with General Riedesel's illness made him "grieve the more over his situation," wrote Mrs. General. The local doctor suggested that she take him to "Frederick-Spring," and when she approached General Phillips about this idea he said to go ahead and he would come along himself as soon as he could.

Jefferson gave the Riedesels a passport to "visit several medicinal springs, in Louisa, Berkeley and Augusta [Counties]. You will be pleased in this to follow your own inclination, passing from one to another of them by such roads and making such excursions on the road or at any of the springs as may be agreeable to yourself," Jefferson wrote, dating his letter July, 1779. The letter released Riedesel from his previous parole, "prescribing certain limits which might have restrained you from visiting these springs. You are also at perfect liberty to take with you such of your family as you choose to be attended by, who shall be considered as included within the same dispensation. I shall be obliged to you, however, for their names at a time before you set out, for the information of the commanding officer of the garrison that I may be able to guard them from molestation." A more generous permission could hardly have been devised.

"Frederick-Spring," now called Berkeley Springs, was a fashion-

323

able resort not far from the Potomac in what is now West Virginia. As was the case with most of the warm springs, the Indians were supposed to have discovered curative powers in the water. Unlike most mineral springs, however, the water was pleasant, rather sweet-tasting. George Washington surveyed the land around Berkeley Springs for Lord Thomas Fairfax in 1746 and the area was granted to Virginia as public domain. General Gates bought a plot in the nearby town of Bath — as did Washington, whose nephew, Major John Augustus Washington, took the waters in the vain hope of a cure for tuberculosis. Makeshift cottages, shelters and tents dotted the narrow hollow where the springs rise, below Warm Springs Ridge and Hogback Mountain.

Mrs. General thought the waters did her husband no good at all and might have harmed him. He "probably increased his disorder by always getting his head wet before bathing," she said, "and in spite of all we could do his hair would remain damp." The air was hot and humid — and for a man who liked a cold, dry climate this was torture. The poor General could not sleep at night, so his wife "read to him in a drowsy tone." This put him to sleep but if she stopped reading he woke again. "His feet and hands were constantly blue and cold as ice," no matter how hot and uncomfortable he felt.

The books the Riedesels read were in French and had belonged to Mazzei. *Candide* was among them and this Lady Fritz returned. Mazzei complained that she kept others, and doubtless this troubled her conscience very little. Mazzei's profiteering had not been forgotten.

Worried as she was about her husband, Lady Fritz could not help having a good time. One day "a Virginian came into my room," she said. He wanted to have a look at a German woman. She laughed and told him to go ahead and look. "He eyed me from head to foot," and when he asked to see her husband, she took him to the General. But the idea of being stared at like a

circus freak brought tears to the General's eyes and she was overcome with remorse. "Everything irritated him," she knew that —
it was just that she had had a good laugh and wanted him to
laugh too.[1]

Members of General Washington's family were at Frederick-
Spring, but the Baroness refrained from comment. However, there
was a Mrs. Carroll,[2] "an ardent American patriot, but reasonable."
The inference might be that the Washingtons were unreasonably
patriotic. But in any case Lady Fritz and Mrs. Carroll "became
great friends." Her husband had come to take the waters. The
official bathing and water-drinking time was in the morning, so
Mrs. Carroll and the Baroness spent their mornings together. Captain Geismar had come as one of General Riedesel's aides, and he
had brought his violin, so he played "and I sang Italian arias to
the great delight of Mrs. Carroll," said Lady Fritz.

One day "a peasant came in. As Americans generally are fond of
music, he listened attentively" and when the Baroness finished
her song he asked her to sing again. She knew this man, because
he was a neighboring farmer from whom she had attempted in
vain to buy butter. Having a little fun with him, therefore, the
Baroness asked him what he would give her to sing. "Two pounds
of butter," he replied quite seriously.

Lady Fritz laughed and began to sing again. Once more she
received an encore, only this time the farmer said he wanted something lively. "At length I sang so much," she said, "that the next
morning he brought me four or five pounds of fresh butter." He
had his wife with him because he wanted the Baroness to sing
for her too. "I succeeded in winning their affection," she said,
"and afterwards I lacked for nothing." She thought that "the best
of the joke" was that these people imagined they really paid her
to sing for them. "They wondered much when I paid them for
the butter they thought they had sold."

Like most foreign visitors, Lady Fritz generalized from details she observed. "The Virginians are generally languid, a fate which they attribute to their hot climate," she said. "But on the slightest inducement, in a twinkling they will leap up and dance about and if a reel is played for them the men immediately catch hold of the women who then jump up [and dance] as if possessed. But as soon as they are led back to their chairs they sit on them like blocks of wood."

The Baroness was told tales of incest among mountain folk, and she seemed to think it was common practice everywhere. She did not mention German deserters, but there were many who slipped off into the Blue Ridge Mountains, took unto themselves more or less lawful wives, and brought German names among a people who accepted the newcomers with respect and affection.

Desertion was again one of the problems troubling General Riedesel's mind. As General Phillips wrote him, "The difficulty of discovering the motives of this great desertion[3] or the means made use of to get away is very great — whoever the men are who act as guides or who plan the taking-off of soldiers, they are possessed of much cunning and caution." General Phillips discovered that the Convention soldiers were running off to join a group of Americans called "Goodrich's Privateers." The Americans "engage themselves by oath to bring the men safe to the vessels which lie in the Rappahannock River." It took three days to go through the woods from Charlottesville, by way of an unfrequented path near which they had a log house where were collected provisions for two hundred for two days. "The route taken is toward Augusta, over the blue ridge, and down the Rappahannock to the vessels."

There was still another method of escape, by which Phillips was sure some of the deserters were getting safely away. "A man who lived in the mountains and found a brother in the 9th Regiment, has undertaken to conduct men of that regiment to Halifax, they are gone off some days," he said. "The guides appear in the

Barracks as sellers of whiskey. There is reason to believe a good many have got off safe, as the Soldier has returned and six days ago took off 40 more men with him." This kind of desertion would seem to be with Phillips's blessing.

The Riedesels had been expecting from day to day that General Phillips would join them, but he had his troubles back at Charlottesville, not only with deserters but with Colonel Bland, the American in charge of the prisoners — whom he called "Alexander the Great." "My soul is already there [at Frederick-Spring]," he wrote. "Only my miserable body remains at Blenheim. . . . Adieu my dear Riedesel — lay me at the feet of Madame and be assured of my entire attachment."

Captain Edmonston, who had reluctantly parted from the Riedesels, was on his way to England, having been exchanged. He had with him a bill of exchange of 1050 pounds sterling, "several officers wishing to send money to England," and he had gotten as far as Philadelphia when he wrote that "Generals Phillips and Riedesel are about to be exchanged."

"I don't believe a word of it," wrote Phillips, but on August 13 there was definite news. General Clinton wrote to Phillips that "an exchange on parole is agreed upon, the officers which the enemy are to receive for you and General Riedesel are already gone . . . with respect to your final exchange, we must talk of that when we meet."

Now all was excitement. It was decided that General Riedesel must go back to Charlottesville to wind up his affairs. He was to sell provisions, wine, house furnishings and the piano. The Baroness, with Captain Freeman, her husband's English-speaking aide, her children, her coachman Rockel and the servants, would fare forth alone. Loaned to her among the servants was Giovanni, one of Mazzei's Tuscan boys, who carried a cage full of redbirds or caridnals on his back. He was called Giovannetti.

Their friend Mrs. Carroll had invited the Baroness to come to her plantation in Maryland, to stay until she had word that her husband awaited her at York, Pennsylvania.

This journey toward New York was far more pleasant than the one from Cambridge to Charlottesville, but it was not without hazard. "Before we arrived I was overturned in my carriage," said Lady Fritz, "but I was not at all hurt." Mrs. Carroll "sent a man on horseback" to meet the Baroness, on the main highway, and they drove through "a pretty hamlet inhabited by pure Africans, each of whom had his garden and understood some handicraft."

Lady Fritz was not aware that she was the guest of people of distinction. Mrs. Carroll's family consisted of "an old father-in-law, eighty-four years of age, of a sprightly humor and most extreme neatness . . . four perfectly lovely grandchildren and their kind, beloved mother, our amiable hostess." The "old father-in-law" was Charles Carroll of Annapolis. "Although not now decked with titles, we derive our descent from princes," he once told his son. He was one of the great Catholic leaders in Maryland who joined the American patriot cause at the very beginning. The "four lovely grandchildren" were Polly, age nine; Charles, aged four; Anne, three years old; and Catherine, only a year and a half. Charles Carroll of Annapolis had a fine Georgian mansion in Annapolis, where George Washington was often his guest.

But it was "the country-seat" where the Baroness Riedesel was entertained. This would be "Doughoregan," about sixteen miles northwest of Baltimore. Begun about 1727, the two-story house was eventually three hundred feet long and thirty feet wide.

"We drove through a large courtyard to a very beautiful house, where the whole family gave us a joyful welcome," said Lady Fritz. "We were served upon silver and entertained, not, it is true, with much display, but with taste. Nothing was wanting for our comfort.

"The garden was magnificent, and on the following day she

[Mrs. Carroll] drove us out to look at her vineyard which was splendid and displayed great taste, in fact exceeding my expectations. First we went through a great fruit garden. Then we ascended the vineyard by a winding path which led up to the top of the hill. Between every vine a poplar-rose and an amaranth grew. The effect of this arrangement was to give a magnificent appearance to one looking down from the top." Lady Fritz said she never saw its equal for beauty anywhere else in America. "The husband of Mrs. Carroll had traveled abroad and had gathered ideas for the laying out of grounds in England and France."

Doughoregan Manor contained 13,360 acres. Mrs. Carroll's husband had indeed traveled abroad — he had been sent to Europe to study at the age of ten because, under English rule, Catholic schools were unlawful in Maryland. When he returned at the age of twenty-eight, his father gave him a great deal of land and he became known as "Charles Carroll of Carrollton" because he had a cousin, "Charles Carroll the Barrister." His mother had died before Charles got home and he understood that he must marry a Catholic girl, pleasing to his father. He had found a girl he loved, but she died just before the wedding.

It seems probable that Mary Darnall, aged nineteen, was chosen to be Mrs. Carroll of Carrollton by her father-in-law. "She brings no dowry but she is of good family, beautiful, sweet-tempered, virtuous and sensible," wrote the bridegroom at the end of a long letter on political matters.

Lady Fritz did not care much for Carroll of Carrollton. He might be the first signer of the Declaration of Independence, statesman, defender of the Catholic faith — but these things would not commend him to her, if she knew about them. To her "he was not very lovable, but rather brusque and miserly and not at all suited to his wife, who," although she never said anything, "did not appear very happy. She loved her father-in-law very much." That Carroll of Carrollton was parsimonious was mentioned even by one of his most admiring biographers. Charles

Carroll would "send out of the house for change" rather than "overpay a bill by a very few cents. . . . He was also painfully accurate."

"Not far from this estate was a town called Baltimore," wrote Mrs. General. They told her it "was very pretty and inhabited by many amiable families. We received a visit from an intimate friend of our hostess. Both these women reminded me of Rousseau's Héloise." Lady Fritz thought that Mary Carroll "was as full of tender feeling" as Héloise, and "would gladly have had a Saint Preux for a husband."

The visit lasted eight or ten days, and as a parting gift for their hostess, Captain Freeman designed and built "a temple adorned with flowers and dedicated to Friendship and Gratitude." Later, Mrs. Carroll wrote the Baroness that they always kept the little temple decorated with fresh flowers. "Our parting was sad," said Lady Fritz. "The lovely, agreeable Mrs. Carroll is now dead." She died in 1782 at the age of thirty-three, eleven days after the death of her father-in-law, to whom, say the records, "she was deeply attached."

Mrs. Carroll piled the Baroness's wagon "with provisions of the best quality, enough to last a long time." But Lady Fritz did not really need much, because there were many royalists along the road through Maryland who "furnished her with every needful thing."

The weather was not kind, however. Not far from Lancaster, Pennsylvania, the Baroness and her retinue were passing through a great forest when they were "overtaken by a violent thunderstorm. A tree broke and fell between the carriage-box and the horses, and here we sat fast aground because none of our servants were strong enough to move the tree." Lightning flashed, close-followed by the crack of thunder which hardly diminished into rumbles before the next shock came. "The lightning struck in several places around us and another and larger tree threatened to crush us."

There was nothing Mrs. General could think of to tell her army of servants to do to get her out of the forest, and she said all of them, including Captain Freeman, seemed to have lost their heads. But Augusta, "only eight years old at the time," had a suggestion. "Just unhitch the horses, put them behind the carriage and you can drag it backward." They did this, it worked, and somehow or other they got around the fallen tree and on their way again. They all "asked each other, 'Why didn't *we* think of this?'"

The storm swept on over "Yorktown" — or York, Pennsylvania — and when Mrs. General and her little army got there she found her husband very anxious about them "because of the vivid lightning." Next day they "rode through magnificent country, and passed . . . a very well cultivated section inhabited by the Moravian brethren." In Bethlehem they "found a right good tavern" and rested there to wait for some more officers from Charlottesville to catch up with them. Then they pushed forward, for they were all eager to get to New York, which had come to seem like a Promised Land. Frederika Riedesel was especially anxious to get there before her expected child came — a place where she could have "good nursing" and be among friends and allies instead of "the enemy."

They came at last into New Jersey, and "to the house of a family who gave themselves out as Royalists." The name was Van Horne. "They showed us much kindness and begged us to recommend them to General Cornwallis . . . and General Clinton." The Van Horne daughters were young and pretty.

But things had been going too well for the Riedesels — until they reached Elizabeth, New Jersey, or "Elizabethtown" as they called it, General Phillips and part of his staff with them by now. Sitting down to dinner among "many Royalists who welcomed us joyfully, toasts were drunk and we believed we should cross over to New York and be restored to Freedom that same evening. . . .

"Suddenly the door opened and an officer sent by General

Washington stepped in and handed General Phillips a letter." It was addressed to Joshua Messereau, Esq., Deputy Commissary of Prisoners. "You will remove General Phillips and the officers of the Convention Troops under your care, with their families and attendants, to Chatham, where you will have proper quarters pro- vided for them till you receive further orders for their destination," the letter said.

General Phillips flew into a rage. He pounded the table with his fist and shouted that this was what you could expect from people who were all of them rascals. Then he "seized" Lady Fritz's hand and told her not to lose courage and to notice "how collected" he was.

If her recollection of the scene was accurate, Lady Fritz told General Phillips to stop making a spectacle of himself — people were laughing. When he was "in a passion" he could get into "still more trouble." He calmed down and thanked her. Actually, the withdrawal of parole to go into New York was his own fault. It was again an affair of money — a little matter of unpaid bills and gratuitous insults on Phillips's part. Had the Baroness been in Charlottesville instead of Berkeley Springs, it is possible she might have influenced Phillips to behave himself better while there.

James Mulligan, authorized by the Continental Congress, had presented Phillips with a bill for the expenses incurred by the prisoners since the last settlement. "I assure you I have not 2000 pounds in the military chest," Phillips had told him, then un- fortunately he added that if he had the "power to procure all the gold in the province of America," he would not pay Mulligan's bill. The demand was for "eighty-five thousand five hundred pounds sterling, being the expense" of the prisoners from March through August, 1778. Mulligan explained all the charges and Phillips replied to his demands in an increasingly haughty tone. So Congress decided to halt the Generals within sight of British- held New York.

Phillips was still not as calm as the Baroness would have liked when he sat down on September 30 to write to General Washington. Riedesel, who had often persuaded him to moderate his style in his letters to General Heath, was not asked to revise this one.

"I do not allow of any conduct of mine or Major-General Riedesel's deserving this treatment and I hope, Sir, from your known candour and honour an Explanation."

Perhaps he had no idea what was wrong; but he did have debts a trifle on his mind, because on that same date he wrote to Colonel Bland, the American officer in Charlottesville, regarding a debt of honor: "General Phillips sends his compliments to Colonel Bland he quite forgot to send the paymaster general to him, *relating to the bet*. He has commissioned Mr. Hoaksley to wait upon Colonel Bland with five hundred pounds currency."

The Riedesels now returned along the road they had so recently and hopefully traveled. Again they stayed at the Van Hornes', but this time, "we found a nephew of General Washington's there with a lot of other American officers. Three days had wrought a wonderful change in the sentiments of these people." The Baroness saw "the daughters of these pretended Royalists on a most familiar footing with the anti-Royalists and allowing them all sorts of liberties." There was a wild party, in the course of which everybody sang " 'God save Great Washington, God damn the King' all night long."

The activities of the Van Horne young ladies were fairly well known, and at one time the Americans had threatened to jail their father because of his Tory sympathies. It would have been interesting if the Baroness had happened to mention her former shipmate, Mrs. Hannah Foy, who had been a Miss Van Horne. The girls who were so impartial in their favors to officers of both sides were Hannah's cousins; the house belonged to her uncle Philip — the manor nicknamed "Convivial Hall." When she left next morning, Lady Fritz "could hardly conceal" her "indignation."

Although ordered to Chatham, the Riedesels were allowed to go back to Bethlehem, Pennsylvania, at their own request. They now had at least "sixteen people, four house servants and about twenty horses"; and they all put up at the inn which Lady Fritz had liked so well on her way north.[4]

The Baroness was much impressed by Bethlehem, as well she might be. The Moravian buildings which are now such marvels of stone masonry were all of them already built and were no longer new even in 1779. They were said to be larger than any other buildings in America at that time and the heavy stone buttresses, the high walls, the bell tower, gave the town the look of a mediaeval German city. Riverbanks were steep and wooded at the point where Monocacy Creek and the Lehigh River join, so that Bethlehem seemed miraculously transported from Europe to a wilderness. But away from the riverbanks, Moravian industry had cleared great fields, rolling into the distance — acre after acre, unlike any German counterpart.

At Bethlehem "all sorts" of hand-crafted merchandise was for sale, "dressed leather as good as that of the English but less expensive" and "magnificent embroidery" which had been taught to the Moravian settlers by a German woman. Frugal as she was, Lady Fritz could not resist buying some embroidery. There were "workers in steel, excellent blacksmiths and cabinetmakers of great skill."

But best of all was the music. For the previous thirty years, Bethlehem had had a "Collegium Musicum" and some of the scores of Bach were said to have been played at Bethlehem before they were printed in Europe. "Flutes, oboes, French horns and trumpets accompanied the organ" in church on special days, and the Riedesels "went to church often and enjoyed the splendid singing."

In the peaceful cemetery, avenues of trees had been planted. Headstones were laid level with the turf so that no brother or sister should have a monument rising higher than another. While the Riedesels were in Bethlehem, "the wife of the minister died" and Lady Fritz observed a strange custom. They saw the body "laid out in a separate enclosure with bars" awaiting burial, because "they never keep a dead body in the house." The bars were to keep away wolves.

The Riedesels lived in Bethlehem for six weeks, and the Baroness would have been very happy except for her anxiety over her husband's health. He suffered "greatly the whole time from constant pains in his head and at night could scarcely breathe." She suggested that he stop smoking and try taking snuff, "a practice which he regarded with the greatest aversion." He thought she was joking, but he tried it, "and the very next instant felt relief so that he gave up his pipe for a snuff box."

The children had been wonderfully well during their long journey from Brunswick, Germany, to Canada and on the long march which ended so disastrously at Saratoga. The heat in Virginia, which their parents complained of, agreed with them perfectly. But now in Bethlehem, in November, 1779, little Caroline developed "a choking cough" and was very ill. It seems not to have occurred to her mother at first that this was whooping cough, and when the other children came down with it later she was much surprised.

For the first time, however, Mrs. General began to be uneasy about herself. She was "far advanced in pregnancy," she said. At last, after many letters had been exchanged, word came that Congress would allow Phillips and Riedesel to go to New York on parole, and General Riedesel set out around the twentieth of October. He left his wife in Bethlehem, where she must stay until he found suitable quarters for her. New York was a crowded city — with more than 3000 Loyalist refugees added to Tory citizens, and a fair number of rebel agents and spies.

A house was still to be found; but, toward the end of November, Mrs. General set out, in charge of her little army as usual, responsible for the welfare of them all. She was determined not to stop over at the Van Hornes' again because "I despise double-dealing people," she said. But fate played her a mean trick. "Our wagon broke down before their very door" and she was forced to stay with them "until the damage could be repaired." She refused to spend the night, however, and when they "again asked me to recommend them and assured us of their devotion to the King, I said I didn't believe they needed any recommendation. They could take that as they pleased."

Mrs. General "came once more to Elizabethtown" and was "kindly received," as before. Poor Giovannetti was not allowed to go into New York, and so he turned back to Charlottesville. The redbirds or cardinals he had carried in the cage on his back had all died, and Mrs. General grieved for them. One of her packing boxes had been broken, and her collection of butterflies which she had made in Virginia was ruined. She vowed she would never try to make another.

General Pattison, Commandant of the City of New York, sent a boat for Mrs. General and her party. They "embarked upon the Hudson" and arrived very late at night. A soldier was waiting "at the gateway" to the fortifications which the British General Henry Clinton was engaged in strengthening — being much afraid that the Americans planned to attack him. The soldier had been sent by General Riedesel, who was at a supper party with Lord Cornwallis — a command invitation, as his wife understood. Still it was a disappointment not to be met by him, and when the soldier took her "to a very great and beautiful house" she was not happy. The innkeeper at Bethlehem had charged her a great deal too much, she thought, and now she supposed she was in some sumptuous hostelry which would cost still more.[5]

"I was too busy putting my children to bed and too tired to ask where I was," said Lady Fritz.

Next morning a servant came to inquire what the Baroness

would like to order for dinner, how many members of the family would be there, and how many guests. "I told him six in all, myself, my children, my servant, and Pastor Mylius." Pastor Mylius was chaplain of Regiment Riedesel and he was now the children's tutor "in everything useful." General Riedesel and his aides were not dining at home — and "three dishes" would be plenty for just the family.

The servant said that "six large and four small dishes" had already been ordered. "I decidedly forbade such profusion," said Lady Fritz. She was horrified.

Callers were announced before the Baroness could get her boxes unpacked. Lord Cornwallis came first, and then General Clinton. General Pattison also arrived to apologize for not having found a house for Mrs. General. The servant who had announced the Generals had led her to a sumptuous drawing-room to receive them. A fire blazed on the hearth, she was seated in a luxurious wing chair upholstered in brocade; the whole end of the room was of paneled oak, the overmantel carved with a great garland of fruit. Lady Fritz anxiously asked General Pattison about the tariff, for never had she seen such an inn! After some hesitation, General Pattison told her that she was the guest of General Tryon, Royal Governor of New York, who was living on Long Island temporarily. "He had asked that his hospitality be anonymous, for fear I might not accept it," Lady Fritz said.

Now that she was free of anxiety about money, the Baroness enjoyed the mansion that was hers for the time being. It was known to New Yorkers as the "Walton house," and it was on Queen Street (now Pearl Street) just south of the present approaches to the Brooklyn Bridge. Built in 1752, the Walton house was considered the handsomest private home in the city; the lavish entertainment provided by William Walton, merchant, had caused comment in the British parliament — to the effect that if the colonists could afford to live like this, they could pay more taxes to the Crown. When Washington came into New York,

William Walton prudently withdrew to a New Jersey estate. Sir William Howe "invited him to return and he opened his house freely to British officers" — or so it was said.

Over the front door were "two angels carved in oak, bearing a shield" with the Walton coat of arms — a chevron painted red, the "heads of griffins" black, a knight's helmet surmounted with "a crest, a savage man, proper." Some people thought the "savage man" was Hercules because he had a club on his shoulder. The front door was carved oak and the entrance hall was paved in varicolored marble with a wide staircase leading to the ballroom. All the rooms were wainscoted in oak, except the library, which was paneled in "rare wood from Spanish America." There were many luxurious bedrooms, a "morning breakfast-room and family parlor."

Governor Tryon was on Long Island, organizing raids on the Connecticut coast. During 1779, he ordered the burning of Fairfield and Norwalk, leaving copies of "an Address to the Inhabitants of Connecticut" to tell the settlers to mend their ways and be loyal to the King. One day a "General" was announced. The Baroness did not understand his name, but said she would see him. "In the course of conversation, he asked me, among other things, whether I was satisfied with my quarters. My heart was full of gratitude for all the kindness which had been shown me," she wrote. She explained that she had forced General Pattison to tell her who her benefactor was — that she did not know General Tryon personally, but that she would "give anything to be able to thank him."

At this point, General Riedesel came in. "This is the man who has given us the use of this beautiful house," he told his wife. "I could not find words to express my feelings and General Tryon was very much affected," said Lady Fritz. She had made another of her conquests and "invariably received the greatest proofs of his friendship."

Later, General Henry Clinton's call produced mixed emotions.

He told the Baroness that the city of New York was full of small-pox and offered her his country house, where she could go to have her children inoculated. This was kind of him, but inocula-tion for smallpox was a perilous undertaking. Vaccination was a discovery nearly twenty years in the future, and inoculation often resulted in severe cases of smallpox or death from blood poisoning because of unsanitary methods of procedure. But Clinton was sure the children would be "safer" in the country, and their mother began to pack boxes again.

Clinton's house in the country was the Beekman mansion. Standing near the foot of the present Fifty-second Street and the East River, it had been built by Dr. James Beekman in 1764 and had been used as headquarters for General Howe in 1776. Nathan Hale was tried and condemned to death in Dr. Beekman's green-house, and Commissary Loring had the house for a while, but it had been Clinton's summer home since 1778. It was an hour-long journey from the Walton house near the Battery to the Beekman house.

The Riedesels had replaced their knave of a cook with another one, probably drawn from the ranks of the German troops. They were to stay in the country two weeks while the children had their inoculation-induced smallpox, so their mother sent the cook out to buy provisions enough to last. It was to be hoped that this cook was honest, but, taking no chances, the Baroness gave him ten guineas, which she was sure would be ample but not enough to tempt him. He came back almost at once. "The money I had given him would buy enough for only about two days," she dis-covered — and it was not her servant's fault. New York was a hungry city.

People had come in to New York, from New Jersey and Pennsylvania after the evacuation of Philadelphia and from upper New York state in the wake of Burgoyne's army. They told pathetic and true tales of having supplied Burgoyne only to be left to the mercy of angry neighbors who would not give them so much as a crust of bread. Clinton and his officers lived lavishly, three-course dinners with six side-dishes being the rule, not the exception, but the poor were starving and the moderately wealthy found that "fifty dollars would not keep a family for two days."

Mrs. General thought the country house was "perfectly beautiful." Its lines were somewhat classic, with a triple window over the front door and an ornamental wooden balustrade at the upper angle of the gambrel roof. Four chimneys, two at each end, indicated a goodly number of fireplaces, and they were needed — for the house had been built for summer occupancy in a cool location, which proved bitter cold in December.

General Riedesel had sent one of the German doctors from the army to his family, and the inoculation went well. In about two weeks they "had nothing more to fear from the infection," and they got ready to go back to town, sending the servants on ahead. Then in the night it snowed.

The storm roared so that they thought "the whole house would go over." There was a terrible crash and in the morning: they saw that half the balustrade on the roof had come down from the weight of the snow and the force of the gale. There were "four or five feet of snow on the level and eight feet in drifts," they could not get out "without sledges," and there was nothing to eat.

"I went to work to hunt up something for dinner," said Mrs. General. There were fourteen people to feed but she was always equal to emergencies. "I found an old hen that had been forgotten and it served us for soup." General Clinton's gardener provided some potatoes, and there was "a little salt meat left from our provisions."

But that afternoon, after dinner, Mrs. General stood at the window staring out at the white, trackless road "feeling thoroughly perplexed." What in the world was she going to do for another meal? This was as bad as the Blue Ridge Mountains. Then she saw something moving far down the road, making slow progress toward the house. It was a man on horseback, and when he came in at the gate she could tell that it was her cook.

"Filled with joy, I turned around to the rest of the company to tell them the news. When I looked back, I could not see or hear anything of the cook or his horse!

"Terrified by this disappearance the gentlemen rushed out — and found the cook and his horse completely buried in snow." Lady Fritz thought that her cook could never have gotten out of that drift without help — but he had "brought provisions for the evening meal."

Next day Captain Willoe arrived[6] with "two large sledges" to take them back to the city. The children's mother was worried about taking the children out "on account of the terrible cold" and "because their pocks had not entirely dried up." Little Caroline "had lost her whooping cough during inoculation" but it "came back and lasted a whole year." Otherwise the sleighride did them no harm, and never were New Yorkers more happy to get back to town.

25

Miss America

THE Riedesels returned to New York to find their house ready and waiting for them. John Marston, one-time Deputy to the Provincial Congress, was politely but firmly told by General Pattison to get out of his large, three-story brick home on the corner of Broad and Water streets and to let General Riedesel have it.[1] Old Dutch houses, their stair-step gable ends facing the street, alternated with new Colonial mansions or small frame buildings on Broad Street, one of the few streets to escape the fire of 1776. The Riedesels' New York home was only about two blocks from the Walton house, their temporary home, and a block from the fort where the General was to spend much of his time.

The Marston house was beautifully furnished in mahogany throughout, and there were carpets on the floors — a luxury still rather frowned upon in Germany. Of course the frugal Mrs. General asked about the price of all this. The house was to cost her nothing, General Pattison smilingly assured her — the British government would bear the expense. The furnishings had belonged to some rebel or other, had been confiscated and stored and were now all hers.

Mrs. General had been extremely nervous and anxious to get to New York because of being "far advanced in pregnancy." But she never really believed in worrying about anything for very long, and now she was feeling very well indeed. A big celebration was coming up. She determined to go to the Queen's birthday ball.

Queen Charlotte's birthday was really in summer, Lady Fritz explained — but so was the King's. For the benefit of the tradespeople, therefore, the Queen's birthday was celebrated in January. "Partly to please General Phillips and partly to make me forget my own sufferings," the British officers chose the Baroness Frederika von Riedesel to be Queen of the Ball, and this great honor was really a great surprise as well.[2]

The "General, field and staff officers of the army" were giving the party for "the garrison and principal ladies and gentlemen of the city." It was costing them four hundred guineas. Of course they wanted "to please General Phillips," but by now they had all met Mrs. Riedesel and they wanted her for Queen to please themselves, most of all. The "wife of General Cornwallis's adjutant was a lady of noble birth" who outranked the Baroness and was therefore supposed to be Queen. The difficulty was solved rather curiously. The British lady was also expecting a child so the officers told her she ought not to go out in her delicate condition! Madame de Riedesel's "expectations" were not quite so "imminent," it was explained.

Festivities began at noon on the eighteenth of January, 1780, "with the firing of a Royal Salute from Fort George." This was followed at one o'clock by another royal salute from "His Majesty's ships of war in New York Harbor." Ladies were not invited to "the public dinner given by General Tryon to his Excellency General Knyphausen, Major-General Phillips, Baron Riedesel, commander of the troops of his Serene Highness the Duke of Brunswick, Major-General Pattison, Commandant of the City and the other general officers of the garrison. Many public toasts were drank beginning with 'Her Majesty the Queen, the most amiable, exemplary and beloved Princess on earth,'" although the poor Queen had been a disliked, unhappy princess for many years.

"The day was spent in hilarity," so the officers must have been in a fairly mellow mood when they arrived in the afternoon at the ladies' reception, given at Governor Tryon's house. Here the Baroness was "received with all ceremonies," she said, enjoying herself tremendously. General Tryon "introduced me to all the ladies, some of whom were envious of the honor which was shown me." But Lady Fritz told them that she was given precedence over them all for the day alone and because she "represented the Queen just this one time. . . . 'I will always give place to ladies older than I, in the future,' the Baroness promised, and "as there were quite a number present who were my elders, my explanation conciliated them. Their faces quickly brightened up and I was soon on a pleasant footing with all of them." Pointing out a lady's advanced age might not seem the best way to "conciliate." But Lady Fritz, brought up at the court of a small German principality, knew what she was about.

At six o'clock in the evening it was time to start for the ball. The Baroness was escorted to a carriage and seated between Generals Tryon and Pattison. They drove to Hicks Tavern, once the De Lancey Mansion at 115 Broadway, where "the public rooms were . . . entirely new painted and decorated in a Stile that reflects honor on the taste of the Managers." Over the main door "A Doric pediment was erected" which enclosed "a transparent painting of their Majesties in their Royal Robes, over which was an emblematical piece, encircled with the motto of *Britains Strike Home*. The whole [was] illuminated with a beautiful Variety of different colored Lamps." As Lady Fritz drove up, she was "received with kettle-drums and trumpets."

"The ball was opened at eight o'clock by the Baroness de Riedesel and Major-General Pattison, Commandant of the City and Garrison," according to the New York *Mercury* for January 24, 1780. "I had not wanted to dance," the Baroness herself said, "as I was far advanced with child. But I was obliged to open the ball . . . by a formal minuet. My situation, as well as my bashfulness, made me think myself very awkard. But in order to banish my timidity, they all assured me that I did very well and must dance once more. The result was that I danced several English dances."

At half past nine the "country dances began." Now the music grew more lively, and instead of the stately advance and retreat, the bow and curtsey of the minuet, couples whirled in partnership or sidestepped gaily in a big circle, singing the tunes the fiddlers played. They leaped high as they "set and turned single" and they skipped nimbly through the "ladies and gentlemen's hay." It was all too much of a workout for Lady Fritz — but this did not keep her from enjoying herself. Her foot tapped to the music, her blue eyes sparkled and she gave the officers who crowded around her something to laugh about and a smile to remember. There had been time for her to have a new dress made, and silks and satins were available in New York. She could have had her hair powdered in the popular style if she thought it became her; and no matter what she wore she was a pretty woman by all acounts — and in her element at a party.

At midnight the company adjourned for supper in "the two Long Rooms. The tables were "ornamented with parterres and Arbours displaying an elegant assemblage of natural and artificial flowers, China images, etc." and "the supper consisted of three hundred and eighty dishes." They led Lady Fritz to the supper rooms. "And as I represented the Queen, I was made to sit under a canopy and drink the first toast," she said. "I was touched at all the marks of friendship I received. Although extremely tired, still, in order to show my gratitude, I stayed . . . till two o'clock in the morning." The ball lasted until three A.M. but it was no haughty queen who withdrew an hour early, but a warm-hearted, happy and popular young woman.

"I was loaded with kindness and I passed the winter very pleasantly except for suffering very much from the cold," the Baroness wrote. She thought it was just because "the commissary had not had a sufficient quantity of wood cut" and she did not realize that "the oldest man in this country does not remember such a long continuance of very severe cold" — William Smith, a lawyer and a Tory, but an increasingly critical one, said that the ink was freezing on his pen as he wrote those words.

Lawyer William Smith also wrote that "General Tryon is distressed by the scarcity of fuel — has but a load himself — orders old hulks of transport vessels rotten at the wharves to be cut up. There are 3000 cords at the opposite Landings but we can't have it till there is a Thaw to open access to the Landings. . . . 'Tis said that this Island will be totally deforested in a week. . . . Many reputable People lay abed in these Days for Want of Fuel."[3]

The Baroness Riedesel went to call on the "noble British lady" whose place she had taken at the Queen's birthday ball. The lady's child had arrived, and she was in the "lying-in chamber," which was so dark that Lady Fritz could not see who else was there. There seem to have been quite a few callers, and the talk naturally turned to the bitter cold. Like other "reputable people, the three Riedesel children had to stay in bed to keep warm. Their mother had borrowed wood from General Tryon for Saturday and Sunday, promising to pay it back on Monday if she could get any wood.

"The next day, as I was looking out of the window, I saw a number of wagons full of chopped-down trees standing in the street. Each wagon held two cords of wood." She went into the small room where Pastor Mylius sat with the little girls, huddled over the fireplace "where our last stick of wood was burning." The children were wrapped in cloaks and blankets but they were shivering, trying hard not to cry. Little Caroline was coughing.

"I have never been envious in my life," their mother told the chaplain of Regiment Riedesel, "but there are four wagonloads of wood in the street right now, in front of our very door. How happy I would be if I had only some of it!"

There was a knock on the door. "A servant had brought a mes-

sage from a Major Brown." He had sent those four loads of wood
to the Baroness de Riedesel with his compliments, and when she
needed more she was to let him know. Major Brown was in the
Commissary Department. He had been a caller at the other lady's
lying-in chamber, but Lady Fritz had "scarcely seen his face."
What she wanted now was to find him and thank him.

"Some days after, I was at a ball where he also was expected.
He had been described to me as a man with a very prominent,
turned-up nose" so Lady Fritz kept looking everywhere "for such
a person." Major Brown was shy — he hid out; but she found him,
and thanked him "right heartily." He told her he couldn't sleep
for thinking about her and worrying about her children, so next
morning he had ordered "some trees cut in the great avenue in
front of the city."

This friendship with Major Brown was "of immense advantage
to us," said Mrs. General. "My husband was supplied with many
kinds of provisions, with Indian meal, part of which we used for
bread and part for cake, and also with salted meat." General
Riedesel was issued more meat than he needed, some of it not fit
to eat anyway. His wife at first gave it away to get rid of it. But
Major Brown told her what the other Generals did — they exchanged surplus meat for butter and spermaceti candles "which
burn better and are much more beautiful than tallow candles."
Soldiers got the surplus meat, for which they were doubtless grateful regardless of what shape it was in, and "we saved considerable," said Mrs. General. But no matter how carefully she managed, Lady Fritz could afford to give only one "gentlemen's dinner
party a week" because "everything was so terribly expensive in the
city," she said. Generals Phillips, Tryon and Pattison were her
constant guests.[4]

It was no secret that the Baroness wanted a boy, and long before her child was born his name had been chosen. He was to be
called "Americus" in honor of the place of his birth. The God-
fathers had been selected: General Phillips, General Knyphausen

and Colonel Wurmb. And then, on the seventh of March, 1780, a little girl was born. "My husband wished very much for a son," wrote Lady Fritz — just as though she hadn't wanted one herself just as much. "But the baby was so pretty that we were soon consoled." They named her "Amerika (America)." Henceforward, many would be the affectionate inquiries in letters concerning "Lady Fritz" and "Miss America."

Miss America was only six weeks old when General Riedesel "persuaded" his wife to go to General Tryon's to dinner with him. Tryon was soon to leave for England and Lady Fritz never missed a party if she could help it, anyway. But when she got home she noticed that her husband seemed extremely anxious about the baby. He kept "going to look at the child," and kept saying " 'Don't you think she's pale?' " Or he would feel of her forehead and shake his head and say " 'She is certainly ill.' " Suddenly a suspicion "darted into my mind," said Lady Fritz. "I rolled back the baby's little sleeves and there were two pocks on each arm."

It had all been part of a plot on the part of the two Generals, Riedesel and Tryon. "An English doctor had inoculated the baby" while her mother was out. "I must confess that for a moment I was quite angry," said Lady Fritz. "But when the baby became so ill that we were afraid we would lose her, my husband was inconsolable and kept accusing himself" of causing a tragedy. He had only done what he thought was right and he had wanted to keep his wife from anxiety, but now "I had all I could do to keep up his spirits," she said. And "God be praised, it came out all right." The baby recovered perfectly and Miss America would never have to be ashamed of a pockmarked face.[5]

As soon as it was reasonably safe for sailing vessels to cross the Atlantic, General Tryon set out for England. He made the Baroness a parting gift of "magnificent furniture, tapestries, oriental rugs, curtains and a set of silk hangings." It would seem that they came from the Walton house.

Everyone had been looking forward to spring. There were those, like Tryon, who were going to England; supplies from England were expected, and a new campaign would open. But the city of New York — fought-over and fire-ravaged, its poor starving and suffering from the cold — became, with the spring thaw, a city of pestilence. As soon as the snow melted, the soldiers, who had been living in huts underground, found themselves sinking to their knees in mud. The mud had a horrible stench. All winter long, a common sight had been servants carrying on their heads great tubs filled with sewage from their masters' houses. These they emptied on the ice in the river. As the ice melted this accumulation spread everywhere — through the open waterway now Canal Street, into all the overflowing brooks of well-watered Manhattan Island.

Soldiers fell ill, were accused of malingering — and died by the hundreds. Efforts were made to get them out of their horrible quarters, but the survivors were mostly too weak to work on the new huts, to be built aboveground on land laid waste by fire. No one paid any attention to the civilians, "sick of a fever," or to the prisoners — whose condition was the worst of all. There were "fifty or sixty fresh burials every day," and in the graveyards during the winter frozen bodies had been stacked up which must now, somehow or other, go underground.

In the Riedesel household "twenty fell ill, eight of them dangerously." Among the dangerously ill was "my daughter Augusta," her mother wrote. "Augusta had such violent paroxysms of fever that she begged me to hold her tightly, and when the chills and the fits of shaking came she shook me with her in the bed." Someone told the little girl's mother that people were "most likely to die during these shaking fits."

The medication ordered was "salts of wormwood mixed with lemon juice, sugar and water" which the children's mother mixed herself because "all our servants were sick and I was obliged to do everything." The only time she had to rest was while she was nursing the new baby, and when she lay down on the bed with America she often "fell asleep," she was so exhausted.

Augusta recovered but the children's father had the same infection and "became so ill" that his family lost hope. They were now back in Clinton's summer home, the Beekman house, but the pestilence had followed them. General Riedesel was taken with "severe diarrhea and constant vomiting, and when his wife tried to give him "sago water," which the doctor had prescribed, he begged her to let him die in peace.

One day when the doctor came out from New York to see General Riedesel, Lady Fritz begged him to tell her the truth: Was there any hope for her husband? " 'Certainly there is,' " the doctor said. "And at this confident answer" the two oldest little girls who had been hiding in order to hear what the doctor said came out from under the table and "kissed his hands." Before this, the doctor "had visited us very punctually, and now he redoubled his attentions."

While the doctor was there, Lady Fritz kept her watch in her hand. She thought the doctor's visits benefited her husband in direct ratio to the length of time he stayed, and when he "remained three minutes, then five, then fifteen and finally a whole half hour" she was happy. Now she knew that her beloved husband must surely get well! Pastor Mylius and "our trusty jaeger Rockel" proved immune to the infection. They took turns watching at night by General Riedesel's bedside and at last the Baron and his little daughter Augusta both recovered.

"I was well, and blessed with a cheerful, happy temperament," said Lady Fritz. "At length all who were sick were restored to health, and not one died — a result that abundantly repaid me for all my trouble."

It pleased Lady Fritz to have General Clinton come out to see her. He came informally, dressed "like a huntsman," she said, instead of in his uniform. At first, he had seemed cold and distant, but she put this down to British reserve or possibly shyness. If she heard anything about Clinton's private life in New York City, she said nothing about it.

But Thomas Jones, Tory Supreme Court justice, collecting material for his *History of New York in the Revolution,*[6] had become completely disillusioned with the way Great Britain conducted their war in the colonies, and with Sir Henry Clinton in particular.

"In 1780 it was thought necessary (nobody, the Generals excepted, knew for what) to rebuild all the demolished forts . . . and to add a number of new ones. This was done, the work performed, that is the laboring part, by the inhabitants. . . . The General also thought it necessary, for his own safety no doubt, as no one else apprehended any danger, to have beacons erected all around the island [of Manhattan], a circumference of at least 30 miles, and upon every hill or eminence . . . not less than 300 were erected, with a tar barrel" at each beacon, and a guard, "the whole project costing £150,000. As a further security to the General's person, 25 galleys were purchased and moored in a line in the North River within 50 yards of His Excellency's quarters. With the city surrounded by men of war and armed ships, with 25 armed galleys in his rear, a captain's guard in his front, 300 beacons upon the island to set fire to upon an alarm, 20,000 good troops upon York Island, at Kingsbridge, upon Long Island and Staten Island, with at least 10,000 militia and refugees embodied and perfectly disciplined, he thought himself pretty secure — wallowed in the arms of Mrs. Badely, entertained the daughters of Blundell. . . ." Their father had been a butler in General Clinton's house at some time while his father was governor of New York (1741-1753).

One of Mrs. General's callers, "the Hessian General Loos," hurt her feelings. Lady Fritz had known General Loos ever since she was a little girl, and "when he came to see me he looked me over from head to foot," she said. " 'Why, what has become of your slender waist, your beautiful complexion and your fair white hands?' " he exclaimed. " 'They are all gone! But you have seen many lands. When you get home all your friends will ask you to tell your adventures. They will be envious, but behind your back they will say that your story is tiresome. They will play with their fans and declare, 'This woman can talk of nothing but America.' "

" 'Thank you for the warning,' " said Lady Fritz, and the old General ought to have noticed that her eyes still flashed when she was angry. She had a word of advice for him. " 'Don't tell a woman she has lost her looks — she might not take it as well as I do.' "

General Phillips stayed in New York and either escaped the fever or had it only lightly — but he also had advice to offer, this time to General Riedesel:

"I hear you drink no wine," he wrote. "I do not quite approve of it — I would allow you in twenty-four hours one pint of wine with one half pint of water and no other drink. No walking exercise — but moderately so on horseback. To eat moderately at dinner of roast meat but no sausages or high dishes — no roots or greens with rich gravy or forced meats — no tea except sasafras very strong with milk. A strict Regimen altogether with Bark in discretion and Vitriol drops and Purging Physic every week and the Cold Bath but not till August — moderate study but no deep or serious reading — never exposed to the sun. . . .

"I hear Susan and Ann are with you. You must not play with girls, dear Riedesel. It is very bad for you."

No doubt this was all good advice, but a piece of good news had a much better effect on General Riedesel. General Benjamin Lincoln, who helped Stark to surround Burgoyne's troops, had himself been trapped by Clinton in Charleston, South Carolina. He was taken prisoner and on July 19, 1780, General Clinton communicated with Lincoln.[7] He trusted there "would be no difficulties attending your exchange. As it must, however, involve that of Major General Phillips and Riedesel, and as there are many . . . circumstances to be discussed, I propose either Amboy, Elizabeth Town or at General Phillips' Quarters on Long Island."

Galloping couriers carried letters back and forth, and time went by. Clinton finally agreed to Elizabeth, New Jersey, as the place of meeting, and so did Lincoln, but by now it was September. Another month passed. At last, the exchange of Phillips and Riedesel for Lincoln went through on October 13, 1780.

General Riedesel was given a post on Long Island and methodically he went to work to make a survey of the efforts of refugees to fortify and garrison Long Island towns.

"I have been south as far as Schmidts Point," he reported to Clinton. This was "four miles on the other side of Fire Place where the rebels surprised the refugees this winter. The refugees made their fort on poor ground but the location of their new fort nearby will be extremely useful in the forwarding of intelligence from East Hampton. . . .

"From Schmidt's Town I went to Lloyd's Neck. The antipathy of the inhabitants on the other side of Schmidt's Town as far as South Hampton . . . was inconvenient. Without exaggeration, there are ten rebels to every Loyalist. My advice is to keep a sharp eye on them."

General Riedesel found that his Brooklyn headquarters "were not habitable in winter," because only a few rooms could be heated. He returned to New York every night. But when spring came, Mrs. General announced that the Brooklyn farmhouse was just the place for the whole family.

26

Progress in the American Rebellion

"MY ATTENTION had been for some time directed to the drawing out of the enemy's hands, by every possible means, the troops of the Saratoga Convention," wrote Sir Henry Clinton, in the narrative in which he tried to explain his part in the "American Rebellion." But to Burgoyne, Phillips and Riedesel, it seemed as though Clinton was giving little or no thought to the matter.

Clinton explained how he had tried to acquire more American prisoners so as to place himself in a better bargaining position:

"An attempt was made to surprise one of their brigades that lay at Elizabeth Town . . . but unfortunately, some untoward accidents retarding the progress of the detachments . . . allowed the whole brigade" to get away. "In another little excursion from King's Bridge under General Tryon . . . toward Horse Neck and Greenwich, a number of saltpans and a quantity of military stores and provisions were destroyed, a few vessels burned and some cattle collected. We were not fortunate enough, however, to acquire many prisoners with either."[1] Small-scale raids upon the Connecticut coast continued, and on July 22, 1781, for example, a foray into a tiny settlement known as Middlesex Parish netted only a few horses and certain civilian prisoners — taken in church with their minister and ardent patriot, the Reverend Moses

354

Mather. These men were secured aboard prison ships, where many died. They were of no use for purposes of military exchange.

In his *Narrative,* Clinton said he could have exchanged officers but would not leave the troops leaderless with no one to protect them, "exposed" as they were to "such arts as the enemy might use to incite them to enter into their service." This sounds well, but does not exactly correspond with what was said in letters at the time. The emphasis was all on exchanging officers, and it was General Riedesel who had a splendid idea for liberating extra officers so that they could go to Canada, to command the German troops left there and others due to arrive.

Riedesel described his scheme in a letter written in French and marked "to be put in cypher." In the British army, each major-general was entitled to 12 servants, a brigadier was allowed 6, a deputy adjutant general 4, a deputy quartermaster the same, an adjutant 2 — and so on down the line, with a second lieutenant being entitled to one servant. "If the rebels absolutely refuse to exchange rank and file . . . under the guise of 'servants' we can exchange as many officers as possible." Riedesel added a schedule of the number of officers who could masquerade as servants of those properly exchanged, and came up with a total of 222 men.[2]

General Horatio Gates, the great superseder, had taken over the Southern Department after Lincoln's capture. In August, 1780, he was defeated by Lord Cornwallis at Camden, South Carolina. It would have been poetic justice if he had been taken prisoner like Burgoyne, but on the evening after the battle Gates reported the disaster from Charlotte, North Carolina, seventy miles away. But many rank and file Americans had been captured and things looked brighter for an exchange of prisoners from now on.

General Phillips, on active duty since his and Riedesel's exchange in October 1780, wrote to Lord George Germain that he thought the Convention Troops might be exchanged, if bills for their subsistence were paid. "A sum not exceeding Twenty-five Thousand Pounds Sterling will fully answer," he suggested, and

"bring about the exchange of perhaps the whole of the troops."
This would liberate "sixteen hundred rank and file . . . most of
them in full health, inured to the climate and all the changes
of it." It would be cheaper in the end than "recruiting and sending
over the same number of men."

This plan took infinite patience to put into effect. But at last
a small vessel named the *General Riedesel* carried "money, great
and small uniforms and provisions" to the Brunswick troops. The
ship sailed from New York on the nineteenth of March, 1781,
and arrived in Virginia about ten days later. The Troops of the
Convention were no longer in Charlottesville. Because of the
British campaign against the South they had been moved to Win-
chester, about eighty miles north of Charlottesville. In his letter
concerning the liberation of the prisoners, Riedesel asked Jefferson "to allow such of them as are" invalids, "properly certified by
the Physicians of the hospital, to embark on board the flag of
truce vessel and come to New York, from whence it will be in my
power to send them home."[3]

Jefferson granted this request, but there were many delays. The
New Jersey *Gazette* of November 28, 1781, carried the report of
"the wreck of a sloop, bottom up, on a bar off Corson's Inlet with
30 or 40 souls on board." Thirteen bodies were either taken out
of her or cast ashore, and papers found on them identified them
as "prisoners of war on parole, bound from Virginia for New
York." The name of the vessel was not given, but it would seem
that this might be the end of the little ship *General Riedesel*.

Upon his exchange, General Phillips had been given command
"of the grenadiers, the light infantry, and the 42nd British infantry." It was "the *élite* corps of the army. He is full of joy," General Riedesel commented, not without a touch of envy.

Early in March, 1781, Phillips commanded an expeditonary
force of about 2000 men leaving New York and heading for the
coast of Virginia. The Prince Frederick infantry regiment was
among this force, and it seemed to Riedesel as though Germans

were forever being taken out of his care. From this regiment "the convalescent, tired, sick and womenfolk" were left behind, as well as heavy baggage.

This leaving of "womenfolk" was nothing new. Back in 1779, when troops set out to attack the Southern coast line, "all women and children left in New York by the different regiments" had been sent to Cork, in Ireland, whether they came from Ireland or not. But now, in 1781, the "womenfolk" stayed in New York; and the husbands of many would never return.[4] There were girls who had been children when the war began who were now grown; there were some fatherless, some orphaned, who had no means of livelihood save to turn to prostitution. A barracks master named Clarke "interested himself" in these "poor girls," but orphanages were filled to overflowing and nothing could be done about them. Houses where German women established themselves were tolerated until someone complained, whereupon the women were dispersed perhaps to find themselves shelter in some garret or cellar. Jobs were scarce; it was a lucky girl who found someone who would let her work for food and shelter.

The troops were "ordered on board the fleet" on March 2, and good-bys were said. Then came such bad weather that it was March 20 "during the evening" when the "strong winds abated" and, under convoy of nine men-of-war, the fleet, 42 sail in all, passed through the channel."

"I have not time to say all I feel and think," General Phillips had written to the Riedesels on March 8. "Be assured of my continued solicitude for you and my dear Madame de Riedesel and all your family — Augusta in particular. . . . Be careful of your health and believe me ever your sincere friend. . . ." There would be time for several more messages, but this was almost the last letter General William Phillips would ever write.

Benedict Arnold had arrived in New York. He was now wearing the uniform of a British general, Phillips had been placed in command over him and now sailed to meet him in Portsmouth, Virginia.

"I know not by what means they have corrupted the famous American General Arnold," Riedesel had written the previous autumn. "He had promised to make us masters of the fortress of West Point. . . ." Troops had been ready to go up the North River and "Sir Henry had sent, with the consent of Arnold, his adjutant general, Major André, to see West Point and make a plan of it. Unfortunately, André was taken by a patrol of Militia, having a passport from Arnold in his pocket. Arnold, seeing that his secret was betrayed, saved himself and came to New York. They say that he will be employed." Arnold was indeed employed, but the Riedesels did not call on the new General. Major André had called on the Baroness Riedesel when she was at General Clinton's summer home. Everyone liked André and the honors with which Arnold hoped to be received were never forthcoming.

General Phillips did not mention Benedict Arnold in his letters to Riedesel, but he wrote from Portsmouth, Virginia: "It would take a volume to describe the confusion, difficulties and want of arrangements I found here — troops *à la debandade* — works in ruin — Departments all running different ways — no amity."

The Prince Frederick Regiment had a journal of events which told in more detail exactly what happened. "Contrary winds and storms" kept Phillips from moving up the James River "aboard large, long-boats expressly built by the orders of General Arnold." They finally got under way, however, and proceeded, "severely damaging different storage places of the enemy." From the American point of view, this was described as "pillaging, burning and raiding" and some of the rebels said that Arnold purposely delayed Phillips because when Phillips arrived he would lose his chance "of enriching himself with plunder."[5]

On May 14 General Phillips was at Petersburg, Virginia, on the Appomattox River, not far from the James. He was planning to fortify a post here when he was taken suddenly ill with "a severe inflamation of the gall bladder," according to the German chronicler. Others called it "a fever" and a few tried to spread the wild rumor that Arnold had him poisoned.

General Phillips had written Riedesel that Lafayette was in Baltimore, but on May 10 Lafayette appeared on the heights opposite Petersburg and cannonaded British headquarters at "Bollingbrook." They moved General Phillips, desperately ill, to the cellar of this house — taking him there just in time before a cannon ball went through the room where he had been lying. On May 14, General William Phillips died, and was buried in the old Blandford Churchyard in Petersburg.[6]

The Riedesels were shocked and saddened by this news. Even Thomas Jefferson, who got on better with Phillips than other Americans, characterized him as "intolerably insolent and haughty"; but Lady Fritz said, "We have always mourned his loss. He was a very brave man and true friend to his friends."

General Clinton made Riedesel "Lieutenant General with the corresponding English allowance," which was higher pay than he had been getting. The raise was more than welcome, for the cost of living continued to rise. General Pattison, who had been the Riedesels' good friend, had gone back to England and the new Commandant of the City, General Jackson, was out to make his fortune: signs of graft were everywhere. Barrack masters took in "four cart-man's loads" of wood to the cord and then sold three loads to the cord to the army, keeping one load to sell for their own profit at four pounds a cord for oak and five pounds ten shillings for hickory. This was about four times the honest price. Loyalist farmers were paid for "oak, buckwheat, or rye" — whatever produce they brought in — but made to sign blank receipts, which the Collectors of Forage filled in later with false amounts, making "fifty pounds a day with great ease and no expense." The Commissary Department charged the Crown £53,750 a year for the use of 500 horses owned personally by the Commissary and rented to the Crown at "£15 a head," and housed in barns taken from the rebels for no rent at all with the horses' rent charged to the Crown, of course.

This was all such an open secret that when Prince William Henry visited New York in September, 1781, he twitted a young lieutenant on not being under a barrack master or a commissary, so as to "share in the emoluments." The much disillusioned New York Loyalist and historian, Thomas Jones, said that "every two years commissioners in this department returned to England richer than half the princes in Germany."

General Riedesel had great difficulty in collecting claims of money for his officers and men. Before General Phillips left New York, Riedesel had applied to him for eight hundred pounds' subsistence. Phillips replied that he had no jurisdiction over exchanged prisoners; the man to ask was Clinton. But Clinton, after paying the provisions bill for the Convention Troops, was not in a mood to pay any more. It began to seem to Riedesel as though nothing could be done in New York, and he asked to be sent to Canada. The request was granted, but there was a long wait — for transports, for final orders — and for German troops to take along.

The Baroness was "pretty lonesome" over in Brooklyn during 1781. But there was a glorious view from the farmhouse. Every evening she saw the little city of New York "entirely lighted up," with houses "so close to the shore that the lights were reflected in the water." She could hear "the beating of drums" in the fort, and on a windless night she could hear "the calls of the sentinels. We had our own boat," she said, and "we could cross over to New York in a quarter of an hour."

At noon, one day, the English officers under General Riedesel's command were dining with Lady Fritz and her husband. They invited the Baroness to go back with them "to their camp" on Long Island after dinner, and she got into a carriage. When she arrived at the camp, "an officer came up" and asked if she would walk with him "down the line." She said, yes, of course she would. They started out, and then she saw that she was actually reviewing the troops "with all honors even to the beating of drums!"

Extremely embarrassed, Lady Fritz stopped in her tracks. "It is not suitable!" she protested. "A German woman is not accustomed to such distinctions!"

"It was to honor her for all she had done for their comrades at Saratoga," the young officer told her. So Mrs. General marched on, "down the line," while the drums beat.

Mrs. General deserved a happy day. She was on sentry duty every night. No one had been entirely successful in keeping an eye on those Long Island rebels, and a band of them sneaked behind the British lines, snatched the German Major Maybaum out of his bed and carried him off a prisoner. General Riedesel's house, "close to the shore," was "perfectly isolated" and he felt sure he would be the next victim. There were guards outside his house, but he thought the rebels could "overcome them." All night long and every night, "if there was the slightest sound he would wake up" and seize the weapons he had constantly by him. He thought it would break his heart if he were ever a prisoner again, and he determined to die fighting for his personal freedom if necessary. "He lost considerable sleep," said Mrs. General — and as for herself, "I became so accustomed to watching that daylight would often surprise me and then I would lie down for a few hours' rest."

At last, in July, General Riedesel was relieved of this tedious and nerve-wearing command. Now all was hustle and bustle in preparation for departure. The Baroness had laid in a good deal of firewood, and had "saved thirty cords" in case they should have to stay in New York another winter. She tried to return the wood, but Major Brown, the commissary who had been so kind to her, suggested she sell it, and she could have made about one hundred and twenty pounds, supposing it to be hickory, not oak. But the

Baroness refused. She was frugal, constantly worried about expenses, but never a profiteer. Major Brown could have sold it too, but he was evidently not one of the men to go back to England with a princely fortune. He said the wood had been issued and he could not take it back. This was not an age when a social conscience could be said to have developed, but Lady Fritz gave her thirty cords of wood to the poor.

Next, the Baroness sent for the new Commandant of New York and said she was ready to return the fine mahogany furniture so graciously loaned to her. The new Commandant was astonished — it was rebel furniture — why not keep it? Mrs. General said that it belonged to the Crown, and into the Royal warehouse it went, "save for one English bedstead which we kept for remembrance." But she afterwards regretted her decision; the warehouse was burned and all the fine furniture — the highboys, the armchairs, the tea-tables she had loved so much — were destroyed.

Mrs. General had another problem to deal with. The German regimental flags, kept in defiance of the Convention of Saratoga and safely smuggled into New York, were still there — still sewed into the mattress which she and the German tailor had made. Somehow, they must get back to Germany. Mrs. General took charge of them, using that flag-filled mattress for her bed aboard ship.

General Clinton had promised to find the Riedesels a good ship from among the convoy scheduled to leave for Canada — one that "could run away from danger and not be captured on the way." But he turned the matter over to an agent, who was probably bribed by the captain of the *Little Seal*, and they went aboard "one of the smallest and most miserable ships in the whole fleet." The *Little Seal* leaked, she was undermanned and she was loaded so badly that she developed a dangerous list. She fell so far behind the convoy that she finally had to be towed behind a man-of-war.

There was one tragic event just before the Riedesels set sail. They had three Negro servants — "a man, his wife, and a kinswoman of theirs" — who were going to Canada with them. On July 25, 1781, a letter was handed to General Riedesel. "The bearer, Mr. Ludlow, having been Empowered by [former] Governor Bull of South Carolina to take into his possession some of Mr. Bull's Negroes who left Carolina with the King's Troops last summer, hath applied at Headquarters for authority to execute his trust. . . ." Madam Riedesel's opinion of the Loyalist ex-Governor was unflattering. She thought he was a turncoat and that his title to these servants was questionable.[7]

"They had served us faithfully," and their former owner had "treated them shockingly" so that now "the shrieks and lamentations of these poor people were very great. The girl, Phyllis by name, fainted," she said, and the Riedesels offered to buy Phyllis. The agent "demanded thirty guineas for the girl" and in order to compel us to buy all three refused to sell her separately. The sum demanded was too much for our purse, but we afterwards wished we had made the sacrifice."

It was a long, uncomfortable voyage from New York to Halifax. There were storms when everyone was sick, and there were alarms of privateers. But it was "during a calm" when another ship in the convoy sailed too close to the *Little Seal*. A crash, the rending and splintering of wood, and part of their stern came away and sank. "This tore away our little Necessary and it was very fortunate that no one was in it at the time," said the Baroness.

The convoy anchored at Halifax long enough for the usual round of official entertainments. The Governor and his wife gave a dinner — inviting the Riedesels of course — and Lady Fritz was served lobster, a delicacy she had never seen before. They told her that lobsters were good Loyalists because they wore the King's red uniform.

The *Little Seal* somehow stayed afloat and reached the St.

Lawrence River, where she anchored "on account of the ebbing tide." Then she promptly lost her anchor. "They threw out a second anchor, which met with the same fete" and now there was only one left. Provisions were all gone, and "a boat which we had sent on shore brought back only some fowls and eggs."

General Riedesel now took command. He ordered the *Little Seal's* captain to lower the longboat and row his family ashore. "We all got in to it, my husband and myself, our children, both aides-de-camp, my maid servants and two attendants," said Mrs. General. When they reached dry land they "chanced upon a pretty cottage occupied by a peasant," where they were "received in a very friendly manner." At last the land of rebels was far behind them, and they were among proper peasants who knew how to behave.

The General and one of his aides borrowed horses and rode on to Quebec. Mrs. General, once more in command of her little army, arrived there three days later. It was the middle of September, and the journey from New York had taken eight weeks.

"We look upon the Americans as at our feet," exulted Walpole when news of the Southern campaign reached London. Captain Edmonston was now in London and wrote that Burgoyne was "nearly forgotten. He was news at one time, his story is news no longer. . . . He is more miserable here than in America." They were saying that Cornwallis had taken more men from Gates than Gates ever took from Burgoyne at Saratoga. Burgoyne explained that General Benedict Arnold (now on the British side) "advanced without consultation with his general," and really won at Saratoga.

General Riedesel hoped that he had arrived in Canada in time to see action on the rebels' Northern border and to share in a glorious victory. He found a new Governor in Canada — a man much to his taste: Sir Frederick Haldimand, born in Switzerland, a soldier of fortune. He was reputedly austere and unapproachable "but my husband soon gained his affection," wrote Mrs. General. "I soon won his friendship too." She could have put it the other way around. Governor Haldimand, who had never married, was friendly toward Riedesel and enchanted with Lady Fritz, who soon had him eating out of her hand.

No one among the British forces was paying any attention to an American general named Nathanael Greene, who had replaced Gates in the South. On September 17, 1781, at about the time when the Riedesels reached Canada, Lord Cornwallis sent to Clinton for reinforcements. This time there was no story of storms, of troops being ordered into transports and then waiting eighteen days for a favorable wind. But again "the sailing of the fleet was unfortunately protracted," as Clinton put it. After all, there really seemed to be no particular hurry.

Return to Canada

FOR the Baroness, the return to Canada was like a joyful
homecoming. Not only were the peasants docile and ready to
do her bidding but their homes were shining-clean, as she observed
as she traveled up the St. Lawrence by the road to Quebec. Skies
were blue, the air crisp and cool with frosty nights. The City of
Quebec, which she had disapproved of when she first saw it, had
changed for the better.

The Governor's house, which "up to this time resembled a
barrack," was now "furnished and arranged after the English
fashion" and General Haldimand's gardens were "already full of
choice fruits and foreign plants." Lady Fritz could hardly believe
that some of these plants would survive a Canadian winter, but
the Governor, whose house was situated "on a height almost on
the very top" of the great cliff overlooking the St. Lawrence,
had chosen a sunny, protected spot facing southward. His fruit
trees had already survived several seasons.

Lady Fritz revised at least one of her judgments concerning
her husband's friends in Quebec. Before she had first arrived in
1777, the General had assured her that she might not like Lady
Maria Carleton, then Canada's first lady — and that she would be
delighted with Mrs. "Mich" Murray. With feminine perversity,
Lady Fritz had liked Lady Maria but cared very little for Mrs.

Murray. It may easily be that Mrs. Murray was overenthusiastic in her praise of General Riedesel. The Baroness said more than once that she came to America to share her husband's "tour of duty" in order to look after his health. This was true. But she also regarded her stout German husband as handsome beyond compare, charming and irresistible to women. She knew the kind of temptations that would be placed in his path, for she had been an army child and not even Hannah Foy had much to teach her — although she would always be shocked by actual evidence that a general's life was not always a lonely one. But Mrs. Murray, on close acquaintance, proved not only hospitable and friendly but devoted to her own husband — and not vulnerable even to so attractive a German general as the Baron Riedesel. Lady Fritz now moved in with the Murrays, children, servants, baggage and all, and lived with them for a month. When it came time to leave, the Riedesels took the Murrays' young daughter with them to be their guest at Sorel for the winter.

General Riedesel's health improved. He laid this to the invigorating Canadian climate, and to a certain extent he was right; but also, General Haldimand had placed him in command of all the German troops in Canada and had given him work to do, so that now he was a much happier man. This is not to say that he was without problems and frustrations. Sitting down to write to Lord George Germain, he reported carefully on his position and that of the troops as of October 13, 1781 — and mentioned a few difficulties.

Riedesel had arrived in Canada with "British and German exchanged officers, the whole amounting to about 800 men. . . . Had not Mr. Washington without any just cause, broke the promise which he had made to the late Major General Phillips, I should have brought 40 officers more with me," he said.[1] Of course it was not "Mr. Washington" but Congress which had broken off negotiations, over a small matter of unpaid bills. In retaliation, Clinton recalled all American officers on parole from New York City and in daily expectation of exchange. They began to come in, accusations were made that many had broken parole and were fighting again — and then Congress recalled General John Burgoyne, on parole in Great Britain.[2] Clinton promptly reversed his orders. Nothing more was said about Burgoyne's recall, and negotiations continued. General Riedesel did not say how many officers posing as servants got into New York.

If Sir Henry Clinton could have exchanged more "of our prisoners of war, I would have brought above three hundred more of our troops to this Province and the troops of his Serene Highness the Duke of Brunswick, my Master, would now consist of three thousand active men (a number equal to those with whom I crossed the Lake)," Riedesel continued. ". . . But being disappointed by a breach of public faith in the enemy," he would do the best he could with what he had. Riedesel thanked Lord Germain for the "douceur equal to forage money" which His Lordship had granted over Clinton's head "to all officers of the Convention Army."

General Riedesel took up a personal matter in the last paragraph of his letter to Lord George Germain. A new Major General named Clark had just arrived on the Canadian scene. This man "had been only a colonel for more than a year" after Riedesel had "served His Majesty as Major General." But here was this so-called "General" Clark with a commission giving him "local rank" as General since the first of January, 1776, while General Riedesel's "local rank" came from a commission dated eleven days later! "He must command me wherever we meet," wrote the Baron in anguish of spirit. "Your Lordship will not be surprised at my being most sensibly hurt." Riedesel had hoped that his luck would turn. And now this!

Any answer on the subject of General Clark's seniority would be a long time coming from Great Britain, because the ice in the St. Lawrence would soon close all communication. It was hard to have to go on a tour of inspection of frontier posts with General Clark, but orders were orders. That there should be any good word spoken of General Clark in Riedesel's letters would be too much to expect.

Governor Haldimand gave General Clark the command over troops stationed at Quebec, on the Island of Orleans, and on the banks of the St. Lawrence. It was a choice command, close to Quebec for the most part. Haldimand gave Baron Riedesel the Richelieu River, Isle aux Noix and all the most vulnerable approaches that the rebels on the Grants and eastern New York might use. This was a command where action might be expected, and it pleased the Baron. But Haldimand suggested that Madam the Baroness would, of course, prefer to live in Quebec for the winter. Like many another bachelor, he was sure he understood women; and he saw at once that Lady Fritz loved parties, so he promised her plenty of them, and guaranteed she would not miss her husband in the least.

The Baroness upset Haldimand's calculations. Certainly she liked a good time, but she would be off to Sorel, her husband's headquarters, as soon as he could find some sort of house. Gallantly, Governor Haldimand replied, "You must not live in a hovel. I will have a house built for you." He promised that the house would be ready by Christmas and assumed she would stay in Quebec till then. But Mrs. General set out for Sorel as soon as a temporary home was found for her with one of the "inhabitants." "The trees for our dwelling had not been felled, nor the boards sawed," but plans were being drawn and the location had been selected — about a quarter of a mile beyond the town and close to the Richelieu River. The attractive eighteenth-century Government House which now stands on this site, although larger and of cut stone, follows more or less the plans which the Riedesels themselves made. Lady Fritz did not believe that her new house could possibly be finished by Christmas. On Christmas

Eve, however, they moved in, and she spoke as though she were a bride coming into the first home of her own.

"We had a large dining room and nearby a pretty room for my husband, close to which was our sleeping apartment. Then came a cunning little nursery with a small room connected with it for our oldest daughter. Last of all was a large and beautiful parlor, which we used as a sitting room. Overhead were four big rooms, one for the women servants, one for the men servants — and two spare room for guests." There was "an entry" which Lady Fritz described as looking like a "handsome apartment." It had benches along the walls where General Riedesel's personal guard of six men could sleep by turns during the night. They were in constant attendance on him, for he was still mortally afraid of being taken prisoner and he had not forgotten the exploits of the American "vile assassin" Lieutenant Whitcomb, who had kidnapped two officers.

In the entry stood "a great stove from which pipes extended to the ceiling and heated the whole house," Lady Fritz said, describing her primitive hot-air furnace, which she greatly admired. Another luxury delighted her almost as much. "Upon the walls pretty paper hangings were pasted," and this wallpaper, which was such a novelty, kept out a little of the cold. Her heart was almost broken when the walls "warped during the winter, being made of green wood, and the paper hangings were torn, letting in a draft." Eventually, Lady Fritz would design and direct the building of a covered passage leading to the "wash house" and to the kitchen, which was also a separate building. Over the wash house there would be a guardroom.

On Christmas day, 1781, the Riedesels had their Christmas dinner in the dining room of their new house. They had "plum pudding" and Lady Fritz explained in her diary that to eat plum pudding at Christmas was an English custom. All the dinner guests were men, officers of the garrison. But of course there were the Riedesel young ladies — Augusta, Frederika, Caroline and America.

Lady Fritz thoroughly enjoyed setting up housekeeping at Sorel, but there were surprises in store for her. "Inhabitants" came to ask how many chickens she wanted killed to last all winter and how many fish she would need for a full winter's supply. She remembered all too well the putrid meat brought to her in Charlottesville and she was sure that fish, especially, would be much worse. Whereupon the Baroness learned about frozen food. The "loft" would be her frozen-fish locker, because fish would keep better there than in the cellar. She laid in "three or four hundred fish, great quantities of fowls as well as beef and lamb." The meat "was delicious all winter long," but there was a point to be remembered before starting dinner. The food was packed in snow and time must be allowed to chop it out with a hatchet.

Six barrels of apples and a half barrel of pears were shockingly expensive, and Mrs. General blamed herself for not making a firm bargain with the dealer in Quebec before she ordered them. But they kept well in the cellar as long as the barrels were tightly headed, the heads "pasted over with paper." Frozen lemons were good when defrosted, and the Indians brought around "an excellent fruit" for sale. "It grows in water, is red, and as large as a cherry without a stone." The answer to this riddle is "cranberry." Cooked with maple sugar, cranberries made a wonderful preserve.

General Riedesel, meanwhile, had more complicated matters on his mind than frozen food, cranberries or even plum pudding at Christmastime. In the first place, Sorel had changed since he last made it his headquarters before Burgoyne's campaign. Loyalists from northern New York, New Hampshire and Vermont fled over the border into Canada after Burgoyne's defeat. In Sorel, the life of collaborators with the rebels was hard but the life of displaced Loyalists was no easier. That "these immigrants were encouraged by the British government" was the indignant complaint in predominantly French Sorel. To ease the situation, Governor Haldimand bought the "Seigneurie" of Sorel for the Crown, at the cost of about three thousand louis. On these formerly French hereditary lands he established "a contingent of Loyalists," who were still not particularly welcome. The situation, instead of easing, grew more tense. "Captains of parishes" were ordered to build storehouses, barracks and a hospital for soldiers recruited from among the new arrivals.[3] The militia captain in the little village of St. Ours refused — and went to jail.

One of the inhabitants planted red, white and blue flowers in his garden — the "rebel" colors as everyone knew.[4] He was arrested, but finally released without a fine. Where was the law saying what flowers a man might like in front of his house?

New fortifications had been built around the settlement of Sorel — by forced labor from French "inhabitants." General Riedesel found that old settlers distrusted newcomers who spoke only English, and newcomers were arrogant toward "natives," despising their customs based on French tradition. Refugees desecrated the French Catholic cemetery by burying an English Protestant officer there, and disorders would certainly have resulted had not the Parish priest thought of a way to calm the older inhabitants. He reconsecrated the cemetery.

To compound a touchy situation, the Indian agent General Riedesel was given to work with would bear watching. "Lui Schmidt" this man signed himself, and his letters to General Riedesel were scribbled in a French phonetically spelled and atrocious beyond belief.[5] His first communication, dated December 18, 1781, concerned two pairs of moccasins ordered for the little Riedesel girls and an Indian headdress he had "sent to the bay for" and would forward to Sorel later. He had acted as guide at an Indian encampment near Sorel, and said that the "Savages and their wives" had great joy in seeing Madame de Riedesel. This letter was written in excessively flattering terms with a hint that favors might be given and received — a style not at all calculated to please the German General, had "Lui" but known it. Schmidt was next heard from at the village of St. Francis. He had put two soldiers into the house of Merchant Piccard — and he had no right to do this, because the quartering of soldiers was entirely the responsibility of the local militia captain. The militia captain had complained, and Schmidt said he had been planning to tell General Riedesel all about it. Piccard was "a bad Subject of the King" who had "five or six Savages in the village who used to serve his Excellency well," but Piccard "ruined these Savages by the large quantity of liquor which he sold them." In the course of his "explanation," "Lui" committed an error in judgment, however: ". . . And since the women of your troops also sell liquor, for this reason I dared easily to slip some Rum to the Savages to get the news and find out what was going on. . . ."

General Riedesel made it clear to Schmidt that strict orders were going out at once against the selling of rum to the Indians, by anyone, and that penalties would be severe. He would like to know the name "of a single soldier" who sold rum. But Schmidt preferred to accuse women, and his efforts at implicating anyone in particular were unconvincing. On January 11, 1782, General Riedesel reminded Schmidt of his promise to send an Indian guide to the Yamanska Blockhouse to show a scouting party the road to the St. Francis River. Everything was ready; the party would set out as soon as the guide arrived.

But Schmidt replied that nothing could be done until the Indians got over their New Year's celebration. On January 30, the Riedesels being in Quebec on a visit, one of General Riedesel's aides wrote from Sorel to know if Schmidt had as yet had the goodness to send that guide. Schmidt said he had sent the guide on the twenty-first. There was really nothing more he could do for General Riedesel, because the Indians had all gone hunting now. But he sent, with his compliments, "four moose muzzles" and "two moose tongues," because he would like a vacation from his army duties so he himself could go beaver hunting.

Difficulties with the artful "Lui" or Louis Schmidt were not in General Riedesel's official report, of course. He had placed the 44th Regiment in winter quarters, he told General Haldimand. "The fleet," consisting of three vessels, were frozen into the ice at St. Johns, their guns pointed so that they could protect each other and the fort. Each ship had been surrounded with palisades "set on a wall of snow." Garrisons were watchful. Orders had been given to prevent hostile emissaries from coming into the parishes.

It would have gratified General Riedesel to read General Stark's letters to Schuyler at this time, but they did not fall into his hands. Stark was positive that there would be an attack from Canada, and on October 29 he thought they were on their way. "The 10th Massachusetts and the 1st New Hampshire Regiments" had arrived, however, and this "fine body of troops ought to be able to repel every hostile invasion of any enemy this year," Stark wrote. The way General Riedesel heard it, the American rebels were not gathering to oppose an attack — they were the ones massing for a winter invasion.

Two brothers, members of an American scouting party, were caught. "The Lovells, prisoners, are arrived," Riedesel told Haldimand. "I hope from their testimonies and from what . . . fear may draw from the delinquents at Ste.-Thérèse, that useful discoveries may be made — though it is astonishing how unsuccessful we have been in these researches, notwithstanding the pains that have been taken." The inhabitants of the little parish of Ste.-Thérèse could not be made to tell any secrets, although "from their statements, it is but too likely that their wives become willing agents in supplying Rebel Scouts with provisions," Haldimand replied. The men arrested on suspicion should be "enlarged and warned," therefore, because it "would look too much like oppression to detain them." The Lovells refused to talk.

When other rebel scouts who were caught did decide to talk, they told tales of a formidable army on its way to General

Riedesel's posts. Riedesel sent out scouts to look for this army, relying on Louis Schmidt to organize the expeditions. Before long, he discovered that the Indians took the rum issued to them, then went off a little way into the woods to enjoy it, and returned to say they had searched for rebels but couldn't find any. One party, with provisions for twenty days, returned in three days very drunk, with all provisions gone. Schmidt said "the English" had given them rum.

During February, General Riedesel went to Quebec, taking his family with him. They had "cold, snowy, overcast weather with bad roads," he said. However, the trip was taken in such short stages that "Madam and the children did not feel the rigorous climate and arrived in perfect health." Lady Fritz went to a ball, to dinners and other festivities. In March, "Madam and the young ladies went to Montreal." Meanwhile the officers left behind at Sorel started a club where the "bottle was put about very freely" and "the Queen's health drunk many times," but "Sorel was no more Sorel" without Lady Fritz, and "all the gentlemen of the garrison hoped for her speedy return."

The return from Montreal in March was more speedy than safe. Lady Fritz and the children drove down the St. Lawrence on the ice, but the sun was warm and water stood "along the whole of the track." Branches of trees stuck in the ice marked a safe route, but by five in the afternoon when they reached Sorel the water was so deep "it came into the sledge. Next morning when I got up I saw to my horror a ship under full canvas sailing up the river in the very track we had come over the night before," the Baroness said.

When spring really came at last, General Riedesel planted the finest of all the various gardens he had had during his military duty in North America. He set out "1200 fruits trees, 400 lindens" and planted turnips, parsley and carrots. He was disappointed not

to get enough turnip seed to plant an acre. Lady Fritz said she
picked over two hundred cucumbers which she "made into
pickles" and since no one in Canada had ever seen any real German cucumber pickle she made presents of it to all her friends.
"It was, in fact, as if I lived upon a magnificent farm," said Mrs.
General. "I had my own cows, a large number of fowls and Virginia hogs, which are black, smaller than ours and very short-
legged. I also made my own butter.

"This was truly the Promised Land for the soldiers. My husband
gave them seeds and it gave us great pleasure to see the way they
kept house, especially their kitchen arrangements — a pleasure we
often indulged in when we went walking. They exchanged half
of the salt meat they received for fresh; so that they could boil
both kinds together in a big kettle with all sorts of vegetables and
dumplings. . . . My husband also had fishnets made, and each
company took turns going fishing. Every time they went they sent
us some of their catch. They could have fresh fish two or three
times a week and every six days they were issued a bottle of rum,
rice, butter, twelve pounds of Indian meal — and every day they
got either a pound of salt pork or half a pound of beef."

Baron Friedrich von Riedesel might not be the world's most
brilliant General — although he had had scant opportunity to
prove his ability, one way or the other during the rebellion in the
American provinces. But he would have made a fine leader of a
pioneer colony in almost any country.

Wives of the German soldiers here were now so well off and
contented that it was hard for the Baroness to get any of them
to work for her. She tried the wife of a refugee Loyalist, but
thought the woman was lazy. There was nothing like a good German woman; General Riedesel had to see to it that at least one
sergeant having a neat, industrious wife, was always stationed at
Sorel.

When General Riedesel arrived in Quebec he brought with him
a plan for conquering the American rebels. This document was

the result of conferences with Generals Clinton and Phillips in New York. Riedesel laid the plan before General Haldimand and took down Haldimand's reply. The strategy was to "take three or four well-fortified places on the coast, so that the Americans, who are not adapted to making formal sieges and who lack knowledge and armament for such an enterprise, would not be in a position to take them. From these posts, we must harass the Rebels by well followed-up expeditions without insisting on holding posts in the interior of the country. This sort of war would force the Rebels to have armies everywhere. Costs of the war would increase, resources would be exhausted and discontentment would spread. Then the Rebels would finally open their eyes and realize that they are the dupe of European powers. They would join their own compatriots instead of being a whip in the hands of ambitious powers against their own interests."

In accordance with this blueprint for victory, Lord Cornwallis had gone to the South to establish one of those "well-fortified places" — at a place called Yorktown. General Riedesel had been in Canada a little over a month when the Battle of Yorktown was fought and won by those Rebels not adapted to making a siege. This news was slow to reach Governor Haldimand, who relayed it to Riedesel. But neither of them believed it.

There was a special message for Governor Haldimand in the document which Riedesel brought him from New York:

"To this plan, there must be added a new strategy in Canada and a reinforcement of at least 2000 men at the different Posts on the Lakes, at Niagara, Detroit, etc. Under the leadership of capable officers, detachments of five or six hundred men should push toward the Ohio.[6] It would be necessary to add to these detachments Savages, to whom must be given carte blanche to do whatever they will without restriction while striking at the back of the colonies, especially that of Virginia and Pennsylvania.

"Sufficiently cruel though such a plan appears, it is necessary in the present situation. Panic terror would increase among the Rebels and their fine farms and estates would be ruined. Soon subsistence for the army would disappear and since they would be distressed on the coast by the expeditions of our army and exposed in the rear to the depredations of the Savages, they would find no other resource but to submit to their conquerors.

"I don't mean that the Savages should be an army but simply that they should spring out wherever forces assemble against them and fall back on the regular troops posted in their rear. The Savages will love this kind of fighting. Their natural cruelty will be satisfied and they will enrich themselves with booty and be satiated with the flowing of blood. They will regain their former reputation which they had under French rule."

Someone, and it seems probable that it was General Riedesel himself, corrected this document, which was in French, and deleted the part about the "flowing of blood." But the reference to the "fine farms and estates" of Virginia and Pennsylvania sounds like the voice of Riedesel's personal experience as he marched southward, a prisoner of war but still the General, observing enemy territory. The paragraph concluded with the faint voice of conscience: "I will admit that such excess seems extremely cruel but one must sacrifice something to bring about peace and the common good."

Part of Clinton's plan for Haldimand was to "make a diversion against Ticonderoga and Albany while the attack toward the Ohio was going on. Perhaps, as General Riedesel wrote all this down, he visualized himself as succeeding where Burgoyne had failed. Haldimand's "Reply to General Clinton's Proposals as set forth by General Riedesel" — dated September 20, 1781, brought common sense to bear upon the whole ambitious scheme.[7]

The British were supplying the Indians with "4000 rations per day at Niagara alone," Haldimand pointed out. "Supplies for an army of 2000 would have to be conveyed by bateau 200 miles up

rapids, intersected by carrying-places, to the first lake — from
thence to Niagara in vessels, then on over a carrying-place of 7
miles and up a rapid of 18 miles to Fort Erie, from whence they
would proceed to Presqu' Isle. . . ." Moreover, Haldimand was sure
that the inhabitants on the Ohio would fight.

As to Indians — "In all the excursions taken by Indians in this
war, there has not been a single instance where the Indians have
fulfilled their engagements, but influenced by caprice, a dream,
or a desire for protracting the war to obtain presents, they have
dispersed and deserted the troops."

It all made sense, but there was no use in Haldimand's sending
this reply to Clinton. Sir Henry Clinton had delayed so long in
sending reinforcements to Cornwallis that they never set out from
New York until the day of Cornwallis's defeat. After that defeat,
Clinton was recalled and would take up Burgoyne's present occupation — writing out a long explanation of how the Rebels somehow contrived to win decisive victories. *State of the Expedition*
Burgoyne called his narrative. "Disagreeable as is the necessity, I
must here again, in justice to my own army, recur to the vigor
and obstinacy with which they were fought by the enemy," he
said. Clinton entitled his work *The American Rebellion*, and in
it he blamed everyone but himself.

General Riedesel was too practical not to see the logic of Haldimand's refusal to mount an expedition. There were plenty of
frontier forts to be repaired and improved and he occupied himself with this duty.

In April 1782, Governor Haldimand got orders direct from the
War Ministry in London to open a correspondence with Vermont, with a view to annexing that "province," and he turned
the matter over to Riedesel. General Riedesel was "to send a considerable detachment to the frontiers of Vermont in order to
furnish these people with the opportunity of declaring themselves
openly in favor of Government and if necessary to protect them
against the resentment of Congress."[8] Ethan Allen had been ex-

changed. He had presented the claims "of the Independent Republic of Vermont" to join the United States in 1778, but Yorkers in Congress prevailed and he got nowhere. It seemed that here was an ideal spot to drive an opening wedge in the still somewhat disunited United States, and both Haldimand and Riedesel liked the plan. But the whole thing must be done secretly; so Haldimand gave it out that he wanted to build a much larger fort at Isle aux Noix on the Richelieu River. Riedesel gathered provisions and built barracks for troops which arrived at St. Johns "without anyone suspecting the true aim." Part of the plot was to raise recruits in Vermont and bring them to Canada for training.

General Riedesel was at his best while organizing an expedition but the directing of spies was not among his talents. Louis Schmidt wanted to take some Indians and go raiding now that spring had come. But of course this would never do while Vermont was being wooed rather than intimidated. Louis was told to "observe" but not start anything. So Louis and his Indians just went out, observed nothing and came back drunk. Letters were delivered to Ethan Allen at Arlington, Vermont, "by a British soldier in the habit of an American farmer." But "Aaron Boon," who had been sent to "collect recruits . . . was taken prisoner," and did "much harm to our friends in Arlington by endeavoring in a public, unguarded manner to recruit." Boon almost "ruined our principal source of Intelligence," Riedesel was told.

An unsigned letter arrived in Canada from an "emissary going into Vermont disguised as a land agent." "Unfortunately," he said, "on my return with 12 recruits, 3 German soldiers and one Loyalist, besides myself, which made 17 in number, I was discovered by a Rebel lieutenant and one man with him, which for safety we took prisoners, but traveling 8 or 9 miles, one of the prisoners not being pinioned made his escape by running to a Rebel Major's house and broke open the door before we could retake him, which occasioned an alarm in the frontier towns. A body of militia then pursued and took us by which I was obliged to destroy my papers." This man was tried at Sunderland and made "prisoner at large," he said. He promptly set up a letter-carrying service to Canada by which his unsigned letter arrived. But "five of my recruits now lie in close confinement in Bennington jail," he added.

Only a few Loyalist recruits came in from Vermont, and "likewise three or four old, infirm creatures fit for nothing but to consume rations . . . and an enormous assembly of ragged Petticoats and half-naked children to be clothed and receive the hearty benediction of His Excellency."

Whenever General Riedesel set out on a tour of inspection, he left an aide at home to stand guard over his wife and the children.[9] It was now Captain Willoe, who was stationed at Sorel in 1782. He wrote his official communications with all the correct formality of a British officer, but hardly a dispatch went forward to the General without a private note full of affection for the little family under his care. "We had a very heavy shower of rain yesterday and some Thunder which alarmed Madame de Riedesel a little," he wrote on the seventh of June.

As brave as any General when she was under fire at Saratoga, Lady Fritz hated thunder and lightning — particularly just now. She was once more expecting a child. Again she was sure that she would give her husband the son and heir he so much wanted and she was happy — she tried not to be nervous. "The storm soon cleared up," wrote Captain Willoe. He "had the pleasure of seeing her perfectly well in the evening."

28

The Pretty Ship

GENERAL Riedesel heard of a harpsichord "for sale at 16 guineas" and bought it for his wife. She began to give music lessons to Augusta and Frederika, who discovered to their surprise that they must work hard to learn to do what their mother seemed to do so easily. They were impatient with scales and finger exercises but much happier when they were allowed to practice a duet to play for their father as a surprise when he came home.

Of course the new harpsichord meant that the drawing-room must be redecorated, and Lady Fritz had the split and torn wallpaper replaced. It was good to have household projects to think of, because she was worrying constantly about her husband. She could picture him riding through heavy forest on his way from one frontier fort to another or afloat on some rapid river in one of those fearfully unstable canoes. If she had not experienced this kind of travel herself it would have been easier to feel sure he would soon return.

During the summer of 1782, the Riedesels again made a visit to Quebec. They had earned their holiday. Governor Haldimand took them out to see the summer home he had just built for himself beside the falls of Montmorency. "This cataract plunges from a height of one hundred and sixty-three feet," wrote the Baroness. "It made a frightful din." She looked up "at a cleft in the mountain where the water came through" and remarked that it would be wonderful to be able to see it from there. "Three weeks afterwards," when Governor Haldimand invited the Riedesels to Montmorency again:

"We made our way up the steep path, beside the falls, and over pieces of rock that were united by little bridges after the manner of a Chinese garden."

When at last they reached the top, the Governor gave Lady Fritz his hand to help her "into a little building which hung directly over the falls itself. He was astonished when she entered the building "without a moment's hesitation," and commented on her "courage." Perhaps he had hoped she would be afraid and that if the General had not been puffing along up the path too close behind them, he might have held more than her hand. But Lady Fritz said the right thing. "I assured him that I was not in the least afraid when he was with me."

This time the Riedesels did not stay with the Murrays—but this implied no rift in the friendship, it was just that Mrs. Murray had a son, named for General Riedesel, born June 23, 1782. The Riedesels stayed with Dr. and Madam Mabane, who lived a little way up the hill behind the Governor's house. They had dinner with the Governor every day, and this supposedly crusty old bachelor often kept the Riedesel children with him all the afternoon. They played in his garden and he called eleven-year-old Augusta his "little wife." In the evening, after the children were in bed, the Riedesels went back to the Governor's house for supper which was prepared with true French elegance and served with fine wine. Then they played bezique. The language spoken was always either French or German, for Governor Haldimand spoke very little English.

General Riedesel spent most of the winter of 1782 looking for "Hazen's Road." Colonel Moses Hazen, born in Haverhill, Massachusetts, was a veteran of the French and Indian wars. He had settled in St. Johns, Quebec Province, where he had a prosperous farm and a sawmill, but he joined Montgomery in the siege of Quebec and in the retreat from Canada he took Canadian refugees with him and recruited a regiment called "Hazen's Own." Arnold, whose expense accounts were always chaotic, accused Hazen of making off with funds from Montreal; but in a court-martial Hazen was cleared of all charges. With the idea of mounting another expedition from America into Canada, Hazen built a military road from Vermont toward the Canadian border. It would be the proper route for a "protective" force to go into Vermont to annex the present "Republic of Vermont," and so both Governor Haldimand and General Riedesel wanted very much to find it.

Again and again, Louis Schmidt's Indians went out, consumed their rations and returned with no report of any road. Louis explained that the Indians didn't mind taking a canoe down a creek, but they hated to get into the thick forest with all that undergrowth. This was fast developing into an embarrassing situation, when at last came welcome news. The scouts had found blaze marks on trees for a long distance, indicating a wonderfully straight trail in the wilderness. Riedesel wrote all the particulars to Governor Haldimand, feeling pleased with his success.

Haldimand asked Captain Twiss, one of Riedesel's aides, then in Quebec, to explain to Riedesel what the scouts had really found. "The Road you mentioned to be discovered near Point au Fer is neither more or less than the boundary line, marked in 1772 or 73 to divide New York and Canada, its due course is exactly West but the variation will make it appear by compass West and North. Mr. Collins was one of the surveyors who marked it and he tells me they cleared it very wide and that every League they put a square cedar post. On one side was wrote New York, on the other Canada and the distance from any particular place was wrote underneath."[1]

The laugh was on Louis Schmidt — or maybe Louis had known

all about the boundary line and thought he could beguile his German commander with it and not have to go into the unexplored hinterland any more. General Riedesel did not find the affair amusing. But an "emmissary," who got caught in Vermont, broke jail and returned to Canada with the news that "Hazen may be had. He is artful and enterprising. . . ." There was no use bothering any more with searching for Hazen's Road if Hazen himself could be bribed to point it out. Riedesel went back to his business of building a blockhouse at Pointe au Fer and making Isle aux Noix a strong point. Probably he never learned that Moses Hazen remained a staunch patriot — artful and enterprising, to be sure, but on the American side.

General Riedesel was at Pointe au Fer when "in the middle of the night he heard a great commotion." He thought the rebels had discovered where he was and had come to capture him, but a subaltern rushed in shouting, "For God's sake, General, run. The barracks are on fire." Sure enough, he smelled smoke, "the subaltern did not allow him to gather together any of his things so he had to run out naked and barefoot through flames upon the ice." The soldiers got the fire under control, the powder magazine did not blow up after all, and the General "returned and dressed himself." This was his wife's account of the affair.

General Riedesel's report was decidedly more dignified. Someone had built a cook-fire inside the blockhouse, "contrary to orders." Fire spread so rapidly that in a few minutes the whole blockhouse and the fortification on the north were in flames. "But for the extraordinary exertions of the garrison," the whole fort would have burned.

Captain Willoe was very much annoyed because someone told Lady Fritz about the accident and she began strongly to suspect that her husband had met with more narrow escapes than she knew about. "I was perfectly forlorn," she said. "I had been in the habit of dissipating my loneliness by driving out in my carriage," and on the first day of October while she was out riding, labor pains began. She told the driver to turn back, but when she got home the doctor and the midwife, who were already in attendance, thought it was all a false alarm. They told her to sit down at table. "She dined with us, but complained a little and joked with us," said Captain Willoe. "I went home at seven and at nine o'clock Madame was brought to bed." The devoted young aide thanked God that he was able to felicitate his "dear and most honored General" on the happy event — but he never mentioned whether the baby was a boy or a girl.

Two days later, Lady Fritz "felt so well" that she was able to write to her husband herself "announcing the new arrival." It was a little girl. General Riedesel was so sure that this time they would have a son that he thought his wife was joking. But on coming home to Sorel on October 5, he once more "found the little girl so pretty that he was consoled for his disappointment."

This time Governor Haldimand was a godfather, and General Carleton godfather *in absentia,* as were General Spaeth and General Loos — that old friend of the Riedesels who had said that Lady Fritz had lost her lovely white complexion and her slender waist. Mademoiselle de Massow, sister of the Baroness and Lady-in-Waiting to the Queen of Prussia, was godmother and so was the baby's sister Augusta. The baby was christened by Pastor Mylius, still the children's tutor, in the little chapel the Riedesels had fitted up for themselves and the German officers of the Garrison. They named the new little daughter Luisa Augusta Elizabeth Canada; "Canada" was the name they would call her by.

For seven years, Frederika Riedesel had shared the hardships of a military campaign with her husband and her health had been superb. But by the middle of November, she developed an ulcer in her right breast and suffered great pain when nursing the baby. The doctor lanced the ulcer, but pain continued, and at last she was persuaded to wean the baby. It was against her will, and during the first night she thought she heard a voice crying, "You have done wrong!" She "sprang from the bed, tore off the bindings which had been put on her breast to dry the milk and was about to give her "dear little Canada the breast again" when the nurse stopped her. Three days later the baby "was attacked by diarrhea" and the baby's mother was "delirious with milk fever." An English doctor from Three Rivers came and prescribed strange remedies. "He had an old hen killed and took out the entrails, which he had cooked without cleaning them." He gave the baby this horrible concoction, which "at first seemed to infuse new life into her." But little Canada died at the age of five months. The whole family was overcome with grief, and Augusta, the baby's eleven-year-old godmother, was taken dangerously ill — her illness caused by sorrow, her mother felt sure.

The baby Canada was buried in the cemetery at Sorel, and the officers of the garrison promised Mrs. General that they would mark the grave with a stone "which would prevent the inhabitants from taking up the heretic child from consecrated earth." Later, the parish priest came and assured Lady Fritz that because the baby had been christened though not confirmed, she need have no fear. They would take good care of the grave of the child, who was now "one of God's angels."

But now Mrs. General, whose courage had never failed her, grew homesick for Germany. The house, where the height of the growing children was marked on the chimney no longer seemed like home. Army wives and army children never expect to have a place to call home for long, but to her it seemed wrong to bring up four little German girls to speak English and French so much better than German. They could not even remember the land of their forefathers.

By the middle of March, 1783, news from London reached the Murrays in Quebec, who relayed it to the Riedesels at Sorel: "I hear His Excellency [Governor Haldimand] has at last got

the King's Speech, that it breathes nothing but Peace and that he
admits the Independency of the American Provinces and this ends
a seven years' war carried on at immense expense of Blood and
Treasure." The Murrays felt sympathy for "the poor Loyalists,
for their situation must be dreadful indeed."

General Carleton, writing from New York where he was Governor, dated "a letter of farewell to the General and Madam
Riedesel," April 9, 1783. "The preliminaries of a general peace"
had been signed, he said.

Now came the difficult business of rounding up rank and file
who had been prisoners of war. Brunswick soldiers were to be sent
to Halifax so that they could sail home with General Riedesel.
But there was a great shortage of transports in New York; they
would have to wait their turn. Some finally left on the fourth of
July, but the troops imprisoned in Rutland — many of them taken
at Bennington — did not arrive in time and so were sent from
New York direct to Germany. There had been so many who
escaped and deserted that there were only forty men who finally
came from Rutland. Others known to be near Albany and Boston
simply did not report.

Troops of the Prince Frederick Regiment who had embarked
with General Phillips for the Southern campaign were taken at
Yorktown, after his death, and were imprisoned at Frederick in
Maryland.[2] They were in captivity nineteen months, and many
of them hired themselves out to farmers or as artisans. Most of
them were well treated, but some were exploited cruelly. The
regiment marched for New York on May 14, 1783, and on the
way seven noncommissioned officers, three servants, three drummers, and one hundred thirty-two soldiers deserted. Of course not
a word appears in the official records concerning the women and
children left in New York and forbidden to follow the troops
to the Chesapeake. In an age when many women could neither
read nor write, it would be surprising if the women of this regi-

ment ever found their husbands again — or the children, their fathers.

Governor Haldimand asked to be recalled when he got the news of the peace treaty. He was shocked and disillusioned because Detroit and Niagara were given to America, for these posts were of great importance to the Canadian fur trade. He planned to sail for England in the same ship with the Riedesels. His recall did not come in time, but Lady Fritz and the children were in Quebec with him, walking in his garden, when he "pointed out a number of vessels just arriving in the lower city."

"They have come to take us all back home," he said.

The "little ladies" leaned over the garden wall and looked straight down into the lower town and the ships in the river. Frederika — they called her "Miss Fritza" now that she was nine — picked out an especially "pretty ship" and asked, "Can we have that one?"

Governor Haldimand explained that if he hired that ship it would cost the King of England a great deal of money. Frederika thought the King ought not to mind. After all, he had a wife and children of his own, so he would want the best ship for his General's wife and children. Then, judging that this argument was not having much effect, Frederika took another tack. Since Governor Haldimand called her sister Augusta his "little wife" and said he was going to marry her as soon as she was old enough, "Don't you want your little wife to sail home safely?" she asked.

The Governor laughed and said he'd see.

"Two days afterward," Governor Haldimand called at the house "of the good Dr. Mabane" where Lady Fritz was living. "There were tears in his eyes. 'You are to go and I am to stay,' he said. 'I shall miss you very much.'" The Governor's request for recall had been refused.

But Haldimand had already looked over the ship assigned to General Riedesel and found it "unsafe." He had therefore "assumed the responsibility" of hiring the "pretty ship" which little Miss Fritza had chosen. An hour later, Major Twiss came to escort the Baroness aboard so that she could look the ship over and "order it fitted up" exactly as she wanted it. "It was a large West India three-decker in good condition. The captain was also highly praised as an excellent seaman and a courteous, upright man," she said. The Baroness had not forgotten the sea captain who brought her to Canada.

Major Twiss "ordered the cannon which were on the gun deck to be taken away, and a large porthole cut and staterooms built for the gentlemen of General Riedesel's suite." The Riedesels "kept the great cabin," having staterooms partitioned off, one for the children and one for themselves. The governor had "a cow and a calf" put on board so that the children could have fresh milk, and a "place on the upper deck he had filled with earth" to make a garden for growing "salad plants." The Riedesels themselves loaded "many fowls, sheep and vegetables" on board because their official "family" numbered twenty-two officers who would sit down at their table every day.

It was time now for the exchanging of gifts between the departing Riedesels and Governor Haldimand. General Riedesel gave him "his favorite mare and her foal." Governor Haldimand gave Lady Fritz "a magnificent muff and stole of sable" and to his "little wife" Augusta, "a beautiful hunting dog." He hoped that Lady Fritz would stay in Quebec while the ship was being built over for her convenience and while her husband went back to Sorel to wind up his business. But Mrs. General said she was going back to Sorel too.

"You must return soon and give me your company for the little while that will remain to you before you leave," urged the Governor. "He then left me, deeply moved," said Lady Fritz.

General Carleton had replaced Clinton in New York. The Americans felt that he delayed the British evacuation of the city much too long but he was sending American Loyalists to Canada, helping them to make a new start in life. General Riedesel wrote him several times, urging that all German troops, their wives and children then in New York, be sent to Canada at once, but Carleton explained that a lack of transports made this impossible. He promised to send the Germans direct to Europe from New York — sometime. Riedesel was sure that his people would be marooned in New York forever and he was much distressed. As it turned out, however, Riedesel was delayed and the Germans reached the other side of the Atlantic ahead of him. This worried him still more.

General Schuyler wrote to Madam and General Riedesel in behalf of Mrs. Schuyler and himself. He hoped they would go to Europe by way of New York City, taking the overland route, and he wanted to invite the Riedesels to visit him in Albany — no longer as prisoners of war but as friends. It was with real regret that General Riedesel explained that he was to sail from Quebec.

In Canada, Captain Willoe was inconsolable. He had been ordered to Fort Niagara, and Haldimand refused him leave to come to Quebec to say good-by to Lady Fritz and the children. He blamed Haldimand's "cruelty."[3]

The Baroness returned to Quebec a few days before her husband did and found festivities planned for her. The officers of the garrison gave a play and at the end of it they sang a song "wishing us a prosperous journey," she said. Governor Haldimand had attended personally to the alterations on the "pretty ship." There was a final farewell dinner after "the embarkation of the troops" and a last "tea" with Governor Haldimand, before "he carried us himself to the ship, where we took an affectionate and sad farewell."

The Riedesels set sail "about the middle of August" and got as far as the Isle de Bec at the mouth of the St. Lawrence, where they were becalmed for eleven days. After all the farewell parties, the gifts and the tears, it was an anticlimax, and a great disappointment. General Riedesel was upset. He had dispatches from Governor Haldimand for Lord George Germain and day after day went by. Ships setting out from New York might have favorable winds and all the news would reach London before the General. Besides, they were beginning to worry about equinoctial storms.

One Sunday Pastor Mylius was holding his accustomed service on the deck, "praying most fervently that God would grant us a favorable wind and a happy return to our fatherland," Mrs. General wrote, "when the ship began to move." The chaplain said "Amen" just as the "cry went around that the English commodore had signaled for departure."[4]

The passage was tedious, however, because the commodore kept signaling for delays so that slow vessels could catch up with the fleet. The Riedesels' ship was fast but she was under orders to stay in line — until one day when the signal came for "all ships to heave to" and the commodore, speaking through a trumpet, shouted "General, proceed." The General's ship cracked on all sail and sped away. Just as they left, two doves belonging to the commodore's ship flew over to the Riedesel vessel "and could not be driven away." The crew considered this a lucky omen. Whereupon they ran into a storm that continued "with unabated fury" night and day for three weeks. Since the ship stayed afloat, the crew's faith in signs and portents was considered justified. But Lady Fitz marveled at the superstitions of seamen and was very much frightened all during the voyage.

As they approached the coast of Ireland a heavy fog set in. Now the seas were calm and everyone could gather for meals and to enjoy the music of "the hautboys" from Regiment Riedesel. Riedesel's military family and his own family "feasted on beef" because the poor cow, although "fastened into a hammock during the storm," had nevertheless fallen and was so badly hurt she had to be killed. Now that the weather was calm, Lady Fritz and the children really began to enjoy themselves — but General

Riedesel began to worry. He had been calculating the ship's course and his reckoning and the captain's did not agree.

It was whispered among the officers that General Riedesel had calculated the ship's course on the outward-bound voyage before they reached Canada in 1776, and had told the captain that they must have sailed past Canada in the night. This time, "a gust of wind drew aside the fog like a curtain" — and suddenly there was "the Isle of Wight and the whole English coast lying just in front of us." General Riedesel had been right and the captain wrong: they had entered the English Channel, and were much closer to shore than anyone had realized.

Their port of destination was Portsmouth, but as they entered the roadstead known as Spithead there was a grinding shock and the ship struck something underwater where no shoal or rock was known to be. They were stuck fast for about forty-eight hours on the sunken wreck of the man-of-war *Royal George*. On August 29, 1782, the *Royal George*, carrying 100 guns, had been loaded at Portsmouth with supplies, munitions and "about 900 souls including about 200 women and children" bound for Gibraltar. Laden as she was, they heeled her over to make underwater repairs and she capsized "at her anchors," carrying all hands down with her. It was now about the middle of the month of September 1783, and this tragic wreck still remained, a hazard to other ships.[5]

But "our hearts were light as we stepped on shore," wrote Mrs. General, "and I thanked God for the happy return of us all, and especially for His having preserved my husband to me."

They hastened up to London and were "magnificently lodged in a large hotel, the King George. Lady Fritz immediately sent for a dressmaker. She knew that she would be invited to the Queen's Drawing Room receptions, and she hadn't a thing to wear. She could see at a glance that styles had changed: ruffles were in, and so were scarves of gauze or fine linen; skirts were narrower and hats had wider brims. Lady Fritz was not going to

look like a provincial if she could help it, and the clothes she had
brought from Canada would never do — except of course the furs,
but it was not yet the season for them.

Unfortunately, however, the Baroness had made such a favorable impression upon Queen Charlotte that she had not been
forgotten and her summons came too soon. My Lady Howard,
the Queen's first lady-in-waiting, called personally on the Baroness
to invite her to come to St. James's Palace "that afternoon at six
o'clock."

Perhaps only a German Baroness and one quite fond of clothes
would have done such a thing — but Frederika Charlotte Luise
Baroness von Riedesel sent regrets! She had only an *Angloise* to
wear and she just couldn't be seen in it — her new court dress
wasn't ready yet, and she would come later.

The Queen replied, "We do not look at the dress of those
people we are glad to see," and this time Lady Fritz recognized
a command when she heard it. The Riedesels were entertained
at St. James's Palace as informally as though they had been members of the royal family themselves. The Queen, the Princesses,
Lady Howard and the Baroness sat in a semicircle before the fire.
"Tea and cakes were passed around. I sat between the Queen and
one of the Princesses, and they made me tell a great many of my
adventures," said Lady Fritz.

"I have followed you everywhere and have often asked about
you," the Queen told her. "I was always delighted to hear that
you were well, happy and beloved by everyone."

Poor Lady Fritz had "a shocking cough," which Princess Sophia
noticed. "She went herself and brought me a jelly made of black
currants, which she said was a particularly good remedy, and made
me accept a jar full. At nine o'clock the Prince of Wales came in.
His youngest sisters flocked around him and he embraced them
and danced them around." Everything was so informal that it
was like spending an evening "in a cheerful family circle in my
own station in life."

The King and General Riedesel stood in the center of the group, close to the fire, "where His Majesty conversed much about America, and in German."

General Riedesel wrote the details of his private conversation with George III in a letter to Governor Haldimand. His Majesty "took me aside and began to go over the whole of the last war and commanded me to tell him all that I had found out. This I did most faithfully. I admit I never would have believed that the King was so much aware of all that has happened; the mistakes the Ministry has made as well as those of the different Generals and the different factions that have caused projects to fail. Better still did he know to the bottom the capacities and character of all his officers who have been in service, even the German officers — and finally, he knew all the scandalous stories that have been going the rounds in the army, especially in the time of Sir William Howe."[6] It would seem that the reputation of the beautiful, golden-haired Mrs. Loring was international.

George III was so pleased with General Riedesel that he granted him a pension. While in New York, the General's pay was at least two pounds ten shillings a day, and most of his expenses were paid. When Captain Freeman, Riedesel's most trusted aide, went to London he carried funds which he invested for the General. Riedesel went around to Brooks, Watson and Rashleigh, where he found a gratifying balance in his account. The modest items of family jewelry which the Baroness had left with the banker as security for expenses connected with her stay in London and her voyage to Canada were returned to her, and General Riedesel went to a London cabinetmaker, where he ordered fine mahogany furniture for his wife's drawing-room in Germany — such furniture as she had enjoyed in New York and the destruction of which still grieved her.

Distinguished people called on the Riedesels every day of their stay in London. General Tryon was there, and did not fail to put in an appearance. Lord North called, and so did "Mr. Fox."

Charles James Fox had always championed the cause of the American colonies and he had just become British Foreign Minister.

One old acquaintance failed to put in an appearance. Gentleman Johnny Burgoyne was now Commander-in-Chief in Ireland, but had come back to London in 1783 to attend sessions of Parliament. In London, however, Burgoyne's time was at least partly taken up with Miss Susan Caulfield, a singer, who had presented him with a son in 1782.

And there was finally a chance for the Baroness to wear her new court dress, at a formal reception in the Queen's drawing room at St. James's.

But Lady Fritz did not forget old friends. "The very first thing I did, the morning after my arrival, was to hasten to pay a visit to the excellent Mr. Russell who had showed me so much kindness and consideration during my first stay in London," she said. "I took a hackney coach, got in with my four children," and made sure that these good people knew nothing of my intended visit." The Baroness must have made an early call, because Mr. Russell was not yet dressed and his wife was in the shop "weighing out some sugar." Pretending to be a customer, Lady Fritz walked in casually and stood opposite. Mrs. Russell glanced up — then stared at her and cried out: "I can't believe my eyes! Is it really you! But here are four children, and you had only three!"

"I could not restrain myself any longer," said the Baroness. "My tears of joy betrayed me and I fell on her neck. At this point someone grasped me from behind and cried out, 'Pardon, my lady; I must embrace you!' It was the worthy, honest Mr. Russell. The good people wept very much when I left them, but I promised to come back again once more and bring my husband."

29

Mrs. General Comes Home

LADY Fritz went sight-seeing in London. Conscientiously she visited "the most noteworthy objects of interest," taking her three older girls with her and admonishing them to remember Westminster Abbey and London Bridge. "I might have profited still more by my stay," she said, "but the news that the fleet which was to take us to Germany" was ready to sail "changed all our plans. We went to Deal, where we were to embark" and those equinoctial storms "which we so much feared, had already begun."

There was a roadstead at Deal, just north of Dover on the Channel coast, where ships anchored. They were reached by tender from shore, and when the Riedesels arrived waves lashed the wharves and boats put off only at high tide. The storm was a fearsome sight and they decided to wait a day; but next morning it was even worse. The transports had sailed earlier, and General Riedesel now pictured the troops arriving at Stade on the Elbe with no one to take proper charge of them. He decided to go aboard his ship no matter how it plunged and tossed at anchor — so near and yet so far.

A boat was drawn up on the beach and the passengers got into it. Seamen stood alongside ready to help shove off when the highest wave of the high tide should set the boat afloat. "I had my three-year-old daughter Amerika in my lap," said Mrs. General, "and around my boat a number of people were standing." The whole business seemed "an extremely perilous undertaking," and suddenly "Amerika cried out in English, 'Is there nobody here who will take me?' She stretched out both her little arms and an extremely well-dressed woman came running up and was on the point of snatching her from me." At that moment the boat was shoved off — the well-dressed woman must have gotten soaking wet, while the Baroness had all she could do "to keep hold on the little girl."

They rowed safely to the ship, but when they reached it the waves tossed their boat like a cork, the wooden sides of the vessel loomed high as a house, now near, now out of reach, and from the deck dangled only a rope ladder. "I thought with our arrival in England I had escaped all perils," said Mrs. General. "This unlooked-for danger took away all my presence of mind." She said she was going to be the last to leave the rowboat. The others must "climb up first," so that she could see all her family safe on deck.

General Riedesel jumped for the ladder the next time the tender swung close to the ship. He made it and they helped him over the rail. Then a sailor took a child in his arms, another took the next, and these men "climbed with their precious burdens up the little ladder that hung over the side of the vessel." If "one of the sailors had slipped, a child would have been crushed between the ship and the boat," the children's mother said, and she was "in a constant state of anguish." She had not stopped to think how she herself was ever going to climb that ladder, in her long skirts and her voluminous traveling cloak. Moreover, she felt unsure of her balance because she was once more expecting a child. But there was activity on deck and she saw they were lowering a chair for her.

"As soon as I touched the deck the captain came up." He was the same officer who had brought the Riedesels from Canada, and this was the same ship. " 'I congratulate you,' " he said to Mrs. General. " 'You were in more danger just now than on the whole voyage across the Atlantic.' "

It took three days to reach the Elbe, and then they "were obliged to sail to and fro" because they could not make the channel between buoys, "where large ships can sail only at high tide." General Riedesel became so impatient that he had himself set ashore and went ahead to Stade by road. Mrs. General longed to go with him, but she knew that she and the children would only be in the way. She said she would follow when the weather moderated; she waited another day and a night, and still the ship could not get into the Elbe.

The following morning the captain proposed leaving his ship with the first mate and personally taking Mrs. General and the children up the Elbe in the longboat. "I was delighted," she said. "Before leaving, I gave him the present my husband and I had decided upon — two cows, fifteen sheep, six hogs and a considerable quantity of poultry." These were provisions left over from the Atlantic voyage, and "for these presents the captain thanked me warmly."

They set out with six men to row the boat. But the tide was ebbing and it was no joke to row upstream. The men became "so thoroughly exhausted" that Mrs. General was afraid they would have to spend the night in the open boat in the river. It was eleven o'clock when they reached Stade that evening, and they were confronted with still another problem. There were so many transports and merchant ships crowding the wharves that they could not get near enough to land. The captain, by means of much hallooing and passing out of silver, got a bridge of gangplanks laid "from one to the other of three or four ships." Rockel, who had never left his General's wife in all her travels, now carried one of the girls; sailors took the others — and Mrs. General crossed to shore in black darkness with only the flickering light of a lantern to show her the planks strung from one boat to another.

Now they were in Stade, but they had no idea where they would find General Riedesel. Everyone was either drunk or asleep, in that riverport city, Mrs. General found. "I thought in the innocence of my heart that everyone must know the newly arrived General, because he was so dear to me." She was "mortified" and felt she had made herself "ridiculous" in front of her friend the captain, and the sailors, when one man she questioned on the street said " 'We don't know any German General' " and then another laughed, " 'What do we care about *him?*' "

At last a man offered to guide the forlorn little group to an inn where he said a German General had gone. They followed him through so many dark streets that they began to think he was leading them to some den of thieves where they would be robbed and murdered. And then at last they came out on a cobblestoned square — and there, in front of an inn door, was a guard of dragoons. One of them was "a good old man" who, years before, had been particularly fond of General Riedesel. He instantly recognized Mrs. General, stepped forward and took her and the children by the hands. "How good it is to see you safe in Germany," he exclaimed.

Lady Fritz had often been caustic in regard to inns in America. She now expressed herself just as strongly concerning the inn at Stade. She wanted to order some supper for the sea captain and his men, "but the people of the inn were in a snarling humor," she said. The tea was "miserable," the milk had gone sour, the bread was stale and the butter worse. Everything was "served up in such a filthy manner" that she found herself apologizing to the English captain for Germany and its inhabitants. However, in Brunswick it was different, she assured him. He must not judge all Germans by the inn at Stade.

General Riedesel was not yet ready to leave with the Brunswick division, so Mrs. General went on ahead, spending the next night at Zelle in the expectation of being in Brunswick the following morning. She was sound asleep in bed when a light woke her and there was a "soldier with a fierce-looking mustache" standing at the foot of the bed with a lantern. I was "terribly frightened," she said, "and then even more so" when the man handed her a letter. Something dreadful must have happened to her husband, she thought, but the letter only asked her "to change her plan of journey" and go direct to her home in Wolfenbüttel.

It was a hired coach and post-horses to be sure, but Rockel was once more in the driver's seat as Mrs. General and the children bounced over the road to Wolfenbüttel. The Baroness began to think about her home. You do not leave a house with all its contents for seven long years and expect to come back to find everything just as you remember it. The house would be damp and dark, with shutters over the windows, furniture sheeted to keep out the dust. There would be dirt on the floors and cobwebs everywhere. The family silver, locked in vaults, would be tarnished black. A faithful steward had been left in charge of that stone house in the city street, but suppose something had happened to him? The house might have been broken into, and if not actually looted, then damaged and disordered.

As the coach turned into the familiar street, then through the arched gate into her own courtyard, Frederika von Riedesel hardly dared to look. Then she cried out in surprise. The windows were lighted. There was the sound of music. The door was flung open, and friends poured out to greet her. A festive supper had been prepared and everything was bright and shining — in perfect order, "just as I had left it," she said. "I gave thanks to God for having preserved me through so many dangers, for having watched over all my family and for the precious gift of my little daughter, America."

Next day there came a procession of friends to call. Instead of summoning the Baroness to court, her Royal Highness the Princess Augusta, Duchess of Brunswick, came herself to greet the General's wife. She was the granddaughter of George I, King of England, said to be "very affable and remarkably good-tempered," but this was a great honor and the Baroness Riedesel was delighted. Surely it meant that her husband was not out of favor — in spite of Saratoga.

A week went by, and finally Mrs. General heard the sound of hautboys and drums — the music of the Brunswick regiments. General Riedesel was marching into Wolfenbüttel. "It is beyond my power to describe my emotion," said Mrs. General. "There was my beloved husband, who had been so tireless in helping those entrusted to him — standing in the midst of his men, who in turn were surrounded by a joyous and sorrowful crowd of fathers, mothers, wives, children, sisters and friends — all pressing around him to see their loved ones again."

The troops were dressed in new uniforms, after having gone in rags. The women, described by the horrified Hannah Winthrop of Cambridge as tattered and dirty, had been given good clothes and a chance to wash themselves and their children. There were fathers and mothers among the crowd who found themselves the grandparents of children they had never seen before. And there must have been girls who found strange new women following the army from Canada or America — married by the chaplain to the men the German girls had been waiting for. There had been 77 women who marched out with the men; 64 returned, but there were deaths, and new marriages. The fate of some of the Prince Frederick Regiment's women in New York is still unknown. There were many in that crowd who searched in vain, called out a name — and no one answered. Out of four thousand Brunswickers who left Germany with General Riedesel, only two thousand, eight hundred returned.

The Duke of Brunswick graciously signified that he would give these returning men a review.

And so on October 8, 1783, General Riedesel, in dress uniform, was riding at the head of the first division along the road from Wolfenbüttel to Brunswick, with a crowd of people hemming in the troops and marching beside them, when — before they reached Brunswick — they heard cheering ahead. The Duke in person was riding forward to meet them — a great honor indeed!

This was not the same Duke who had reviewed the troops when General Riedesel set out for America. Duke Charles I had died in 1780; it was his son, Charles II, who rode forward, a man of considerable ability whose brother had been Riedesel's special friend and patron. Now it was very clear that General Riedesel was not to be treated like the Hessian, von Heister, who had died "of grief and disappointment" because of his defeat at Trenton. The rulers of the Duchy of Brunswick felt that their General had done the best he could under adverse circumstances. Saratoga meant nothing to them, and they cared little whether there was a new nation or a British colony in North America. Duke Charles II was giving General Riedesel a hero's welcome.

The following day "we all went to Brunswick," said Mrs. General. "We dined at Court, where, in the evening, I met almost all my friends after our long separation. This was great joy." From now on she was "much in demand socially," and the children were "admired everywhere."

General Riedesel's father had died in the year 1780, and the General was now owner of "about seven and a half square miles considered to be a province." The castle of Lauterbach, where he was born, was his; and there were other estates and houses. He longed to go to Lauterbach, "plant cabbages and remember, at my ease, past times," he said. But this was not to be. The new baby was a girl! All these estates and a substantial invested capital would still be inherited by one of the General's two brothers and the General must pay a dowry "conforming to her status" for each of five daughters, including the new little girl named Charlotte! It was a great relief when the Duke of Brunswick "established him lucratively with the title of Lieutenant General." The Riedesels took a house in Brunswick.

Mrs. General loved to be in command of moving into a new house. Her husband furnished this one for her "entirely in the English style." Everything English was fashionable because the Duchess was English, and Mrs. General was glad that she herself had been to London. She hung pictures painted in Canada — Montmorency Falls, General Carleton's house. And now of course it would be a good idea to have everyone's portrait painted.

Tischbein, who had painted Frederika von Massow "representing Spring" at the time of her marriage, had died soon after the Riedesels returned to Brunswick.[1] A different but competent artist did a forthright portrait of Mrs. General, not as "Spring" or even "Autumn," but being just herself: her fine, generous mouth smiling, her wonderfully deep blue eyes still full of fire. If a becoming muslin fichu partly hid a double chin, at least her face was unlined, and a gray-blue silk dress, made in the latest high-waisted style, fitted tightly over a handsome bosom. A white lace scarf covered but did not hide her beautiful white hair — which may of course have been powdered, because the Baroness Riedesel was still only thirty-eight when she moved to her new home in Brunswick.

A German painter named Schroeder, equally honest but less skillful, painted General Riedesel. The General was decidedly overweight. But his smile was cheerful and there was rather a gleam in his eye. "Toward the fair sex he ever displayed . . . knightly gallantry," wrote one of his biographers; and the General, in his portrait, looked as if he were just about to indulge in a little "gallantry." The painter did justice to a red uniform crossed with a broad cerise ribbon, and ornamented with "The Grand Cross of the Order of the Golden Lion" — which was star-shaped.

Of course the girls had their pictures painted, too. They looked young and sweet in white, high-waisted dresses, their shoulders draped in blue muslin — except for Augusta who wore blue draped with white. Little braids perched on top of their heads while short curls floated free around their faces in artful artlessness. But the girls were painted later, perhaps by someone more influenced by the French school.

In May 1784, a young American came to the city of Brunswick. "The roads were so bad that we were four days and two nights coming hither" from Hamburg "with six horses and a light carriage," wrote Francis Coffin to his family back in Boston.[2] "I am now agreeably settled in the Caroline College." There young men from all over Europe were studying for a military career. "Madam and General Riedesel live almost opposite the college so I see them often. They behave in a very kind and friendly manner towards me." General Riedesel saw that Frank was presented at court. But in June the Riedesels left for the castle in Lauterbach, which they made their summer home. Frank was lonely, although in August there was a fair lasting three weeks, "two masquerades, a private Ball" and a public one given by the Duke. He ate at a table with "about six and twenty Englishmen, all of whom except two or three . . . officers in the army," and at table they always spoke French or German. And then in November "General and Madam Riedesel are returned," wrote Frank with evident joy.

"I assure you, my dear Mama," Frank said, "I have often felt the want of a mother since I left you, but that want is in some measure supplied by the good Mrs. de Riedesel whom I am sure you would esteem if you knew her and whom I must beg of you to love for the kindness she has shewn to your son." When the Baroness Riedesel was in Boston, people spat at her in the street. She had not forgotten: she had made a promise to herself, and she was keeping it.

The year 1785 brought a great triumph and a great happiness

to Mrs. General and her husband. On April 27 their son was born![3] What festivities there must have been — with barrels of beer rolled out for all the peasantry on all the estates, crowds gathering in the street in Brunswick, candles in the windows, bonfires in the courtyard. Letters of congratulation poured in. Prince Frederick, later King of Prussia, offered to be the baby's godfather, and from royalty an offer was a command. He doubtless provided a handsome gift. But they named the baby Georg Karl.

All the European powers were looking hungrily at the Netherlands because of their wealth, and in 1788 General Riedesel was sent in command of Brunswick troops "to support the Stadtholder" or Governor in the southern Dutch provinces. He served for six years in Holland, where tact and diplomacy were fully as important as military action, and the Duke of Brunswick was pleased with him. Mrs. General did not share this tour of duty. After all, the provinces of the United Netherlands were only about a hundred and fifty miles from the tiny Duchy of Brunswick, a little less than the distance from Sorel to Quebec or a little farther than from Charlottesville, Virginia, to Berkeley Springs. The North American Continent had amended the Riedesels' ideas of distance, and the General came home fairly often. Besides, it had been perilous enough to take three little girls under five years old to America. Mrs. General was not going to risk their three-year-old only son and heir.

Five years later, General Riedesel at last "retired to his ancestral castle of Lauterbach." Then came the "reign of terror" in France after Louis XVI was executed that September; all the hereditary rulers of all the little dukedoms and principalities soon put their crowned heads together to see what could be done to stop this overthrow of kings. The last thing a professional army officer cared for was a completely secure world, but General Riedesel had hardly time to see that the peasants on his estates were planting better gardens, raising more horses and sending more young men into the army before he was recalled to Brunswick to become Commandant of the City.

This was a position of honor, well paid but by no means merely honorary. With the people of Paris spreading abroad their motto, "Liberty, Equality, Fraternity," what the Duke of Brunswick needed badly was a tactful man to keep an eye on his city. He was considered a liberal ruler, having actually opened schools for children of the lowly born. On certain nights the public was admitted free to the opera which he supported, and he "encouraged agriculture." But now he must take the field against the French, who would all too soon be led by a Corsican named Napoleon Bonaparte.

As the wife of the Commandant, Mrs. General's duty was to entertain a great deal. And if there was anything she liked better than going to a party it was giving one. Besides, she had five daughters. The Caroline College, with its quota of well-born young men intent on a military education, was a great asset, and many were the gay dancing parties where the Riedesel girls could exert their charms under their mother's watchful eye. She was no matchmaker, but with all her heart Mrs. General wished that her girls would marry for love as she herself had done — and be just as happy. When Augusta became the Countess Reuss, there was almost as much rejoicing in the Riedesel family over this first son-in-law as there had been at the birth of their son.[4]

Count Reuss, sometimes referred to as Prince Reuss, was the heir to a good-sized principality. He was attached to the Court of the King of Prussia at Berlin and lived there in winter. So naturally enough Mrs. General took her girls to visit their sister and enjoy a larger social world than their own, from time to time. She felt that her pretty daughters had but to be seen to be appreciated.

It was an American, Gouverneur Morris, ex-minister to France, who described Berlin at this time.[5] "The appearance of this town

is magnificent and at the same time it has an air of dissoluteness
which is striking. . . . I observe on driving through this great
unpeopled town that the greater part of it is built of brick
plastered over to imitate free-stone. The plaster already falling off
in places. The effect is emblematical, I think, of want of solidity
and this power . . . will soon fade away and figure hereafter in
history as one of those grand operas which have amused generations long since mingled with the dust, and of which no traces
are now to be found." The time of year was July, and the city of
Berlin was "unpeopled" partly because so many had gone to
summer homes — the Count and Countess Reuss to Silesia, for
example. Morris remarked that Berlin "is built on such a dead
level that the gutters do not carry off the water, and of course the
stench is great."

Four months later, on February 15, 1797, Gouverneur Morris
returned to Berlin. He changed from traveling clothes and "went
to Court where I am presented to Their Majesties," he said. The
King asked after President George Washington. He had heard
that the first President of the United States would refuse a third
term, but he did not believe it — was it true that Washington
was in bad shape physically? The King seemed to hope so. Morris
told the King of Prussia that Washington, when he last saw him,
was "a hale, robust man, as much as Your Majesty is now, so
how could he be indisposed?" This was to flatter the King, who
looked all worn out, Morris said in his diary.

Morris was just planning to leave so as "to avoid staying to
supper" when "the Queen points out to me a young Mademoiselle
Riedesel who was born in America and christened 'America.' She
is a fine girl and when she comes down to dance I tell her, in the
presence of Her Majesty, that I reclaim my Countrywoman."

Mademoiselle America's birthday was three weeks away. She
would be seventeen. She wore a delicate white muslin dress, high-
waisted in the style made all the rage by Joséphine de Beauharnais

— now one year married to Napoleon. Her blond hair was cut short to curl around her face but she also wore a little braid tucked up on the back of her head. The middle-aged American diplomat was dancing with the future Countess Bernsdorf (Bernstorff): one of Mademoiselle America's descendants would one day be the German Ambassador to the United States.

30

The Letters of Mrs. General

COUNT von Reuss was still the only son-in-law in the Riedesel family in 1799. He and his Countess were visiting at the castle at Lauterbach when he persuaded his lively mother-in-law to tell him about her adventures in America. Mrs. General had not forgotten the warning of old Colonel Loos and she was always watchful lest her reminiscences became a bore. But there was no mistaking the Count's enthusiasm. He said she ought to write a book.

Mrs. General had already written almost everything, in letters to her mother, she said. When the ice closed the St. Lawrence and when she was in the midst of the American wilderness she had written her letters journal-fashion, and sent them on in a large packet with her husband's reports to the Duke of Brunswick. Count Reuss wanted to see the letters.

Nothing was ever thrown away in the great stone castle at Lauterbach; there was endless storage space. There were armoires, some of them with pieces of armor still in them; there were *garde-robes* filled with ancient gowns and uniforms; and there were trunks and boxes full of land deeds, genealogies, and letters. Among the effects of Madame von Massow that were left to her daughter Frederika, the letters were found. They were passed around and read.

Augusta, Countess Reuss, remembered how frightened she had

been in the cellar at Saratoga when cannon balls came through the house and rolled along the floor over her head. Frederika remembered a nice man who could moo like a cow and make little girls laugh instead of cry. But Count Reuss was interested only in Burgoyne's historic surrender, and it was only Mrs. General who remembered that. He was fascinated to find that she had written it all down.

Mrs. General was surprised to find that her husband was also interested in her letters. He got out letters of his own and documents which he had ordered his aides to write for him. Here was that statement of Burgoyne's that he alone was responsible for the defeat and that the Germans had fought bravely. Riedesel had asked all the officers present to sign the paper as witnesses, because he suspected he would need this evidence — and so it proved.

Mrs. General was still not at all sure that she wanted to write a book, but Count Reuss promised to arrange and edit. Then he had another good idea: the General must write his autobiography. At this, the General demurred even more strongly than his wife, but Count Reuss promised to find a scholarly young man who would do all the work. The General agreed to arrange his papers and make some notes.

Not all the time that General Riedesel put in among his papers had to do with his future *Memoirs,* however. On October 14, 1799, while the family was still at Lauterbach, "contemplating the swift passage of human life," he summoned a lawyer and made his will. First of all, he hoped to be buried in the family vault "here at Lauterbach." But "if I should die somewhere else, I should be buried at such place without delay and without undue attention. . . ." General Riedesel assumed that he was not through with active service, although in June he had celebrated his sixty-first birthday, which was an advanced age for his era. There would be no dramatic funeral if he died in action, like Fraser's at the "great redoubt" at Saratoga — fatally delaying the retreat of a whole army.

"I am not permitted to testate about the old family entail and also not about real estate, buildings and jewelry acquired by our grandfather and father's brothers. All this property can be inherited by law only by a male heir," General Riedesel had his lawyer write down. What a relief and joy it was to be able to say, "It will therefore be inherited by my beloved son . . . at his coming of age."

But the will really concerned the property that General Riedesel had himself acquired and which he had a right to dispose of "to my only son and my five daughters." For years, he had been afraid that his girls would be left penniless. The chance to make money had come in America, as he said in his will, without giving details. But furnishings for the house in Charlottesville must have been sold at a profit. Wines were many times ordered from Madeira only to arrive too late because the General had moved on to another post. They sold well. And there was the fur trade, engaged in first by Mrs. General and pursued with success as the General asked young officers to get him "fine marten skins" when they went to frontier posts. Cash credits at the London banker's were invested with the advice of Riedesel's brother, "Imperial Court Assessor Karl Georg Riedesel," who was good at business.

General Riedesel figured that he could give each of his five daughters "10,000 reichsthalers, payable in twenty-gulden pieces, out of my capital," he said. No paper money was to be used — he had seen what happened to paper dollars in America. Riedesel pointed out that Augusta had been given 5000 reichsthalers at the time of her wedding; this was to be deducted from her 10,000 and each girl was to be given the same when she married, "in addition to a dowry conforming to her status."

To Mrs. General was given the "administration of all the property, including the entailed property of her son until his coming of age." Georg was now fourteen, probably no longer studying with tutors at home but away at school. In seven years he must give his mother "her widow's right of 2000 gulden." And during her lifetime, Mrs. General was to have the income from the 50,000 reichsthalers left to her girls. Three guardians were appointed to help her administer what was bound to be a complicated estate. They were Major-General Hans Conrad Riedesel, the brother who had once shot young Captain Friederich's horse from under him — not knowing who the captain was. Court Assessor Karl Georg was another, and a personal friend was appointed to watch over the girls in case their brother died and the interests of another heir should "come into collision" with theirs. It was not easy to provide for a widow and five well-born daughters who could never earn their keep, or marry without a dowry — but General Riedesel had done well.[1]

Four months later, the family were all gathered together again, this time in the city of Brunswick. It was the last day of December, 1799, and the next morning would usher in not only a new year but a new century. There was a big New Year's party at the General's house, with officers from the garrison at Wolfenbüttel, officers from the Court and students at Caroline College all flocking to it, to dance with the General's pretty daughters.

General Riedesel was feeling especially well on that last day of 1799. He rode his favorite horse "in the avenue" and then dressed in his best for the party. The girls enjoyed their new dresses, and their beaux; and when their father appeared they made him "dance a few rounds." Mrs. General danced more than a few rounds and they saluted the year 1800 in champagne.

The General went to the Ducal Palace next day to give Duke Charles his New Year's greeting. He had caught cold, and Mrs. General told him he ought to stay in bed. But only those out of favor would be absent from the royal reception, and General Riedesel had been the trusted friend of the ruling house of Brunswick for many years. His absence would cause comment. The General made his call brief, however, and when he got home he "had to lie down."

On the sixth of January, General Riedesel declared that he was well again. He played whist in the evening. Count Reuss, who had brought Augusta to the New Year's party, was still visiting them and said that Mrs. General's book was at the printer's. There would be a private edition just for family and friends, and Mrs. General was pleased when her husband was excited about it and eager to see it. There was "a joyful 'good-night.'" General Riedesel slept well — never to wake.

Eight years of widowhood lay ahead of Frederika von Riedesel. Friends told her what a comfort her children would be, and this was true. But she had given all her first thoughts to her husband for thirty-seven years. He would always come first in her heart, so now there was a loneliness that never left her.

The Baroness was busy, and for this she was thankful. Her husband, in his will, had directed her to sell furnishings, horses and wine, the Brunswick house, and other houses not entailed, and to live either at Lauterbach or Saxonia. She chose Lauterbach,[2] and there was the task, bound to be sad at times, of disposing of furniture, pictures, jewels, which she and her husband had bought together. But they had talked it over and decided that this must be done to raise cash for the girls' bequests. Then the money must be carefully invested, and Mrs. General would be in charge of that.

There was a renewed pang of loneliness when Mrs. General's book came from the printer. Her husband had wanted to see it. *Extracts from the Letters and Papers of General, Baron de Riedesel and His Wife née Massow, Concerning Their Common Voyage to America and Their Sojourn in That Country* was its title; it was "compiled and arranged by their son-in-law, Count Reuss. Printed as a Manuscript for the family." So the title page read. No one could say that the Baroness had disgraced her sex and her rank by becoming a woman author. And if the family found that Count Reuss had left out too much — as, for example, the name of Burgoyne's mistress in America — Mrs. General was right on hand to explain.[3]

The book was so popular that Carl Spener, a publisher in Berlin, got out a public edition. He decided to call it *The Voyage of Duty to America: Letters of Mrs. General von Riedesel Written to Germany on Her Journey and During Her Six Years' Stay in America at the Time of the War There in the Years 1776 to 1783.* He said he had shortened the title for popular taste. And if Mrs. General had any doubts about a public edition being proper she had but to remember that her husband had wanted her to increase the family capital if she could.

The book found its way to America, where bits of it were translated more or less accurately from the original German and used for the benefit of those writing "reminiscences" of the American Revolution. It is to be hoped that Mrs. General never saw any of those first American quotations from her book. Perhaps it would have amused her to learn that a man by the name of James Wilkinson claimed to know her well. He had been twenty years old at the time of the battle of Saratoga, and as aide to Gates he was somewhere on the scene during Burgoyne's surrender. Mrs. General had not noticed him. But he claimed that he had "more than once seen her charming blue eyes bedewed with tears at the recital of her sufferings."

Strange were the descriptions of her. One author in America mentioned her "small Dresden China figure," while another spoke of her as "Amazonian." Could just the beginning of pregnancy have made all that difference? But when it came to her "distracting rose-bud mouth" or her "wise little button of a mouth," she would merely have needed to look in the mirror or at her latest portrait — and laugh.

Much as her own book pleased her, one thing was still lacking. No studious young man had been found to write her husband's *Memoirs.* The Baroness gave her son the papers and told him to be sure to attend to the matter. At long last, Max von Eelking, Captain in the Saxon-Meiningen Army, wrote the *Life of General Riedesel* and made the history of the German troops in America during the Revolution almost his lifework. But Mrs. General was not to live to see these books written.

Mrs. General was always "the Baroness" now, though she would have liked to hear the name her husband gave her when he raised her to his own rank on setting out for America. Lady Fritz was a name she also liked, having been given it by Lady Carleton and her friends in Canada. But in 1808 no one remembered these things except herself. She was over sixty — older than her husband was when he died, and she knew her children thought of her as old. They were all married — except Caroline. Caroline's brother Georg would have to remember that he was required to give her a home, "hunting and fishing rights, gardens, wood and lumber and food for two horses" at the castle at Lauterbach. Frederika had married Count von Reden; and Charlotte, Major von Schoening.

The Baroness often visited Count Reuss, who was always her favorite son-in-law. She never ceased to love parties, and the King's Court in Berlin amused her. But there was one more grief in store. In 1805 Augusta, Countess Reuss, died in Berlin, aged thirty-four. Gentle, serious and conscientious, Augusta had been the one entrusted with her mother's purse in Canada when she was not quite six years old. She and her mother were especially close, perhaps because she was so much like her father.

In the spring of 1808, the Baroness was planning to go soon to the castle at Lauterbach with children and grandchildren. But on March 29 the Baroness Frederika von Riedesel died suddenly in Berlin. She left no will — only a last request, which was granted. They laid her beside her husband in the family vault at Lauterbach.

Acknowledgments

I want to thank JULIA WARD STICKLEY first of all, for introducing me to the Baroness Frederika Riedesel. No historical account of the Battles of Saratoga is complete without some mention of the Baroness and she always appears in fiction connected with this decisive action in the American Revolution. But Mrs. Stickley piloted me through the intricacies of the National Archives in Washington, where the Riedesels and their children emerged as real people in the Force Papers and other documents.

MR. ROBERT W. HILL, Keeper of Manuscripts, Manuscript Division, New York Public Library, gave me guidance in the early stages of my research and made available a treasure-trove of material in the Riedesel Papers, Bancroft Collection. The many volumes of Brunswick Journals and the Schuyler Papers alone illuminate all printed sources — such as the firsthand accounts of Mrs. General Riedesel and her husband.

At Mr. Hill's direction, I wrote to Colonial Williamsburg and received their kind permission to use in New York the photostats of the British Headquarters Papers, with their "secret documents," letters to be "put into cypher" and letters to be read through a mask. I also want to thank MRS. SHIRLEY SPRANGER for her unfailing assistance in the American History Room, New York Public Library.

I am indebted to the STAFF AT THE NEW-YORK HISTORICAL SOCIETY LIBRARY for much help as I worked with the voluminous

Gates Papers and the smaller collections of manuscripts of officers on Gates's staff. To the NEW YORK GENEALOGICAL AND BIOGRAPHICAL SOCIETY I am grateful for guidance concerning the family background of Americans encountered by the Baroness.

Of great importance as a source are the Canadian Archives at Ottawa, Canada. I wish to express appreciation for the kindness my husband and I received there as we read many volumes of hand-written records and made selections for photostating. In Quebec, our good friend M. JEAN-CHARLES BONENFANT gave valuable information on early Canadian affairs. I wish also to thank ANTOINE PELLETIER, Assistant Librarian of the Provincial Museum of Quebec. In Montreal, M. JULES BAZIN, Head Librarian, Civic Library, City of Montreal, provided me with information I am sure I could not have found anywhere else.

Most important for the American side of this story are the papers deposited by MR. HALL PARK MCCULLOCH at the library of the Bennington Museum. I am especially grateful for Mr. McCulloch's permission to use manuscripts he has collected and to MR. ALLEN D. HILL, Genealogical Consultant, for his assistance. MR. FRANCIS S. RONALDS, Superintendent, Morristown National Historical Park, placed at my disposal the large collection of papers to which I have referred in notes as "Morristown Transcripts," and I am most grateful to him and to MR. HANS MEYER, Librarian, for this addition to my research material. I shall not soon forget the friendly staff at the Morristown museum.

Once more, as so often before, MR. STEPHEN T. RILEY, Director of the Massachusetts Historical Society, has placed me in his debt by calling my attention to unusual manuscripts. I want to thank MISS CAROLINE JAKEMAN, Librarian, Houghton Library of Harvard University, for calling my attention to the Dearborn Papers. At the Alderman Library, University of Virginia, my husband and I met with most cordial assistance. At my own home-town library in Darien, Connecticut, I can always count on the kind efforts of the staff, and at the Ferguson Library in Stamford, Connecticut, MISS GRACE WALMSLEY, reference librarian, always has an answer to my questions.

At the Schuyler House in Schuylerville (once Saratoga), New York, my husband and I had the good fortune to find MRS. DANIEL BARRETT, of the local Historical Society, author of a series of articles on Schuylerville history. Mrs. Barrett told us we must see "the Riedesel house," and arranged an appointment for us with the owner, MRS. KENNETH BULLARD. No one could have been kinder than Mrs. Bullard, and we had the happy experience of coming as strangers and leaving as friends. I am also indebted to Mrs. Bullard for pictures of the Riedesels, as indicated in Notes (Ch. 29).

I want to speak with especial appreciation of my translators, MRS. CONSTANCE BRUZELIUS and DR. CLEMENTINE ZERNICK. Their fine work is noted where their work for this book is used. DR. HAROLD BOWDITCH contributed a translation from a German medical work, as noted, and MRS. LOVELL THOMPSON called my attention to the mention of "Miss America Riedesel" in the *Diary and Letters of Gouverneur Morris*, edited by Anne Cary Morris (New York, 1888: Scribner).

Chapter Notes

1: THE BARONESS

1. Johann Heinrich Tischbein the elder (1722–1789) studied in Paris under Watteau and shows Watteau's influence.

2. Pronunciation "Ree-day-zel" is from *Riedesel*, Stone.

3. Riedesel was an ensign at the age of nineteen, a captain after the battle of Minden. See *Memoirs and Letters and Journals of Major General Riedesel During His Residence in America*, translated from the original German of Max von Eelking by William L. Stone (Albany, 1868: Joel Munsell) — hereafter called *Riedesel*, Stone.

4. Cash paid by Great Britain to the Duke of Brunswick is from *The Hessians and Other Auxiliaries of Great Britain in the Revolutionary War*, by Edward J. Lowell (New York, 1884: Harper) — hereafter called *The Hessians*, Lowell. Cash values have been recalculated for modern currency.

5. Acland is the spelling according the *Encyclopaedia Americana* and other modern sources, although it is Ackland in William L. Stone, B. J. Lossing, Mrs. Elizabeth F. L. Ellet and other early writers.

6. For the numbers of women camp followers, see *The Hessians*, Lowell; also *Women Camp Followers of the American Revolution*, by Walter Hart Blumenthal (Philadelphia, 1952: McManus).

2: MRS. GENERAL

1. Brunswick sent a total of 5723 troops, including later recruits, according to *The Hessians*, Lowell.

2. See "Memoirs of a Hessian Conscript: J. G. Seume's Reluctant Voyage to America," translated by Margarete Woelfel; *William and Mary College Quarterly Historical Magazine*, October 1948, pp. 553-670 (Williamsburg).

3. The ages of the Riedesel children are from *Riedesel*, Stone, Vol. I, p. 8, footnote. Further genealogical material has been culled for me by Dr. Clementine Zernick, from German sources.

4. Beer soup: According to *A Short History of the German People*, by Ernest F. Henderson, Vol. I, p. 201 (New York, 1902: Macmillan). Frederick the Great told his subjects that coffee was bad for them. He put a duty on it of 250 per cent, sent "sniffers" around to detect illegal coffee drinkers, and said that he himself had been raised on beer soup.

5. Material for this chapter comes directly from *Letters and Journals Relating to the War of the American Revolution and the Capture of the German Troops at Saratoga* by Mrs. General Riedesel, translated from the original German by William L. Stone (Albany: 1876: Joel Munsell) — hereafter called *Madam Riedesel*.

3: THEY POINT THE FINGER

1. In response to my query, J. L. Purchase, Secretary to the Lord Mayor of Bristol, England, very kindly sent the following letter: ". . . The Mayor of Bristol in 1776 was Andrew Pope, a sugar-baker. . . . There were several members of the Foy family who were merchants of Bristol in the eighteenth century. One of the most notable was Nathaniel Foy, councillor, 1756–1783, who became an alderman in 1776 . . . Mayor, 1772–1773. . . . By his will, made 21 December, 1779, which is preserved in the City Archives Office, the chief beneficiaries are Hannah Foy, 'widow of my late nephew Captain Edward Foy deceased, and her only child, Nathaniel Foy,' who was a minor in 1779."

2. "Sunday the 26 ult Capt. Foy was married to Miss Hannah Van Horne, daughter of John Van Horne Esq. of Kills-Hall." — *New York Journal*, Aug. 6, 1772.

"The *Arethusa*, Capt. Hammond, is shortly expected" from New York, "in which . . . will come . . . Captains Campbell and Foy and some other ladies and gentlemen." — *Virginia Gazette*, Oct. 8, 1772.

For a description of Van Horne houses near Middlebrook, Bridgewater Township, New Jersey, see *Pre-revolutionary Dutch Houses and Families* by Rosalie Fellows Bailey (New York, 1936: William Morrow).

Children of John Van Horne were Hannah, Elizabeth and Catherine. See *Jan Wallace Cornelius Van Horne and His Descendants*, by Charles Selwyn Williams New York: 1912, Philip Van Horne, brother of John, had four sons and three daughters. The Marquis de Chastellux stopped at the John Van Horne's in 1780 and met "three daughters." References to "five daughters" in some sources must have included some of the Philip Van Horne cousins, who lived nearby.

4: MEANWHILE, THE GENERAL . . .

1. Sir Guy Carleton succeeded Sir James Murray as "Governor of Canada." Carleton is often called "Governor of Quebec," as though someone else out-

ranked him; but this title comes from a royal proclamation of 1763 dividing territory acquired after the French and Indian War into regions called Quebec, East Florida, West Florida and Granada. Carleton's territory included the Ohio and Mississippi River regions. See *The Tercentenary History of Canada from Champlain to Laurier* by Frank Basil Tracy (Toronto, 1908: P. F. Collier and Son).

2. For Canadian background material, I am indebted to *Cinq Femmes et Nous* by B. DuFèbre (Quebec, 1950: Belisle) and *Un Général Allemand au Canada, le Baron Friedrich Adolphus von Riedesel*, by Georges Monarque (Montreal, 1946: Imprimerie Populaire Limité.).

3. Arnold's letter describing the American retreating army is from *The Life and Times of Philip Schuyler*, by Benson J. Lossing (New York, 1883: Henry Holt) — hereafter referred to as *Schuyler*, Lossing.

4. For a description of the British point of view as to what happened at Three Rivers, see *The British Invasion from the North: The Campaigns of Carleton and Burgoyne from Canada, 1776–77, with the Journal of Lieut.17 William Digby of the 53d or Shropshire Regiment of Foot*, by James Phinney Baxter. (Albany, 1887: Joel Munsell) — hereafter referred to as Digby.

5. "Indians . . . walked freely through our camp . . ." See Digby.

6. "Carpenters ordered . . ." See Digby.

In August 1935, work was begun to raise the gunboat *Philadelphia*. This boat, with everything that was in her remarkably preserved, may be seen near Willsboro, New York Route 22.

7. Job Cook's letter is from the Schuyler Papers, Manuscript Division, New York Public Library — hereafter abbreviated as Ms. Div., N.Y. Pub. Lib.

8. Riedesel to the Duke of Brunswick *re* Howe is from the Force Papers, Washington Archives, Washington, D. C. Riedesel spells Howe "*Hau*."

9. Riedesel to the Duke *re* British finances is from the French in the Riedesel Papers, Bancroft Collection, Ms. Div., N.Y. Pub. Lib. All translations from Riedesel's French are my own.

5: THE FIRST THRUST

1. Captain Christopher Carleton "of the 31st English Regiment" was "first Aide-de-Camp to his uncle . . . has lived among the Indians" and "had an Indian wife. His present wife is a very pretty woman, a My Lady, the sister of General Carleton's wife," according to *Letters from America 1776–1779, Being Letters of Brunswick, Hessian and Waldeck Officers with the British Armies during the Revolution*, translated by Ray W. Pettingill, Ph.D. (Boston, 1924: Houghton Mifflin.) — hereafter called Pettingill.

2. For further details of what the Indians did and did not wear, see *Hadden's Journal and Orderly Books, A Journal Kept in Canada and Upon*

Burgoyne's Campaign in 1776 and 1777, by Lieutenant James M. Hadden, Roy. Art., also Orders kept by him and issued by Sir Guy Carlton, Lieut. General John Burgoyne and Major General William Phillips, in 1776, 1777, and 1778, with an Explanatory Note by Horatio Rogers, Brevet General U.S.V. . . . etc. (Albany, 1884: Joel Munsell) — hereafter referred to as Hadden.

3. The Whitcomb story is told in Hadden, in Digby, and in *Riedesel, Stone.* His own report is in *American Archives,* (5 Series) Vol. I, p. 828: "A Journal of a Scout from Crown-Point to St. John's, Chambly etc. etc. . . ." Whitcomb set out with four men, but "the two Frenchmen" were afraid to approach St. Johns so he told them to interview some former neighbors and return to Ticonderoga. He later sent his other men back, with further information; and eventually he returned alone via the west bank of Champlain, which he said was difficult "without a compass."

4. The Battle of Valcour Island is from *The Journal of Captain Pausch, Chief of the Hanau Artillery during the Burgoyne Campaign,* translated and annotated by William L. Stone (Albany, 1886: Joel Munsell) — hereafter called *Pausch.*

5. For the American point of view, see *The Traitor and The Spy* by James Thomas Flexner (New York, 1953: Harcourt, Brace).

6. "Butonmole Bay:" See *Riedesel, Stone,* Vol. I, p. 80. But remains of the *Congress* and four gun boats were found in "Ferris Bay, now called Arnold's Bay" in the township of Paton; "The British arrived before the *Congress* exploded and fired on the men on shore, and at the house of Squire Peter Ferris, which was struck by one cannon ball and several grape shot." Parts of the *Congress* could be seen in the lake, and local citizens did a thriving business selling walking canes made from wood taken from the wreck. See clipping (William L. Stone clipping-book, Library, Fort Ticonderoga, dated Vergennes, Jan. 28, 1861 — an article by Philip C. Tucker).

6: WINTER IN LONDON

1. For a scholarly picture of the period, see *George III, The Story of a Complex Man* by J. C. Long (Boston, 1960: Little, Brown).

2. "Apart from a handful of close friends," Queen Charlotte "was generally disliked." See *Love and the Princess* by Lucille Iremonger (New York, 1960: Crowell). If this is true, then the Baroness was among the Queen's "handful" of friends.

7: WINTER IN CANADA

1. Carleton's marriage, see *Cinq Femmes Et Nous* by B. Dufèbre.

2. All letters from Mich Murray are from the Morristown Transcripts.

These transcriptions were made for William Van Vleck Lidgerwood at the archives at Marburg and Wolfenbüttel, and cover the years 1775–1784. The "Hessian Transcripts" were given by Mr. Lidgerwood to the Washington Association of New Jersey, and by them to the Morristown National Historic Park. They may be consulted at the library of the museum, Morristown, N.J. Letters in German and French have, in some cases, been translated, but for the French I have made my own translation. This valuable material will hereafter be referred to as "Morristown Transcripts."

3. For carioling, see Digby, and Pettingill.

4. The dead "pending burial": See *Travels through the Interior Parts of America in a Series of Letters by an Officer,* by Thomas Anburey, Vol. I pp. 161–162 — hereafter referred to as Anburey. Thomas Anburey was a volunteer in the British army in 1776, with the 29th Regiment of Foot. His book is written as a series of letters, supposedly from the scene of action. Anburey undoubtedly used some of his own letters — but he included incidents observed by others, claiming them as his own experiences, and he borrowed liberally from contemporary travel books. His book was first printed in 1789 with two English editions, three French, and a German edition following. See *Thomas Anburey's 'Travels through America,' a note on Eighteenth-Century Plagiarism,* by Whitfield J. Bell, Jr. in the *Bibliographical Society of America Papers,* 37: No. 1, pp. 23–36, 1943.

5. Rum at Ticonderoga: See Varick to Schuyler, Nov. 20, 1776, in Schuyler Papers, Ms. Div., N.Y. Pub. Lib.

6. Riedesel to the Duke of Brunswick, May 6, 1777, is headed *à mettre en chiffre.* See Riedesel Papers, Bancroft Collection, Ms. Div., N.Y. Pub. Lib.

8: "WELCOME TO THE CANADIAN CONTINENT"

1. For distances in Canada I have used *The Dominion of Canada . . . Handbook for Travellers,* by Karl Baedeker, a 1900 edition. But roads are often rebuilt and all distances are approximate. In *The Brunswick Journal,* kept by officers of General Riedesel's troops, distances are accurately set down according to the German system. *The Brunswick Journal,* partly in French, partly in German, is in the Bancroft Collection, Ms. Div., N.Y. Pub. Lib.

German distances were usually measured in feet and rods. A German mile was 4.6 English miles. "To find the length of a rood in the right and lawful way and according to scientific usage, you shall do as follows: stand at the door of a church on a Sunday and bid sixteen men to stop, tall ones and small ones, as they happen to pass out when the service is finished; then make them put their left feet one behind the other, and the length thus obtained shall be a right and lawful rood to measure and survey the land with, and the sixteenth part of it shall be a right and lawful foot" — according to Koebel. See *The New International Encyclopaedia* (New York, 1916; Dodd Mead).

2. *Les Ursulines des Trois-rivières depuis leur Etablissement jusqu'à nos Jours*, by A. M. D. G. (copyrighted by the Ursulines in 1888) gives an interesting picture not only of the establishment but of the town. *Les Cahiers des Dix*, Number 22, 1957, tells of American prisoners at the Ursuline hospital whose bills were never paid.

3. Neither General Riedesel nor Mrs. General understood place names in Canada accurately, but George Monarque in *Un Général Allemand au Canada* has identified towns and villages mentioned.

9: SECOND THRUST

1. For the mislaid orders to Howe, see *Gentleman Johnny Burgoyne, Misadventures of an English General in the Revolution*, by R. J. Huddleston (Indianapolis, 1927: Bobbs-Merrill).

> Sir William, he, snug as a flea,
> Lay all this time a-snoring,
> Nor dreamed of harm as he lay warm
> In bed with Mrs. Loring.
> —From "The Battle of the Kegs," by
> Francis Hopkinson, lawyer and
> signer of the Declaration of Independence.

3. Joshua Loring; see Vol. XI of the *Dictionary of American Biography* (New York, 1928: Scribner's) — hereafter referred to as D. A. B.

4. All statistics are approximate. For Burgoyne's army, see Hadden, p. LXIV. See also *The turning point of the Revolution, or Burgoyne in America*, by Hoffman Nickerson. (Boston, 1928: Houghton Mifflin Co.).

5. For Governor Livingston's satirical poem, see *Ballads and Poems Relating to the Burgoyne Campaign*, annotated by William L. Stone (Albany, 1893: Joel Munsell).

6. Gilliland or Guilliland wrote a series of letters demanding a guard for his property and demanding "boats or carriages" for his transportation to Albany. See Schuyler Papers, Ms. Div. N. Y. Pub. Lib.

7. The dragoons' gun was "a rifle," according to *The Hessians*, Lowell, p. 195.

8. Brunswick uniform: See *Visits to the Saratoga Battle-ground*, by William L. Stone (Albany, 1895: Joel Munsell series no. 23) — hereafter called *Visits*, Stone.

10: WITHIN THE WALLS

1. For troubles with Congress, see *Schuyler*, Lossing.

For Schuyler as a man, an affectionate father, a much-loved general, see Schuyler Papers, Ms. Div. N. Y. Pub. Lib.

2. Schuyler's integrity is still being debated. I found only one questionable incident. On April 24, 1777, Lt. Moses Robinson wrote to Horatio Gates: "Your Honor may remember that at your request I march'd a part of my regiment to Ticonderoga last October. For which service I never rec'v'd any pay. The pay rolls have been made up and attested to, application made to Genl. Schuyler for a warrant to draw the money — but he refused to sign the same unless we acknowledged we were in the State of New York. Which people on the Grants are not willing." Schuyler Papers, Ms. Div. N.Y. Pub. Lib.

3. For Ticonderoga after Schuyler was superseded, see Gates Papers, New York Historical Society.

4. See *Fort Ticonderoga, A Short History* by S. H. P. Pell. See also *The Narration from Mt. Defiance* by James M. Lonegan; (1953: Historic Mt. Defiance, Inc.).

5. Richard Varick (1753–1831) was devoted to Schuyler and also worshiped Arnold as his hero. He was appointed aide to Arnold at West Point and was "prostrated" by Arnold's treason. Acquitted of complicity with Arnold, he was chosen to record Washington's letters. In 1788 he was attorney general in New York, and was mayor of New York City in 1789.

6. Henry Brockholst Livingston (1757–1823) was aide to General St. Clair as well as to Schuyler. In 1779 he went to Spain as private secretary to John Jay, who was his brother-in-law. On his return he was captured at sea by the British. While awaiting exchange he studied law in New York. He opposed the Jay Treaty, his friend Varick taking the other side.

7. Letters of Varick and Livingston are in the Schuyler Papers, Ms. Div. N.Y. Pub. Lib.; and at the Massachusetts Historical Society. See also *Letters on the American Revolution in the Library at 'Karolfred,'* edited by F. R. Kirkland (New York, 1952: Coward-McCann) — hereafter referred to as *Letters*, Kirkland.

11: THE FALL OF TICONDEROGA

1. William Twiss was exchanged immediately after the Battle of Saratoga and went back to Canada, where he designed and built fortifications. He eventually became a General in the Royal Engineers. See Hadden, p. 171, footnote.

2. Henry B. Livingston to his father after the fall of Ticonderoga: ". . . in short, we retreated or rather fled, so precipitously that not an individual article, except the military chest, was saved, not a single officer saved any of his baggage but what he had on . . ." Sparks transcripts, Houghton Library, Harvard College.

3. For the escape of the invalids, see *The American Revolution from the Commencement to the Disbanding of the American Army: Given in the Form of a Daily Journal . . .*, by James Thacher, M.D. (New York, 1860: American Subscription Publishing House).

4. For Ebenezer Fletcher, see *The Narrative and Sufferings of Ebenezer Fletcher of New Ipswich (New Hampshire) Written by Himself and Published at the Request of His Friends* (1827: Charles L. Bushnell).

5. Oxen "half skinned . . .": See Patrick Cogan to Colonel Stark in *A Life of General John Stark of New Hampshire* by Howard Parker Moore (1949: privately published).

6. For the memorandum of Riedesel to Burgoyne on horses, see Riedesel Papers, Bancroft Collection, Ms. Div. N.Y. Pub. Lib.; in French.

12: THE BARONESS AT FORT EDWARD

1. Many letters of Philip Skene and other documents have been collected by Mr. Hall Park McCulloch and deposited at the Bennington Museum Library. I quote from these papers with Mr. McCulloch's kind permission and I wish I had space to tell Skene's story in more detail. *Philip Skene of Skenesborough*, by Doris Begor Morton (Granville, New York, 1959: Grastorf Press), presents Skene in a more favorable light than his own letters indicate, in my opinion.

2. Fort George is described as "near" Fort William Henry, now carefully restored. On exhibition at Fort Ticonderoga is a charming toy, a whistle made of china in the shape of a shepherd boy, found during excavations. It is supposed that it could have belonged to the Riedesel children. But they did not go to Ticonderoga, and there were plenty of other children with Burgoyne's army.

3. *Old Fort Edward before 1800: An account of the historic ground now occupied by the village of Fort Edward, New York*, by William H. Hill (Fort Edward, 1929: privately printed) contains a careful sifting of fact from legend.

4. *Reminiscences of the Revolution, or Le Loup's Bloody Trail from Salem to Fort Edward*, by Arthur Reid (Utica: 1859) gives details of Indian attacks.

5. At the library at Fort Ticonderoga, in William L. Stone's book of clippings, is a printed letter by Dr. Asa Fitch to Dr. E. B. O'Calligan, 1850. The McNeil house is described as "some 16 feet by 20 in size, built of round logs with a door on the east side only, an old-fashioned fireplace without jambs at its north end, on one side of which were ladderlike stairs leading to a loft overhead and rather to the south of the center of the floor, a trap door opening into an unwalled cellar-hole beneath." It was "demolished in 1809." It was "about 60 rods north of the fort."

13: BENNINGTON

1. "Weights from sundry clocks": See Heath Papers, Vol. VI, Massachusetts Historical Society.

2. The American side of the Battle of Bennington is told in the Hall Park McCulloch Papers deposited at The Bennington Museum Library, Bennington, Vt. (See 1211).

3. Burgoyne's collecting flour sacks is from a letter of Francis Carr Clark, aide to Burgoyne, to Riedesel, August 8, 1777, in Morristown Transcripts.

4. Orders for Baum's detachment . . .: See *Riedesel*, Stone, Vol. I p. 262. See also *The German Allied Troops in the North American War of Independence*, by Max von Eelking, translated by J. G. Rosengarten (Albany, 1893: Joel Munsell) — hereafter called Von Eelking.

5. Baum's orders written down by Riedesel are in the Riedesel Papers, Bancroft Collection, Ms. Div. N.Y. Pub. Lib.

6. References to modern roads are from personal observation, but distances are only approximate because of the many route changes throughout the years.

7. In 1756 "no duty was to be paid on Pot and Pearl Ashes from America," and "British wool manufacturers, glassmakers, linen weavers, clamored for more and more American potash." It was one of the few exports permitted to the colonists, and commanded a high price. See *Vermont Tradition* by Dorothy Canfield Fisher, Chapter 10 (Boston, 1953: Little, Brown).

8. The Bennington expedition cost Burgoyne "between 800 and 850 of all ranks, including Tories and Indians." See *The Turning Point of the Revolution*, by Hoffman Nickerson.

14: THE ROAD TO ALBANY

1. Burgoyne sent Mrs. Higgins to Lord Howe with a letter and a secret verbal message. Howe offered to exchange "her husband and Mr. Clarke, both Deputy Commissaries under the Convention of Saratoga" for one American deputy commissary. Howe referred to her as "the fair lady." See British Headquarters Papers; the Headquarters Papers covering the period of the American Revolution were acquired by Rockefeller for Colonial Williamsburg. They were photostated, one copy being given to the Ms. Div. N.Y. Pub. Lib. I am indebted to Colonial Williamsburg for permission to quote from these papers, which will be hereafter referred as B. HQ. Papers, Photostat, Ms. Div. N.Y. Pub. Lib.

2. "Half Moon" was named for Henry Hudson's ship. Riedesel wrote it "Half Mohn." Camp Van Schaick, or Half Moon, is at the intersection of

Park and Van Schaick Avenues, Cohoes, New York. The Van Schaick mansion, Gates's headquarters, is open to the public. See *New York, A Guide to
the Empire State*, (New York, 1956: American Guide Series, Oxford Press).

3. "Captain Whitcomb returned last evening after a scout of eight days.
He says the main body of the enemy are between Fort Edward and Fort
Anne with their baggage and stores. . . . He had several hair-breadth escapes
but kept himself and his party (consisting of four privates) safe till they got
between this and Fort Miller. They were then surprised by a few Indians
who have taken or killed all his men." See Kirkland, Livingston to Varick,
Aug. 3, 1777; Vol. II, Letter 24.

4. For Skene's financial affairs, see the Hall Park McCulloch Papers,
Library, Bennington Museum Library.

5. Lieutenant (afterwards Admiral) John Schank built the boats for the
Hudson bridge at Crown Point, 70 miles away. He equipped them with
chains, so they could be fastened together, and with mast and sail for the
lake crossing. He is also credited with the invention of the centerboard sail-
boat. See *Hadden*, Appendix 18, also p. LXXVI.

6. "Boundless forests": See Digby p. 235.

7. "Camp life was irksome": H. B. Livingston to Schuyler, September 19,
1777. Schuyler Papers, Ms. Div. N.Y. Pub. Lib.

8. A map of 1877 shows the Schuyler house on the west side of the highway to Stillwater. It is on the east side of the new road at Schuylerville
and is being restored as a public monument, open to visitors.

15: THE BATTLES OF SARATOGA

1. The battle fields of Saratoga attracted visitors as early as 1780. "The
woods continually rise toward the west . . . with eminences but no summits,"
see *Travels in North-America in the Years 1780, 1781 and 1782*, by the Marquis de Chastellux — hereafter called *Travels*, de Chastellux.

"A great part of the battle field was occupied by lofty trees, principally
pine, with here and there a few cleared fields of which the most conspicuous
was Freeman's Farm. . . . Many gigantic trees still remain . . . shew wounds
in their trunks and branches. . . ." See *Remarks on a Short Tour between
Hartford and Quebec in the Autumn of 1819*, by Benjamin Silliman (1820:
Converse).

Today, the Saratoga National Park provides guide service and publishes
information with helpful maps. But the park does not include the field of
Burgoyne's last stand, nor his place of surrender — commemorated by the
Saratoga Monument at Schuylerville (the original Saratoga) and marked
with tablets.

2. *Riedesel*, Stone, contains an account of Saratoga; but I have used a

manuscript in French from the Riedesel Papers, Bancroft Collection, Ms. Div. N.Y. Pub. Lib. as more colorful.

3. The house where the Baroness lived during the action at Freeman's Farm and Bemis Heights was recently burned. A guide at the Saratoga National Park kindly pointed out its location and my husband and I visited the spot — a cellarhole near the Hudson. But the house had been moved; it was once much nearer the great redoubt. A photograph shows the house to have been remodeled in the Victorian manner.

4. Burgoyne to Powell, see Gates Papers, New-York Historical Society. Brigadier Powell to Burgoyne: see B. HQ Papers, Photostat, Ms. Div. N.Y. Pub. Lib.

5. German-American letter, see Gates Papers, New-York Historical Society.

6. It was a *four*-pronged advance at Bemis Heights according to *Visits*, Stone, and *Travels*, de Chastellux. But it looked like three prongs to Riedesel, who did not count Fraser's advance corps.

16:   MRS. GENERAL IN COMMAND

1. The story of Lady Acland's joining her husband after he became Gates's prisoner is told in *The Women of the American Revolution* by Elizabeth F. L. Ellet, Vol. I Chapter X. (New York, 1848: Baker and Scribner). But she was a sort of female Parson Weems, using her imagination freely. Her tales have caused historians a good deal of trouble. Major Acland was not killed in a duel — he died of natural causes. Lady Acland was not "deprived of her reason" for two years because of "the shock of his death," and she did not marry Chaplain Brudenel but remained a widow until her death. Wilkinson in his *Memoirs* and Fonblanque in his biography of Burgoyne both have her married to Brudenel, but William L. Stone wrote to the Acland family in England and "exploded the theory." See Hadden, LV, footnote.

2. William L. Stone includes the first-hand account of "General Ebenezer Mattoon" in his *Visits*.

3. The *Diary of Captain Benjamin Warren on the Battle Field of Saratoga* was transcribed by David E. Alexander, from the Jared Sparks Collection of Manuscripts deposited in the Library of Harvard University, and published in the *Journal of American History*, Vol. 3, p. 201, 1909, no. II second quarter. In 1909, the whereabouts of the original diary were not known. Benjamin Warren was born in Plymouth, March 1740, son of Captain Benjamin Warren, descendant of Richard Warren, Mayflower immigrant.

4. Reynels (Stone) or Reynal (Hadden).

5. *Madam Riedesel*, Stone, says that it was "Captain Thomas Bloomfield" (not "Major Plumfield") who was wounded through his cheeks.

17: TROOPS OF THE CONVENTION

1. For Digby, see Chapter 4 Note 4.

2. An account of the proceedings just before Burgoyne's surrender was written by Heinrich Urban von Cleve, adjutant of the Brunswick troops and aide to Riedesel. This manuscript is in Volume R of the Force Papers, Manuscript Library, Library of Congress, Washington, D.C. There is an abstract in English and, through the kindness of Mrs. Julia Ward Stickley of National Archives, I have had it compared with the original by a German translator. Another account is in the National Archives, Ottawa, Canada.

3. The hollow bullet recovered from Daniel Taylor is on display in the museum at Fort Ticonderoga. Accounts of Taylor's capture are from the Gates Papers, New-York Historical Society, New York City.

4. The burning of Kingston is from the Schuyler Papers, Ms. Div., N.Y. Pub. Lib., and *The American Rebellion, Sir Henry Clinton's Narrative of His Campaigns, 1775-1782, with an Appendix of Original Documents*, edited by William B. Willcox (1954: Yale University, New Haven).

5. Wilkinson in his *Memoirs . . .* places Gates on horseback — not so Digby, nor the anonymous German who described the scene, wigs and all, in Pettingill.

18: OVERLAND JOURNEY

1. The Schuyler mansion in Albany is open to the Public and is well worth a visit.

2. Burgoyne's "Official" letter is from the Canadian Archives, Ottawa, Canada. His "separate and private" letter is from the B. HQ., photostat copy, Ms. Div., N.Y. Pub. Lib.

3. John B. Church was associated with Alexander Hamilton in establishing the National Bank.

4. For "bundling board," see *Bundling, Its Origin, Progress and Decline in America* by Henry Reed Stiles. (Privately printed, no date.)

19: THE BARONESS IN CAMBRIDGE

1. "Colleges illuminated." See *Diary of the American Revolution from Newspapers and Original Documents*, edited by Frank Moore, Vol. II, p. 513 (New York, 1858: Scribner's).

2. General Heath refers to himself as "our General" in his autobiography, *Heath's Memoirs of the American War*, written in 1789 (New York, 1904: and reprinted by A. Wessels Co.). This was supposed to be just a literary device, but Hannah Winthrop's letters show that "our General" was what his neighbors called him.

3. All correspondence to and from Heath is from the Heath Papers, Massachusetts Historical Society.

4. As commander in chief in Boston in 1776, Gage had a salary of ten pounds per day, and Burgoyne, as major general, two pounds ten. B. HQ. Papers photostat, Ms. Div. N.Y. Pub. Lib.

5. The Riedesel house in Cambridge is still standing, Number 149 Brattle Street. Dr. Harold Bowditch and Mr. Howard Turner have kindly supplied me with material concerning it. The house has been moved across Riedesel Avenue from its original site, and extensively remodeled.

6. *The Journal of Ernst Johann Schuler von Senden* was presented anonymously by a descendant to *American Heritage* and given by them to the Morristown National Historic Park. Mr. Hans Meyer, Librarian of the Morristown Museum Library, has compared it with a printed version in German at the New York Public Library and has found interesting variations. He translated portions of it; the untranslated sections relating to my subject I have had translated especially for this book by Mrs. Constance Bruzelius.

20: PEACEFUL CAMBRIDGE

1. In the Morristown Transcripts is a list of articles Captain Willoe bought for General Riedesel. They were received on board the Schooner *Industry*, which was held so long in Halifax that it arrived in Boston after the Riedesels left. There was "a box anchovies and mustard . . . raisins, oranges & citron, A Box Linnen, Chip hats etc.," probably summer hats for the Baroness and the little girls.

2. The description of the Henley trial is from Pettingill, p. 137.

3. Burgoyne's departure is from the *Bulletin of the Newport Historical Society*, No. 86, Jan. 1933: "Newport Harbor and Lower Narragansett Bay, Rhode Island, during the American Revolution," a paper read by Mrs. Elizabeth Covell.

4. The letter describing "masks" for secret communications is from B.HQ. Papers, photostat copy, Ms. Div., N.Y. Pub. Lib.

5. The punishment for desertion was to be "forever degraded and afterwards punished by running the gantlet through 200 men, 12 times in 2 days, 6 times each day." Haldimand Papers, Canadian Archives, Ottawa, Canada.

6. Armand's letter to Riedesel, 31 May, 1778, is in the Gates papers, New-York Historical Society Library. See also, *The New-York Historical Society Quarterly*, Vol. XLV (January 1961), Number 1, "Colonel Armand and Washington's Cavalry," by John H. Stutesman, Jr., with a portrait of this astonishing gentleman by Charles Willson Peale (*c.* 1783).

21: MARCHING ORDERS

1. For the French Fleet, see *Memoirs* of General Heath (Chapter 19, Note 2).

2. For John Hancock's breakfast party, see *The Memorial History of Boston*, edited by Justin Winsor (Boston, 1886: Ticknor).

3. This decidedly mysterious letter, Phillips to Riedesel, ". . . *si nous avions attaqué* . . ." is from Morristown Transcripts.

4. Correspondence with the British concerning money goes on at great length, with itemized accounts, in the B.HQ. Papers, Photostat, Ms. Div. N.Y. Pub. Lib.

5. Angelica Schuyler Church's son: See Schuyler Papers, Ms. Div. N.Y. Pub. Lib.

6. For the departure of Mrs. Harnage, see Gates Papers, New-York Historical Society.

7. Refusal of permission to go into Boston: See above source.

8. The story of the German march southward is from *The Journal of Du Roi the Elder, Lieutenant and Adjutant in the Service of the Duke of Brunswick, 1776–1778.* Translated from the original German Manuscript in the Library of Congress, Washington, D.C., by Charlotte S. J. Epping. *American Germania*, edited by M. D. Learned, No. 15, University of Pennsylvania (New York, 1911: D. Apleton). The University of Pennsylvania Press kindly gives permission to quote.

22: THE LONG ROAD

1. I have endeavored to identify the places mentioned by Du Roi on a modern road map and my husband and I took the journey to Charlottesville by the route described. It was a long road, even by car, but a most interesting one.

2. Robert Troup to Gates, Gates Papers, New-York Historical Society.

3. John Laurens (1754–1782) was born in Charleston, South Carolina. He had been studying law at the Inner Temple in London, but came home to join in the American struggle for independence, becoming a volunteer aide to Washington in 1777. He was "angered by the constant personal abuse of Washington" by Major General Charles Lee, according to the official story. It was said that Lee used his slight wound to avoid duels with other challengers, and everyone seemed to forget that Washington had forbidden dueling. John Laurens was taken prisoner at Charleston, South Carolina, exchanged, and sent to France as "envoy extraordinary" at the age of twenty-six. "Recklessly" brave, he stormed a British redoubt at Yorktown, and was eventually killed in the "irregular warfare" which thereafter continued in South Carolina.

23: THE BARONESS IN VIRGINIA

1. Two water color sketches by von Senden show a Charlottesville hut

before and after completion. They accompanied von Senden's *Journal* and are at the library of the Museum at Morristown.

2. Negotiations for Colle are from the Morristown Transcripts.

3. Letters to and from General Riedesel are in the *Papers of Thomas Jefferson*, edited by Julian P. Boyd, Vol. II (Princeton, 1950: Princeton University Press).

4. Some of the prisoners borrowed books from Jefferson's library. Other young officers quartered in Charlottesville underestimated the potency of peach brandy and one "Robt. Dobson" was obliged to apologize. "I am informed I made use of the word Reptell," he wrote. He said he had not meant it to be "injurious to my acquaintance in Virginia." Bland Papers, University of Virginia Library, Charlottesville, Virginia.

5. For weather, see *Thomas Jefferson's Garden Book*, 1776–1824, annotated by Edwin Morris Betts (Philadelphia, 1944: The American Philosophical Society).

6. For Mazzei's auction, see *William and Mary College Quarterly Historical Magazine*, William and Mary College Press, Vol. IX, second series, October, 1929, No. 4, second installment, "Memoires of Philip Mazzei" translated by Dr. E. C. Branchi.

7. Monticello as the Baroness saw it, see *Old Pictures of Monticello*, by James A. Bear, Jr., Curator of Monticello, University of Virginia Press, 1957.

8. Because there is no mention of the Jeffersons in Madame Riedesel's published journal and because of Jefferson's assumption that Riedesel's horses ruined Mazzei's grapevines, it has been concluded that the two families were not friends. Letters indicate the contrary. See Riedesel Papers, Bancroft Collection, N.Y. Pub. Lib.

24:   THE NEW YORKERS

1. Descriptions of Frederick or Berkeley Springs are from *George Washington, a Biography*, by Douglas Southall Freeman, Vols. III and VI, (New York, 1954: Scribner's).

2. In Madam Riedesel's published journal the name is "Mrs. Garel." When a search of Maryland records failed to uncover such a name, it was my husband's idea to consider Carroll. A check showed that Mary Darnall Carroll was twelve years younger than her husband (Charles Carroll, signer of the Declaration), that she had four children at the time of the Baroness's visit, that she was living at Doughoregan Manor with her father-in-law as one of the family. He was Charles Carroll of Annapolis of the "princely family of the Carrolls of Ely of Carroll, Kings County, Ireland," seventy-seven rather than eighty-four — which was the only item which does not fit Madam Riedesel's description. See *The Life of Charles Carroll of Carrollton*, by Kate

Mason Rowland (2 vols.; New York, 1898: Putnam's); *Charles Carroll of Carrollton*, by Joseph Gurn (New York, 1932: Kenedy); *History of Carrollton Manor*, by William J. Grove (Frederick, Md., 1928: Marken and Bieldfield); *History of Maryland*, by J. Thomas Scharf (Baltimore, Md., 1879: J. B. Piet).

3. "Great desertion" is from Morristown Transcripts. Mention of Halifax may refer to Halifax, North Carolina.

4. In the Sparks Papers, Houghton Library, is a list of officers and servants "belonging to Major General Riedesel and his Family." It is dated Sept. 12, 1779, and therefore refers to their journey toward New York. Women have no names!

Return of the names of the Officers and Servants belonging to
General Riedesel and his Family

Lady Riedesel & three children one Chamber Maid

Rubel	*Cook*
Rockel	*Servant*
Glockenthen	*Coachman*
Fisher	*Postillion*

Lieut. Freeman, Aid-de-Camp to General Riedesel

Backer
Forrens   *Servants*

(are now at the Spring and meets with General Riedesel at Leesburg)

Major General Riedesel goes with General Phillips

| Miller | *Servant* |
| Paez | *Groom* |

Capit. (sic) Poellnetz Dep.\u2019 Adjt. Gen.\u00b9 goes with General Riedesel

John Hueter
Hallman   *Servants*

Dr. Pralle goes with General Riedesel

Carl Roetger
Foerster   *Servants*

Buerig, Steward to General Riedesel goes with the Baggage and the following Servants

Cruse
Valentin
Nordez
two kitchen women

The list continues with aides Gerlach and Cleve, each with two servants; Pastor Mylius and Secretary Langemeyer, two servants apiece; two clerks attended by one servant.

5. Information leading to the identification of the houses given the

Riedesels for quarters is from *Iconography of Manhattan Island,* Vol. V, by Isaac Newton Phelps Stokes (New York, 1915–1928: Dodd Mead) at New-York Historical Society — hereafter referred to as *Iconography.* Mr. Arthur Carlson, New-York Historical Society, Map Room, most kindly found a water-color of the John Marston house for me.

6. *Captain Willoe.* Captain Sam Willoe was a member of General Riedesel's military family for seven years, by his own account. This was however an interrupted service. He was sent to Canada to forward officers' baggage to Cambridge, Massachusetts, General Burgoyne requesting a pass-port for him, February 11, 1778, according to British Headquarters Papers. The passport was not granted until June 14, 1778, and on October 2 "nothing further is known" of Captain Willoe, sent to Canada. This does not mean that the young man wrote no letters. He wrote to General Riedesel, heading his letter Quebec, June 16, 1778 (Morristown papers) . . . "Judging of the state that your trunks might be in, from the miserable condition in which I found my own, I had them brought to the Grand Vicaire's and opened; I was agreeably surprised to find everything safe and Madame de Riedesel's large Band Box in very good order and dry to the bottom." Willoe was afraid he could not have "all the fine things" packed up "in the same good order."

Willoe was in Quebec October 7, 1778 — still trying in vain to expedite baggage. "I hope Madame de Riedesel and the three dear little Graces are well" he wrote. He was not exchanged as he expected and in August 24, 1779, he was still in Quebec, "extremely unhappy at not having the Honor of hearing" from General Riedesel. On October 9, he headed his letters "New York," and was "concerned and surprised" because Burgoyne "omitted to mention" him to Howe. He was finally exchanged September 6, 1780.

Captain Willoe was once more aide to General Riedesel when the Baroness arrived in New York — although still a prisoner of war. He negotiated for "a Pipe of Madeira" for the General on October 20, 1779, and carried the message from General Phillips that Riedesel was invited by Haldimand to dine "at Black Sam's at four o'clock . . ."

25:   MISS AMERICA

1. See note 5 previous chapter.

2. The Queen's birthday: See *New York Mercury,* January 24, 1780, also *Iconography* and *The Memorial History of the City of New-York from its First Settlement to the Year 1892,* edited by James Grant Wilson (New York, 1892: The New-York History Company). See also *The Memorial History of the City of New-York,* Vol. II, p. 300: "The oppulent De Lanceys occupied many fine mansions in the city and vicinity. The founder of the family built that which later became Fraunces' Tavern on the

corner of Pearl and Broad streets. . . . Stephen De Lancey also built a large house on Broadway just above Trinity Church, which later became the City Arms." See also *Iconography.* The De Lancey mansion, 115 Broadway was the Province Arms; New York Arms; City Arms; Hull's Tavern (and had still other names.) It was taken by W. Hick on January 17, 1778 and the name changed to The Bunch of Grapes — but called (William Smith's Diary) Hick's Tavern. Supper given there in honor of the Queen's Birthday, Jan. 18, 1780.

3. William Smith (1728–1793) was born in New York City, graduated from Yale College in 1745 and studied law in his father's office. His *History of the Province of New-York from the First Discovery to the Year M.DCC. XXXII* was published in London in 1732. He continued to write, but the years covering the Revolution remain in manuscript in the New York Public Library. When New York was evacuated, William Smith went to England, then to Canada where he became a chief justice. Quotations are from Smith's manuscript as published in the *Iconography.*

4. Letters of General Pattison are in The New-York Historical Society Collections, Vol. 8, 1875.

5. Dr. Harold Bowditch has sent me a translation from *The Physician and the Healing Art in Past Days,* Herman papers, Leipsig, 1900. Seite 200. "However, the inoculation with the human smallpox lymph seems to have been very risky. The wife of General Riedesel . . . experienced a smallpox epidemic in New York. In her letters she writes that her child nearly lost its life owing to inoculation. . . ."

6. Thomas Jones (1731–1792) was born on Long Island, graduated from Yale College and "probably" studied law with his father. He was a Loyalist with much to lose, "a fine residence called Mount Pitt on the highest point in lower Manhattan," and "a magnificent country place" at Fort Neck, Long Island. For suspected Loyalist activities, he was imprisoned and parolled by Governor Trumbull of Connecticut. During the period of his parole he wrote *The History of New York during the Revolutionary War and of the Leading Events of the Other Colonies,* 1879. His estates were confiscated and he went to England.

7. For exchange of Phillips and Riedesel for Lincoln, see B.HQ. Papers, Photostat, Ms. Div. N.Y. Pub. Lib.

26: PROGRESS IN THE AMERICAN REBELLION

1. "This service was performed with a trifling loss, and the men who are missing, through excessive fatigue, are hourly expected in." — *Rivington's Gazette* Mar. 4, 1779.

"I ordered the few troops that came from Stamford to pursue them, thinking they might have an opportunity to pick up some stragglers. In this I was not disappointed, as Your Excellency will see by the list of prisoners." — General Israel Putnam to Washington, in *Diary of the American Revolution*, by Frank Moore.

2. For scheme for liberating officers, see Riedesel Papers, Bancroft Coll. Ms. Div. N.Y. Pub. Lib.

3. Riedesel to Jefferson; for flag of truce for ship *Riedesel*, see Jefferson Papers, Vol. 5.

"Captain Gerlach begs me to interest myself for him with your Excellency as he is excessively sick at sea, to permit him to return to this place by land as soon as his affairs are settled." Dearborn Papers, Houghton Library, Harvard. General quartermaster of the Brunswick infantry, Captain of Engineers Heinrich von Gerlach, came home safely and became Commander of artillery in Brunswick. He died in 1798. See *Riedesel*, Stone, Vol. II, p. 265.

4. On August 22, 1781, there was a total of 23,489 men, 3615 women and 4127 children "victualled at New York and the outposts." In the "Germanic Regiments there were 10,251 men and 679 women." See *Women Camp Followers of the American Revolution* by Walter Hart Blumenthal, MacManus, Philadelphia, 1952.

5. Delays in sailing: See *The American Rebellion*, by Sir Henry Clinton.

6. For death of Phillips, see Hadden, Appendix I. Lafayette's father was killed at Minden at the age of twenty-seven. Lafayette believed that his father was killed by a ball from the battery commanded by General Phillips, and he thought that a ball from his own battery killed General Phillips. See *Adrienne, the Life of the Marquise de La Fayette* by André Maurois. (New York; 1961: McGraw-Hill).

7. "Mr. Ludlow . . ." Morristown Transcripts.

27: RETURN TO CANADA

1. "Had not Mr. Washington without any just cause. . . .": See Canadian Archives, Ottawa, Canada.

2. "By the United States in Congress Assembled. April 3, 1781. *Resolved*, That the Commander in Chief be and is hereby directed to recall Lt. Gen. Burgoyne . . ." B. HQ., photostat copy, Ms. Div., N.Y. Pub. Lib.

3. "Other than the officers, none of the Convention troops were restored to their native countries until the war was over." *History of Prisoner of War Utilization by the United States*, 1776–1945, by Lieutenant Colonel George G. Lewis and Captain John Mewha. Department of the Army pamphlet No. 20-213. Hereafter called *Utilization*.

4. Red, white and blue flowers — Canadian Archives, Ottawa.

5. Letters from "Lui" or Louis Schmidt: See Morristown Transcripts.

6. "Plan of an Expedition to the Ohio": See Riedesel Papers, Bancroft Collection, Ms. Div., N.Y. Pub. Lib.

7. For "Reply to General Clinton's Proposals . . .": See Vermont Historical Collections; Haldimand Papers, Vol. 2, p. 343, 20 Sept. 1781. Canadian Archives, Ottawa, Canada. Hereafter called Haldimand Papers.

8. Riedesel offered amnesty to all deserters if they would come in. (July 19, 1782, Morristown Transcripts.) Driven to desperation by fresh desertions, Riedesel also offered a "reward of Half a Joe [Johannes] for every Deserter or Deserter's scalp" from St. Johns Blockhouse, or Isle aux Noix. (Dec. 30, 1782 Haldimand Papers, Canadian Archives, Ottawa, Canada.) A Johannes was a Portuguese goldpiece worth about sixteen dollars.

9. Letters to and from General Riedesel and General St. Leger concerning St. Leger's son, "petit Jean": See Morristown Transcripts. Petit Jean played a German version of drop-the-handkerchief with the Riedesel little girls. But a servant girl played a different sort of game with "petit Jean," and he was sent home in disgrace. It was childish innocence on the boy's part, and his father arranged for the doctor to explain matters. General Riedesel's letter (in French) was most tactful: "In the eleventh year, he feels what I only began to feel when I was fourteen, my joy then being one of my mother's maids."

28: THE PRETTY SHIP

1. See the *Vermonter*, Nov. 1906, "Hazen's Road," by Frederick W. Baldwin.

2. Advertisements were put in local papers to recall prisoners who had found jobs for themselves. "German soldiers . . . were permitted to ransom themselves for 80 Spanish milled dollars . . . Those who could not raise the money usually found some Americans who were willing to advance it in return for labor for a fixed term . . . Approximately 6000 Hessians [Germans] remained in the United States after the Revolutionary War." *Utilization*, p. 20. No distinction between Hessians and Brunswickers is made here.

3. While in Canada with the Riedesels, Willoe found himself ordered to Fort Niagara. At Fort Erie on the 5th of July, 1783, he learned that he would not be allowed to say good-by to the Riedesels. He was in "a State of Mind and Agitation of Spirits not easily described . . ." (Morristown papers.)

Captain Sam Willoe remained devoted to the Baroness and the General, as the last letter from him in the Morristown papers shows. It is headed London, December 14, 1786, and he was doing errands as usual. "I have sent two pairs of spectacles and four pairs of glasses (of different focuses) to be changed in case these now in the frames should not suit her R. Highnesses Eyes . . ." It seems probable that "her R. Highness" was the Duchess of Brunswick and that the Baroness Riedesel has been extolling the virtues of English glasses. Willoe "bespoke the Spectacles at Mr. Watkins's, who, wishing to execute her R. H.'s Orders in the best manner, desired a few days' time."

4. Madam Riedesel tells the story of the voyage home, as indicated.

5. *The Royal Navy* by Sir William Laird Clowes, Sir C. Markham, A. T. Mahan and others (London, 1899-1903: S. Lowe, Marston and Co.), Vol. 4, tells of the foundering of the *Royal George*, a hundred-gun ship. Rear Admiral Kempenfelt and Captain Martin Waghorn were lost, but of course there is no record of rank and file and women and children who were drowned.

6. Interview with King George: See Haldimand Papers.

29: MRS. GENERAL COMES HOME

1. When Count Bernstorff was Ambassador to the United States he visited Schuylerville, New York, to see the house where his ancestress, the Baroness Riedesel, had taken refuge during Burgoyne's last stand. Afterwards, he ordered copies in oil of the portraits of the General and of Mrs. General, which he presented to Mrs. Kenneth Bullard's father, owner of the house. Mrs. Bullard kindly allowed me to have the portraits photographed. Photographs of the portraits of the daughters, reproduced here, were sent from Germany at the same time. No artist is given but, with the exception of Augusta, they seem to be by the same hand.

2. Letters from Francis Coffin are in the Massachusetts Historical Society.

3. Information on the birth date of Georg Karl and other family dates for this period has been painstakingly gathered for me by Dr. Clementine Zernick.

4. Georg Karl married a cousin, Caroline Friederike, in 1808. He was twenty-three and she a year younger. The marriage month is not given, so it is impossible to say whether Georg's mother lived to enjoy this happy occasion. Their daughter, Marie Caroline, was born July 4, 1809. I am indebted to Dr. Clementine Zernick for her search in German genealogies and to Widener Library, Harvard College, for sending rare German volumes to the New York Public Library for her use.

5. *The Diary and Letters of Gouverneur Morris*, edited by Anne Cary Morris (New York, 1888: Scribner's). Vol. 2 (1797) tells of his meeting with Miss America.

30: THE LETTERS OF MRS. GENERAL

1. A photostat of the will of General Riedesel was sent to me by Baron Dr. von Galera, from Lauterbach. The handwriting, the archaic German and the legalistic language made it most difficult to translate; but Dr. Clementine

Zernick, herself a lawyer, has made a most excellent English translation for me.

2. A note in *Riedesel*, Stone, tells how the castle at Lauterbach was burned in the insurrections of 1848. Baron Dr. von Galera, in a letter to me, says that it was only the woodwork inside the castle which was burned and that "the fortress itself, under the rebellion, did not suffer."

3. It seems that we have Count Reuss to thank for the suppression of the name of "the wife of the commissary" who was Burgoyne's mistress in America.

Index

Index